EXPLORER'S GUIDE

COLORADO

D0168312

EXPLORER'S GUIDE

COLORADO

THIRD EDITION

MATT FORSTER
with photographs by Matt & Kim Forster

THE COUNTRYMAN PRESS
A division of W. W. Norton & Company
Independent Publishers Since 1923

For information about permission to reproduce selections from this book,
write to Permissions, The Countryman Press,
500 Fifth Avenue, New York, NY 10110

For information about special discounts for bulk purchases, please contact
W. W. Norton Special Sales at specialsales@wwnorton.com or 800-233-4830

Library of Congress Cataloging-in-Publication Data

Names: Forster, Matt, 1971– author.
Title: Explorer's guide Colorado / Matt Forster.
Description: Third edition. | New York : The Countryman Press,
a division of W. W. Norton & Company, [2017] | Includes index.
Identifiers: LCCN 2017016667 | ISBN 9781581574951 (pbk.)
Subjects: LCSH: Colorado—Guidebooks.
Classification: LCC F774.3 .S43 2016 | DDC 917.8804—dc23
LC record available at https://lccn.loc.gov/2017016667

The Countryman Press
www.countrymanpress.com

A division of W. W. Norton & Company
500 Fifth Avenue, New York, NY 10110
www.wwnorton.com

978-1-58157-495-1 (pbk.)

1 2 3 4 5 6 7 8 9 0

For Abby and Nathan, who make every trip a joy.

EXPLORE WITH US!

Welcome to the third edition of *Explorer's Guide Colorado,* the definitive guide to the Centennial State. From the expansive eastern plains to the Rocky Mountains, this guide covers the best there is to see and do in Colorado. Travelers will find important information on where to stay, where to eat, which attractions to see, and which activities are available in every region of the state. Like the other titles in the Explorer's Guides series, this book covers the usual worthwhile attractions as well as some out-of-the-way local favorites.

WHAT'S WHERE In the beginning of the book you'll find an alphabetical listing of important information and state highlights—everything from avalanches and altitude to wildlife and wineries.

LODGING The hotels, B&Bs, cabins, and campgrounds in this book have been included because they have a proven reputation for being great places to stay—no one pays to be listed in these pages. From season to season, rates across Colorado fluctuate greatly; so a range of rates is included with each listing. For accurate travel planning, it's essential to call ahead. Every attempt has been made to provide the most current lodging rates, but the old saying holds true that the only constant is that everything changes.

KEY TO SYMBOLS

- ✎ **Child friendly.** The crayon indicates that a place or event is family friendly and welcomes children. Most upscale restaurants do not do a good job of accommodating children, and many B&Bs restrict kids (especially kids under 12).
- & **Handicapped access.** The wheelchair icon denotes a place that has indicated it has access that complies with the Americans with Disabilities Act (ADA) standards.
- ❡ **Liquor.** This symbol indicates that the restaurant in question has a bar.
- 🐾 **Pets.** The dog's paw icon identifies lodgings that allow pets. Be sure to make arrangements in advance. Most lodgings will charge extra for pets and will often restrict certain breeds.
- ☂ **Rainy day.** The umbrella icon points out places where you can entertain yourself but still stay dry in bad weather.
- ⚭ **Wedding friendly.** The wedding rings icon denotes places and establishments that are good venues for weddings.
- ((ᵩ)) **Wi-Fi.** This symbol indicates that a lodging, restaurant, or coffeehouse offers free wireless Internet access.

RESTAURANTS The eateries in this book have been separated out into two sections: Dining Out and Eating Out. Dining Out listings are typically (although not always) the most expensive. These are where you find fine cuisine. Eating Out listings are typically cheaper, family dining establishments—where you find good grub. A range of prices is included for each entry. Colorado has a statewide ban on smoking in bars and restaurants.

We would appreciate any comments or corrections. Please write to:

Explorer's Guide Editor
The Countryman Press
A division of W. W. Norton & Company
500 Fifth Avenue
New York, NY 10110

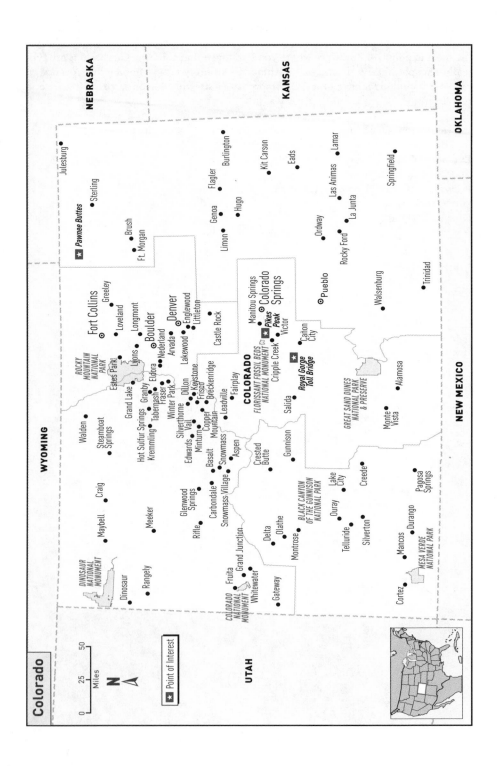

Colorado

N

Miles
0   25   50

UTAH

WYOMING

NEBRASKA

KANSAS

OKLAHOMA

NEW MEXICO

Julesburg

★ Pawnee Buttes

Sterling

Brush
Ft. Morgan

Burlington
Flagler
Kit Carson
Eads
Las Animas   Lamar
Genoa
Hugo   Springfield
Limon
Ordway
Rocky Ford   La Junta

Greeley

Fort Collins
Loveland
Longmont
Boulder
Nederland   Denver
Arvada   Englewood
Lakewood   Littleton
Castle Rock

ROCKY
MOUNTAIN
NATIONAL
PARK
Estes Park
Lyons
Eldora

Walden
Steamboat
Springs

Grand Lake
Granby
Tabernash
Fraser
Winter Park
Silverthorne   Dillon
Vail   Keystone
Kremmling   Frisco
Minturn   Copper   Breckenridge
Edwards   Mountain
Basalt   Snowmass   Leadville
Snowmass Village   Aspen
Fairplay

Hot Sulfur Springs

Manitou Springs
Colorado
Springs

★ Pikes
Peak
Victor
Cripple Creek   Cañon
City

★ Royal Gorge
Toll Bridge

Pueblo

Walsenburg

Trinidad

FLORISSANT FOSSIL BEDS
NATIONAL MONUMENT

COLORADO

Salida

GREAT SAND DUNES
NATIONAL PARK
& PRESERVE

Monte
Vista   Alamosa

Gunnison

Crested
Butte

Lake
City   Creede

Pagosa
Springs

BLACK CANYON
OF THE GUNNISON
NATIONAL PARK

Maybell   Craig

Meeker

Glenwood
Springs

Rifle   Carbondale

Delta
Montrose   Olathe

Ouray

Telluride
Silverton

Durango
Mancos

Cortez

MESA VERDE
NATIONAL PARK

DINOSAUR
NATIONAL
MONUMENT

Dinosaur

Rangely

COLORADO
NATIONAL
MONUMENT
Fruita
Grand Junction
Whitewater

Gateway

CONTENTS

EASTERN COLORADO | 261

MAPS

INTRODUCTION

My wife's family goes back several generations in Colorado. Her great-great-grandfather, Ole Halvorson, moved here from Minnesota and settled in the plains east of Denver near the tiny farming town of Genoa. He dug a hole in the ground for shelter—a cellar that became the basement of the family farmhouse—built a barn for the livestock, and began to turn the land over for planting. It wasn't long before he sent for his family. From those humble beginnings, four generations of Coloradans were born. The stories from those days on the farm are exciting. Genoa was a hopping place for a time. There were stores, a restaurant, a school, and dances on the weekends where my wife's grandfather, Lawrence, played piano or fiddle, whatever was needed. There were even baseball teams from towns all over eastern Colorado that traveled from ball field to ball field on warm summer evenings.

Today Genoa is a quieter place. The few kids who live here have quite a bus ride to school. It's a different picture than the usual tourist poster with a family skiing down freshly powdered slopes, peaks towering in the background, but it illustrates the great diversity you will find in Colorado, all of which is worth exploring.

My fascination with Colorado began long before I met my wife and her family. It began when I was a boy, listening to *An Evening with John Denver* on my parents' record player. Although the album isn't all about Colorado per se, songs like "Rocky Mountain High" left indelible impressions about Colorado in general and the Rocky Mountains in particular. Growing up in the Midwest, trips that took us west of the Mississippi were rare, but greatly enjoyed. And although I found myself in the Rockies several times, Colorado was somewhat elusive. By the time I was in college, my only experience with the state was an ill-fated road trip that left me stranded for a week north of Dotsero. It wasn't until I moved to Denver to get married that I finally got a chance to appreciate all the state has to offer. Over the years, that appreciation has continued to grow.

Like all travel guides, this one divvies up the state into regions. Determining which cities and towns fit into each region is a bit tricky. Do you group towns by activity—all the ski towns in this group, and all the rest over here? Or do you do it by terrain—all the mountain towns in one group, the plains in another? You could divide them up by culture in a sense, with agricultural towns separated from industrial and college towns. Soon, however, all these classifications run into an inevitable obstacle. As you begin to examine the people, activities, and culture, you soon discover that each town, village, and hamlet should have its own region. They are all too different to be lumped together.

Consider the chapter "Southwest Colorado." Durango has a distinct Old West feel. The historic downtown, the narrow-gauge railroad, and the annual Cowboy Gathering all feed into the town's vibe. Just an hour or so east is Pagosa Springs. It's a relaxed place, with easygoing people, and the entire town evokes a strong Southwest feel—like a mini Santa Fe. Head north of Durango, and you have a touristy mountain town such as Silverton, and just over the mountain from there is Telluride, one of the state's chicest ski resorts.

A FARM IN EASTERN COLORADO

In the end, I decided to create five regions that loosely follow the six already established by the state tourism office. Maybe this will help you avoid some confusion when juggling the guidebook and travel brochures as you head down the road.

To research this book, I jumped in the car and traveled all over the state. I visited hotels, B&Bs, lodges, and resorts. I ate in fine Italian restaurants, roadside barbecue joints, old-school diners, and, of course, steakhouses. I visited the zoos, explored the caves, hiked trails to hidden falls, and jumped on every train I could. In the end, it really is impossible to do everything and eat everywhere—in Denver alone you could eat every meal at a new place for more than two years—so I talked to people, too. Lots of people. Folks who live in Colorado are more than happy to tell you about their favorite restaurants, the ones where they take their own out-of-town guests. They are also more than happy to tell you about the places that aren't so good. The input provided by hundreds of strangers gave me excellent leads and confirmed much of what I learned on my own. None of the businesses mentioned in the book paid for their inclusion. They're here because they have a proven reputation for providing a great experience.

One of the things I like best about Colorado is the sense of the state's unique history, which is very evident as you travel from town to town. This history doesn't just add to the tourist experience; it *is* the tourist experience. Even before Colorado was part of the Union, tourists made their way here. As early as 1854, men came west with large hunting parties to what is now Colorado, set on seeing how many grizzly bears, bison, antelope, and deer they could mow down in a month. This early form of "recreational tourism" might not seem quite kosher today, but it illustrates how quickly people came to appreciate this mountainous region on the country's frontier. Ever since the 19th century, tourists have been enticed to Colorado for the mountains, which offer opportunities for recreation, scenery for contemplation, and a climate conducive to good health.

The city of Colorado Springs was established in 1871 as a resort community. Not only did the town cater to tourists looking to explore the local natural wonders, but to thousands of people suffering ailments such as tuberculosis and rheumatism who came to take the waters in Manitou Springs or simply sit on a wide, shady porch and breathe that dry, fresh mountain air. Soon after the turn of the century, Pikes Peak had a road to its summit, paving the path, so to speak, for the millions who subsequently rode and eventually drove to the top.

In the mountains, the story is much the same. In 1860, the first American to "discover" Glenwood Springs was followed less than 20 years later by the first permanent settler. By the 1880s, the town's legendary Hot Springs Pool had been established, complete with a sandstone lodge and the world-class Hotel Colorado across the street.

The turn of the century brought continued development to the state's tourism industry. Mesa Verde National Park was established in 1906. Seven years later, Rocky Mountain National Park (RMNP) was created near Estes Park. Visitors making their way to Estes Park not soon after would have been able to stay at the luxurious Stanley Hotel, which F. O. Stanley built in 1909. In fact, the way up through the Big Thompson Canyon had been significantly improved by Stanley, allowing him to eventually offer an early motorized shuttle to his resort.

Much of this growth was driven by the wealth pouring out of the mountains in the latter portion of the 19th century. Gold, silver, and other precious metals fueled an economic boom that is evident by the number of Victorian buildings throughout the state. When mining fell off, the state's mining towns struggled. The smaller towns soon became ghosts, with a few dilapidated structures left to indicate that people once lived there. The towns that served as mining centers—Leadville, Aspen, Breckenridge—somehow continued on.

In 1912, a Norwegian skier by the name of Carl Howelsen moved to Steamboat. He brought with him a passion for cross-country skiing and ski jumping. By 1913, Steamboat had a ski jump, and soon a ski hill. Howelsen is credited with bringing skiing to Colorado. By 1937, Berthoud Pass became the state's first ski area with a tow lift. The rope was hauled uphill by a Ford V-8 engine. Other ski areas were eventually built, and by the 1960s and '70s, the ski industry in Colorado was booming.

A MOUNTAIN MAN TENDING HIS WARES

As you explore Colorado, there are countless opportunities to learn more about the state's rich history. From the Ute and other Native Americans who called this region home and the mountain men and French trappers who scouted the frontier to the farmers, ranchers, and prospectors who followed, the story of this land is complex and compelling.

The book begins with a "What's Where in Colorado" section. This highlights some of the unique things you can find in Colorado. It also points the way to other sources of information. The remainder of the book describes Colorado, region by region. No individual section of the book can tell the whole story of this wide and varied state. It is my hope, however, that as a whole the book paints a pretty decent picture of what travelers can expect to find here.

I imagine you reading this book sometime in the future while planning a trip to Mesa Verde to see the cliff dwellings, or maybe on a ski vacation in Vail, or just pulling into Estes Park after the first leg of your trip, looking for a place to eat. No matter what the scenario, I envy you. As soon as I return home after exploring some new part of Colorado, I begin to look forward to the next trip. My hope is that this book will be helpful in your own travels and will open up new vistas for you and your family in Colorado.

As you travel, I welcome your feedback. I am always researching for the next edition of *Explorer's Guide Colorado*. You can e-mail me (colorado@big-words.net) or stop by my website (big-words.net) to see other travel projects I am working on!

GASTHOF GRAMSHAMMER

WHAT'S WHERE IN COLORADO

General Information

ALTITUDE West of I-25, altitude is everywhere. When travelers come from lower altitudes, they often do not understand the effect it can have on their body. Dehydration and sunburn are easy enough to deal with—drink plenty of water, wear a hat, and use sunscreen. But no matter how healthy you are, altitude can affect anyone, and altitude sickness is something emergency rooms see a lot of here. Watch for symptoms such as dizziness and headaches, and head to a lower elevation (and continue to drink water) until they disappear. If symptoms do not go away, seek medical attention.

AVALANCHES Every year avalanches close sections of road in the mountains. Nearly 70 people will be caught in an avalanche in an average year; of those about six will die. To prevent avalanche disasters, the Colorado Department of Transportation does avalanche control along the major highways. This involves identifying and stopping potential avalanches. In extreme cases, explosives are used to create a

THE SCENIC MAROON BELLS, NEAR ASPEN

controlled avalanche. Within the ski resorts, ski patrols do the same kind of work. In backcountry areas, it's up to individuals to understand the dangers and take necessary steps to protect themselves and their travel partners. The **Colorado Avalanche Information Center** (avalanche.state.co.us) is an organization that provides up-to-date avalanche forecasts, educates the public on avalanche safety, and looks into avalanche fatalities.

BED & BREAKFASTS Colorado has amazing B&Bs. With few exceptions, the innkeepers here are incredibly hospitable. Those listed throughout the book come highly recommended. For a complete listing of B&Bs throughout the state, you might want to look online at **Colorado Bed & Breakfast, "On the Web"** (colorado-bnb.com) or **Bed & Breakfast Innkeepers of Colorado** (1-800-265-7696; innsofcolorado.org).

DAMS Throughout Colorado, various rivers have been dammed to control flooding and to provide water for the state. Often what is called a lake is in fact a reservoir—and as you drive around these reservoirs, you will often find yourself driving across the top of a dam. Since 9/11, the Department of Homeland Security has tightened security around the nation's dams, and parking on dams is not permitted. Therefore, if you stop on a dam to take a picture or enjoy the view, it will not be long before someone in an official-looking vehicle pulls up and asks you to move along.

GEOLOGY Colorado is defined by its geology more than anything else. The Colorado Rocky Mountains are home to all of the range's highest peaks, those more than 14,000 feet. A dozen fossil sites speak to the region's deep geological history. To fully appreciate Colorado's natural history, begin by learning a bit more about its geology. I found

Hiking Colorado's Geology and *Roadside Geology of Colorado* particularly informative. Whether hiking through the mountains or taking a family road trip, these are great resources to find examples and descriptions of Colorado's unique geological past.

HIGHWAYS Travel in the mountains, and across the plains, can be dramatically affected by the weather. Storms in Colorado have been known to shut down highways. The **Colorado Department of Transportation** maintains a website, cotrip.org, that tracks road conditions across the state, so you can make adequate preparations before you leave. Still and streaming cameras give drivers a chance to view traffic conditions in real time.

RAILROADS For a time, railroads were the lifeline for many towns across Colorado. Fortunes could be made if the railroad came to town. This fact was not lost on the railroad companies themselves, who would often build a town of their own for a depot, several miles down the track from a neighbor. Today, trains offer passengers a unique vantage point for enjoying Colorado's stunning landscape. Colorado's most popular train may be either the **Royal Gorge Route** (719-276-4000 or 1-888-724-5748; royalgorgeroute.com) that takes passengers into the towering canyon walls of the Royal Gorge or the **Durango & Silverton Narrow-Gauge Railroad** (1-888-872-4607; durangotrain .com), which follows the Animas River to Silverton. Other trains to ride are highlighted throughout the book.

SNOW Skiing is all about the snow. Several websites provide current snow reports on all of Colorado's ski areas. **Colorado: Ski Country USA** (colorado ski.com) is a good place to start. Just click on the "Snow Report" link.

SOUTH PARK If you watch a lot of Comedy Central, you might expect to find the town of South Park nestled somewhere in Colorado's mountains. You won't. South Park is a grassland basin, located in the Rockies, southwest of Denver. The largest town in South Park is Fairplay, along the Mosquito Range. Driving from Denver, west on US 285, you will climb about 5,000 feet through the mountains. The road is full of twists and turns, and mountains rise on either side. Suddenly, the landscape seems to recede and the horizon expands dramatically. Stretched out in front of you is grassland—nearly 1,000 square miles of it—edged in by distant peaks. This is South Park—and a drive through the high plains is not soon forgotten.

TOURISM For a ton of information on traveling to Colorado, there's no better resource than the **Colorado Tourism Office**'s website, colorado.com. It has a directory of nearly every attraction, restaurant, and hotel in the state. It also posts numerous itineraries and advertise different promotions.

Entertainment

AMUSEMENT PARKS The most popular amusement park in Colorado is **Elitch Gardens** (303-595-4386; elitch gardens.com), 2000 Elitch Circle. In 2015, Elitch Gardens celebrated its 125th season. In that time, the park has undergone many changes. Developed back in 1890 as a zoological park on the outskirts of Denver, the park spent its first 40 years without rides, attracting summer guests for great performances and dancing. In 1928 the carousel was built, and in 1936 came the Ferris wheel. Roller coasters followed. Then in 1995, the whole outfit moved to downtown Denver. Today, the park has a mess of roller coasters and other rides. On hot days, its water park is a nice way to cool off. The water rides, however, are no match for those at **Water World** (303-427-7873; waterworldcolorado .com), 8801 N. Pecos St., Federal Heights. Located north of Denver, this water park has acres of slides, wave pools, and a relaxing Lazy River.

ART MUSEUMS The **Denver Art Museum** (720-865-5000; denverart museum.org), 100 W. 14th Ave. Pkwy., is one of the finest in the country. For western art, consider the **A. R. Mitchell Memorial Museum and Gallery** (719-846-4224; armitchellmuseum.com), 150 E. Main St., in Trinidad. Most major Colorado cities have some art museums. Those in Colorado Springs, Boulder, and Fort Collins are worth a visit. In the mountains, Aspen has a non-collecting museum that features contemporary art, the **Aspen Art Museum** (970-925-8050; aspenartmuseum.org), 590 N. Mill St.

COWBOY MUSIC Two ranches in Colorado offer chuck wagon suppers and quality cowboy entertainment. The **Flying W Ranch** (719-598-4000; flyingw .com), in Colorado Springs, features the Flying W Wranglers. Out of commission for several years following the Waldo Canyon Fire of 2012, the ranch has been going through a rebuild and is set to begin receiving visitors again in 2017. Out west in Durango, you will find the Bar D Wranglers playing regularly throughout the summer at the **Bar D Chuckwagon Suppers** (970-247-5753; bardchuckwagon.com).

GAMBLING There are three primary destinations for folks looking to give away their money in Colorado. **Cripple Creek** (west of Colorado Springs) and **Central City** (west of Golden) are two old mining towns that have been taken over by casinos. In both places, the town's historic structures have been preserved, and you still get a sense of what the towns were like back in the day. **Black Hawk**, down canyon from Central City, is less unobtrusive, but perhaps the most popular since the casinos are more modern and the closest to Denver.

MELODRAMA I am not sure what it is about the mountains, but there's nothing like visiting an old mining town that gets you geared up for a melodrama. Several theater companies in the state put on an exceptional show. All include audience participation— hooting and hollering, booing and hissing are accepted. The shows typically begin with a sing-along and end with an olio. What's an *olio*, you ask. It's a hodgepodge of vaudeville-style singing, dancing, and comedy. In Manitou Springs, shows are regularly scheduled at the **Iron Springs Chateau Melodrama Dinner Theater** (719-685-5104; ironspringschateau.com). Farther up in Cripple Creek, where a melodrama seems to make even more sense, **Thin**

Air Theatre Company puts on shows at the **Butte Opera House** (buttetheater .com).

Nature & Outdoors

CANYONS Colorado has some of the most scenic canyons in the world. The **Colorado National Monument** (970-858-3617, ext. 360; nps.gov/colm), just south of Grand Junction, has many unique geological features, including rocky towers jutting up from the canyon floor. The **Black Canyon of the Gunnison National Park** (970-641-2337, ext. 205; nps.gov/blca), west of Gunnison, has stunningly tall walls and a relatively narrow span. For centuries the canyon was considered impenetrable, and even today those who want to get to the canyon floor must have plenty of experience hiking and climbing, and must blaze their own trail. The most popular canyon, however, must be the Royal Gorge, west of Cañon City. The **Royal Gorge Bridge and Park** (719-275-7507 or 1-888-333-5597; royalgorge bridge.com) has the highest suspension bridge in the world and offers great perspective on the gorge itself.

CLIFF DWELLINGS Many stop by the Manitou Cliff Dwellings in Manitou Springs to get an idea of what cliff dwellings are like. For the true experience, you must visit **Mesa Verde National Park** (970-529-4465; nps.gov /meve), west of Cortez in the southwest corner of the state. There you can climb down to the famous Balcony House and Cliff Palace. If you want more, take a side trip to **Chimney Rock Archaeological Area** (970-883-5359; chimneyrockco .org), west of Pagosa Springs, which has several structures a walking tour of Archaeological ru from the mountai

COLORADO TRAIL The Colorado Trail stretches across the state from Denver to Durango. Two books by the **Colorado Trail Foundation** (coloradotrail.org) are almost required reading for anyone feeling inspired to walk all or part of the trail. They are *The Colorado Trail: The Official Guidebook* and *The Colorado Trail: The Trailside Databook*. The former gives an overview of each section of the trail, pointing out landmarks and giving advice from those who have walked this terrain before. The latter has detailed GPS data that will help keep your path straight (or winding, when appropriate).

DUDE RANCHES Dozens of dude ranches around the state provide guests with all sorts of prepackaged vacations. The more traditional ranches have guests riding horses and helping with the daily running of a ranch, everything from roping calves to driving cattle. More and more ranches have become like summer camps for the whole family. Horseback trail riding and fly fishing are common activities, as are white-water rafting, swimming, and nightly cowboy dinners and bonfires. Then there are the more upscale ranches that have a chef on hand to provide fine dining; there are wine tastings and gourmet cooking classes, and large outdoor pools and hot tubs. Very few ranches are covered in this book, but you can still find a ranch vacation that's right for you by checking with the **Colorado Dude Ranch Association** (coloradoranch.com). The association has a list of most of the ranches in the state, along with information on what they offer.

ELK Many people come to Colorado with expectations of seeing wildlife. If prairie dogs are your idea of wildlife, you won't even have to head to the mountains—just drive by an empty lot in metro Denver. If bigger game is what you're into, however, you may have to be a little purposeful. For elk, Estes Park is the spot. Elk wander freely through town—especially in the fall, winter, and spring, when herds literally stop traffic.

FISHING Rivers and lakes all across the state are great for fishing, and every angler has a favorite spot. Whether you choose one of the reservoirs on the plains such as Lake Pueblo State Park or a fast-moving stream in the mountains such as Chalk Creek southwest of Buena Vista, if you are 16 or older you need a fishing license. These are readily available at sporting goods stores. Check out the state wildlife website for more information: wildlife.state.co.us/fishing.

FOREST SERVICE CABINS & LOOKOUTS The U.S. Forest Service has nearly 20 cabins and fire lookouts throughout Forest Service land in Colorado's Rocky Mountains—and they are available for rent. Roberts Cabin near Como in South Park, for example, is a rustic cabin built for the railroad back in 1880. It's a two-story log cabin that sleeps six. A complete list of accommodations and rates can be found on the Forest Service website: fs.fed.us/r2/recreation/rentals/index.shtml.

FOUR-WHEEL DRIVING Many companies in Colorado take passengers on four-wheel-drive trips for sightseeing in the mountains. **Switzerland of America Tours** (970-325-4484 or 1-866-990-5337; soajeep.com) works out of Ouray and has numerous tour schedules. In the fall, Cripple Creek, in the mountains above Colorado Springs, offers autumn **Aspen Tours** (719-689-2169). For about three weeks, folks can come up to Cripple Creek to celebrate the changing colors of the season, and the town offers free Jeep rides into the mountains to see the foliage.

MOUNTAIN-BIKING CAPITALS Driving through Colorado, you will hear the phrase "mountain biking capital" tossed around quite a bit. The moniker has been tagged to Durango, Crested Butte, and Fruita, and a few years back, Winter Park had the title printed on banners that were hung on nearly every lamppost in town.

So what to make of it all? Durango holds a special place in bikers' hearts because it was the site of the first professional UCI Mountain Bike & Trials World Championships in 1990. It also is surrounded by more than 2,000 miles of trails—hundreds of miles of singletrack. Crested Butte, on the other hand, has a mountain biking lineage that goes back even farther to the legendary Pearl Pass–to–Aspen ride in 1976. The ride is commemorated annually with a repeat of the tour and stands as the oldest mountain bike event in the world. Mountain bike fanatics in Fruita have worked for years to create miles and miles of excellent singletrack that have earned the respect and admiration of riders from all over the country. Winter Park is a newcomer to the list, but its 600 miles of mountain singletrack are not to be taken lightly. It also enjoys the benefit of being a short drive from Denver. Check out the Outdoor Activities section in each of these town's respective chapters for more information on finding the best trails.

PARKS, MONUMENTS, & NATIONAL HISTORIC SITES The list of National Parks in Colorado is impressive. The most popular remain **Rocky Mountain National Park** (970-586-1206; nps.gov /romo), west of Estes Park, and **Mesa Verde National Park** (970-529-4465; nps.gov/meve), near Cortez. The **Dinosaur National Monument** (970-374-3000; nps.gov/dino) in northwest Colorado and the **Great Sand Dunes National Park and Preserve** (719-378-6300; nps.gov/grsa), near Alamosa, are both a little off the beaten track but well worth the visit. **Bent's Old Fort National Historic Site** (719-383-5010; nps.gov/beol) is not particularly known for its scenery, rather, for its hands-on view of history, allowing visitors to really feel what life might have been like on the plains.

PARKS, STATE The **Colorado Department of Natural Resources** (parks.state.co.us) operates more than 40 state parks. These parks are often home to some of the state's best recreational lakes. Many have campground facilities. Day passes cost $7–8 (at most parks); annual park passes are $70. Passes can be purchased at all state parks and regional offices. They are also available at the Denver and Littleton offices.

ROCKY MOUNTAINS Many newcomers driving in from the east stop at the **WELCOME TO COLORADO** sign on I-70 or I-76 and stare in disbelief. Dreary hours in the car have been spent yearning for the mountains, and all they see is flat, all the way to the horizon. Don't get discouraged, Colorado isn't likely to run out of mountains anytime soon. However, they only fill two-thirds of the state map, and you have a few more hours of driving before the mighty Rockies rise from the plains.

SKIING There's plenty of skiing in Colorado. In fact, there is probably more skiing than you can imagine. Of course, the stellar ski areas such as Vail offer alpine (a.k.a. downhill) skiing. And every town in the mountains seems to have a Nordic center that focuses on cross-country skiing. But don't forget the renegade sports such as freeskiing and snowboarding. Vail, for example, has ski-biking. Several Nordic centers have trails set aside for skijoring (pulled on your skis by a dog), and Steamboat has an interesting variation with people pulled by horses.

VISITORS LOVE THE DENVER ZOO

WATERFALLS Cascading water is strangely inspiring. No two waterfalls in Colorado are the same. Many Rocky Mountain towns have waterfalls within view of Main Street. Idaho Springs has a small waterfall visible high up across I-70. Telluride has Bridal Falls. In Ouray, just blocks from downtown, there are two waterfalls. One is seen from town; the other, the compact and powerful Box Canyon Falls, is within walking distance. In Steamboat, drive out Fish Creek Road and make the short hike to Fish Creek Falls, which plummets more than 280 feet. Finally, one of the most photographed falls in the state is right off the highway west of Creed in the San Juans, North Clear Creek Falls. Visitors will notice signs pointing out various waterfalls as they tour the state. Be sure to stop at as many as you can.

WHITEWATER RAFTING Although there are plenty of rivers for rafting in Colorado, Salida remains the state's whitewater capital. Local outfitters, such as **Dvorak's Rafting & Kayak** (719-539-6851; dvorakexpeditions.com), in Nathrop, take paddlers down the Arkansas River. Every June, Salida throws the **Blue Paddle FIBArk Whitewater Festival** (fibark.com). FIBArk stands for "First in Boating the Arkansas," and the festival has all sorts of water events. Farther in the mountains, whitewater outfitters guide trips down the Colorado and other regional waters—check relevant chapters for outfitter info.

WILDLIFE (THE SCARY KIND) There are no tigers in Colorado, except at the zoos, but the mountains are home to mountain lions and black bears, as well as other wildlife. In most cases, you will never see a mountain lion as you are hiking or biking along the trails. In most cases, you don't want to. If you come face to face with a lion or bear, there are a few rules that will help keep you and your family safe: (1) Do not run, scream, or turn your back; (2) make yourself look as large as possible; (3) put children between adults; (4) speak firmly and back away slowly; and (5) if attacked, fight back. For more information on staying safe around mountain wildlife, see the Colorado Division of Wildlife website, wildlife .state.co.us.

Food & Drink

BREWERIES Even before actor Mark Harmon walked beside a mountain stream in winter, proclaiming the Rocky Mountain purity of Coors, beer has been a big deal in Colorado. This is even truer today, following a decade of

growing appreciation for microbrews. By last count there were something like 284 craft breweries in the state. Most offer people a chance to tour their facilities and taste the end product. Some of the better tours will be noted throughout this guide. Denver has more than 90 kinds of beer brewed locally, and Fort Collins has created its own brewery culture, with the visitor center offering a brochure that outlines a day of brewery hopping.

CANTALOUPE Over the years, Rocky Ford in southeast Colorado has built up quite a reputation for growing the world's best cantaloupe. When the fruit is in season, in August, you can find growers selling their cantaloupe and watermelon on the side of the road. Just look for handmade signs and pickup trucks loaded with fresh melons.

PEACHES Start talking about peaches with Coloradoans, and they get a certain gleam in their eye. Many childhood memories feature trips out to Grand Junction or Palisade to load up on bushels of fresh peaches, followed by weeks of peach pie, peaches and cream, and peach cobbler. Whatever was left over got canned for winter. While in Palisade, stop by **Herman Produce** (970-464-0420; hermanproduce.weebly.com), 753 Elberta St. They sell the region's succulent peaches as well as other Colorado gourmet foods.

ROCKY MOUNTAIN OYSTERS Not many visitors to Colorado are adventurous enough to tackle this uniquely western culinary experience. If you see them on a menu, be advised: Rocky Mountain oysters are bull testicles. Either pounded flat or sliced into ovals, they are then deep-fried and served with hot sauce. People who like 'em, like 'em—that's all the insight I can offer.

They are so popular a dish that Bruce's Bar in Severance (now closed) used to serve 20 tons of the delicacy every year. You might also find them called prairie oysters, Montana tendergroins, and swinging sirloin. They are featured on menus across the state. To try them fancy, call ahead at **Briarhurst Manor** in Manitou Springs (719-685-1864), 404 Manitou Ave.

WINERIES & VINEYARDS Colorado's regional wine industry has been growing by leaps and bounds during the past decade. The **Colorado Wine Industry Development Board** (coloradowine .com) has a list of state wineries and a helpful locator map. It has also organized a series of wine trails, giving travelers a handy itinerary for visiting wineries. Most of Colorado's grapes are grown in the Grand Valley (the Grand Junction/Palisade area). The **Grand Junction Visitor and Convention Bureau** (visitgrandjunction.com) has a list of local wineries and vineyards, many of which offer tours.

THE FRONT RANGE

DENVER

BOULDER

FORT COLLINS

ESTES PARK

DENVER

As you come across the plains from the east, the skyline of Denver rises dramatically against the backdrop of the Front Range. Denver is the gateway to Colorado, securely settled on the plains within reach of the mountains, at the crossroads of two of the region's major interstate highways. Sitting at an altitude of 5,280 feet, Denver is quite literally the Mile High City.

The city is located at the confluence of Cherry Creek and the South Platte River and was once a seasonal campground for Ute, Arapaho, and Cheyenne tribes. In the 1850s, gold was found in the waters. As the news spread, tens of thousands of prospectors headed west to make their fortune. Various settlements sprang up and faded on both sides of the South Platte River. The mining settlement of Auraria was doing quite well when Gen. William Larimer staked a claim on the opposite side of the river. He named the new settlement Denver City in hopes that James Denver, the governor of the Kansas Territory, would make it the county seat. Ironically, Governor Denver had already submitted his resignation and would never step foot in the town that bears his name.

The gold that drew thousands, however, ran out before they started panning, and the promise of riches didn't materialize for most prospectors. In 1859, when gold was discovered in the mountains, the miners again packed up and headed west, nearly emptying the town overnight. Denver was quickly transformed into a trade center, and in time it became the requisite stop for everyone and everything heading in and out of the mountains.

The Colorado Territory was formed in 1861, and in 1865 Denver City became the territorial capital. "Denver City" was shortened to "Denver," and in 1876 when the state was admitted into the Union, Denver became the state capital.

Throughout its history, Denver has grown in spurts, and this growth has not always been welcomed with open arms. The rejection of the Olympics in 1972 by state voters sent the message that residents were hesitant to see the state, and by default Denver, lose its uncrowded, easygoing character in exchange for unbridled expansion.

Growth, however, has come to Denver, welcomed or not. A mild climate with 300 days of sunshine, great job opportunities, and the possibility of living close to the great outdoors are just some of the factors that have fueled the incredible jump in population that Denver has seen, to some extent, since the 1950s. For a decade now, the city has seen over 2 percent growth every year. With nearly 3 million residents in the Denver-Aurora metro area, it's no surprise that Denver has become one of the country's leading metropolitan centers.

With this growth, Denver has developed into a world-class city. Within walking distance, the city has Elitch Gardens, the Pepsi Center, Coors Field, and the INVESCO Stadium at Mile High. In 1997, President Clinton invited the Summit of Eight to meet in Denver, and in 2008, the Democratic National Convention was held at the Pepsi Center.

In 1995, Denver International Airport opened northeast of Denver. With 53 square miles of property, it's the largest international airport in the United States. Catering especially to the thousands of guests who pour into the state bound for ski vacations in the mountains, the airport has special ski and snowboard conveyors for quick gathering of winter sports gear.

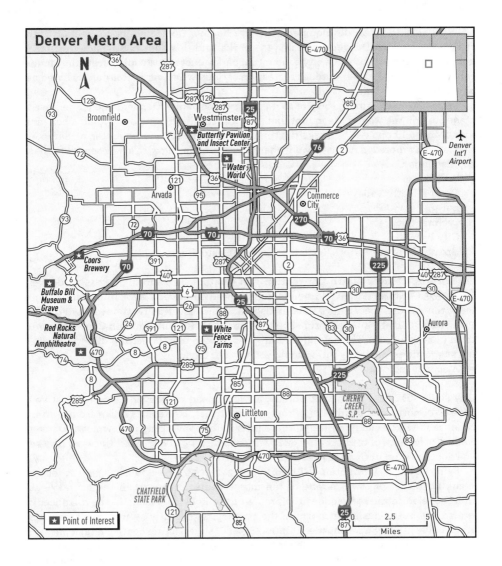

Denver Metro Area

N

Broomfield

Westminster

★ Butterfly Pavilion and Insect Center

★ Water World

Arvada

Commerce City

★ Coors Brewery

★ Buffalo Bill Museum & Grave

Red Rocks Natural Amphitheatre ★

★ White Fence Farms

Aurora

CHERRY CREEK S.P.

Littleton

CHATFIELD STATE PARK

Denver Int'l Airport

★ Point of Interest

0   2.5   5
Miles

In a little more than a decade, what was Denver's skid row became the city's central business and shopping district. With the creation of the 16th Street Mall in LoDo (Lower Downtown), people from all over the metro area drive into the city for fine dining, shopping, and theater. Real estate prices have skyrocketed, and older industrial areas have been transformed into hip condos and shopping centers. With eight professional sports teams and numerous intercollegiate rivalries, Denver can boast more sporting events than almost any city in the country.

Every year, thousands move to Denver from outside the state. The city's Hispanic population has surpassed 30 percent and serves to highlight just one facet of the area's diverse ethnic landscape. This diversity continually adds vitality to the city's cultural offerings.

With all this urban development, the city has not neglected its connection with the great outdoors. Denver maintains 155 parks, and this does not include the area's county and state parks or the city's mountain parks. Just 15 to 20 miles from the mountains, residents take their outdoor recreation seriously. Denver is continually listed as one of the nation's thinnest cities.

From Old West mining town to 21st-century metropolis, Denver is no longer just a stage stop on the way to the mountains. It is a destination in its own right. When you visit Denver, I hope you will take the time to soak in its unique character, a character that is firmly rooted in its history but changing and adapting with a new sense of urban sophistication.

Sections of town:

Central Platte Valley

LoDo

Larimer Square

City Park

Greater Denver—Aurora, Littleton, Golden, Castle Rock

GUIDANCE **Denver Metro Convention and Visitors Bureau** (303-892-1505; denver .org), 1575 California St. In addition to maintaining a Denver Visitor Information Center at the airport, the Visitors Bureau also has a nice location right downtown on the 16th Street Mall at 1600 California St.—the **Official Visitor Information Center–Downtown** (303-892-1505). The helpful staff are a great resource for getting directions, dining suggestions, or simply introducing you to their city.

Also visit: colorado.com.

GETTING THERE *By car:* In Colorado, all roads lead to Denver. East and west you have I-70; north and south, I-25. From the northeast, I-76 comes down from 1-80 in Nebraska. As you can imagine, all these interstates converging in downtown Denver can make for a lot of traffic. On weekday afternoons, rush hour is in full swing by 3 PM and doesn't let up until after 7 PM.

By air: **Denver International Airport** (303-342-2000 or 1-800-247-2336; flydenver .com), northeast of town, is one of the most beautiful airports in the country—its white tension fabric roof echoes the profile of the Rockies, visible in the distance. It is also one of the busiest airports in the country, with nearly 50 million passengers served every year. **SuperShuttle** (1-800-258-3826; supershuttle.com) can take passengers from DIA to Denver. **SkyRide** (303-299-6000 or 1-800-258-3826; rtd-denver.com /airport.shtml), which is operated by the DIA, also offers affordable transportation to and from the airport.

By train: **Amtrak's** (1-800-872-7245; amtrak.com) California Zephyr, which travels from Chicago to San Francisco, makes a key stop at Union Station (1701 Wynkoop St.) in downtown Denver.

By bus: The **Greyhound** (303-293-6555; greyhound.com) station is located at 1055 19th St.

GETTING AROUND *By car:* Getting around Denver by car can be difficult, but it's the way most people get from place to place. There are plenty of parking lots and structures downtown that charge anywhere from $5 to $25 per day. The streets downtown run diagonally, parallel with the Platte River—contrary to the rest of the metro area, where streets run east and west, north and south. Add the number of one-way streets, and a newcomer can get turned around rather quickly. Bring a good map, and you will be fine.

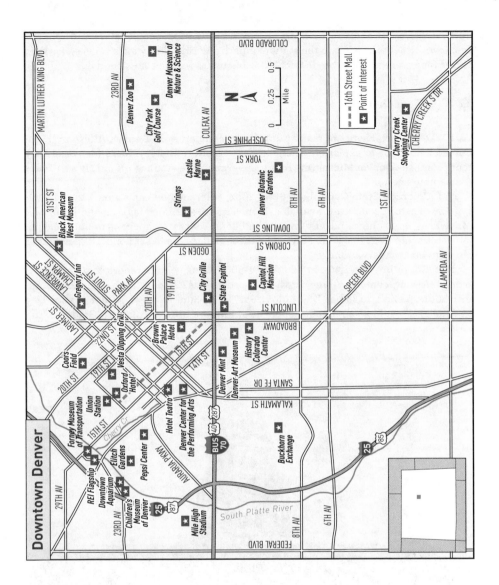

By bus: **Denver Regional Transportation District** (303-299-6000; rtd-denver.com) maintains an extensive bus system that can get you anywhere in the metro area. See its website for a complete schedule and route information. Fares $2.60–4.50 ($9 for the airport).

By bus (in LoDo): Denver's free bus service, **RTD's MallRide** (303-299-6000; rtd-denver.com), runs the length of the 16th Street Mall. The first generation of buses—which had logged 200,000 miles on this 1-mile route—were recently replaced by a fleet of electric buses. On weekdays, buses come by every five minutes or so from 5 AM (5:30 and 7 on Sat. and Sun., respectively) to 1:35 in the morning.

By light rail: The light rail system operated by **Denver Regional Transportation District** (303-299-6000; rtd-denver.com) connects downtown Denver with the Denver

Tech Center, south of town, and with various suburbs. Most people taking the light rail into town either take a bus to the station or park and ride. One way is $2.25–5. Parking is free for cars registered "in-district." Out-of-staters will pay $2–4 per day.

✱ To See & Do

GUIDED TOURS There are many guided tour companies in Denver. A few are highlighted below, but to explore further, check out **Denver History Tours** (denverhistory tours.com), the **Denver Microbrew Tour** (denvermicrobrewtour.com), and **My 420 Tours** (my420tours.com).

    ♿ ⬆ **Colorado State Capitol** (303-866-2604; colorado.gov/capitoltour), 200 E. Colfax Ave. Historic tours are available Mon.–Fri. 10–3 (Aug.–May), on the hour, and Mon.–Fri. 9–3:30 (June and July), on the half hour. Tours take about 45 minutes. Legislative tours are available Jan.–May, when the legislature is in session; call the number above to make reservations.

    ♿ 🐾 **Coors Brewery** (303-277-2337 or 1-866-812-2337; millercoors.com/breweries /coors-brewing-company/tours), 13th and Ford streets, Golden. Tours available. Summer hours (June 1 to Labor Day): Mon.–Sat. 10–4, Sun. noon–4. Winter (Labor Day to June 1): Thu.–Mon. 10–4, Sun. noon–4. The Coors brewing plant in Golden is the

COLORADO STATE CAPITOL

DOWNTOWN DENVER

world's largest single-site brewery. Sitting on 2,000 acres, it produces nearly 2 million barrels of beer per day. This may seem to be an incredible claim, until you take the tour. For guests 21 or older (with an ID), there is beer tasting at the end of the tour as well as a gift shop to pick up Coors memorabilia. Tours are free.

    ♿ ♟ **Denver Mint** (303-405-4761; usmint.gov), 320 W. Colfax Ave. Take a look at a penny, and you will see a small letter stamped beneath the year. West of the Mississippi, more and more of these pennies have a small *D*, which means they were minted here in Denver. Tours of the Denver Mint are available Mon.–Fri. 8–2 on the hour. Reservations are required and can be made online or at the reservation booth at the U.S. Mint Visitor Center on Cherokee Street (between 14th and Colfax avenues). Try to schedule your tour early in your trip as spots tend to fill up quickly. Tours are free.

MUSEUMS ♟ **Black American West Museum & Heritage Center** (720-242-7428; blackamericanwestmuseum.org), 3091 California St. Open Fri.–Sat. 10–4. Since 1971, the museum has commemorated the contribution of African Americans in the Old West. You can learn about famous black cowboys and pioneers—O. T. Jackson, for example, founded the black pioneer town of Dearfield, which thrived east of Greeley from 1910 until the Great Depression—or see exhibitions that tell the story of the Buffalo Soldiers or the Tuskegee airmen. This museum offers a unique and necessary perspective on the region's history. Adult admission $10, seniors $9, and children 12 and under $8.

    Byers-Evans House Museum (303-620-4933; historycolorado.org/museums/byers-evans-house-museum), 1310 Bannock St. Open Mon.–Sat. 10–4, Sun. 1–4. Built in 1883, the Byers-Evans House was designed in the Italianate style. Two prominent Denver families lived here, and the house has been restored and includes furniture original to the Evans family. The site includes an art gallery and a gift shop. Guided tours (the only way to view the house) are offered about an hour apart, six times a day (three tours on Sunday). Adults $6, seniors $5, children (6–12) $4, under 6 free.

✂ ♿ ♦ **The Children's Museum of Denver** (303-433-7444; cmdenver.org), 2121 Children's Museum Dr. Open Mon.–Fri. 9–4 (Wed. until 7:30), Sat. and Sun. 10–5. The museum caters to children from birth to 8 years old, using creative play experiences to help kids learn and prepare for life. This of course means that this place is a blast for kids. They can climb all over a real fire truck, put on a puppet show or perform a song, or learn about nutrition as they "shop" at My Market. Admission ages 2–59 is $8, age 60 and over $6, age 1 $6, and children under 1 free.

Clyfford Still Museum (720-354-4880; clyffordstillmuseum.org), 1250 Bannock St. Open Tue.–Sun. 10–5 (open until 8 on Fri.). Sitting in the shadow of the Denver Art Museum is the less celebrated Clyfford Still Museum. The museum contains the works of Clyfford Still, an influential 20th-century American abstract impressionist. Nearly 95 percent of what the artist created in his lifetime is housed here in a two-story, 28,500-square-foot facility that was designed specifically for this purpose. The museum opened in 2011. Adults $10, seniors $8, youth under 18 free.

♿ ♦ **Denver Art Museum** (720-865-5000; denverartmuseum.org), 100 W. 14th Ave. Open Tue.–Thu. 10–5, Fri. 10–8, Sat. 10–5, and Sun. 10–5. The art museum has housed Denver's finest collection of paintings and sculpture since 1893. More recently, the museum itself has become a piece of art. In 2006, an addition was completed that houses the museum's Modern & Contemporary and Western American Art collections. Designed by Daniel Libeskind, the building's radical lines and titanium exterior raised a few eyebrows. The city has come to terms with the newcomer, which really is a fantastic space in which to view art. Colorado residents: adult admission $10, seniors and students $8, youth (6–18) and children (under 6) free. Unlike the major art museums in other cities—Chicago, New York, Boston—DAM kind of sticks it to out-of-state visitors. Nonresidents: adult admission $13, seniors and students $10, youth and children free.

Denver Firefighters Museum (303-892-1436; denverfirefightersmuseum.org), 1326 Tremont Pl. Open Mon.–Sat. 10–4. The Denver Fire Department goes back to 1866. That original department was called the Volunteer Hook and Ladder Co. #1. In 1909, Fire Station Number 1 was built in Denver, and that is where you find the museum today. The museum educates visitors on the history of firefighting—from how people spread the alarm to how communities responded. There is also a lot to learn here about the Denver Fire Department in particular, and there is a lot of great information on fire safety. Adults $7, children (2–12) $5.

✂ ♿ ♦ **Denver Museum of Nature & Science** (303-370-6000; dmns.org), 2001 Colorado Blvd. Open daily 9–5. Located down the street from the Denver Zoo in Denver's City Park, the Museum of Nature & Science covers everything from Egyptian mummies to North American Indian cultures. You can explore human biology from DNA to organs in the Hall of Life exhibition, and kids can tackle hands-on activities in the Discovery Zone. In addition, the museum has an IMAX theater and planetarium with regular shows. Adult admission $14.95, juniors (3–18) $9.95, and seniors $11.95; does not include IMAX or the planetarium.

♿ ♦ **Forney Museum of Transportation** (303-297-1113; forneymuseum.com), 4303 Brighton Blvd. Open Mon.–Sat. 10–4, Sun. noon–4. The museum began as a private collection of antique cars. Today there are more than 500 exhibitions celebrating all sorts of transportation, from trains to automobiles—as they say, "anything on wheels." You can see Amelia Earhart's "Gold Bug" Kissel and one of the last remaining Big Boy locomotives. Adult admission $11, seniors $9, children (3–12) $5, and children under 3 free.

♿ ♦ **History Colorado Center** (303-866-3682; coloradohistory.org), 1200 Broadway. Open daily 10–5. Several years back, the Colorado History Museum moved, and changed its name. In early 2010, the museum moved from 1300 to 1200 Broadway.

DENVER ART MUSEUM

Renamed the History Colorado Center, the new location opened in 2012. This museum strives to preserve and educate guests about Colorado history. You can learn about women and their role as settlers and pioneers. There is an exhibition on the creation of the 10th Mountain Division and their contribution to the United States' efforts in World War II. The museum has numerous pieces of mining equipment and an original Conestoga wagon—the "prairie schooner" used by countless settlers on their westward journey. (I think you will be surprised by the size of this wagon up close. It can carry eight tons of cargo!)

　☂ **Molly Brown House Museum** (303-832-4092; mollybrown.org), 1340 Pennsylvania St. Open Tue.–Sat. 9:30–3:30 and Sun. noon–3:30 in the summer (June–August; check website for exact dates). Otherwise Tue.–Sat. 10–3:30 and Sun. noon–3:30. Few characters in Colorado history have continued to intrigue the public as has Molly Brown. Born in Hannibal, Missouri, Molly Brown made her way to Leadville, Colorado, where she married J. J. Brown. They grew wealthy in Leadville, primarily due to J. J.'s hard work and ingenuity. As their family grew, they moved to Denver, where they hoped to enjoy more social opportunities, eventually setting up home at 1340 Pennsylvania. Tours of the home are given throughout the day. The hours above indicate when the last tour begins. Exhibitions include items that belonged to Molly Brown and artifacts dating from the turn of the century when the Browns lived in the home. Adult admission $11, seniors, college students, and veterans $9, and children (6–12) $7.

　Museo de las Americas (303-571-4401; museo.org), 861 Santa Fe Dr. Through traveling exhibitions and exhibitions pulled from the museum's permanent collections, Museo de las Americas preserves and promotes an understanding of Latin American heritage. Exhibitions celebrate Latin American art and culture, both from the past and the present. Open Tue.–Sat. 12–5. General admission $5, seniors and students $3.

　♿ ☂ **Wings over the Rockies Air and Space Museum** (303-360-5360; wingsmuseum .org), 7711 E. Academy Blvd. Open Mon.–Sat. 10–5., Sun. noon–5. Located in a hangar in the old Lowry Air Force Base, the museum exhibits more than three dozen airplanes and space vehicles. It has everything from small civilian planes and military fighter planes to a 16-foot model of the Titan II launch vehicle. Adult admission $12.50, seniors and veterans $9, children (4–12) $6, and children under 4 free.

  ♿ **Buffalo Bill Museum and Grave** (303-526-0744; buffalobill.org), 987½ Lookout Mountain Rd., Golden. Open May 1–Oct. 31 daily 9–5; Nov. 1–April 30 Tue.–Sun. 9–5. According to his wife, Buffalo Bill always wanted to be buried on Lookout Mountain when he died, much to the chagrin of the folks in Cody, Wyoming, the town Buffalo Bill founded. The top of Lookout Mountain affords great panoramic views of Denver, and the trail to the gravesite is free. The museum, however, charges admission. Adults $5, seniors $4, children (6–15) $1, and children 5 and under free.

  ⍃ ♿ **Colorado Railroad Museum** (303-279-4591 or 1-800-365-6263; crrm.org), 17155 W. 44th Ave., Golden. Open daily 9–5. If you like trains, there is a lot for you to enjoy here. Driving into the parking lot, you are surrounded by trains—engines, cars, cabooses. Inside, there are exhibitions illustrating the history of the railroad in Colorado. Outside, tons of railroad equipment have been preserved from around the state, such as narrow-gauge locomotives that once served the mining industry up in the mountains and observation cars that once catered to tourists. Adult admission $10, seniors $8, children (2–15) $5, and children under 2 free.

  Cussler Museum (303-420-2795; cusslermuseum.com), 14959 West 69th Ave., Arvada. Open summers (May–Sept.) Mon. and Tue. 10–7. If you have read the adventures of Dirk Pitt, you know that author Clive Cussler likes his cars, and he does more than write about them. He's an avid collector and has an impressive stable of more than 75 of the world's finest vehicles—from a Stanley Steamer, to a passel of classic boat-tails, to a '65 Corvette Stingray. You can see them for yourself at the Cussler Museum in Arvada, a short drive from Denver. Adult admission $10, seniors $8, and children (under 12) $5.

THEME PARKS ⍃ ♿ **Elitch Gardens** (303-595-4386 for general information and 303-595-4386 for season passes or group sales; elitchgardens.com), 2000 Elitch Cir. Open May–Oct. daily 10–9. Early and late in the season, the park is closed most weekdays; see website for complete schedule. Elitch Gardens has been a Denver institution since 1890. Originally located at 38th Avenue and Tennyson Street northwest of town, the park opened at its present location in downtown Denver in 1995. From 1998 to 2007, it was branded Six Flags Elitch Gardens, but "Six Flags" was dropped after a change in ownership. This is a compact little amusement park that packs in more rides and attractions than its 70 acres would suggest is possible. The park has everything from a classic wooden roller coaster to the Flying Roller Coaster, which has guests hanging beneath the tracks sprawled out like Superman. General admission, which includes access to the Island Kingdom Water Park, is $49.99 at the gate (only $35.99 if you order online). Guests under 48 inches tall have limited access to rides and pay only $31.99.

  ⍃ ♿ **Lakeside Amusement Park** (303-477-1621; lakesideamusementpark.com), 4601 Sheridan Blvd. Gates open at noon (rides at 1). During weekdays the adult rides aren't running until after 6 or 7. For more than 100 years, families have been trekking to Lakeside in northwest Denver to be amused at this classic amusement park. From the highway the park looks a bit run-down, but up close its die-hard fans will tell you it's all about charm. (This park isn't a pair of starch-pressed Dockers; it's a pair of well-worn jeans, if you get my meaning.) The rides include a classic wooden roller coaster, a Ferris wheel, and more than a dozen rides just for little kids. Unlimited rides and gate admission $16 (weekdays), $25 (weekends and holidays). Or pay $3 gate admission and buy coupons for individual rides (coupons cost 50¢, rides take anywhere from one to six coupons).

FERRIS WHEEL AT ELITCH GARDENS

✎ ♿ **Water World** (303-427-7873; waterworldcolorado.com), 8801 N. Pecos St., Federal Heights. Open late May–early Sept., daily 10–6. This 64-acre water park is not to be missed. With 43 water attractions and 12,300 feet of water slides, there is enough here to keep you and the family busy all day. You can spend hours just float-ing around the Lazy River in your inner tube or try the Lost River of the Pharaohs, the first water ride to combine whitewater rafting with a themed animatronic attraction. Plenty of wave pools, places to sunbathe, and heart-pounding slides. Lines can get pretty long in the afternoon, so be sure to bring sandals, as the ground gets hotter and hotter as the day drags on. General admission $41.99, children 40–47 inches tall $36.99, and seniors $10.99. After 2 PM, sunset pricing goes into effect and tickets are significantly cheaper.

WINERIES & WINE TASTING **Balistreri Winery** (303-287-5156 or 1-866-896-9620; balistreriwine.com), 1946 E. 66th Ave. Open daily for winery tours and wine tasting noon–5. Close to the intersection of I-25 and I-76, Balistreri Winery is a short drive from downtown. The winery is located on a nice stretch of property that includes a patio for guests and greenhouses.

♿ **Creekside Cellars** (303-674-5460; creeksidecellars.net), 28036 CO 74, Evergreen. Open daily 11–5. The café at Creekside serves food until 4. Located along Bear Creek, about 30 miles west of Denver, Creekside Cellars makes for a great day trip. The café serves food inside or on the deck overlooking the water. Its Italian antipasto platter, a collection of cheeses, deli meat, and vegetables and olives, is the perfect snack after a wine tasting.

ZOOS & NATURE EXHIBITIONS ♂️♿ **Denver Botanic Gardens** (720-865-3500; botanic gardens.org), 1007 York St. Open daily in the summer 9–8; open daily in the winter 9–5. A wide walking path makes a winding loop through the numerous horticultural displays at the Botanic Gardens. The individual gardens are thematically organized. The Japanese Garden, for example, uses large ponds, carefully placed rocks, and plants to create a balanced atmosphere. In addition to the more exotic displays, indigenous plants are highlighted in the Plains Garden. Be sure to check out the tropical plants in the Boettcher Memorial Tropical Conservatory. To make a day of your visit, head over to the Monet Garden for lunch at the Monet Deck Café. Adult admission $12.50, seniors $9.50, youths (4–15) and students $9, and children 3 and under free. All rates cheaper in fall and winter.

Denver Botanic Gardens Chatfield (720-865-4346; botanicgardens.org/chatfield-farms), 8500 W. Deer Creek Canyon Rd., Littleton. Open daily 9–5. In the Denver suburb of Littleton, the botanic gardens maintains a working farm and native-plant refuge on 700 acres. Passenger vehicle pass $5.

♂️♿ **Denver Zoo** (303-376-4800; denverzoo.org), 2300 Steele St. Open daily, year-round. Summer 9–5, winter 10–4. Located in City Park, this 80-acre zoo receives over 1.5 million visitors every year. Guests come to walk the zoo's shady paths and to see the impressive collection of animals from around the world. The zoo is home to a three-ton rhinoceros named Mshindi that paints pictures—they are on display in the Pachyderm House. Every day in the summer, at 11, zookeepers bring out the elephants for a demonstration. They talk about the animals and field questions from the crowd. Also be sure to check out Bear Mountain, which when it was built in 1918, was the first exhibition in North America that tried to replicate an animals' natural habitat. It has since been placed on the National Register of Historic Places. Adult admission $13, seniors $11, children (3–11) $9, and children 2 and under are free. Admission rates are a few bucks cheaper from Nov. through Feb.

♂️♿🍴 **Downtown Aquarium—An Underwater Adventure** (303-561-4450; aquarium-restaurants.com/downtownaquariumdenver), 700 Water St. Open Sun.–Thu. 10–9 and Fri. and Sat. 10–9:30. When Denver's Ocean Journey went belly-up after less than three years, there was fear Denver would soon be without an aquarium. In 2002, however, the site was purchased by Landry's Restaurants, and a full-service seafood restaurant, bar, and ballroom were added. In addition to the million gallons of underwater exhibitions that focus on various ecosystems and the importance of conservation, the center-piece of the restaurant is a 150,000-gallon tank that holds an impressive variety of fish. Adult aquarium admission $19.50, seniors $18.50, children (3–11) $13.50, and children 2 and under free.

♂️♿🍴 **Butterfly Pavilion and Insect Center** (303-469-5441; butterflies.org), 6252 W. 104th Ave., Westminster. Open daily 9–5. If you have kids who are crazy about bugs, the Butterfly Pavilion is the perfect place to spend an afternoon. This insect zoo lets visitors get up close to invertebrates from around the world. It has a petting tank, called Water's Edge, where you can see and touch sea stars and other ocean dwellers. Or you can step into

FLOWERS IN BLOOM AT DENVER BOTANIC GARDENS

the tropical conservatory, a warm and humid greenhouse that is home to more than 1,200 butterflies. Adult admission $11 (adult residents of Westminster $9), seniors $9, children (2–12) $6, and children 1 and under free.

✳ Outdoor Activities

ALPINE SKIING **Loveland Ski Area** (303-569-3203 or 1-800-736-3754; skiloveland .com), 3877 US 6, Georgetown. Loveland is right off 1-70 at exit 216, 13 miles west of Georgetown. One of the most accessible ski areas to Denver, Loveland is less than 60 miles away. The ski area comprises two sections: Loveland Basin and the gentler Loveland Valley. Because Loveland has never developed a resort, it's seen primarily as a spot for locals to go day skiing. This means fewer amenities, but it also translates into cheaper lift tickets and shorter lines. With 77 trails on 1,385 skiable acres, there is terrain here for everyone. About 20 percent is rated for beginners; the rest is split between intermediate and advanced skiers. For free-skiers and snowboarders, there is a terrain park with some nice features.

BICYCLING There are hundreds of miles of bike paths, trails, and bike lanes throughout Denver. The city's 200-plus parks are all connected by bike routes. One of the most popular is the **Cherry Creek Path**, which runs about 15 miles from the Cherry Creek Reservoir in Aurora to downtown Denver, following Cherry Creek until it meets the South Platte River. This paved path is wide enough that even on the busiest days, there's plenty of room for everyone.

    Campus Cycles (303-698-2811; campuscycles.com), 2102 S. Washington St. Open in the summer Mon.–Fri. 10–6, Sat. 10–5, and Sun. 12–5. Winter Mon.–Thu. 10–6 and Fri. and Sun. 10–5 (closed Sat.). This company offers rental bikes, both cruisers and mountain bikes.

    Golden Bike Shop (303-278-6545; goldenbikeshop.com), 722 Washington Ave., Golden. Open Mon.–Fri. 10–6 and Sun. 12–5. Outside of Denver proper, the Golden Bike Shop has road bikes, mountain bikes, and cruisers for rent. A 24-hour rental runs $60 (metal frame) or $100 (carbon frame).

GOLF There are more than 70 golf courses in the greater Denver area. While a number of these are private, there are, nonetheless, enough public courses to keep you playing fresh greens for a long time.

    Arrowhead (303-973-9614; arrowheadcolorado.com), 10850 W. Sundown Tr., Littleton. Located in the foothills, Arrowhead features rolling terrain with stunning geological features. Greens fees $29–145.

    City Park (303-865-3410; cityofdenvergolf.com/golf-course/city-park), 2500 York St. This fine public course, owned by the city, is located right in town across from the zoo and the Museum of Nature & Science. Greens fees $27–39.

    The Ridge at Castle Pines North (303-688-4301; theridgecpn.com), 1414 Castle Pines Pkwy., Castle Rock. The rolling greens have been carved out of the region's natural covering of scrub oak and pine. The courses, two loops were designed to allow wildlife to pass through an untouched natural corridor. This is one of the most highly regarded courses on the Front Range. Greens fees $60–145.

    Riverdale Golf Courses (303-659-6700; riverdalegolf.com), 13300 Riverdale Rd., Brighton. The courses at Riverdale, the Dunes and the Knolls, have been longtime favorites of Front Range golfers. The Dunes is a great beginners' course, whereas the

A DAY IN THE MOUNTAINS

Although the mountains are right there for all to see, they are still 15 to 20 miles from downtown Denver. A great day trip is to head west on US 6 into the mountains from Golden. An easy detour en route leads up CO 119 to Black Hawk and (eventually) to the charmingly historic town of Central City. These towns are known today for gambling. Black Hawk looks as if a Vegas developer decided to plop some resort casinos in a Colorado canyon. Central City, however, has maintained its architectural heritage. It's downright old-timey. Most of the gaming here is tucked into the town's original structures. The casinos have saved this town from becoming a ghost town, but they've also left their mark. Be sure to stop by the **Central City Visitors Center** (303-582-3345; colorado.gov/centralcity; 103 Eureka St.) for stories about the real Central City, the town once known as the "Richest Square Mile on Earth" for its gold-mining operations. The visitor center is open daily 10–5.

Continuing on US 6 you will come to the small towns of Idaho Springs and Georgetown. Idaho Springs is familiar to thousands of Denverites who have stopped there on the way home after a day on the slopes. Many have made it a tradition to dine at **Beau Jo's Pizza** (303-567-4376; beaujos.com, 1517 Miner St.) for dinner on their way home. This pizzeria is a Colorado institution. Chicago has deep dish; New York has thin crust; and Colorado has the legendary mountain pie: pizzas here have a tall crust to hold the piles of toppings. Beau Jo's may be the first pizza place to stock tables with honey to drizzle on the remaining crust—it's sort of like dessert.

HISTORIC DOWNTOWN STRETCH OF CENTRAL CITY

THE PHOENIX MINE IN IDAHO SPRINGS

For a day in Idaho Springs, consider a hard-rock mine tour at the Phoenix Gold Mine (303-567-0422; phoenixmine.com). Just west of town on Trail Creek Road, this mine was first discovered in 1871. The tour takes around an hour, and the path is an even walk. There are no ladders to climb, so wheelchairs and strollers can make the trip with a little finagling.

A little farther up the interstate is Georgetown, a quaint mountain town full of shops and restaurants catering to day-trippers. Railroad Art by Scotty (303-956-7208; railroadartby-scotty.com), 509 Sixth St., features original prints of classic locomotives—many recapture the spirit of the early art deco posters. Right next door is Georgetown Rock Shop (303-569-2750), 501 Sixth St. At the back of the rock shop is the Russian Room, selling authentic antique icons and samovars from Eastern Europe.

A nice afternoon activity is a ride on the Georgetown Loop Railroad: Historic Mining & Railroad Park (1-888-456-6777; georgetownlooprr.com), 646 Loop Dr., Georgetown, CO 80444. This railroad makes a round trip to the old mining town of Silver Plume. On the way, the train stops at the Lebanon Silver Mine, where guests can get a guided tour.

For more information on Idaho Springs and Georgetown, visit the Clear Creek County Chamber of Commerce online at clearcreekcounty.org.

This trip can be amended with a return through Evergreen, following Bear Creek Canyon Rd. back into Denver (see "Another Day in the Mountains" later in this chapter). This route was a popular scenic drive in the early days of the automobile and is called the Lariat Loop in visitor bureau literature.

Knolls provides more challenging play. Greens fees for the Dunes are $39–49 for 18 holes; the Knolls $27–30.

HIKING There are a number of great places in the Denver area for hiking. Chatfield Lake State Park has numerous trails and hooks up with Waterton Canyon. Waterton Canyon is the eastern terminus of the Colorado Trail, which climbs up and through Colorado, ending near Durango. Closer to the mountains, there are trails at Red Rocks Park, and south of town there's the 2-mile loop at Roxborough State Park. (See *Green Space* for more details on the parks.)

HORSEBACK RIDING There are trails to ride and horses to rent at **Cherry Creek State Park** and **Chatfield Lake State Park**. The stables at both parks can be found at the same place online, chatfieldstables.com. This outfit maintains the Chatfield Stables on N. Roxborough Rd. in Littleton and the Paint Horse Stables on S. Parker Rd. in Aurora. Check out the website for a list of guided rides and lessons.

PADDLING **Confluence Kayaks** (303-433-3676; confluencekayaks.com), 2373 15th St. Open Mon.–Fri. 10–8, Sat. 10–6., and Sun. 12–5. This paddling outfit offers kayak lessons at Chatfield Lake State Park and on the South Platte River. Confluence rents everything you need for a day on the water, from wetsuits to kayaks. If you are new to the area, be sure to ask about guided tours and bike rentals.

Geo Tours (303-756-6070 or 1-800-660-7238; georafting.com), 229 CO 8, Morrison. The closest whitewater rafting to Denver is on Clear Creek near Idaho Springs. Geo Tours offers tours for rafters of all levels on Clear Creek. It also does trips on the upper Colorado and Arkansas rivers. Day trips and multiday trips available.

✲ Green Space

City Park, located east of downtown between York St. and Colorado Blvd., north of Colfax, is home to some of Denver's busiest attractions: the Denver Zoo and the Museum of Nature & Science. The 330-acre park goes back to the 19th century when the state gave Denver acreage to create parks throughout the city. City Park was (and still is) the biggest in Denver. It was designed in a classic style, reminiscent of Central Park in New York City. Considering how many people flock to the park's museum and zoo, it is surprising to find the park rarely crowded. So there is always plenty of room to toss the Frisbee, host a picnic, or simply roll out a blanket and take a nap. There are two lakes in City Park, and you can rent a paddleboat and toodle around to your heart's content.

Confluence Park is located downtown, across the river from REI and at the confluence of the Platte River and Cherry Creek. When settlers first arrived to the area, the South Platte River ran much wider and shallower than it does today. At one point, this section of the waterway was so polluted that it was avoided with a vengeance. Today the water here flows so clean that you will often see swimmers venturing in for a dip.

Cherry Creek State Park (303-690-1166; cpw.state.co.us/placestogo/Parks/cherry creek), 4201 S. Parker Rd., Aurora. Located 1 mile south of I-225 on Parker. Open daily 5–10. More than 1.5 million people visit Cherry Creek every year. The 840-acre reservoir is chock-full of trout, walleye, and pike (just to mention a few of the species sought here). You can rent a boat or boat slip at the **Cherry Creek Marina** (303-779-6144). A swim beach on the east side of the lake stays pretty busy in the summer. A system of trails runs throughout the 4,300-acre park. Horseback riding can be arranged through

WHAT'S THE STORY WITH MARIJUANA?

In 2012, Colorado voters passed Amendment 64, which allows folks to possess, use, and sell marijuana. (Interestingly, just four years earlier in 2007, the state legislators were arguing whether John Denver's "Rocky Mountain High" was an appropriate state song because of the suggestive lyric, "Friends around the campfire and everybody's high." Seems pretty darn appropriate now.)

Since then, dispensaries have sprung up all over the state, and along the Front Range in particular. The state's new attitude toward cannabis use has not only been a boon to those selling marijuana, it has sparked a sub-industry of pot tourism. Many of these tourists might be confused by the various rules and regulations surrounding marijuana use.

A few of the basics: You must be 21 in order to possess or consume marijuana in Colorado—and you must be able to prove your age. You don't need to be a resident to purchase pot, but transporting your purchase over state lines is a big no-no. There are limits to how much you can purchase and rules about when and where you can partake. The laws can be confusing, but stop by any dispensary and you can get a run-down on the ins and outs. There are also numerous online resources. The Colorado Pot Guide website (coloradopotguide.com), for example, is aimed at the cannabis-inclined tourist. The site outlines the basics of the law regarding marijuana and offers lists of dispensaries, pot-friendly (or 420-friendly) lodgings, and tours.

(It should be noted that marijuana is still illegal under federal law. Different administrations may are or not choose to enforce those laws.)

TOUR COMPANIES

My 420 Tours (my420tours.com) offers grow and dispensary tours, cannabis cooking classes, and more.

Lighthouse Cannabis Project (lighthousecannabisproject.com) takes guests on a two-hour exploration of the cannabis industry, called the "Seed to Sale" tour.

Paint Horse Stables (303-690-8235; chatfieldstables.com). The website has a complete list of available lessons and trail rides. You can also use the paved paths for bike riding and in-line skating. Campground details can be found under Lodging. Daily park pass $7 (except from Labor Day until the end of Sept. when it is $8).

Chatfield Lake State Recreation Area (303-791-7275; cpw.state.co.us/placestogo /parks/chatfield), 11500 N. Roxborough Park Rd., Littleton. Open daily 5–10 in the summer. The main entrance to the park is right off CO 470, just 1 mile south on Wadsworth. This is the most popular park in the Denver area. The centerpiece of the park is the Chatfield Reservoir, a beautiful lake for boating, fishing, or swimming. For boaters, the lake has two boat ramps and the full-service **Chatfield Marina** (303-791-5555; chatfieldmarina.com), where you can rent boats and boat slips. On the west side of the lake, the park maintains a swim beach with restrooms—open all summer, Memorial Day to Labor Day. More than 10 miles of trails (paved and unpaved) are open to hiking, biking, and horseback riding. You can rent horses and ponies at the **Chatfield Stables** (303-933-3636; chatfieldstables.com). There are several scheduled trail rides and lessons—details are on the website. Campground details can be found under Lodging. Daily park passes $5.

Roxborough State Park (303-973-3959; cpw.state.co.us/placestogo/parks/roxborough), 4751 North Roxborough Dr., Littleton. Call ahead for seasonal hours. Take Carpenter Peak Trail up to the top for fantastic views. The trail is 6.4 miles and takes you to an elevation of 7,160 feet. For a less strenuous hike, try the Fountain Valley Trail.

This 2-mile trek winds through the rock formations that really make the park unique and worth visiting.

Castlewood Canyon State Park (303-688-5242; cpw.state.co.us/placestogo/parks /CastlewoodCanyon), 2989 South CO 83, Franktown. Call ahead for seasonal hours. This day park offers plenty of opportunities to explore Castlewood Canyon. A paved trail along the canyon rim, the Canyon View Nature Trail, is perfect for walkers of all abilities. For more of a challenge try Rimrock Trail, an unpaved 2-mile hike. Creek Bottom Trail, a 1.7-mile hike, takes you to the canyon bottom.

Hayden Park on Green Mountain (303-697-6159; lakewood.org/HaydenPark), 1000 S. Rooney Rd., Lakewood. Open daily 5 AM–10 PM. Hayden Park features 2,400 acres of open space. There are miles of trails, and from the peak of Green Mountain, there are stunning views of Denver. Free.

Mount Falcon Park (303-271-5925; jef.co.us/open-space/parks/mount-falcon-park), Morrison. There are two trailheads with parking for Mount Falcon Park. On the east side of the park, there is a trailhead on Vine Street in Morrison. On the west side, you take Mount Falcon Rd. to the parking area. There is some excellent hiking to be found here with views of Denver and the Rocky Mountains. An interesting historical footnote is a marker you can hike to that identifies the location of the "Summer White House." This was a short-lived plan to build an estate here for U.S. presidents seeking to escape the humidity of the capitol. The endeavor did not get past the laying-the-foundations stage, but it's nice to hike and see what might have been. Free.

Waterton Canyon (denverwater.org/Recreation/WatertonCanyon), located on W. Waterton Rd., Littleton. Located on the south end of Chatfield Lake State Recreation Area, the Waterton Canyon trail follows the S. Platte River 6.5 miles up to the Strontia Springs Dam. The canyon is home to bighorn sheep that climb the steep walls. The trail can be used for hiking, biking, and horseback riding. Dogs are not allowed due to the bighorn sheep. It is one of the most popular day hikes in the Denver area. It is also the eastern terminus of the Colorado Trail, which continues on to Durango (see *Durango* for more information).

✽ Lodging

The Brown Palace, The Queen Anne B&B, and numerous other hotels and inns throughout Denver offer room service through **Delivered Dish** (303-991-3400; d-dish.com/denver). This service allows you to order off the menus of more than 50 local restaurants and have the food delivered directly to your room.

HOTELS ♿ (((•))) **The Brown Palace Hotel** (303-297-3111 or 1-800-321-2599; brown palace.com), 321 17th St. It says some-thing about The Brown Palace that it has a hotel historian and archivist on-staff. The hotel opened in 1892, during the days when men got rich mining in the mountains, and came to Denver to settle into "society." In the years since, it has hosted many of the rich, powerful, and famous, including several U.S. presi-dents. Teddy Roosevelt was the first in 1905. Historical tours are offered for $10 on Wed. and Sat. at 3. For private tours outside these two times, there is a charge. Not just a place to tour, however, The Brown Palace has 241 rooms, 33 executive staterooms, and three presi-dential suites. It offers 24-hour room ser-vice, twice-daily maid service, and a full-time concierge. The service is impec-cable, worthy of the hotel's near-legend-ary status in Denver. Rooms $229–329 and suites $329–1,400.

♿ (((•))) **Hotel Teatro** (303-228-1100 or 1-888-727-1200; hotelteatro.com), 1100 14th St. The hotel has 110 rooms, each with 12-foot ceilings and luxurious furnishings. The building was built in 1911 and originally housed the Denver Tramway Company. For guests who come to town to enjoy the theater, the hotel is directly across from the Denver Center for the Performing Arts. Rooms $169–1,500.

  The Magnolia Hotel Denver (303-607-9000 or for reservations 1-888-915-1110; magnoliahoteldenver.com), 818 17th St. The Magnolia in Denver opened in 1983 in the American National Bank Building, which was built in 1910. The hotel has 246 rooms. In the evenings, fresh chocolate chip cookies and milk are available in the Club Room. One of the nicer features of the hotel, the Club Room has plenty of comfortable seating and a beautiful fountain. Rooms $150–280.

  The Oxford Hotel (303-628-5400 or for reservations 1-800-228-5838; theoxfordhotel.com), 1600 17th St. The Oxford Hotel has been taking care of guests in this grand style in Denver since 1891. The hotel's spacious accommodations are decorated with European antiques and fine linens, and amenities include a full-service spa and babysitting services. Unique among hotels of its time, The Oxford has an atrium that allows daylight to fill the lobby and guest rooms. Rooms $200–260.

  Sheraton Denver Downtown Hotel (303-893-3333 or 1-800-325-3535; sheratondenverdowntown.com), 1550 Court Pl. Previously an Adam's Mark property, the Sheraton in downtown Denver is the largest hotel in the city. Its 1,225 rooms, 92 suites, and 133,000 square feet of meeting space make it a popular place for conventions. This is a full-service hotel with all the expected amenities, from free wireless Internet in the lobby (not in the rooms) to self-service guest laundry to 24-hour room service. The hotel has several options for dining and drinking. Rooms $127–339.

BED & BREAKFASTS   **Bud & Breakfast at the Adagio** (1-866-200-2837; budandbfast.com/bbadagio), 1430 Race St. For cannabis aficionados, the Adagio has transitioned from a traditional B&B to a pot-friendly inn that features a "Wake and Bake Breakfast." Located just south of Colfax in the Wyman Historic District, the Adagio has six guest suites, all decorated in bright colors and named after composers. Close to City Park and downtown. Guests must be 21 or older. If you like the concept, Bud & Breakfast has locations in Colorado Springs and Silverthorne. Rooms start at $299.

  Capitol Hill Mansion (1-800-839-9329; capitolhillmansion.com), 1207 Pennsylvania St. A few blocks from the Colorado State Capitol, the Mansion has five guest rooms and three two-room suites. From the moment you walk in the door, you will appreciate the simple elegance of this bed & breakfast. The inn's eight rooms are colorfully decorated. The Snowlover Balcony Room, however, stands out with a bold, 28-foot mural depicting an alpine forest in winter. Amenities include cable TV, wireless Internet, and private baths. You can ask for a room with a whirlpool bath or a fireplace if that suits your mood. Rooms $164–249. Children 2 and up are an extra $25.

  Castle Marne (303-331-0621 or 1-800-926-2763; castlemarne.com), 1572 Race St. Castle Marne is decorated in high Victorian fashion. The dining room, with its cherry paneling and beautifully hand-painted ceiling, is a thing to behold. Three of the nine rooms have their own private hot tubs. The Presidential Suite has a whirlpool for two and a sitting room in the castle tower. The inn serves a gourmet breakfast, and dinner is also available if you call ahead. Rooms $179–329 for double occupancy; elegant candlelight dinner $85 per guest.

  The Holiday Chalet (303-437-8245; theholidaychalet.com), 1820 E. Colfax Ave. Centrally located in the city's historic Wyman District, this restored Victorian brownstone is within easy reach of many of Denver's more popular attractions. The Museum of Nature & Science is just up the street, as is the Denver Zoo. LoDo is just a short drive or bus ride away. There are 10 rooms. You have several options when it comes to breakfast, such as French crepes or cowboy pancakes. Dogs are welcome and there is a cannabis-friendly smoking patio. Rooms $99–170.

((ᵖ)) **Lumber Baron Inn and Gardens** (303-477-8205; lumberbaron.com), 2555 W. 37th Ave. Each of this inn's five rooms features a private bath and Jacuzzi tub. The spacious home was built in the Potter Highlands neighborhood of Denver in 1890. The rooms are tastefully decorated to bring out the home's historic character. Note that all the rooms are located on the second floor, and there is no elevator. Rooms $159–249.

((ᵖ)) **The Queen Anne Bed & Breakfast Inn** (303-296-6666; queenannebnb .com), 2147-51 Tremont Pl. Ten rooms and four suites all decorated with their own theme, the most unusual of which is the Aspen Room with a wraparound mural depicting an aspen grove. (The furniture is also made out of aspen wood.) Old wooden floors throughout have a reassuring creak. In addition to breakfast, the inn serves Colorado wines in the evening. Amenities include a phone, but not cable TV. Several rooms have special bathtubs, and the Rooftop Room has a private deck with hot tub. Rooms $155–230 and suites $225–230.

CAMPGROUNDS **Chatfield Lake State Recreation Area** (303-791-7275; cpw.state .co.us/placestogo/parks/Chatfield), 11500 N. Roxborough Park Rd., Littleton. Natural grassland surrounds the four camping areas at Chatfield. There are a total of 197 sites divided in four sections, loops A–D. The majority of sites have full hookups, but 77 sites in loops B and C have only electrical. Restrooms and showers are centrally located, and each loop has its own laundry facility as well. If you are traveling with horses, campers can over-night their animals in Chatfield

Stables. Sites with full hookups $30; with just electrical $26.

Cherry Creek State Park (303-690-1166; cpw.state.co.us/placestogo /parks/CherryCreek), 4201 S. Parker Rd., Aurora. Cherry Creek has 125 sites, from basic tent sites to those with full hookups. Showers and laundry facilities are located conveniently throughout the campground. Sites with full hookups $30 and tent sites $20.

((ᵖ)) **Denver East/Strasburg KOA** (303-622-9274 or 1-800-562-6538; campdenver.com), 1312 Monroe St., Strasburg. Located about 40 miles east of downtown Denver, the Strasburg KOA has an outdoor swimming pool and hot tub for campground guests. There are facilities for all sorts of campers—you can park your RV, pitch your tent, or rent a Kamping Kabin. Plenty of trees make for comfortable camping. Rates begin at $25 for a basic tent site (with electricity), and go a little over $40 for a site with full hookups.

✳ Where to Eat

Denver is second only to San Francisco in the number of restaurants per capita, and you will find restaurants everywhere in the greater Denver-Aurora metro area. All these restaurants competing for a piece of the pie, so to speak, has resulted in top-notch dining. It seems every strip mall and shopping center has unique offerings for breakfast, lunch, and dinner.

DINING OUT ♿ 🍸 **Bistro Vendôme** (303-825-3232; bistrovendome.com), 1420 Larimer Sq. Dinner Mon.–Thu. 5–10; Fri. and Sat. 5–11; Sun. 5–9. Brunch Sat. and Sun. 10–2. If you are longing for a taste of the Old World, look no farther than Larimer Square's Bistro Vendôme. The European feel of this French bistro begins with its location. Tucked away from the busy streets and bustling crowds, to get there you walk through the Kettle Arcade to the Sussex breezeway. White table linens and intimate dining spaces complete the feel. The menu features traditional French bistro fare, with appetizers such as steak tartare, escargots, and French onion soup. For a main course, the steak frites comes highly recommended. And for the perfect complement to your meal, the bar has more than 60 different French wines. Dinner entrées $19–28.

♿ 🍸 **Buckhorn Exchange** (303-534-9505; buckhorn.com), 1000 Osage St. Open for lunch Mon.–Fri. 11–2; dinner (or as they say, "supper") Sun.–Thu. 5–9, Fri. and Sat. 5–10. First opened in 1893 by Henry "Shorty Scout" Zietz, one of Buffalo Bill Cody's frontiersmen, the Buckhorn Exchange is truly a living piece of Colorado history. It is a history you feel when you walk in the front door, with mounted animal heads and walls covered with historic memorabilia. Be sure to check out the liquor license on the wall—it was the first the state issued back in 1949. The house specialty is steak, but there's plenty of variety for the adventurous diner. From rattlesnake and Rocky Mountain oysters to buffalo prime rib and elk, game is a centerpiece of the menu. Dinner entrées range from $25–56. Lunches are less pricey. The authentic Dutch Lunch—bean soup, bratwurst, ribs, brisket, baked beans, and slaw—is a mere $14.50.

♿ 🍸 **Elway's** (303-399-5353; elways .com), 2500 E. First Ave. Open Mon.–Thu. 11–10; Fri. and Sat. 11–11; Sun. 11–9. Part steakhouse, part classy sports bar, Elway's has become a popular place for dining in the Cherry Creek area. Cofounder and local hero John Elway (former quarterback for the Denver Broncos, for those who don't keep up with sports) has been known to visit the bar and sign autographs from time to time. Although its specialty is steak, which is always well commented on, it has great burgers, too—try the smash burger, if you get a chance. Most dinner entrées (excluding steak) under $40.

Mercantile Dining and Provisions (720-460-3733; mercantiledenver.com), 1701 Wynkoop St. Dinner served daily from 5 PM. The idea behind Mercantile Dining and Provisions is to tell the story of food. The restaurant provides the climax and denouement, but the backstory and some character development is served in the adjoining market. In addition to selling specialty foods, the market is open for breakfast, lunch, and snacks from 7–5 and serves sandwiches and salads. The restaurant, in its turn, serves "elevated comfort food" in a casual dining room. Entrées are around $30, and the menu also includes family meals.

🍸 **Mizuna** (303-832-4778; mizuna denver.com), 225 E. Seventh Ave. Open Tue.–Sat. 5–10. The menu changes monthly, but fine food is a constant at Mizuna. Dishes represent a mixture of culinary traditions—Italian, French, American—and diners are never disappointed. Dinner entrées around $40.

♿ 🍸 **Panzano** (303-296-3525; panzano-denver.com), 909 17th St. (at Champa). Breakfast Mon.–Fri. 6:30–10; lunch Mon.–Fri. 11–2:30; and dinner Mon.–Thu. 5–10, Fri. and Sat. 5–11, and Sun. 4:30–9. Italian food, excellent pizza, and salads. Dinner entrées $26–44.

♿ 🍸 **Rioja** (303-820-2282; riojadenver .com), 1431 Larimer St. Open for dinner daily at 4. Lunch Wed.–Fri. at 11:30. Brunch Sat. and Sun. at 10. Located in Larimer Square, Rioja has helped establish the reputation the neighborhood has for fine dining. For over a decade, the chefs at Rioja have used locally sourced ingredients to prepare their Mediterranean-inspired menu. The dining experience is upscale without pretension. They also have an excellent wine list. Dinner entrées $19–40.

♿ 🍸 **Stoic and Genuine** (303-640-3474; stoicandgenuine.com), 1701 Wynkoop St. Open Sun.–Thu. 11–10, Fri. and Sat. 11–11. Here in Denver, you are pretty much as far from the oceans of the world as you're ever going to be, but that doesn't mean you must pass on fresh seafood. Stoic and Genuine is perhaps the best place in town for fresh fish, shellfish, clams, and oysters from around the world. The cuisine is modern. The restaurant also has a raw bar. Entrées $18–28.

&. Ÿ **Tamayo** (720-946-1433; richard sandoval.com/tamayo), 1400 Larimer St. Lunch Mon.–Fri. 11–2; dinner Sun.–Thu. 5–10 and Fri. and Sat. 5–11. Richard Sandoval is a celebrated chef, and he has restaurants throughout the country. Tamayo is known for its creative Mexican menu, and people simply rave about the margaritas. Dinner entrées $13–29.

&. Ÿ **Vesta Dipping Grill** (303-296-1970; vestagrill.com), 1822 Blake St. Open for dinner Sun.–Thu. 5–10 and Fri. and Sat. 5–11. Beneath every entrée on the Vesta Dipping Grill menu you will find a list of suggested sauces for dipping—or you can choose from any of the 30 sauces on offer. It is a fun concept that might get tired if the food weren't so darn good. This is considered required dining for people who enjoy food and can make it to Denver's Lower Downtown. Vesta has dedicated menus for people with various allergies and food intolerances—lactose, nut, wheat, etc. Dinner entrées $24–36.

&. Ÿ **The Fort Restaurant** (303-697-4771; thefort.com), 19192 Hwy. 8, Morrison. "Gates open" for dinner Mon.–Fri. at 6, Sat. and Sun. at 5. Walking into the replica of Bent's Fort feels like a step back into the early 1800s. In keeping with the décor, the menu strives to replicate the diet of the early mountain men, trappers, and pioneers who made their way to the original Bent's Fort on the Santa Fe Trail to buy and sell goods. Buffalo is its specialty (the Fort serves more than 50,000 buffalo dinners every year), but the entire menu gets rave reviews—it includes beef and seafood, game, pork, and poultry. Some of the items are unique, such as roast bison marrow bones as an appetizer and rosemary-infused panna cotta with huckleberries for dessert. Call for pricing.

&. Ÿ **The Old Stone Church Restaurant** (303-688-9000; oscrestaurant.com), 210 Third St., Castle Rock. The Old Stone Church Restaurant is located in the first church built in the town of Castle Rock, a good 25 miles south of downtown Denver. The architecture goes back to 1888, but the cuisine is all New American. Fine dining that's worth the drive. Rainbow trout and lamb shank top a menu that is anchored by duck tacos and buffalo burgers. Entrées $11–28.

EATING OUT &. **Biju's Little Curry Shop** (303-292-3500; littlecurryshop.com), 1441 26th St. There are some great little Indian places in Denver. Biju's stands out for its relaxed, quirky atmosphere and simple menu. This location is northeast of Coors Field in RiNo (River North Art District). If you enjoy the flavors of southern India, this places serves an excellent spicy chicken vindaloo bowl. Dishes $10–14.

&. **Brother's BBQ** (720-570-4227; brothers-bbq.com), 568 Washington St. Open every day 10–10 (later if there is a crowd). Founded in 1998 by two brothers from England, Brother's BBQ is considered by many to be Denver's best barbecue. The menu combines various barbecue traditions from around the country, so there's something here for every barbecue fanatic. There are now five locations around metro Denver. Most entrées $7–14.

&. Ÿ **Cart-Driver** (303-292-3553; cart-driver.com), 2500 Larimer St. Open daily, noon to midnight. Cart-Driver serves southern Italian cuisine. The name is inspired by the guy who delivered produce from Italian farms to villages, stopping to prepare meals along the way. The restaurant is housed in a shipping container, bringing the food transportation theme up to date. The house specializes in wood-fired pizza and fresh clams, the latter flown in daily. Pizzas $9–18.

✐ &. **Casa Bonita** (303-232-5115; casabonitadenver.com), 6715 W. Colfax Ave. Open Sun.–Thu. 11–9 and Fri. and

DENVER CHEFS TAKE FINE DINING TO THE STREETS

Street food has been part of the dining scene in Denver for decades. For a time, some of the best Mexican food you might find was sold out of a pickup truck in the Kmart parking lot. For example, there's a cart at the corner of Quincy and Gun Club Road in southeast Aurora that sells a killer breakfast burrito, and I've always counted on street vendors (perhaps sometimes unadvisedly) for the best hot dogs. But times have changed, and the bar has been raised quite a bit. The Denver truck/street food scene is off and running, and you now find some of the best food in town on the street.

For years folks have known about **Biker Jim's Gourmet Dogs** (bikerjimsdogs.com) at 16th and Arapahoe downtown. The business expanded to another cart on the Auraria Campus and recently opened a restaurant at 2148 Larimer. Foodies love the place. The likes of Anthony Bourdain rave on Biker Jim's unique dogs. The wild boar hot dog and one with reindeer are favorites with regulars.

Hang around the city long enough, and you're bound to catch sight of the **Steuben's Food Truck** (steubens.com/truck) driving by. Fans follow the truck's location on Twitter and Facebook, or they just call (303-475-9636). The menu is simple enough—burgers, pulled pork sandwiches, and BLTs with fries and wings or a wedge salad, among other things—but the quality is as good as what guests would expect to find at the Steuben's sit-down venue on 17th Ave.

Dessert lovers are not left out in the cold, either. The **Denver Cupcake Truck** (303-861-4912; cake-crumbs.com) is often on hand, dishing out its sweet cakes to the satisfied masses. (With more than 10,000 followers on Facebook, you know it's doing something right!)

Of course, there are others. Just to name a few, don't miss out on the **Brava! Pizzeria Della Strada** (303-835-1611; bravapizza.com), which travels with a wood-fired oven on the back of a pickup, making great pizza, and the **Biscuit Bus** (720-459-3846; denbisco.com), offering unbelievably comfortable comfort food.

Sat. 11–10. There is an online joke that says something like, "You know you're from Denver if the only time you visit Casa Bonita is when you have out-of-town guests." There's some truth to this. Although the restaurant has seen better days, it's still worth a trip, and kids *love* this place. With seating for 1,100 people, it has been said to be the largest restaurant in North America. The food isn't bad, but what people come for is the experience. The exterior of Casa Bonita gives just a hint of what you will find inside: a Mexican village at night. The over-the-top dining entertainment features a large pool with cliff divers, an old-time cowboy shootout (with the villain inevitably falling off a cliff into the pool), Black Bart's Cave, and an arcade. Sopaipillas come with every meal. Platters around $14; kid meals $5.

& ￥ **CityGrille** (303-861-0276; citygrille.com), 321 E. Colfax Ave. Open Sun.–Thu. 11–11, Fri. and Sat. 11–midnight. CityGrille is known for dishing up the best burgers in Denver (at least the editors of *5280* thought so). The menu offers three takes on the traditional hamburger—the Steakburger, the Buffalo Burger, and the crowd-pleasing CityGrille Burger. Or you can go Mexican with *chiles rellenos*, smothered in their award-winning green chili. Burgers around $10–13; other entrées $10–15.

& **Jack-n-Grill** (303-964-9544; jackngrill.com), 2524 N. Federal Blvd. The first time a lot of folks hear about Jack-n-Grill it has something to do with its seven-pound breakfast burrito and the standing challenge for anyone who would dare finish this beast solo. What often gets neglected, until later, is just how great its breakfast burritos are.

Everything here is great, from the breakfast tacos, to the huevos rancheros—and the lunch/dinner menu isn't too bad, either. The family behind the restaurant hails from New Mexico, and it shows in the delicious pork green chili. The menu includes $2 breakfast burritos to go. The big breakfast burrito is $15, but most breakfast entrées are $9–12. Lunch and dinner plates $9–13.

& **Parisi** (303-561-0234; parisidenver .com), 4401 Tennyson St. Open Mon.–Thu. 11–9, Fri. and Sat. 11–10. The dining experience at Parisi is casual—you order at the counter and either find a table in the dining room or take your food to go. Even though it's laid back, it serves up some of the best Italian food in Denver. You have to try one of Parisi's wood-oven-baked pizzas. Most entrées and pizzas $10–19.

& **Pete's Kitchen** (303-321-3139; petesrestaurantstoo.com/petesKitchen .html), 1962 E. Colfax Ave. Open 24 hours a day, every day. Since 1942, diners have been coming to Pete's Kitchen on Colfax. If you need a late-night bite, there is no place better in town. Pete's serves a traditional "Greek diner" menu of gyros and hamburgers, kebab sandwiches, and chicken-fried steak. The green chili is outstanding. The breakfast burrito is always a contender for "best in Denver" awards, and like the rest of the breakfast menu it is served all day—and all night, for that matter. Entrées $11–14; sandwiches and breakfast all under $10.

& **Racca's Pizzeria Napoletana** (303-296-7000; raccaspizzeria.com), 2129 Larimer St. Open Sun.–Thu. 11–10, Fri. and Sat. 11–11. Originally called Marco's Coal-Fired Pizza, the restaurant has expanded to four locations and changed its name. Racca's is the only restaurant in Colorado that serves authentic pizza Napoletana (as certified by the Italian Associazione Verace Pizza Napoletana). And it's every bit as good that designation suggests it should be. Keep it simple and try the Campania to experience the greatness of this pizza in its subtlety.

Just as all "champagne" made outside the Champagne region of France is just sparkling wine, all other pizza Napoletana in the state is just thin crust. (They also serve an excellent gluten-free pie.) Pizzas $14–19.

& **Spicy Pickle Sub Shop** (spicypickle .com), 1875 Lawrence St. The Spicy Pickle came and spread throughout the land. The chain launched from a single location but was soon spotted in 12 states. There were 16 locations in Colorado alone. Then, just as quickly as they spread, Spicy Pickle locations began to close their doors until none were left in Colorado, and you could only find shops in Nevada, Qatar, and Kuwait. But the tide is turning once again, and the Pickle has come home to Denver. As before, "spicy" is the optimal word to describe the eats—not hot, but spicy. Everything on the menu, from panini to salad, has a particular zing that makes it a standout place for lunch. The chicken Caesar salad may be the best I have ever had. The corn and green chili bisque is pretty good, too. Panini, subs, and large salads all around $10.

& Y **Steuben's Food Service Uptown** (303-830-1001; steubens.com), 523 E. 17th St. Open Mon.–Thu. 11–11, Fri. 11–12, Sat. 10–12, Sun. 10–11. Steuben's secured its position on the Denver dining landscape in 2006. The restaurant (and the sister location in Arvada) serves regional American favorites, from Nashville fried chicken to Maine lobster rolls. In addition to the two restaurant locations, keep an eye out for the Steuben's food truck. Dinner and entrées $12–20. Sandwiches $5–10.

& **WaterCourse Foods** (303-832-7313; watercoursefoods.com), 837 E. 17th Ave. Open daily 9–11. The vegetarian menu at WaterCourse Foods is extensive—relying heavily on mushrooms, seitan, and tofu—making it a favorite spot for local herbivores. The po' boy sandwich is highly praised, as is the tempeh burger. All dishes can be served vegan. Dishes $12–14.

DOG TOWN?

Few cities can match Denver when it comes to the breadth and depth of dining options you will find here. From steakhouses specializing in wild game to street vendors selling wood-fired pizza, there's not much it doesn't have. You might expect to find a couple of hot-dog joints, but Denver goes one better and offers a passel of wiener vendors. Here are a few favorites:

Billy's Gourmet Hot Dogs (303-284-2714; billysgourmethotdogs.com), 2445 Larimer St. Billy's has a fine collection of the usual dogs, plus some extras—the Healthy Fish Dog, for example. Sausage lovers won't go away disappointed, either. I am especially fond of the gourmet extras, such as the Garlic Pesto Blue Cheese Fries. There's also a location on Broadway in Englewood. Hot dogs $4, with fries $6.

Mile High Vienna Stand (720-379-4600; milehighvienna.com), 258 Santa Fe Dr. The original location is on Santa Fe, but you can also visit Mile High Vienna Stand in LoDo at 1312 21st St. The menu here is all Chicago, from the Chicago dog to the Juicy Beef sandwich. The stand even puts the two together in the Combo sandwich. A Chicago-style hot dog, fries, and a drink will run you $4.50.

Mustard's Last Stand II (303-722-7936; mustardslaststandcolorado.com), 2081 S. University Blvd. I first discovered Mustard's Last Stand in Boulder. It has great hot dogs and burgers. I come for the hand-cut fries. These potato sticks shame all others by comparison.

Steve's Snappin' Dogs (303-333-7627; stevessnappindogs.com), 3525 E. Colfax Ave. Steve's has the Chicago Dog, and the Atlanta Slaw Dog, and the quintessential Bronx Dog, but a few options look to give Denverites a dog of their own. The Rippin' Rockies Dog at Steve's is deepfried and topped with green chili, grilled red onions, sour cream, jalapeño peppers, and yellow mustard—then topped with diced red onions. You sleep alone after this one. There's also the Denver "Burrito" Dog, which is more of a burrito than anything else. Steve's also does a lot for local charities. Hot dogs $4.55.

And don't forget **Biker Jim's**, mentioned in the "Street Food" sidebar (page 47).

& **White Fence Farm** (303-935-5945; whitefencefarm.com), 6263 W. Jewell Ave., Lakewood. Open Tue.–Fri. 4:30–8, Sat. and Sun. 11:30–8. Although the business is expanding to new locations, the original restaurant southwest of downtown is still the best. It is the perfect place for a family dinner—especially if you have a large group. The menu has plenty of options, such as steak and seafood, but nearly everyone orders the Family Style Farm Chicken. The chicken comes with a mess of sides that include coleslaw, cottage cheese, corn fritters, and farm-made gravy (especially nice on the mashed potatoes), all served family style. Most nights there is live country and bluegrass music playing in the American Barn. Reservations are a good idea. Dinners run $11–26 and Family Style Farm Chicken is $16.95 per person—and White Fence sometimes has coupons online.

Work & Class (303-292-0700; workandclassdenver.com), 2500 Larimer St. Open Sun. and Tue.–Thu. 4–10, Fri. and Sat. 4–11. The food at Work & Class is a blend of Latin- and American-influenced dishes. For starters, there are meatballs served on poblano grits, and peppers served all different ways. The main menu features roasted goat and lamb, braised pork, and fried trout. You will order entrées in quarter-, half-, or one-pound servings—enough for a single diner or a larger party. Quarter-pound dishes run $8.75–11.75.

BAKERIES & COFFEE SHOPS & (ᵂⁱ-ᶠⁱ)

Hooked on Colfax (303-398-2665; hookedoncolfax.com), 3213 E. Colfax Ave. Open

ANOTHER DAY IN THE MOUNTAINS

Begin your trip at **Red Rocks** (720-865-2494; www.redrocksonline.com). Widely known as a music venue, locals know it is one of the prettiest places you'll find for hiking and biking. The Trading Post Trail winds 1.4 miles through this unique terrain. Here where the Great Plains meet the Rocky Mountains are acres and acres of deer and other wildlife. Trails take you through the area's iconic geology, past dinosaur fossils, prairies, and pine. Take your bike out on the Red Rocks Trail to hook up with 6 miles of riding, which include the trails of the adjacent Matthews/Winter Park Open Space.

The west side of the park abuts Bear Creek Canyon Rd. After your time at Red Rocks, follow the scenic canyon into the mountains, to the town of Evergreen. For lunch, consider stopping at **Da Kind Soup** (303-674-7687; www.dakindsoups.com), 27833 Meadow Dr. Owners Dustin and Ariane Speck offer guests a selection of house-made soups—from the traditional tomato

THE AMPHITHEATRE AT RED ROCKS

"every freakin' day" 7–10. In addition to its great coffee, Hooked on Colfax gets kudos for "going green" with corn cups and straws. It also sells books. Great place to kick back and read. The basement is finished up nicely and can be reserved for meetings or study groups.

♿ (◎) **Lube & Latte** (303-274-0713; lubeandlatte.com), 2595 Kipling St. Café open Mon.–Fri. 7–6 and Sat. 9–5. People who are waiting for work on their car don't want to sit in dirty, industrial waiting rooms, drinking two-day-old coffee and reading two-year-old magazines. So Eilis and Dustin McNamara-Olde came

BUFFALO HERD AT GENESEE PARK

and chicken noodle to less familiar options such as mushroom rosemary and carrot lentil—and sandwiches. For a more touristy experience, try dining at the **Little Bear Saloon** (303-674-9991; www.littlebearsaloon.com) in downtown Evergreen. The raised wooden sidewalks of Evergreen truly hark back to the town's earlier days. Open for lunch at 11. The crowd can get a bit rowdy after the sun goes down, especially on nights when a band is playing.

Just west of the downtown strip, Bear Creek is dammed, which has created Evergreen Lake. There is a walking path along the north rim of the lake, and at the far end is the **Evergreen Nature Center** (www.evergreenaudubon.org). Restrooms next to the parking lot are a godsend for families who have spent the better part of a day hiking and sightseeing.

If you decide to stay on overnight, put yourself up at one of Evergreen's B&Bs. The **Bears Inn** (303-670-1205 or 1-800-863-1205; www.bearsinn.com), which is about 3.5 miles south of town off CO 73, began in the 1920s as a teahouse. Today there are 11 rooms, each uniquely decorated with a private bath.

On the way back to Denver, take I-70 and pull off at exit 254 to watch the Denver buffalo herd at Genesee Park.

up with the idea of a coffee shop that is also an auto service station. Brilliant! And you don't even need to have anything wrong with your car to stop by and enjoy mocha or Lube & Latte's very own 10w-20 (coffee with a couple of shots of espresso).

ICE-CREAM SHOPS ♿ **Little Man Ice Cream** (303-455-3811; littlemanicecream .com), 2620 16th St. Let's be honest, taking the kids out for ice cream is often much more about the experience than the treat itself. That said, if the s'cream falls flat, it's not worth the trip. Little Man exceeds expectations on both counts. Not only does Little Man small-batch craft its own ice cream, the oversized milk can the shop calls home is a local landmark.

BARS, TAVERNS, & BREW PUBS ⅄ ⅋

Wynkoop Brewing Company (303-297-2700; wynkoop.com), 1634 18th St. Open every day 11 AM–2 AM (the kitchen closes at 11 on Mon.–Thu., at midnight on Fri. and Sat., and at 10 on Sun.). When a small army of entrepreneurs was beginning to breathe life back into Denver's lower downtown, the Wynkoop brew pub was one of the first places to set up shop. The brew pub opened in 1988, founded by a group of entrepreneurs, including one John Hickenlooper, who would go on to become the mayor of Denver. Wynkoop's has live theater, the Denver Center for the Performing Arts (DCPA) is often a key stop for touring Broadway productions. All the big shows are here, so

check out its site to see what's on the schedule while you are in town.

Brik on York (303-284-6754; brik.bar), 2223 E. Colfax Ave. Open Tue.–Fri. 4:30–close, Sat. and Sun. 11–close. Located east of downtown on Colfax, Brik on York is a great place for a drink. Brick walls, vintage bric-a-brac, lots of folks with tats. It's also a great place for a meal. The food is incredible, from small plates like oozing burrata and upscale deviled eggs with pork belly to wood-fired pizza and *carne e formaggio*.

MUSIC ⅊ **Red Rocks Amphitheatre** (720-865-2494; redrocksonline.com), 18300 W. Alameda Pkwy., Morrison. Everyone who's anyone has performed at Red Rocks. Bono waving a large white flag during U2's legendary concert in 1983 is just one of many iconic images that have secured the place of Red Rocks in rock-and-roll history. The park's natural amphitheater, formed by two 300-foot monoliths, creates perfect acoustics, and performers have been coming to the site since the early 1900s take advantage of its unique qualities.

⅄ **Grizzly Rose Saloon & Dance Emporium** (303-295-1330; grizzlyrose.com), 5450 N. Valley Hwy. This is the area's best-known country music nightclub. A lot of stars have played the stage here—Willie Nelson, LeAnn Rimes, and John Michael Montgomery, to name a few. Weekly dance lessons teach everything from line dancing to the two-step.

Opera Colorado (303-778-1500; operacolorado.org), 695 S. Colorado Blvd., Ste. 20. The opera company puts on performances at the Ellie Caulkins Opera House, which is part of the Denver Center for the Performing Arts.

❋ Selective Shopping

REI–Flagship (303-756-3100; rei.com/stores/denver.html), 1416 Platte St. Open Sun. 10–7, Mon.–Sat. 9–9. Occupying the old Denver Tramway Power

CLIMBING WALL AT REI'S FLAGSHIP STORE IN DENVER

Company Building, REI's flagship store sits right on the South Platte River across from Confluence Park. Before you even walk through the door, you get a sense of REI's outdoor spirit. The landscaping, with a thick grove of aspen and a boulder for climbing, captures the natural feel of Colorado. There's even a singletrack bike loop for customers looking to test the new mountain bikes. More than 5 million bricks were used when the building was originally built. Three stories tall, half of the space indoors was left open, leaving room for a massive climbing wall. Everything you could want for any outdoor adventure is here. So if you can't find what you're looking for, be sure to ask.

Rockmount Ranch Wear (303-629-7777 or 1-800-776-2566; rockmount.com), 1626 Wazee St. Open Mon.–Fri. 8–6, Sat. 10–6, and Sun. 11–4. Rockmount is the home of western fashion. The store was founded in 1946 by Jack Weil, who, up until his death in 2008 at the age of 107, still went to work every day. It was Jack who revolutionized the cowboy uniform, introducing the distinctive slim-fitting western shirt with snaps instead of buttons. Rockmount clothing is still predominantly made in America. Be sure to check out the store to get a glimpse of living history as it continues to thrive in downtown Denver.

Savory Spice Shop (303-477-3322 or 1-888-677-3322; savoryspiceshop.com), 1537 Platte St. Open Mon.–Fri. 10–6, Sat. 10–5, and Sun. 11–4. When we first discovered Savory Spice Shop, it was a revelation. Apparently word has caught on because there are now more than two dozen shops across the country. The original location is near 15th and Platte Streets, and in my opinion, it's still the best. This store is a real delight for aspiring cooks. It carries a large assortment of spices that are ground right there in the shop. The selection is amazing—there are at least a dozen different kinds of peppercorns alone. There are also spice mixes of the shop's own creation. A personal favorite of mine is the Mt. Massive steak seasoning. Shopping for your kitchen might feel a little strange if you are on vacation, but everything is available on its website when you get home.

Tewksbury & Co (303-825-1805; tewksburycompany.com), 1512 Larimer St., R-14. Open Mon.–Fri. 10–7, Sat. 11–6, and Sun. noon–5. This tobacconist shop on Larimer carries a fine selection of cigars and pipe tobacco, as well as other tobacciana. It also has a wide selection of wines from a number of Colorado's wineries. Every day from 1:30–5, the shop hosts a wine tasting. This is a great opportunity to sample several local wines if you can't make the trek to each individual winery.

✳ Special Events

January: **National Western Stock Show** (303-295-6124; nationalwestern.com), 4655 Humboldt St. The two-week stock show begins with a parade—complete with longhorn cattle walking the streets of downtown Denver. Livestock shows, the rodeo, and plenty of activities for kids all make this a required annual event for families.

May: **Downtown Denver Arts Festival** (303-330-8237; denverartsfestival.com), Stapleton Northfield. Once held downtown, the Denver Arts Festival now sets up on the site of the former Stapleton International Airport east of Denver. More than 125 Colorado artists come to participate in this fine art and craft exhibition.

September: **A Taste of Colorado** (303-295-6330; atasteofcolorado.com), Civic Center Park. Held every year over Labor Day Weekend, the festival brings together great food by local eateries, an art fair, and a full weekend of musical performances.

BOULDER

Part university town and part upwardly mobile hippie enclave, Boulder has a character all its own. The city touts cultural resources found nowhere else in the state—this is the only town I know of that has its own pottery studio. The residents of Boulder as whole are passionate about the outdoors and outdoor recreation. This in turn translates into a passion for the environment and healthy living. Boulder residents lead North America in organic food consumption. A quick look at a list of corporations that call Boulder home reveals many familiar names—Celestial Seasonings, Wild Oats Market, and Horizon Organic Dairy—all companies known for their promotion of natural goodness. Maybe this is why Boulder is regularly touted as the happiest city in the country.

On a warm day, the city's parks, bike paths, and sidewalks are full of people jogging, in-line skating, and riding their bike. A stroll through Boulder's Pearl Street Mall on a spring afternoon finds buskers making their music wherever they can—audience or not. During my last trip, it was a cold day and there were still four guitarists, two percussionists, and a guy wailing on the sax, all adding their signature sounds to the laid-back atmosphere of downtown.

Part of Boulder's vibrancy comes from the University of Colorado at Boulder. Not only is the university one of the largest employers in Boulder County, but the annual influx of nearly 30,000 students means the population, to some extent, is always changing—and Boulder seems to be a town that is not at all afraid of change.

Boulder's history goes back to the 19th century. In 1858, prospectors looking for gold settled near the mouth of Boulder Canyon. Soon the town of Boulder City was established. The town came to be a trading post of sorts, supplying the many miners heading into the mountains with gear and equipment. With the growth of retail, saloons and houses of ill repute were established to cater to miners and their vices. Rail service came in 1873, and in 1874, Boulder became home to the new University of Colorado.

In the 20th century, Boulder continued to grow and change. Tourism, which had been an industry in Boulder from early on, was greatly boosted by the building of the Hotel Boulderado in 1909. Several decades later at the end of World War II, the university's enrollment swelled with folks taking advantage of the GI Bill.

In recent decades, numerous tech companies have come to make Boulder their home. Sun Microsystems and IBM are two of the county's largest employers. Not only does the city provide the kinds of cultural, recreational, and entertainment activities that help attract the best employees, but the nearby university is constantly bringing the brightest and best students and faculty to study and do research.

Shopping and business districts such as the Hill and the Pearl Street Mall, and recreational opportunities in the nearby mountains and Boulder Canyon, mean visitors can mountain bike in the morning, enjoy a bowl of soup at The Kitchen before hiking into the Flatirons, and be back for fine dining at the Dushanbe Teahouse for dinner.

GUIDANCE Boulder Convention & Visitors Bureau (303-442-2911 or 1-800-444-0447; bouldercoloradousa.com), 2440 Pearl St. In addition to its main office on Pearl St., the Visitors Bureau maintains two visitor kiosks in Boulder. One is located right downtown

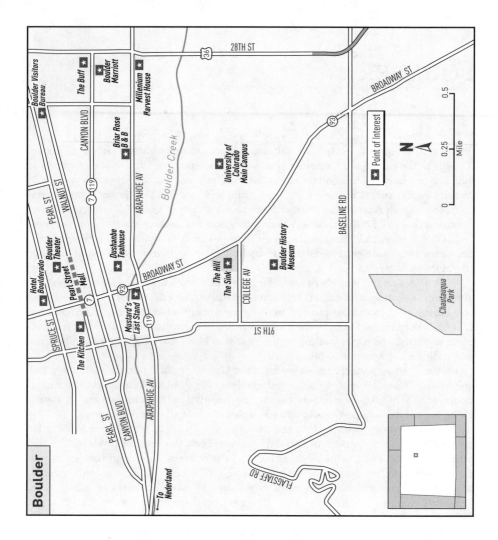

Boulder

on the Pearl Street Mall, in front of the courthouse. The other is several miles southeast of town on US 36.

More websites:
boulderdowntown.com
getboulder.com

GETTING THERE *By car:* From Denver, take I-25 north to the Denver–Boulder Turnpike (US 36), which takes you right into the city. From the north, take exit 240 off I-25 onto CO 119. That will take you west to the Diagonal Highway (still CO 119), which leads directly into Boulder.

By air: **Denver International Airport** (303-342-2000 or 1-800-247-2336; flydenver .com) is about a 45-minute drive from Boulder. **Super-Shuttle** (1-800-258-3826; super shuttle.com) takes passengers from DIA to Boulder. And the DIA operates **SkyRide**

THE UNIVERSITY OF COLORADO AT BOULDER

(303-299-6000; rtd-denver.com/airport.shtml), which also offers affordable transportation to and from the airport.

By train: **Amtrak** (1-800-872-7245; amtrak.com) does not have direct service to Boulder, but does operate its Thruway bus service that stops at the Greyhound stop at the gas station at the corner of 30th and the Diagonal Highway.

By bus: **Greyhound** (1-800-231-2222; greyhound.com) has a regular stop in Boulder at the gas station at the corner of 30th and the Diagonal Highway. Tickets are not available at this stop and must be bought in advance.

GETTING AROUND *By car:* Getting around by car is no problem in Boulder. There is plenty of parking downtown, including a number of parking structures.

By bus: The Denver RTD operates the bus system in Boulder. The routes are named for easy identification—Hop, Skip, Jump, Bound, Stampede, Dash, and Bolt. Hop makes a regular tour down Pearl Street.

✷ To See & Do

GUIDED TOURS **Banjo Billy's Bus Tours** (banjobilly.com). To be fully immersed in the weirdness that is Boulder, take one of Banjo Billy's bus tours. There are several from which to choose. History tours (my favorite), ghost tours, and brewery tours are all conducted from the crazy hillbilly shack on wheels. Not your run-of-the-mill drive through town. The tours are entertaining as well as informative. Tickets in the $15–25 range. (They have also started giving tours of Denver.)

MORK & MINDY

In 1978, a young Robin Williams made a cameo on the sitcom *Happy Days* as the alien Mork. (The show had literally jumped the shark at the beginning of the fifth season. Mork appeared later that season.) When *Happy Days* began its sixth season in the fall of 1978, the spinoff *Mork & Mindy* debuted on ABC. The show took place in Boulder. Presumably, the idea was that an alien who wore rainbow-striped suspenders, drank with his finger, and slept upside down would not stand out among the other crazies in Boulder. Although the show was shot on a set, the outdoor shots of the house they lived in were from Boulder. The house is still there of course—two blocks off Pearl on Pine Street, near the corner of 16th and Pine. Remember that this is someone's home, so please don't go knocking on the door asking for a tour of Mork's loft.

MORK & MINDY'S PLACE

HISTORIC SITES ♿ **Chautauqua National Historic Landmark** (303-442-3282; chautauqua
.com), 900 Baseline Rd. In the late 19th century, there was a movement in the United States
to promote adult education. The movement began in upstate New York at Chautauqua Lake
with a meeting of Sunday school teachers. At first, the intention was to improve teacher
education, but soon the mandate was to bring a "college outlook" to the working masses
and the middle class. In 1898, the Colorado Chautauqua opened in Boulder as a retreat
for educators. Today, Chautauqua continues to entertain and educate thousands through
countless concerts, lectures, art exhibitions, and other programs. The park offers free tours
of historic Chautauqua. In addition to the Auditorium and the Dining Hall (both built in
1898), the site has numerous historic buildings, including 98 cottages. Tour times vary, so
check the website for current details. Admission is free.

Mapleton Historic District. The Mapleton Hill neighborhood dates back to the late
19th century. The neighborhood is centered around Mapleton Avenue, which runs east
to west three blocks north of downtown Boulder. It is bordered on the west and east,
respectively, by Fourth and Broadway. Concord marks the northern and Spruce the
southern boundaries. As Boulder continued to grow and expand into the 20th century,
wealthy residents tended to build homes south of Mapleton Avenue, while working
class families filled out the north side of the neighborhood. The neighborhood preserves houses of both historic and aesthetic value.

Historic Boulder (303-444-5192; historicboulder.org), 1123 Spruce St., is an organization that works to preserve historic sites in Boulder. At its office on Spruce Street
you can get self-guided walking tour brochures for this neighborhood. It also has brochures that will guide you through Columbia Cemetery, the University of Colorado, the
Whittier Neighborhood, Chautauqua, Historic Downtown Boulder, and the University
Hill neighborhood. Guided tours are offered during the holidays.

MUSEUMS ♿ 👆 **Museum of Boulder** (303-449-3464; museumofboulder.org), 2205
Broadway. In 2017, the Boulder History Museum moves from their old location in the
Harbeck-Bergheim House on Euclid Avenue to a new facility on Broadway. The name
changes too. Check the website for hours. In the 60-odd years since the museum's creation, more than 35,000 objects, all with significance to the story of Boulder, have been
donated by local families. To keep the museum fresh, displays are changed several
times a year. Adult admission $6, seniors $4, children and students $3, and children
under 5 free.

♿ 👆 **Boulder Museum of Contemporary Art** (303-443-2122; bmoca.org), 1750 13th
St. Open Tue.–Sun. 11–5. Back in 1972, local artists created the Boulder Arts Center to
support and promote the visual arts. Over the years, the mission of the center broad-
ened, and the name changed to the Boulder Museum of Contemporary Art. Today, the
BMoCA includes art from all over the world and has become a venue for performance
art as well. See website for current shows and exhibitions. Admission is $1.

♿ **Leanin' Tree Western Art Museum** (303-530-1442 or 1-800-777-8716; leanin
treemuseum.com), 6055 Longbow Dr. Open Mon.–Fri. 8–6, Sat. 9–5, and Sun. 10–5.
First and foremost, Leanin' Tree is a manufacturer of greeting cards. It began back
in 1949 with four western-themed Christmas cards, and today has more than 3,000
different cards for sale at numerous independent outlets around the country. The company maintains a fantastic museum with extensive western paintings and sculptures.
Outside is a sculpture garden to display large-scale works. A quick walk around will
not take a lot of time, and it's a great stop to make before or after taking the tour at
Celestial Seasonings. Admission is free.

NATURAL ATTRACTIONS **Boulder Falls.** Driving west up CO 119 to Nederland, there are signs along the road for Boulder Falls. It's about 11 miles west of town. Parking is on the south side of the road and the falls are on the north. This 5-acre park holds a real gem of a waterfall, often referred to as the "Yosemite of Boulder Canyon," just a short walk from the highway. Water cascades down 70 feet to the canyon floor. The park is open dawn to dusk.

Flatirons. Located to the southwest of town, there is no geological feature more synonymous with Boulder than the Flatirons. They are conglomerate sandstone that has been heaved up at an angle and subsequently exposed by erosion. Geologists estimate that these formations were heaved up to their current position 35 to 80 million years ago. The largest have been numbered north to south, one to five. For a view of the Flatirons, try driving south on CO 93 south of town. Or try the Flatirons Vista Trail (see "Hiking" under *Outdoor Activities*).

SCENIC DRIVES **Boulder Canyon.** The drive up to Nederland on CO 119 (a.k.a. Boulder Canyon Dr.) follows Boulder Creek up to the Barker Reservoir. There are many places to pull over and take in the scenery.

Peak-to-Peak Scenic and Historic Byway. This 55-mile drive through the mountains begins in Black Hawk/Central City and makes its way north to Estes Park. The byway is easy to get to from points all along the Front Range and offers views of the Continental Divide.

BOULDER FALLS

TOURS ✐ ♿ ☂ **Celestial Seasonings** (1-800-434-4246 or 303-581-1202; celestial seasonings.com), 4600 Sleepytime Dr. Visitors to Boulder should make an effort to tour the Celestial Seasonings factory. The facility cranks out enough tea to make 1.2 billion cups a year, making it the largest herbal tea manufacturer in North America. Factory tours take about 45 minutes and include a short informative video. Visitors get to see tea in many of its incarnations, from the dried leaves that arrive in crates to the sifted form that makes it into the tea bags. A highlight of the tour is the stop in the mint room, where peppermint and spearmint clear your sinuses. Tours begin on the hour at 10, with the last at 3. On Sunday, the first tour is at 11 and the last is at 2. Space is limited and openings are doled out on a first-come, first-served basis. After the tour, take a look around in the tea shop or grab lunch in the café.

✐ ♿ ☂ **National Center for Atmospheric Research** (303-497-1000; scied.ucar.edu /visit), 1850 Table Mesa Dr. Open Mon.–Fri. 8–5 and Sat. and Sun. (and holidays) 9–4. Tours on Mon., Wed., and Fri. at noon. Scientists at the NCAR, which is primarily a research facility, study such things as the world's changing climate, the science of hurricanes, and how to come up with better models for predicting floods and tornados. For the public, NCAR offers guided and self-guided tours of the Mesa Lab. The visitor center has several exhibitions that teach about the sun, weather and climate, and instrumentation and technology. The Walter Orr Roberts Weather Trail is also a popular hike. The trail is paved and wheelchair accessible. Admission is free.

WINERIES & BREWERIES ♿ **Augustina's Winery** (303-545-2047; augustinaswinery .com), 4715 N. Broadway, B-3. Open Fri. and Sat. 1–7, Sun. and Thu. 1–5. This small winery north of Boulder has a tasting room. Tasting hours vary, so call ahead. For your convenience, the wines at Augustina's have been nicely paired with some down-to-earth foods and activities. The Boulder Backpacking Wine, for example, is the perfect complement to an evening campfire after a day of hiking, and the WineChick Pinot Noir "goes well with activities involving peanut butter." If things aren't too rushed, someone would be happy to give you a tour of the facilities.

♿ **BookCliff Vineyards** (303-449-7301; bookcliffvineyards.com), 1501 Lee Hill Rd. Tasting room open year-round, Thu.–Sun. 1–6. Locals John Garlich and Ulla Merz grow grapes on the weekends out in Palisade. Most of their grapes go to other wineries, but they keep a third for their own winery here in Boulder. As their reputation grows, so does their wine production. On Friday evenings in the summer they often have live music until 9:30.

Oskar Blues (303-776-1914; oskarblues.com), 1800 Pike Rd., Longmont. Open Mon.–Fri. 10–8, Sat. and Sun. noon–8. If you have pretensions, it's best to leave them behind when visiting the Oskar Blues brewery. Known for taking craft beer and putting it in a can, the folks here struck a blow against less-than-fresh beer and launched a truly classic brew to boot. Dale's Pale Ale was the first and most popular, but others have followed. You can learn more about all of that with a tour. Meet at the Tasty Weasel Taproom Fri.–Sun. The brewery offers four free tours on each of those days. Check the website or call ahead for an up-to-date tour schedule.

Redstone Meadery (720-406-1215; redstonemeadery.com), 4700 Pearl St. #2A. Tasting room open Mon.–Fri. noon–6:30 with tours at 1 and 3; Sat. noon–5 with a tour at 12:30. The brewing of mead, or honey wine, goes back at least to 1100 B.C. Aristotle wrote of mead, and warriors in the epic of Beowulf sang songs and told their tales in the mead-hall. And yet there are few places in the world where mead is still brewed today. Luckily, one of those places is in Boulder. At Redstone Meadery you can taste the fruit of the bee and get a tour of the facilities.

✳ Outdoor Activities

One of the reasons people give for moving to Boulder is the accessibility of the great outdoors. Runners, hikers, rock climbers, and cyclists have a seemingly endless number of trails, paths, and climbs for their recreational pursuits, many of which are close to town. If there is nothing here that strikes your fancy, the staff at most of the hotels and inns in Boulder can direct you to local trailheads, or stop by one of the outfitters or shops listed below. These folks live the outdoors and are happy to share their local knowledge.

ALPINE SKIING & SNOWSHOEING **Eldora Mountain Resort** (303-440-8700; eldora .com), 2861 Eldora Ski Road #140, Nederland. Take CO 119 up to Nederland, follow CO 119 to the south for 1 mile and then turn right on CO 130. Lifts run Mon.–Fri. 9–4; weekends and holidays 8:30–4. The elevation at the top of Eldora is 10,800 feet, making it 1,600 feet above the base of the resort. There are 680 skiable acres, which includes 55 trails, 12 lifts, and a Terrain Park. With 300 inches of snow falling annually, the resort relies little on snowmaking. The RTD out of Boulder operates regular bus service to and from Eldora during ski season.

BICYCLING The city of Boulder has 38 miles of trails open to off-road cyclists. In addition, the 7-mile **Boulder Creek Path**, which runs from Boulder Canyon out to Arapahoe Road near the Valmont Reservoir, is a cyclist's dream, allowing bikes to access the heart of Boulder without having to drive in the street.

Community Ditch Trail. Starting at the Doudy Trail trailhead, located west of CO 93 on Eldora Springs Dr., the Community Ditch Trail runs east to the Marshall Reservoir. The 4-mile route is a combination of trail and dirt roads. There are not many trees along this route, so it's best ridden in the morning or evening when there is some respite from the sun. The views of the Flatirons are impressive. At its eastern terminus, the trail connects with the **Greenbelt Plateau Trail**, which offers another 1.6 miles of riding through open grasslands.

Switzerland Trail. The trail is built on the old railroad bed of the Switzerland Trail Railway, and as such, it's popular with the four-wheeling crowd. To get there, take CO 119 west out of Boulder. In about 3 miles turn right on Fourmile Canyon Road (CO 118). Continue 10 miles to Sunset. Turning right in town will put you on the Switzerland Trail. Riding south takes you to Bald and Sugarloaf mountains. Or you can start at Sugarloaf Mountain Road trailhead and go north to Gold Hill.

The Bikesmith (303-443-1132; boulderbikesmith.com), 1668 30th St. Located at Arapahoe and Folsom. Open daily 10–5 (summer), Mon.–Sat. 10–5, Sun. noon–4 (winter). The Bikesmith rents full- and front-suspension mountain bikes, cruisers, road bikes, and even recumbent bikes. The shop also offers service if you need a repair or just a tune-up. Rentals for 24 hours run $35.

University Cycles (303-444-4196 or 1-800-451-3950; ubikes.com), 839 Pearl St. Open Mon.–Sat. 10–6, Sun. 11–5. University Cycles rents town cruisers, mountain bikes, and some really nice road bikes. The shop also has all the service and parts support a cyclist could need. Rentals for 24 hours run $35–90 (electric bikes $70).

FISHING Several local lakes are popular with anglers. **Boulder Reservoir** (303-441-3461; ci.boulder.co.us), 5565 51st St., is north of town off the Diagonal Highway. **Barker Reservoir** is just east of Nederland at the top of Boulder Canyon. Public access to the lake on the west and north shores provides opportunities for bank fishing. **Brainerd**

ELDORA SKI AREA OUTSIDE NEDERLAND

Lake is found in the Roosevelt National Forest and is the centerpiece of the Brainerd Lake Recreation Area. High in the mountains, the scenery around Brainerd is simply beautiful. The recreation area also has a number of trails for hiking. **Walden Ponds Wildlife Habitat** (east of town at 75th and Valmont streets) was built up on the site of old gravel pits. Five ponds were created, and great effort went into making the area a fitting wetland for local wildlife. The ponds are stocked with several species including large and smallmouth bass, bluegill, and channel catfish. Bass are catch-and-release only. One pond, Wally Toevs Pond, is set aside for seniors and the handicapped and requires a special pass.

Rocky Mountain Anglers (303-447-2400; rockymtanglers.com), 1904 Arapahoe Ave. Open Mon.–Fri. 9–6, Sat. 9–5, and Sun. 9–4. The folks at Rocky Mountain Anglers offer everything from gear to fully guided fishing trips. They also report on the conditions they find on the waters they fish on their website. A fully guided day trip for one person runs $270.

GOLF **Flatirons** (303-442-7851; flatironsgolf.com), 5706 Arapahoe Ave. The Flatirons first opened in 1993. This is the closest golfing to Boulder. Golfers enjoy mountain views and a course lined with old-growth trees. Greens fees during peak season $34–39 for 18 holes.

Indian Peaks (303-666-4706; indianpeaksgolf.com), 2300 Indian Peaks Tr., Lafayette. This course, designed by Hale Irwin, features 1,200 trees, 87 bunkers, 6 lakes, and a couple of streams. While working around these obstacles, golfers enjoy beautiful views of the nearby Indian Peaks. Operated by the city of Lafayette. Greens fees $45–53 for 18 holes.

HIKING There are so many trails and paths in and around Boulder—and up in the mountains—that it is nearly impossible to keep track of them all. The **City of Boulder Open Space & Mountain Parks** (303-441-3440; osmp.org) maintains miles of paved paths and trails throughout Boulder and the surrounding area. There are 33 trailheads—nearly half of these permit bicycles, and less than half permit horseback riding. Complete information, including an interactive map, can be found on the website.

Boulder Creek Path (303-413-7200) runs from Boulder Canyon in the west to Arapahoe Road near Cherryvale. The 7-mile path is mostly paved but turns to dirt and gravel in the canyon. Following Boulder Creek, the path connects a number of city parks and runs through the heart of Boulder. It is open to pedestrians and cyclists. Speed limit signs are posted along the way.

Chautauqua Park. A network of trails connects Chautauqua Park with Flagstaff Mountain, Saddle Rock, and Green Mountain. One loop is particularly enjoyable, and pretty easygoing—the **McClintock–Enchanted Mesa Loop**. Start behind the Chautauqua Auditorium at the McClintock trailhead. Take the trail out about a mile, and come back via the Enchanted Mesa Trail. This 2.1-mile hike has views of the Flatirons and Bear Peak. Another hike, one of the more difficult you will find in Boulder, is the **Royal Arch Trail**. This trail begins at the Bluebell picnic shelter, about a half-mile up Bluebell Road from the Ranger Cottage at Chautauqua. From there the trail climbs into Bluebell Canyon on its way to the Royal Arch, a unique geological feature in the mountains. In all, the trail climbs 1,200 feet in 3 miles. There are plenty of steep sections, but the views are incredible.

Eldorado Canyon State Park (303-494-3943; cpw.state.co.us/placestogo/Parks /eldoradocanyon), 9 Kneale Rd., Eldorado Springs. Open sunrise to sunset. There are more than 12 miles of trails at Eldorado Canyon State Park, many capitalizing on the park's namesake canyon. The Streamside Trail is an easy, wheelchair-accessible path for half a mile along Boulder Creek. Others, like Eldorado Canyon Trail and Rattle Snake Gulch Trail, are longer and offer some strenuous uphill hiking.

Flagstaff Mountain. Located west of Boulder; take Baseline Avenue west. Just before it ends, veer left on Flagstaff Road and begin climbing. From the summit of Flagstaff Mountain, overlooking Boulder, there are a several trails of varying difficulty. Trailheads at Realization Point (at the turnoff for Flagstaff Summit Road) and one at the summit offer several short hiking options. The **Boy Scout–May's Point Loop** is a 1.2-mile circuit that most hikers find relatively easy to handle. The trailhead is off Flagstaff Summit Road about a half-mile from Realization Point. A little more difficult is the 1.1-mile **Ute–Range View Loop**. The trailhead for this easy-to-moderate route is at Realization Point. Both hikes offer views of the Indian Peaks. A daily parking permit on Flagstaff Mountain is $3. There are six self-serve stations on the way up the mountain. No biking on these trails.

Flatirons Vista and **Doudy Trails**. The Flatirons area is popular with hikers, and with more than 650 climbing routes, it is not unusual to find rock climbers making their arduous way up the Flatirons themselves. For a nice trail, try the Doudy Draw Trail, which is south of town on CO 93, just south of the intersection with CO 128. It's a moderate trail, and the loop around is just over 3 miles.

PADDLING As all paddlers know, the best conditions for rafting or kayaking are found when the winter snows melt and rivers swell with spring runoff. **Boulder Creek** is very popular with local kayakers. Near the mouth of Boulder Canyon, the city maintains a kayak course on the creek with 20 slalom gates. The put-in is at the west end of Arapahoe Avenue where it meets Canyon Boulevard. The city of Lyons also has a whitewater park on the North St. Vrain River. It is in Meadow Park across from Lyons Town Hall. The park is about 400 yards long and features eight drops and a rodeo hole.

Boulder Outdoor Center (303-444-8420; boc123.com), 2525 Arapahoe Ave. Suite E4-228. The BOC has everything a paddler needs from gear and boat rentals to solid information on local conditions. The center offers indoor kayaking instruction and organizes paddling trips around the state. You can get connected with other paddlers on the BOC website—buy and sell used gear or read about trips others are planning.

Whitewater Tubing (720-279-2179; whitewatertubing.com), 1717 15th St. (the Watershed School). Tubes can be rented June–Labor Day, daily 10–6. It's not technically paddling, but tubing is a great way to enjoy the water and to keep cool. Tube rental $16–21, or you can buy a tube for not much more.

✳ Green Space

Boulder County Open Space & Mountain Parks (303-678-6200; bouldercounty.org /dept/openspace), 5201 St. Vrain Rd., Longmont. The county of Boulder is committed to maintaining green spaces for the public's enjoyment. There are numerous parks, trails, and scenic areas throughout the county. The website has a map of all the open space in the county.

City of Boulder Open Space & Mountain Parks (303-441-3440; osmp.org) P.O. Box 791 Boulder, CO 80306. The Open Space & Mountain Parks website has information on all the city's parks and trails. It also includes information on trail and park usage—regulations for dogs on city property, where bikes and horses are allowed, and so on. The city also hosts several free nature hikes, and the site has the current schedule.

Eldorado Canyon State Park (303-494-3943; cpw.state.co.us/placestogo/Parks /eldoradocanyon), 9 Kneale Rd., Eldorado Springs. Open sunrise to sunset. Kayakers come to Eldorado to ride the rapids in South Boulder Creek. Anglers come to fish those same waters. One of the biggest draws to Eldorado Canyon is the nearly 500 rock climbing routes up the canyon walls. There are also some great trails here for day-hikers, including the impressive Eldorado Canyon Trail, which connects the Inner Canyon section of the park with Crescent Meadows to the west. This 3.5-mile hike gains 1,000 feet in elevation, and sections of the trail are considered difficult hiking. Just south of Boulder, Eldorado makes a great day trip, whether you go for the activities or just to picnic in this beautiful park. Day vehicle pass $8; walk-in pass $3.

✳ Lodging

HOTELS ♿ ((ᵗ)) **Boulder Marriott** (303-440-8877; marriott.com), 2660 Canyon Blvd. You will find the Marriott in the heart of Boulder. Most of the hotel's 152 rooms and 5 suites offer mountain views. Guests will appreciate the indoor pool and fitness area. It also provides numerous amenities for business travelers. Rooms $185–259.

((ᵗ)) **The Bradley Boulder Inn** (303-545-5200 or 1-800-858-5811; thebradley boulder.com), 2040 16th St. This cozy boutique hotel is located right in town, just a block from the Pearl Street Mall. The Great Room, with its large stone fireplace, decorated in original art donated by local galleries, sets the tone. The inn's 12 rooms are all tastefully decorated and extremely comfortable. Everything is included in your room rate, from the parking to breakfast and wireless Internet. Rooms $225–300.

♿ ((ᵗ)) **Hotel Boulderado** (303-442-4344 or 1-800-433-4344; boulderado .com), 2115 13th St. Borrowing design sensibilities from the Palace Hotel in San Francisco and The Brown Palace in Denver, the Hotel Boulderado opened its doors on New Year's Day 1909. The original investors hoped that bringing first-class accommodations to Boulder would stimulate growth and establish Boulder's future. Keeping with the grand tradition of opulent Victorian hotels, the Boulderado features a stained-glass canopy ceiling and a stunning cantile-vered cherry wood staircase that reaches from the basement to the fifth floor. Each of the hotel's 160 rooms is individually decorated. Amenities include cable TV, wireless Internet, and air-conditioning. Rooms $279–359.

  ♿ ☀ ((ɣ)) **Millennium Harvest House** (303-443-3850 or 1-800-545-6285; millenniumhotels.com/millennium boulder), 1345 28th St. In keeping with the desire to offer guests western hos-pitality, beds at the hotel are decorated in "a unique pioneer look." The beds are dressed in patchwork quilts and the pho-tos on the walls are often of local scenes. None of this is overwhelming, however, and the furniture and décor are all classy. No knotty pine dressers here. The hotel offers several getaway packages that highlight activities in Boulder, like the Take a Hike package, which includes lodging, a picnic lunch, trail maps, and transportation to and from the trailhead. There are even backpacks you can use. Rooms $129–459.

  ♿ ((ɣ)) **St. Julien Hotel & Spa** (720-406-9696 or 1-877-303-0900; stjulien .com), 900 Walnut St. Located across from Boulder's Central Park, the St. Julien Hotel is a relative newcomer to Boulder. The hotel opened in early 2005 and brought 200 rooms and 11,000 square feet of meeting space to the heart of the city. The hotel also holds a spa and fitness center. Everything about St. Julien is high-end, from the elegant and comfortable guest rooms to the tiled pool area. The hotel caters to business travel-ers and tourists alike. Rooms $249–549.

  ((ɣ)) ♿ **Niwot Inn** (303-652-8452; niwot inn.com), 342 Second Ave., Niwot. This small hotel, located halfway between Boulder and Longmont right off Diag-onal Highway (CO 119), has the feel of a B&B. The 14 rooms are named after famous Colorado 14-ers. Wireless Inter-net is available throughout the inn, including the 740 square feet of meeting space. Many rooms have jetted tubs and

fireplaces. For a romantic stay, consider the Crestone Suite. Rooms $159–189.

BED & BREAKFASTS ((ɣ)) **The Alps Boul-der Canyon Inn** (303-444-5445 or 1-800-414-2577; alpsinn.com), 38619 Boulder Canyon Dr. This inn has a long history, going back before 1870, when it was a stage stop for people traveling in and out of the mountains. Today, it is one of the better B&Bs in Colorado, recently voted the best in Boulder. The inn is found a short drive west of town, a couple of miles into Boulder Canyon. The property has fishing in Boulder Creek. All 12 rooms at the Alps Inn have private baths, fireplaces, satellite TV with DVD players, and both wireless and Ethernet Internet connections. Most rooms have two-per-son whirlpool tubs. In addition to receiv-ing an outstanding breakfast, guests are served dessert nightly, and the inn's famous cowboy cookies are served throughout the day. The breakfasts are outstanding. Rooms $159–279.

  ((ɣ)) **Briar Rose Bed & Breakfast** (303-442-3007 or 1-888-786-8440; briarrosebb .com), 2151 Arapahoe Ave. From the outside, the Briar Rose looks like a quiet country cottage, and happily, that sensibility is carried throughout the house. What is unexpected is that such a secluded and peaceful retreat can be found right in the middle of town, just several blocks from the Pearl Street Mall. Guests can relax in the parlor or out in the beautiful gardens. In recent years the inn has worked hard to offer the "green-est" lodgings in Boulder. From organic meals to organic sheets, from composted food and yard waste or cleaning supplies that are easy on the environment, a stay at the Briar Rose allows you to leave as small a footprint as possible when you visit Boulder. Amenities include wireless Internet, fireplaces, TVs, and air-condi-tioning. Double occupancy $129–234.

CAMPGROUNDS Roosevelt National Forest has numerous campgrounds in the mountains. Those listed here have restrooms and drinking water, but none has showers. All sites can be reserved online at reserveusa.com or by calling 1-877-444-6777. Following are a few of those closest to Boulder.

&. **Camp Dick Campground** (Boulder Ranger District office, 303-541-2500). From Lyons, head 12 miles west on CO 7, and then south on CO 72 for 4 miles. At an elevation of 8,600 feet Camp Dick offers 41 sites for both tents and RVs near the Middle St. Vrain Creek. This is a wheelchair-accessible campground, including accessible facilities and fishing. Sites run $17 for a single, $20 for large sites.

Kelly Dahl Campground (Boulder Ranger District office, 303-541-2500), 3 miles south of Nederland on CO 119. The 46 campsites are right on the Peak to Peak Scenic Byway. There are trails for hiking and horseback riding. Sites $17/night.

Peaceful Valley Campground (Boulder Ranger District office, 303-541-2500). From Lyons, head 12 miles west on CO 7, and then south on CO 72 for 3.5 miles. Located near Camp Dick, Peaceful Valley is a smaller campground with only 17 sites. Campers can enjoy mountain biking, hiking, fishing, and other outdoor activities. Sites run $13 for a single, $16 for large sites.

CABINS & COTTAGES **Colorado Chautauqua Association** (303-442-3282; chautauqua.com), 900 Baseline Rd. Sixty of Chautauqua's historic turn-of-the-century cottages are available for rent. There are even several cottages that have been designated Heritage Cottages, meaning they have been well preserved or well restored, and each has a unique story to tell. (For more on Chautauqua, see "Historic Sites" under *To See & Do*, page 59) Cottages rent for $152–303.

✳ Where to Eat

DINING OUT &. **The Boulder Dushanbe Teahouse** (303-442-4993; boulder teahouse.com), 1770 13th St. Open daily 8–9. Teatime daily 3–5. The teahouse was a gift from Boulder's sister city, Dushanbe, in Tajikistan—more than 40 Tajikistani artisans worked on the teahouse, which was then shipped to Boulder and assembled. From the carved cedar columns to the Fountain of the Seven Beauties to the remarkably detailed ceiling, the teahouse is simply stunning. The menu is a potpourri of international influences, including Indian, Cuban, Italian, and Asian dishes. Breakfast $9–10, lunch $10–16, and dinner $14–23. Afternoon tea $22 (children under 9 $14).

&. Ψ **Flagstaff House Restaurant** (303-442-4640; flagstaffhouse.com), 1138 Flagstaff Rd. Open for dinner Sun.–Fri. 6–10 and Sat. 5–10. If you are looking for an excellent dining experience with fabulous views, be sure to make reservations at the Flagstaff House Restaurant, which stands 1,500 feet above Boulder with a view of the city. When anyone is asked about fine dining in Boulder, the Flagstaff always gets first mention. This elegant restaurant has been around since 1951 and has a reputation for its excellent menu, service, and ambience. Dishes include seafood, steak, and chicken, as well as buffalo, venison, and quail. The dress code is business casual. First course $14–28; main course $38–74.

&. Ψ **The Kitchen** (303-544-5973; thekitchen.com/the-kitchen-boulder), 1039 Pearl St. Lunch Mon.–Fri. 11–3. Happy hour Mon.–Fri. 3–5. Dinner daily at 5. Brunch Sat. and Sun. 9–2. The Kitchen uses locally grown organic produce whenever possible; as a result, the menu changes daily based on the seasonal availability of various ingredients. Recent items included Wisdom Farm chicken and butternut squash ravioli made with Munson Farm summer squash. Community is central to the founders' philosophy. As the restaurant has expanded to new locations, they have created the nonprofit Kitchen Community, which works to introduce kids to real food through learning gardens (200 such gardens so far). If anything, you should come for the tomato soup—maybe the best I've ever had. Dishes $20–30.

  ♿ ♉ **The Mediterranean** (303-444-5335; themedboulder.com), 1002 Walnut St. Open daily at 11. Happy hour daily 3–6:30. Since it opened in 1993, The Mediterranean has been impressing patrons with its extensive menu, which offers everything from tapas to pizza to paella. It seems the entire Mediterranean region, from Greece to Morocco, is represented here. The décor is bright and inviting and seems alive with geraniums. Tapas $4–8, pizzas $8–10, and main dishes $14–27. These are dinner prices; lunch is cheaper. During the happy hour, tapas are very affordable.

  ♿ ♉ **Gold Hill Inn** (303-443-6461; goldhillinn.com), 401 Main St., Gold Hill. Open for dinner Fri. and Sat. 6–9 and Sun. 5–8. *Gourmet* magazine wrote in 2004 that Gold Hill Inn "must be one of the best restaurant values in America." That in itself should be enough to inspire diners, but add to that live music and a richly historic setting, and this restaurant is a must if you are in the mountains outside Boulder. The dining hall was built in 1924 to match the neighboring 19th-century log hotel, so the feel is rustic and elegant. Dishes include such highfalutin fare as roast lamb venison and coquilles Saint-Jacques. The atmosphere, however, is warm and inviting. A six-course meal is $37, three-course $29.

  ♿ ♉ **Lyons Fork** (303-823-5014; lyons fork.com), 450 Main St., Lyons. Open daily. Dinner 5–9. Brunch on Sat. and Sun. 9–2. The owners of Lyons Fork, Wayne and Debbie, have a long history in the craft beer industry. So it shouldn't be a surprise that the beer list features some of the country's best brews from Pennsylvania to California. What might be a surprise is the high-end menu.

Guests dine on entrées like grilled lamb loin with truffled celery root ravioli or the Haystack goat cheese gnocchi. Dinner $12–28.

EATING OUT ♿ **The Buff** (303-442-9150; buffrestaurant.com), 1725 28th St. Open for breakfast and lunch Mon.–Fri. 6:30–2 and Sat. and Sun. 7–2. The Buff is a great place for breakfast. It has the usual bacon and eggs, but also offers interesting diversions such as salmon and eggs or banana bread French toast. You can even get a breakfast panini. Dishes $8–14.

  ♿ **Café Gondolier** (303-443-5015; gondolieronpearl.com), 4800 Baseline Rd. (used to be on Pearl St.). Open Mon 4:30–9, Tue.–Thu. 11:30–9, Fri. and Sat. 11:30–9:30, and Sun. 11:30–9. The oldest family-owned restaurant in Boulder, Café Gondolier has been serving fine homestyle Italian food since 1960. Hand-cut pasta, freshly made sauces, and a fantastic thin-crust pizza have kept it thriving for over 45 years. Patrons rave about the food and the service. Tuesday and Wednesday are "all-you-can-eat spaghetti" nights. Be sure to check out the 100-year-old espresso machine in the main dining room. Recently retired, it had been serving espresso in Boulder since the late 1940s. Pasta $8–12, dinner entrées $12–16.

  ♿ **Mustard's Last Stand** (303-444-5841; mustardslaststandcolorado.com /history/boulder), 1719 Broadway St. Open Mon.–Fri. 10:30–9 and Sat. and Sun. 11–9. Every university town worthy of the name has at least one great hot-dog joint. Mustard's Last Stand, across from the amphitheater, is Boulder's great hot-dog joint. In addition to Chicago-style hot dogs, it serves a nice charred burger. And you certainly will appreciate Mustard's handmade fries. With a row of stools facing the street, it's also a great place to people watch. Hot dogs and hamburgers with fries go for around $8.

 ♿ The Sink (303-444-7465; thesink .com), 1165 13th St. The restaurant is open 11–10, and the bar 11 AM–2 AM. The Sink has been around in one form or another since 1923. It began as a European-style restaurant, served as a bar for a time, and even became sort of an artist showroom with its off-the-wall gallery. In 1955, it secured permanent status as a top-notch burger joint with the creation of the Sink Burger, and since have solidified its place in the hearts of Boulderites with its pizzas and famous Buddha Basil Pie. The Sink was featured on Food Network's *Diners, Drive-Ins, and Dives* with Guy Fieri and was visited by President Obama and Anthony Bourdain. Burgers around $10 and pizzas $16–29.

 ♿ **Wild Mountain Smokehouse & Brewery** (303-258-9453; wildmountainsb .com), 70 E. First St., Nederland. Mon.–Thu. 11:30–8:30, Fri. and Sat. 11–9, and Sun. 11–8:30. Up Boulder Canyon to Nederland, this is one of the best spots for good eats. Wild Mountain Smokehouse & Brewery serves up a full menu of pulled pork, prime rib, ribs, and game sausage. The brewery cranks out several different beers, such as Mountain Siren Cherry Wheat and Otis Pale Ale. All go great with an appetizer such as the large soft pretzel served with whole-grain beer mustard.

THE SINK BURGER IN BOULDER

Dinner entrées under $20, burgers and sandwiches $9–13.

BAKERIES & COFFEE SHOPS ♿ **Breadworks** (303-444-5667; breadworks.net), 2644 N. Broadway. Open Mon.–Fri. 7–7 and Sat. and Sun. 7–6. For many locals, this is the best spot in town for great artisan breads.

The Laughing Goat Coffeehouse (303-440-4628; thelaughinggoat.com), 1709 Pearl St. Open Mon.–Fri. 6–11 and Sat. and Sun. 7–11. The folks at The Laughing Goat serve up a great cup of coffee. They also keep the grand coffeehouse tradition alive with weekly open poetry readings and nightly live music. See website for a schedule of events. There are a half-dozen coffee shops on Pearl Street in Boulder, including The Laughing Goat. **Ozo Coffee** (1015 Pearl St.) and **Boxcar Coffee Roasters** (1825B Pearl St.) are both worth a visit if you have a couple of days to try something different.

Moe's Broadway Bagel (303-444-3252; moesbagel.com), 2650 Broadway. Open daily 5:30–5. The ambience at Moe's is true to Boulder—from bright colors inside to its "flower power" bumper stickers—but the bagels are all New York. It's the bagels, cooked fresh every morning, that bring in the regulars. There are now three locations in Boulder and two in Denver. People really love these bagels.

BARS, TAVERNS, & BREW PUBS ♿ **Dark Horse Bar** (303-442-8162; dark horsebar.com), 2922 Baseline Rd. Open daily 11–2. The Dark Horse has been serving Boulder's drinking public since 1975. Locals like to gather on game day and watch the Buffs with friends. On other nights the bar has dancing, karaoke, DJs, and live music. Some would argue this place deserves a mention under "Eating Out." The Dark Horse has received plenty of attention for its great burgers and wings.

 ♿ **Oskar Blues Grill & Brew** (303-823-6685; oskarbluesfooderies.com /grill-and-brew), 303 Main St., Lyons.

Food served Sat.–Sun. noon–8, Mon.–Fri. 10–8. Bar open later. Known for its craft-beer-in-a-can, Dale's Pale Ale, Oskar Blues created a classic brew pub in Lyons. Menu features burgers and barbeque, the Giant Burrito, and brick-oven pizzas. You can't miss the Cajun specialties, from po' boys to jambalaya and dirty rice. Jazz, blues, and bluegrass are played downstairs in the basement "juke joint." Entrées $9–16.

✳ Entertainment

& **Boulder Chamber Orchestra** (1-888-397-6952; boulderchamberorchestra .org), 4641 10th St. One of the things that defines Boulder is an intense appreciation for the arts. This has been illustrated by the quick success of the Boulder Chamber Orchestra, which has only been in existence since 2004. Season runs Oct.–April. Concerts are held at First Baptist Church (1237 Pine St.), Broomfield Auditorium (3 Community Park Rd., Broomfield), and First Congregational Church of Boulder (1128 Pine St.). See website for schedule of performances.

& **Boulder's Dinner Theatre** (303-449-6000; theatreinboulder.com), 5501 Arapahoe Ave., at the corner of 55th St. and Arapahoe. Dinner begins Wed. at 5:30 and Thu.–Sat. at 6:15. The Sunday matinee starts at 12:00, dinner at 6:15. (See website for other select performance times.) The show starts 90 minutes after seating for dinner. Since 1977, the good folks at Boulder's Dinner Theatre have been mixing fine dining and Broadway-style entertainment. In the true dinner theater tradition, the performers are also the waitstaff. Tickets $41–60, which includes meal.

Boulder Philharmonic Orchestra (303-449-1343; boulderphil.org), 2590 Walnut St. Concerts are held at the Macky Auditorium on the CU campus. In the summer, the orchestra holds a series of outdoor concerts that are free to the public.

Chautauqua Auditorium (303-442-3282; chautauqua.com), 900 Baseline Rd. Several years ago, we saw one of our

CHAUTAUQUA AUDITORIUM

BREDO MORSTØL

Up in the mountains in Nederland, there's a frozen dead guy in a Tuff Shed. His name is Bredo Morstøl. When Morstøl died in 1989, his grandson, Trygve Bauge, had him cryogenically frozen in the hope that someday medical science will be advanced enough to reanimate his body and fix whatever it was that caused him to have his fatal heart attack in the first place.

In 1993, Bauge brought his grandfather to Nederland, where he stored the body in a shack behind the house of his mother, Aud (Morstøl's daughter). No one knew there was a frozen dead guy up there, but then Bauge was deported back to Norway for overstaying his visa. Then Aud was evicted from her unfinished home because it's illegal to live in a house without electricity or water. Suddenly there was a crisis—who would keep Morstøl from thawing out? Aud, who has since been deported herself, let the authorities know about the body and suddenly it was the town's problem.

After passing some laws to make it illegal to store a frozen body in your backyard, the town still had to decide what to do about Morstøl, who was grandfathered in under the new ordinance (no pun intended). Over time, volunteers stepped up and began helping out. Tuff Shed donated a new shelter for the old man, replacing the deteriorating shack that had been his home for several years. Others gave and continue to give their time, regularly loading the shed with dry ice.

In 2002, Nederland decided to celebrate its most distinguished citizen, and the idea of Frozen Dead Guy Days (frozendeadguydays.org) was born. A bit irreverent, the festival is quite a party and worth the trip.

favorite performers at Chautauqua. This is a fantastic venue. The inside has a rustic, homey feel. During the day, you can see sunlight peaking between the boards that make up the auditorium walls. Musicians and fans alike have commented on the building's acoustics—because of its wooden construction, there are few places where music carries so well. Although it can seat more than 500 people, there's not a bad seat in the place. This, of course, makes it the perfect location for the Colorado Music Festival (see *Special Events*). Check out the website to find a current schedule of performances.

eTown Radio Show (303-443-8696; etown.org). Music fans across the country listen to eTown every week on National Public Radio. Hosted by Nick and Helen Forster, the show features musical guests from across the musical spectrum—they are always great. Usually recorded locally at the Boulder Theater (303-786-7030; bouldertheater .com), 2032 14th St. Be sure to check the

schedule as they sometimes take the show on the road.

✳ Selective Shopping

The Hill (facebook.com/thehillboulder), located just west of the CU Boulder campus, the Hill business district is centered along 13th Street, south of Broadway. The Hill claims to be a virtual extension of the CU campus, and it is. Surrounded by sorority and fraternity houses and off-campus housing, the Hill is right in the thick of student life. Plenty of shopping and restaurants, but parking can be tough.

Pearl Street Mall and Downtown Boulder (303-449-3774; boulderdowntown .com). Downtown Boulder has numerous shops, art galleries, and restaurants. The centerpiece of the city is the Pearl Street Mall. Several blocks of Pearl Street were closed to cars and laid with brick for foot traffic. On any given afternoon or evening, a stroll down this tree-lined street will reveal couples walking hand in hand, families window shopping, and the sound of buskers playing on the corners.

Boulder Arts & Crafts Cooperative (303-443-3683 or 1-866-656-2667; boulder artsandcrafts.com), 1421 Pearl St. In 1976, a group of artists rented space to display and sell their work on the recently constructed Pearl Street Mall. Today, 42 local artists own and operate this co-op, and an even greater number of artists sell their wares here.

Boulder Book Store & Café (303-447-2074; boulderbookstore.com), 1107 Pearl St. Open Mon.–Sat. 10–10 and Sun. 10–8. This four-story bookstore on Pearl Street is a bit of a surprise. It honestly doesn't look all that big from the outside. But 20,000 square feet of retail space offers a lot of selection. Next door, and connected to the bookstore, is the café—itself a great place to read with a nice cup of coffee.

Boulder Map Gallery (303-444-1406; bouldermapgallery.com), 607 S. Broadway. This place has maps, lots of them—everything from wall maps and posters to globes and reproduction antique maps. Especially of interest to people traveling around Colorado, they have trail maps from all over the state.

Into the Wind (303-449-5356; into thewind.com), 1408 Pearl St. Open daily, hours are seasonal. Into the Wind sells more than just kites; there are all sorts of wind-up toys and novelties here. That said, the store is one of the biggest mail-order kite sellers in the country—if you have any kite questions, this is the place to go.

Boulder Furniture Arts (303-443-2030; boulderfurniturearts.com), 1200 Pearl St. Open daily at 10. Closes at 8 on Wed.–Sat. and Mon., 7 on Sun., and 6 on Tue. Lew Collins at Mountain Furniture Arts makes some of the finest furniture on the Front Range. His showroom is right downtown in Nederland. The pieces in his showroom represent several styles—Mission, Shaker, and many have a Southwest feel. He also does a lot of custom work If you like what you see, but don't see what you like.

❋ Special Events

May: **BolderBOULDER** (303-444-7223; bolderboulder.com), 5500 Central Ave. As 10K races go, this is a big one. In 2007, nearly 50,000 runners joined the fray, making it the third-largest road race in the United States and fifth in the world. In fact, when the runners gather at Folsom Stadium for a tribute to veterans at the end of the race, it's the largest Memorial Day gathering in the country.

Boulder Creek Festival (bceproductions .com/boulder-creek-festival). Three days of food and entertainment, capped off by the annual rubber duck race.

June–August: **Colorado Music Festival** (303-449-1397;.co.usic.org), 900 Baseline Rd., Cottage 100. The six-week music festival features regular concerts at Chautauqua Auditorium. The performances showcase everything from children's choirs to klezmer quartets to chamber orchestras.

Colorado Shakespeare Festival (303-492-0554; coloradoshakes.org). For 50 years, Boulder has been keeping the work of Shakespeare alive with this fantastic festival. Forty-five minutes before each show, there's a prologue where a member of the CSF company comes out and tells the audience a little about the play they are about to see. For outdoor performances, you can bring a picnic or purchase a gourmet picnic supper from Falstaff's Fare.

FORT COLLINS

I n 2006, *Money* magazine listed Fort Collins as the number one place to live in the United States (and in 2010, the city placed in the top ten). A decade on, the town keeps getting better and better. A great job market, lots of outdoor activities, plenty of culture, and that fresh mountain air all set Fort Collins apart. At its heart, Fort Collins is a college town, the home of Colorado State University. The university goes back to 1879, when it was called the Colorado Agricultural & Mining College (the name changed in 1957). The university remains the largest employer in Fort Collins.

The town goes back to the 19th century as well. In 1862, the Ninth Kansas Volunteer Cavalry built a post along the Cache la Poudre (pronounced POO-der) River called Camp Collins in the present-day town of Laporte. They were there to protect the nearby Cherokee Trail and the Overland Stage Line. In 1864, a terrific flood swept away the entire encampment. No lives were lost, but the troops were faced with finding another place to rebuild. A couple of months later, Fort Collins was established along the river, in the area of today's Willow Street. The military left the fort in 1866, but farmers and ranchers who had settled nearby remained. Since 1860, farmers had been pulling water out of the Cache la Poudre via a growing system of irrigation ditches. In 1877, the railroad came to Fort Collins, in a way assuring the town's future.

The original town streets ran parallel to the river. The new part of town is aligned with the points of the compass. A good part of the old town has been preserved as an historic district, and Old Town Square at the corner of College and Mountain avenues is booming. Restaurants and shops, not to mention a thriving art community, continue to bring vitality to the local economy. Annual festivals and events bring in more than a half-million people to the city each year. Fort Collins also enjoys a temperate climate, perfect for enjoying nearby Horsetooth Mountain and Reservoir or any of the town's 40 parks and 23 miles of trails for biking and walking.

GUIDANCE **Fort Collins Convention & Visitors Bureau** (970-232-3840 or 1-800-274-3678; visitftcollins.com), 19 Old Town Sq., Suite 137. Open Mon.–Thu. 8:30–5, Fri. 8:30–6, Sat. 9:30–6, Sun. 11–5. The Visitors Information Center is located right in Old Town Square—you can't miss it.

Colorado Welcome Center at Fort Collins (970-491-4775; colorado.com/colorado-official-state-welcome-center/colorado-welcome-center-fort-collins), 3745 E. Prospect Rd. (exit 268 off I-25). Open daily in the summer 8–6, other times of the year 8–5. In addition to the plethora of brochures, maps, and visitor guides, the Welcome Center in Fort Collins is home to the Rocky Mountain Nature Association bookstore. There's also a couple of hundred acres of nature preserve around the center, complete with trails.

More websites:
downtownfortcollins.com

GETTING THERE *By car:* Fort Collins is 60 miles north of Denver on I-25. It's the last big town before Wyoming.

By air: **Denver International Airport** (303-342-2000 or 1-800-247-2336; flydenver.com) is about an hour's drive from Fort Collins.

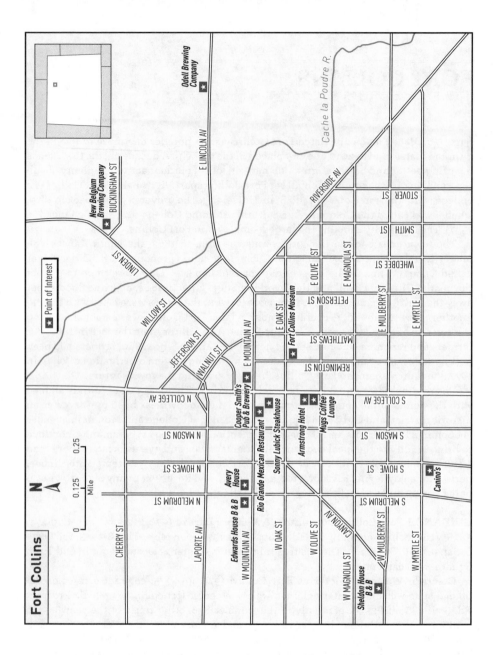

By train: **Amtrak** (1-800-872-7245; amtrak.com) does not have direct service to Fort Collins, but does operate its Thruway bus service that stops at the Greyhound Station at 250 N. Mason St.

By bus: **Greyhound** operates regular service to and from Fort Collins from the **Fort Collins Greyhound Station** (970-221-1327 or 1-800-231-2222; greyhound.com), 250 N. Mason St.

GETTING AROUND *By car:* The town is fairly car friendly with plenty of on-street parking as well as a parking structure a couple of blocks west of the Old Town Square off Mountain Avenue.

By bus: The city operates a bus system, **Transfort** (970-221-6620; ridetransfort.com), which offers numerous routes connecting the whole town.

✳ To See & Do

BREWERIES ♿ ↑ **Anheuser-Busch Brewery** (970-490-4691; budweisertours.com), 2351 Busch Dr. Tours given daily 10–4. This is the big daddy of breweries in Fort Collins. No microbrew here—it's all macrobrew. To see the famous Budweiser Clydesdales, come on the first Saturday of every month for Clydesdale Camera Day.

♿ ↑ **Fort Collins Brewery** (970-472-1499; fortcollinsbrewery.com), 1020 E. Lincoln Ave. Tavern open daily. Guided tours are given on Saturdays at the top of the hour, starting at 1. Can't make it on a Saturday? Call ahead for a tour on Fridays. (There's often a brewer around happy to talk about the process any day if you're interested.)

♿ ↑ **New Belgium Brewing Company, Inc.** (970-221-0524 or 1-888-622-4044; newbelgium.com), 500 Linden St. Guided tours daily. The tours are free, but reservations must be made online beforehand (and they fill up weeks out). Tasting room is open every day 11–8. New Belgium is the brewer of Fat Tire, a beer known and loved by mountain bikers and beer drinkers the world over. It is also the greenest brewery in Fort Collins. In 1998, the employees at New Belgium agreed to use money from their bonus pool to convert the brewery to wind power, ending the operation's reliance on the local power plant (a big source of CO_2 emissions). The plant reuses water and is outfitted with many green innovations to cut waste and maximize resources.

♿ ↑ **Odell Brewing Company** (970-498-9070 or 1-887-2797; odellbrewing.com), 800 E. Lincoln Ave. Tasting room open Sun.–Tue. 11–6, Wed.–Sat. 11–7. Tours daily at noon, 1, 2, and 3. When Doug Odell started brewing commercially in 1989, the Odell Brewing Company was only the second microbrewery in Colorado. The company started with 90 Schilling, a fantastically light Scottish ale. The beers on tap in the tasting room change from week to week. There is live music on Wed. evenings.

OTHER ATTRACTIONS ↑ **Avery House** (970-221-0533; poudrelandmarks.com), 328 W. Mountain Ave. Open for tours Sat. and Sun. 1–4. As one of the town's early residents, Franklin Avery wore many hats. He surveyed Fort Collins in 1873, founded the First National Bank, and worked to develop water projects that benefited local farmers. His house, built in 1879 out of local sandstone, still stands at the corner of Mountain Avenue and Meldrum Street.

🐾 **Farm at Lee Martinez Park** (970-221-6665; fcgov.com/recreation/thefarm.php), 600 N. Sherwood St. There is a lot for kids to enjoy at the farm—including plenty of animals, from turkeys and geese to horses and goats. There are pony rides and hayrides and opportunities to feed the animals. Picnic spots and playgrounds make this a nice place to bring lunch. And if it rains, there's always the farming museum and Silo Store. Admission $3.35 (ages 2 and older).

♿ ↑ **Fort Collins Museum** (970-221-6738; fcmod.org), 408 Mason Ct. Open Tue.–Sun. 9:30–6. Since 1941, the museum has been educating the public on the history of Fort Collins and the Cache la Poudre River valley from prehistoric times to the present. There is an extensive collection of artifacts, including a courtyard and four historic buildings from the 19th century. Children's (3–12) admission $6, adults (13–59) $9.50, and seniors (60+) $7.

HISTORIC AVERY HOUSE

 ♯ **Fort Collins Museum of Art** (970-482-2787; fcma.org), 201 S. College Ave. Open Wed.–Fri. 10–5, Sat. and Sun. noon–5. The museum, which resides in the old Fort Collins Post Office, began in 1990 as the Once West Contemporary Art Center. The museum presents new works in an ever-changing series of exhibitions. Adult admission $6, seniors and students $5, youth (7–18) $2.

✳ Outdoor Activities

FISHING The **Cache la Poudre River** offers some nice holes for fishing, as do the **North Platte** and **Laramie** rivers. **Horsetooth Reservoir** has several boat ramps and is regularly stocked with fish.

Rocky Mountain Adventures (970-493-4005 or 1-800-858-6808; shoprma.com), 1117 N Hwy 287. These folks offer guided fly-fishing trips on the Big Thompson River, Rocky Mountain National Park, the Cache la Poudre River, and other spots. One-person trips $135 and $225 for half- and full-day outings.

St. Peter's Fly Shop (970-498-8968; stpetes.com), 202 Remington St. St. Pete's has a great reputation with anglers. Everyone who works at the shop is intimately knowledgeable about the nuances of fly fishing in northern Colorado and southern Wyoming. The staff lead guided fly-fishing trips and offer instruction for beginners.

GOLF **Collindale Golf Course** (970-221-6651; fcgov.com/golf/collindale.php), 1441 E. Horsetooth Rd. Collindale is a municipal course close to town. There is a new clubhouse with a full-service grill. Greens fees $26–38 for 18 holes.

HIKING & BIKING **Horsetooth Mountain Park** (970-679-4570; larimer.org/parks /htmp.htm) has 29 miles of trails for hiking and biking. Parking and the trailhead are 6.5 miles west of Taft Hill Road on Harmony (a.k.a. CO 38E). The hike to Horsetooth Falls is an easy 2.5-mile round-trip that takes you into the foothills. Mountain bikers might enjoy a lengthier ride—there's a nice 5-mile loop that follows Soderberg Trail up and around via Wathen Trail. See website for an excellent trail map.

Lory State Park (970-493-1623; cpw.state.co.us/placestogo/Parks/lory) 708 Lodgepole Dr., Bellvue. Parking at the Timber Group Picnic Area, mountain bikers can start at the Timber Trail trailhead and take the trail up to the ridge just beneath Arthur Rock. The trail is moderately difficult and makes for a nice 7-mile trip. Hikers might enjoy the 3.4-mile round-trip up to Arthur Rock, with its fantastic views of the Front Range. Start at the southernmost parking area and follow the Arthur Rock Trail to the top. It's not an easy trail, but the view is worth the huffing and puffing. Lory State Park also has an impressive Mountain Bike Park with all sorts of tracks and jumps.

Devil's Backbone Open Space (larimer.org/parks/bbone.cfm). Larimer County maintains a number of parks and open spaces. The Devil's Backbone Open Space, 3 miles west of Lake Loveland on CO 34 in Loveland, has some distinct features—most notable is the sharp spine of rocks that juts up for about a mile to the northwest. There are several trails at the site. More adventurous hikers and mountain bikers can connect up with the Blue Sky Trail. It's a 9.6-mile hike from Devil's Backbone to the Soderberg trailhead, which is in Horsetooth Mountain Park; it's the trail following the Inlet Bay of Horsetooth Reservoir. You will climb nearly 500 feet on the Blue Sky Trail, so know your limitations.

HORSETOOTH RESERVOIR

Recycled Cycles (970-223-1969 or 1-877-214-1811; recycled-cycles.com), 4031-A S. Mason St. If you need to rent a bike while you are in town, this shop sells and rents used bikes at affordable rates—it usually has everything from mountain bikes to cruisers. Day rental about $25–40.

PADDLING & RAFTING The Cache la Poudre River that runs through Fort Collins is known for its whitewater. A few outfitters in town offer guided rafting trips.

A-1 Wildwater Rafting (970-224-3379 or 1-800-369-4165; a1wildwater.com), 2801 N. Shields St. A-1 takes people rafting down the Poudre River. Depending on the section of river the company is riding, you can see class II to IV rapids. For fun on the water on your own, you can also rent kayaks and duckies.

Mountain Whitewater Descents (970-419-0917; raftmwd.com), 13289 N. CO 287. The guides here will take you down the Poudre River on full- or half-day trips. Paddlers can encounter rapids from class II to IV.

✳ Green Space

Boyd Lake State Park (970-669-1739; cpw.state.co.us/placestogo/parks/BoydLake), 3720 N. CR 11-C, Loveland. Open all day, every day. Quiet hours daily 10 PM–6 AM. This is a busy park down in Loveland, with plenty of swimming, boating, and other water sports. The park sponsors a series of outdoor concerts every summer. Day pass $8.

Colorado State Forest State Park (970-723-8366; cpw.state.co.us/placestogo /Parks/stateforest), 56750 CO 14, Walden. So far west of Fort Collins on CO 14, the Colorado State Forest State Park might rightly belong in the Northwest Colorado section of this book. But the access from Fort Collins is the easiest route even though it is 76 miles away. The state forest has 71,000 acres of rugged mountain wilderness. It's a prime destination for backcountry hikers and skiers. The park maintains nine yurts and huts and six cabins. These shelters can accommodate larger groups, some up to eight people. Two cabins hold 15 and 21 lodgers. The yurts are managed by the **Never Summer Nordic Yurt System** (970-723-4070; www.neversummernordic.com), 247 CR 41, Walden.

In addition to numerous trails and roads, the park keeps things lively with geocaching. Eight geocaches have been set up around the park for participants to find with their GPS devices (available for rent at the Moose Visitor Center). The visitor center, which is an excellent introduction to the park, is also a place you might see moose. It is located near Gould on CO 14. Daily park pass $7.

Horsetooth Reservoir (970-679-4570; larimer.org/parks/horsetooth.cfm), located due west of Fort Collins. Both CO 42C and CO 38E head up to the reservoir. Centennial Drive runs along the east shore of the reservoir. This 1,900-acre lake is bordered by 2,000 acres of public land. There is swimming, boating, camping, hiking, biking, and rock climbing throughout the area. Daily auto pass $7. Same for boat passes.

Lory State Park (970-493-1623; parks.state.co.us/parks/lory), 708 Lodgepole Dr., Bellvue. Open daily 6–10 in the summer (5–8 otherwise). Mountain bike trails, dirt bike jumps, and the Corral Center Mountain Bike Park make Lory a great excursion for mountain bikers. Boaters can access Horsetooth Reservoir, which borders the park on the east. (See "Hiking & Biking" under *Outdoor Activities*.) Daily pass $7/car or $3/individual.

✴ Lodging

HOTELS ♿ 🐾 ((ᵠ)) **Armstrong Hotel** (970-484-3883 or 1-866-384-3883; the armstronghotel.com), 259 S. College Ave. Built in 1923, this hip hotel is located a few blocks from Old Town Square, right in the heart of things. The 37 rooms have been decorated in a mix of vintage and modern styles. Rooms $139–199.

BED & BREAKFASTS ((ᵠ)) **Edwards House Bed & Breakfast** (970-493-9191 or 1-800-281-9190; edwardshouse.com), 402 W. Mountain Ave. This B&B was built in 1904 and is decorated throughout with antique furnishings. The full breakfast includes a selection of fresh fruit and baked goods. The eight rooms are all spacious and comfortable. Rooms $200–250.

CAMPGROUNDS ((ᵠ)) **Fort Collins Lakeside KOA** (970-484-9880 or 1-800-562-9168; fclakesidecg.com), 1910 N. Taft Hill Rd. The campground has a swimming pool for summer use, a sauna and hot tub, and a beautiful gazebo overlooking the lake. Not a lot of trees, but the campground is clean and orderly. Tent sites around $42–50, RVs around $55–95, and Kamping Kabins $73–92.

Fort Collins Poudre Canyon KOA (970-493-9758 or 1-800-562-2648; koa.com/campgrounds/fort-collins-poudre-canyon), 6670 N. US 287. The Poudre Canyon KOA has a swimming pool for use in the summer, cabins for rent, and an outside covered kitchen area for campers. The campground has some trees for shade. Rates $40–100 (tent sites on the low end, Kamping Lodge on the high).

Riverview RV Park and Campground (970-667-9910 or 1-800-447-9910 for reservations; riverviewrv.com), 7806 W. US 34, Loveland. Located alongside the Big Thompson River west of Loveland, the campground has plenty of sites, many next to the river, for RVs (pull-through and back-in) as well as tent sites. It also maintains several cabins that sleep four (double bed and a bunk bed)—remember to bring your own bedding. RV and tent sites $27–48. Rates depend on hookups, on the river or off-river, number of people and vehicles in your party, and so on. Cabins are $76 ($54 off season), more for "deluxe" cabins.

RANCHES ♿ ((ᵠ)) **Sylvan Dale Guest Ranch** (970-667-3915; sylvandale.com), 2939 N. CR 31D, Loveland. Sylvan Dale Guest Ranch is west of Loveland, just north of US 34, along the banks of the Big Thompson. During the summer, the ranch offers six-night vacation packages—giving guests a chance to get the whole dude ranch experience. Activities include horseback riding, whitewater rafting, fishing, overnight pack trips to cow camp, and a ranch party. Throughout the rest of the year, the ranch is available for folks looking for more of a B&B experience. Adult six-day rate $1,595–2,295. Call for bed & breakfast room rates.

✴ Where to Eat

DINING OUT ♿ **Canino's** (970-493-7205; caninositalianrestaurant.com), 613 S. College Ave. Open daily 7–9. In 1976, Clyde Canino opened his Italian restaurant in Fort Collins. The one-time residence that houses the restaurant is an historic landmark, built in 1903, and contributes to the cozy atmosphere. For Italian cuisine in Fort Collins, there are few places better. Dinner entrées and pizza $14–24.

Sonny Lubick Steakhouse (970-484-9200; sonnylubicksteakhouse.com), 115 S. College Ave. Open daily for dinner at 4. From 1993 to 2007, Sonny Lubick led the CSU Rams football team as head coach. When Nico's Catacombs closed in 2008, it created an opening in Fort Collins for a new enterprise. The steakhouse moved into the old subterranean dining room, and another local hotspot was born. The menu features a raft of steaks, as well as seafood and chicken, and lighter fare such as the steak burger or prime rib dip. Steaks and other entrées $22–40.

EATING OUT ♿ **Austin's American Grille** (970-224-9691; austinsamerican grill.com), 100 W. Mountain Ave. Open Sun. 10–9, Mon.–Thu. 11–9, and Fri. and Sat. 11–10 (open an hour later all week in the summer). Located right at the corner of Mountain and College, Austin's is in the thick of things. The menu is good old American fare, with such appetizers as coconut shrimp and iron-skillet corn bread and dinner entrées such as St. Louis ribs and buffalo meat loaf. People get excited about the ribs. Entrées $13–25.

♿ **Café Bluebird** (970-484-7755; cafe bluebird.com), 524 W. Laurel St. Open Mon.–Fri. 6:30–2, Sat. and Sun. 7–2. This is one of the best places for breakfast in Fort Collins. It may seem your typical restaurant, but the menu is full of unique twists on traditional dishes. You can play it safe with a couple of eggs and grilled homemade wheat toast, or try something different, such as the Corgie Street Benedict (poached eggs with grilled smoked salmon, tomatoes, and fresh spinach). The restaurant also serves lunch. Breakfast and lunch dishes $8–12.

♿ **Rio Grande Mexican Restaurant** (970-224-5428; riograndemexican.com), 143 W. Mountain Ave. Open Sun.–Wed. 11–close and Thu.–Sat. 11–midnight. For summer dining, the Rio Grande has a shaded patio and a pleasant fountain. The menu is Tex-Mex, and diners will go on and on about the fresh chips and salsa, the green chili, and the Rio's famous margaritas. Dinner entrées $12–16.

♿ **Silver Grill Cafe** (970-484-4656; silvergrill.com), 218 Walnut St. Open for breakfast and lunch daily 7–2. Silver Grill Cafe has been serving breakfast and lunch since 1933. The café has an extensive espresso menu. Always save room for one of its giant cinnamon rolls. Breakfast and lunch dishes $8–12.

♿ **Suehiro Japanese Restaurant** (970-482-3734; suehirofc.com), 223 Linden St. Open Sun.–Thu. 11–9:30, Fri. and Sat. 11–10. Suehiro has been voted the best sushi in Fort Collins. Carry-out is available. Be sure to make reservations during the school year because the place packs out with college students. Entrées $12–15.

Nordy's BBQ (970-461-9227; nordys bbq.com), 4360 Saint Cloud Dr., Loveland. Open Mon.–Fri. 11–10, Sat. and Sun. 11–midnight. Ten miles south from Fort Collins, just off I-25, Nordy's offers barbeque that's worth the drive. Not the usual BBQ hole-in-the-wall, this place has a huge dining room and an efficient army of waitstaff. The kitchen serves the kind of slow cooked food you dream about. There's brisket and smoked sausage. Raise their ribs to your mouth and the meat will actually fall right off the bone. And don't miss out on their unique sides, like the pasta slaw or Aunt Judy's beans. Sandwiches come in under $10–12. For barbeque entrées, you're looking at $14–16. Rib platters up to $24.

BAKERIES & COFFEE SHOPS ♿ ((ꜱ))
Mugs Coffee Lounge (970-472-6847; mugscoffeelounge.com), 261 S. College Ave. Open daily 6–9. Coffee, tea, and "blendies" are the key to the menu at Mugs. It also has a huge food menu, including breakfast and lunch eats. The pizza-on-a-pita is pretty good.

BARS, TAVERNS, & BREW PUBS ♿
CooperSmith's Pub & Brewery (970-498-0483; coopersmithspub.com), 5 Old Town Sq. This place is hopping all weekend long. All the beer is brewed right on the premises. CooperSmith's has nearly 20 brews on tap, including hard cider and a raspberry mead. There are different menus for the pub and the billiard room. Both serve CooperSmith's wood-fired stove pizzas. The pub side has excellent pub grub—bangers and mash and an

interesting take on shepherd's pie called Highland Cottage Pie. Sandwiches $10 and dinner entrées $20.

  ✦ **Sundance Steakhouse & Saloon** (970-484-1600; sundancesteakhouse.com), 2716 E. Mulberry St. Sundance Saloon could be listed under Entertainment—it may be the most popular place in northern Colorado to hear, and dance to, country music. On Wednesdays, there are dance lessons earlier in the evening. Instructors teach line dancing and couples dancing (only $5/person). Live music is a regular feature of Sundance. The steakhouse serves up a nice steak as well as burgers and such. Dishes $14–20.

✳ Entertainment

✦ **Avogadro's Number** (970-493-5555; avogadros.com), 605 S. Mason St. Although named after a "constant" only chemists would readily recognize, Avogadro's Number is all about music. Local bands play here regularly, as do some big names in folk, jazz, and bluegrass. There is also a rather ordinary menu for breakfast, lunch, and dinner—standouts would be the tempeh burgers and falafel.

Mishawaka Amphitheatre (970-482-4420; themishawaka.com), 13714 Poudre Canyon Hwy., Bellvue. The Mish has a regular schedule of live outdoor performances throughout the summer. The remainder of the year, concerts are held inside with a smaller audience. The Kitchen at Mishawaka has indoor and outdoor seating, and a fine menu to make your evening more of a "dinner and a show" kind of event. Parking is tight, so the theater prefers that you buy tickets in advance instead of at the box office, as the latter just makes things more congested.

✳ Selective Shopping

Old Town Square (downownfortcollins.com) is the restored shopping district in the heart of old Fort Collins. It's located at the northeast corner of Mountain and College avenues. There are plenty of restaurants and art galleries and other shops for a pleasant afternoon of shopping. The website lists all the festivals and events planned for the area.

First Friday Gallery Walk (970-482-2232; downtownfortcollins.com/events/first-friday-featuring-gallery-walk), downtown Fort Collins. The first Friday of the month, from 6–9 in the evening, the downtown art galleries stay open later for a gallery walk. Refreshments are served at the galleries as you take a self-guided tour to see their new exhibitions. Maps available at almost all the galleries in town and the visitor center in Old Town Square.

Illustrated Light (970-493-4673; illustratedlight.com), #1 Old Town Square, Ste. 103. Open daily 10–6, Sun. noon–5. This gallery specializes in photographic arts. Contemporary as well as vintage photographs are on display, and the images are simply stunning.

Trimble Court Artisans (970-221-0051; trimblecourt.com), 118 Trimble Ct. Open daily 10–6, Sun. 11–5. This artist co-op features all local artists, with a great selection of pottery, watercolors, and so on. All the artists take turns watching the store, so you will find them very knowledgeable and passionate about the art on display.

✳ Special Events

June: **Colorado Brewer's Festival** (970-484-6500; downtownfortcollins.com/events/colorado-brewers-festival), downtown Fort Collins. In a town that celebrates beer, this annual festival is a big event. Beer sampling and live music are the main attractions. Participating breweries are all from Colorado.

June/July: **Greeley Stampede** (970-356-2855 or 1-800-982-2855; greeleystampede.org). Touted as "the world's largest Fourth of July rodeo and western celebration," the Stampede is one of Colorado's biggest annual events. Located just east of Loveland in Greeley, home of the University of Northern Colorado, the event runs during the weekends leading up to July 4 and brings some of country music's biggest names for a series of concerts.

August: **Bohemian Nights at NewWest-Fest** (970-484-6500; bohemiannights.org /bohemian-nights-at-newwestfest.html), downtown Fort Collins. This annual festival brings more than 50 musical acts to Fort Collins to perform on five stages over three days. Recent headliners included Earl Scruggs and Melissa Etheridge. Other entertainment includes belly dancing, ballet, Mexican folk dance, and other acts. For the kids, there are puppet shows and magic shows.

ESTES PARK

In some ways, Estes Park is a town with a bit of a split personality. You can spend a ritzy weekend at the Stanley, play a round of golf on a world-class course, and enjoy fine dining at a number of high-end eateries. Or you can buzz into town with a passel of kids in tow, park your RV (or rent a cabin) at the local KOA, spend your days at the tourist shops in town, and splurge on pizza for dinner. Or simply stop in town for supplies and to arrange plans with an outfitter before heading into Rocky Mountain National Park for a bare-bones backcountry camping trip. Whatever your idea of a great mountain vacation, Estes Park can fit the bill.

The beautiful Estes Valley has attracted people for centuries. Nearly 12,000 years ago, the first people to arrive on this continent used the valley as a hunting ground. Later, the Ute and Arapaho set up camp here in the summers. And from early in the 19th century, mountain men trapped on local rivers and hunted game throughout this region. They were followed by the miners who were drawn to Colorado by the discovery of gold in the Denver area. Soon the mountains were swarming with miners hoping to find an elusive gold vein of their own.

It was in 1859 that one man, Joel Estes, who had made a fortune of his own mining in California, stumbled upon the valley. So taken was he with this lush meadow, he moved there with his wife and 13 children. They brought with them a herd of cattle and stayed for six years. By the late 1860s, Estes had found cattle ranching to be impractical. The Earl of Dunhaven came to buy the entire valley to create a hunting preserve and resort.

His plans were shot down by the valley's other residents, but the tourism potential of what was now called Estes Park had been recognized. Soon the Elkhorn Lodge was catering to guests looking for a mountain retreat. By 1909, F. O. Stanley had built the landmark Stanley Hotel, which brought big-city luxury lodging to town. And in 1915, Rocky Mountain National Park was established.

Stanley proved to be a real asset to the burgeoning tourist industry in the valley. He made the first auto road to Estes Park and operated an early shuttle service bringing guests into the mountains via the Big Thompson Canyon.

Within the past 30 years, two floods have devastated the area. In 1976, a sudden storm inundated the Big Thompson River. As a wall of water swept down the canyon toward Loveland, 145 people lost their lives. Four hundred homes were destroyed, as were many businesses. Just six years later, in 1982, there was the Lawn Lake Flood. The natural dam that held Lawn Lake in the mountains broke. Unlike the Big Thompson flood, which caused almost all its damage downriver of town, the flood of 1982 devastated downtown Estes Park.

Today Estes Park has been rebuilt, and the town is a thriving tourist destination seen as the gateway to Rocky Mountain National Park. There are hundreds of hotels, motels, campgrounds, cabins, lodges, and resorts catering to thousands of annual visitors.

GUIDANCE **Estes Park Visitors Center** (970-577-9900 or 1-800-443-7837; visitestes park.com), 500 Big Thompson Ave. Right near the intersection of Big Thompson and St. Vrain avenues, the visitor center can be your first stop whether you are coming from Loveland or Lyons. Helpful staff, plenty of brochures, and clean restrooms make for a good start in town.

ENTERING ESTES PARK

More websites:
estes-park.com
estespark-colorado.com
estespark.us

GETTING THERE *By car:* From Loveland in the east and Grand Lake in the west, US 34 is the main route to and through town (in town it's called Big Thompson Avenue). Coming up from the south, take I-25 to exit 243 and head west on CO 66. In Lyons, stay to the right on US 36 and arrive in Estes Park from the south on St. Vrain Avenue.

By air: **Denver International Airport** (303-342-2000 or 1-800-247-2336; flydenver .com) is a 1.5-hour drive from Estes Park.

By shuttle: **Estes Park Shuttle and Mountain Tours** (970-586-5151; estesparkshuttle .com) offers shuttle service to and from Denver International Airport, as well as several locations in Boulder, Lyons, and Longmont.

GETTING AROUND *By car:* Downtown Estes Park is entirely walkable once you get there. There is plenty of parking behind the shops on the south side of Elkhorn Avenue. If you get to town early enough in the day to pick your spot, park east of Moraine Avenue, near the Riverside Plaza, where trees keep the lot shady.

By shuttle: **Estes Park Shopper Shuttle** (970-577-9900 or 1-800-443-7837; colorado .gov/pacific/townofestespark/shuttles) operates a free shuttle that makes stops all around the Estes Park area, even out to Rocky Mountain National Park. All routes begin at the visitor center on Big Thompson Avenue.

✷ To See & Do

Enos Mills Cabin Museum & Nature Trail (970-586-4706; enosmills.com), 8 miles south of Estes Park on CO 7. Open all year. Summer hours Wed.–Fri. 11–4 and other days completely at random. Call ahead for an appointment in winter. Enos Mills is called "the father of Rocky Mountain National Park" for his efforts in convincing Congress to protect and preserve this section of the Rockies. At age 14, Mills left his family in Kansas and came to stay in Estes Park with relatives. He was resourceful, and the museum resides in the log cabin he built in 1885, when he was 15 years old. A friend of John

Muir, an avid outdoorsman, and passionate conservationist, Enos Mills is the history of Estes Park. The museum has many exhibitions that illustrate his impact. Adult admission $20.

Estes Park Aerial Tramway (970-586-3675; estestram.com), 420 E. Riverside Di. Open summers, daily 9–6. The tramway takes you right up to the top of Prospect Mountain. It has a great view of Estes Park and panoramic views of the surrounding peaks. There are some trails for hiking and a deli for lunch. Adults $10, seniors $9, children (6–11) $5, and children under 6 free.

♂ GET MARRIED Weddings are a big deal in Estes Park; 3,000 to 4,000 couples get married here every year. The first thing you need is a marriage license, which you can get from the **Larimer County Clerks Office** (970-577-2025), 1601 Brodie Ave., for $30. It is open Mon.–Fri. 8–4:30. There is no waiting period, you just need your ID, and if you've been married before, you will need to state who issued the divorce or death certificate. Everything else you could possibly need for the wedding—from a live band and a champagne fountain to a ring and a preacher—can be found through the businesses listed on the **Estes Park Wedding Association** website, estespark weddings.com.

☂ **Historic Fall River Hydro Plant** (970-586-6256; estesnet.com/hydroplant), 1754 Fish Hatchery Rd. Take US 34 northwest toward RMNP, and then turn left on Fish Hatchery Road, which dead-ends at the Hydro Plant. In the summer (Memorial Day–Labor Day), the plant is open Tue.–Sun. 1–4. Call for an appointment in the winter. This historic facility was built by F. O. Stanley to power the Stanley Hotel, making it the first fully electric hotel in the country. Free admission.

MacGregor Ranch (970-586-3749; macgregorranch.org), 180 MacGregor Ln. Museum open summers, Tue.–Fri. 10–4. MacGregor Ranch has 42 buildings, 28 of which are listed on the National Register of Historic Places. As the last working ranch in Estes Park, visitors can experience a true piece of living history. A museum puts the ranch in historic context, and guests can take self-guided tours of the blacksmith shop, milk house, and other buildings and exhibitions. Free admission, but donations keep the ranch running.

♿ ☂ **The Stanley Hotel** (970-586-3371 or 1-800-976-1377; stanleyhotel.com), 333 E. Wonderview Ave. The Stanley Hotel has a longstanding reputation for being haunted.

HISTORIC STANLEY HOTEL

National Park (970-586-1206 from 8-4:30 or 970-586-1222 for a recorded ... ours a day; nps.gov/romo), 1000 US 36. The park is open 24 hours a day, ... ere are six visitor centers; most are open daily in the summer. Check web-... ours.

... n National Park (RMNP) was established by an act of Congress in 1915. The original inten... of the park was to set aside a portion of the Rocky Mountains so that its scenic and natural beauty could be enjoyed for future generations. The park is truly majestic and includes canyons, meadows, and soaring peaks. Over the years, many cultural assets have been discovered and preserved, including ancient trails that hint at the park's deep past and old cattle ranches that look back a century or two.

For a quick overview of the park, Trail Ridge Road (US 34) runs west of Estes Park, through the park, and over the Continental Divide, and then descends on the other side to Grand Lake, terminating in Granby. (In the east, US 34 ends in Berwyn, Illinois.) It is the highest continuous paved road in the United States—12,183 feet at its highest point—with 11 miles of road above tree line. The views are phenomenal.

For a nice trip without going all the way to Grand Lake, drive up to the Alpine Visitors Center. At 11,796 feet, the air here is awfully thin, especially for people who have only been as high as Estes Park for a day (watch for signs of altitude sickness—shortness of breath, dizziness—and head back down the mountain if you need to). The road is closed from winter into early spring—plowing starts in April with a goal of having it all cleared for the opening on Memorial Day.

For more scenery, head up to Bear Lake. If you park at Glacier Basin, a shuttle will take you up Bear Lake Road.

To really experience the park, however, you have to get out of your car. The Lawn Lake Flood of 1982 devastated Estes Park and created a unique alluvial fan in Horseshoe Park. When the water came bellowing down the mountain, it brought with it tons of debris. When it hit the wide Horseshoe Park, the flood dropped the thousands of boulders it had been carrying. What remains now is a river that cascades down a slope of rocks. This is especially worth a visit in the spring and early summer, when the water levels are higher.

If you have time for more than a quick stop, RMNP has more than 355 miles of hiking trails. There are four campgrounds within the park. These are pretty bare-bones, with just water

Stephen King's stay in room 217 was the inspiration for his novel *The Shining*. The ABC miniseries was filmed here. As the story goes, most of the ghosts reside on the fourth floor. The hotel gives one-hour ghost tours for $28 (no one under 10 years old). The ghost tours are very popular, and the hotel recommends calling ahead (970-577-4110) and making reservations two weeks before your visit. There are also hotel tours and a new show, "Illusions of the Passed," which combines history and magic.

 & ⚲ **Stanley Museum** (970-577-1903; stanleymuseum.org), 40 School St., Lower Stanley Village. Open Tue.–Sun. 11–4. The Stanley Museum tells the story of F. O. Stanley, the Stanley Steamer, and the historic Stanley Hotel. The museum also manages historic tours of the hotel.

✳ Outdoor Activities

FISHING For fly fishing, **Fall River** and the **Big Thompson River** stretch for miles and have plenty of secluded spots for the avid angler. **Lake Estes** and **Mary's Lake** and toilets. There are no water, sewer, or electric hookups at any of the sites. Backcountry camping is allowed, but you must purchase a permit in advance.

The park operates a shuttle service, **Rocky Mountain National Park Shuttle** (970-586-1206; nps.gov/romo/planyourvisit/gettingaround.htm), which takes visitors to stops along the main road at campgrounds, trailheads, and scenic stops.

AN ALLUVIAL FAN IN ROCKY MOUNTAIN NATIONAL PARK

are popular as well. There are several fishing outfitters in town with guides who have extensive local knowledge.

Estes Angler (970-586-2110 or 1-800-586-2110; estesangler.com), 338 W. Riverside Dr. In addition to offering guided fishing trips with access to private water, Estes Angler also posts up-to-date fishing reports on its website. One-person trips $150 and $245 for half- and full-day outings. Gets cheaper if you bring along a friend or two.

FOUR-WHEEL TOURS **Wildside 4X4 Tours (aka Rocky Mountain Rush Tours)** (970-586-8687; rockymountainrush.com), 212 E. Elkhorn Ave. Four-wheeling is a great way to experience Rocky Mountain National Park. This company specializes in photo tours and rates drives by the level of thrill—from mild to wild. Some tours include alcohol, some a hot dog roast. Check out the site for all the details. Generally tours cost adults about $70 apiece.

GOLF **Estes Park Golf Course** (970-586-8146 or 1-866-586-8146; evrpd.com/18-hole-golf-course), 1480 Golf Course Rd. Located south of town, this 18-hole course offers fantastic views of the surrounding mountains. It is considered one of the most beautiful courses in the country. Don't be surprised to find deer and elk wandering the course. Greens fees $28–40 for residents, $35–51 for nonresidents.

Lake Estes 9 Hole Executive Course (970-586-8176; evrpd.com/9-hole-golf-course), 690 Big Thompson Ave. Summer season runs mid-April–Oct. This nine-hole course is close to town on the western tip of Lake Estes. Greens fees $11–14 for residents, $13–18 for nonresidents.

HIKING & SNOWSHOEING Rocky Mountain National Park offers some of the most spectacular trails and scenery for hiking, and in the winter, cross-country skiing and snowshoeing. Up in the mountains, the season for winter sports lasts well into the spring. The snow cover on the east side of the park is better suited for snowshoeing, and the park offers free ranger-guided walks. Gear and other guide services can easily be found in Estes Park through various shops and outfitters. (See Rocky Mountain National Park sidebar for more information.)

Estes Park Mountain Shop (970-586-6548 or 1-866-303-6548; estesparkmountain shop.com), 2050 Big Thompson Ave. Open daily 8–9. The Mountain Shop rents everything for outdoor adventure in Estes Park. For winter it has cross-country skis and snowshoes. For summer trips you can find everything from mountain bikes and trailers to backpacks and tents. The shop also has rock-climbing lessons and fly-fishing lessons.

Outdoor World (970-586-2114; rmconnection.com), 156 E. Elkhorn Ave. Open daily 9–9. The shop rents equipment for hiking, camping, and snowshoeing. The staff are very knowledgeable about regional conditions and the proper use of equipment.

The Warming House (970-586-2995; warminghouse.com), 790 Moraine Ave. Close to RMNP on Estes Park's west side, this outfitter rents equipment for hiking, snowshoeing, and camping. Its staff also lead guided trips in winter and summer.

LOCAL WILDLIFE

HORSEBACK RIDING Sombrero Ranch–Estes Park Stable (970-586-4577; sombrero .com), 1895 US 34. East of Estes Park on Big Thompson Ave., right across from Lake Estes, Sombrero Ranch's Estes Stables have one- and two-hour trail rides, as well as four- and eight-hour rides, on its private 1,000-acre ranch. Trips also take guests into the nearby national forest. For added interest, there are also breakfast rides and steak-fry rides, sleigh rides, and wagon rides. Prices range from $35 for the one-hour ride to $180 for the complete overnight camping package. Sombrero also maintains two stables within Rocky Mountain National Park—**Moraine Park Riding Stables** and **Glacier Creek Stables**. See website for more information on rides right in RMNP.

MOUNTAIN BIKING Colorado Bicycling Adventures (970-586-4241; colorado bicycling.com), located at the Elkhorn Lodge. Open by appointment. To really get an insider's look at what the area has to offer mountain bikers, take one of the off-road or downhill tours offered by Colorado Bicycling Adventures.

Estes Park Mountain Shop (970-586-6548 or 1-866-303-6548; estesparkmountain shop.com), 2050 Big Thompson Ave. To tour on your own, stop by, rent a bike, and get advice on where to ride. Mountain bikes run $25 for a full-day rental and up to $80 for three days.

BOATING, PADDLING & RAFTING Lake Estes Marina (970-586-2011; evrpd.com /marina/marina-info), 1770 Big Thompson Ave. Located at the east end of Lake Estes, the marina has a ton of boats for rent—motorboats, large and small pontoons, paddleboats, kayaks, and canoes. The large pontoons can hold up to nine people for a party on the lake. The marina also rents bikes.

Rapid Transit Rafting (1-800-367-8523; rapidtransitrafting.com), 161 Virginia Dr. Rapid Transit takes guests on rafting trips on both sides of the Continental Divide. In the west, you can ride the Colorado River with class II and III rapids. Closer to town, the Cache la Poudre running toward Fort Collins has class II–IV rapids. Full-day trip on the Colorado $85, and half-day trip on the Cache la Poudre $55.

✳ Lodging

HOTELS (ᯤ) **Boulder Brook on Fall River** (970-586-0910 or 1-800-238-0910; boulder brook.com), 1900 Fall River Rd. Two standard suites and three themed suites. Open year-round right on Fall River. Each suite has a private riverfront deck, and there are jetted tubs, fireplaces, cable TV, and DVD players. Peak season rates: suites $199–249. Much less in the shoulder and off seasons.

✍ ६ ☀ (ᯤ) **Estes Park Center–YMCA of the Rockies** (970-586-3341; ymcarockies .org), 2515 Tunnel Rd. (See *Northwest Colorado* for the Winter Park portion of YMCA of the Rockies, Snow Mountain Ranch.) Estes Park Center offers visitors lodge rooms, cabins, and vacation homes. Jackson Stables (jacksonstables.com),

are also on site. Rooms $79–169 and cabins $129–389.

✍ (ᯤ) **Fawn Valley Inn** (970-586-2388 or 1-800-525-2961; fawnvalleyinn.com), 2760 Fall River Rd. Frontage on Fall River for fishing. Cable TV and DVD player, heated pool, and hot tub. A huge DVD library of over 1,000 movies. With such a wide selection of accommodations—condos, suites, and cabins, all with different amenities—rates also range widely: $90–375.

६ ☀ (ᯤ) **The Stanley Hotel** (970-586-3371 or 1-800-976-1377; stanleyhotel .com), 333 E. Wonderview Ave. In 1903, F. O. Stanley, maker of the famous Stanley Steamer, moved west for his health. He arrived in Estes Park, and by 1907 had decided to build a hotel. The Stanley Hotel was completed in 1909, and many of the original buildings are still in use.

THE VIEW FROM YMCA OF THE ROCKIES

The hotel stands as an iconic landmark of Estes Park. Rooms $209–499 (in season) and $139–459 (off season).

& (((•))) **Taharaa Mountain Lodge** (970-577-0098 or 1-800-597-0098; taharaa .com), 3110 S. St. Vrain Ave. This lodge/B&B has nine rooms and nine suites. Each room has a fireplace and a fantastic view. Every morning, guests enjoy a full gourmet breakfast. Rooms $155–199 and suites $195–349.

BED & BREAKFASTS **Anniversary Inn** (970-586-6200; estesinn.com), 1060 Mary's Lake Rd. This 100-year-old log inn has three rooms and one Sweetheart's Cottage. The cottage and two of the rooms have Jacuzzi tubs. Full breakfast is served on the enclosed porch every morning. Less than 2 miles from downtown Estes Park. Rooms $150–200, cottage $230.

& (((•))) **Baldpate Inn** (970-586-6151; baldpateinn.com), 4900 S. CO 7. Built in 1917, the inn has always been an inn—12 rooms in the main lodge and 4 cabins. Located 7 miles south of Estes Park, Baldpate sits on Twin Sisters Mountain. Rooms all have double or twin beds and have shared or private baths. The cabins all have private baths. The inn boasts of having the world's largest key collection—there is an interesting story about how this collection came about, so be sure to ask about it when you visit. Rooms $120–140 and cabins $220.

(((•))) **Mountain Valley Home** (970-586-3100; amountainvalleyhome.com), 1420 Axminster Ln. This is a newer home (2002) with five suites. Enjoy wine and appetizers in the Tuscan Wine Room. There is a kitchen for guest use, and a gourmet breakfast is served. Hosts Lynn and Paul know Estes Park, and they can offer help finding places to eat and things to do. A great way to start the morning is with breakfast on their back porch. Be sure to ask Lynn to surprise you with a favorite tea. Enjoy beautiful views, fresh mountain air, and the occasional elk wandering by. Rooms $179–239 (summer) and $149–199 (winter).

    ♿ ☀ (((ŋ))) **Romantic RiverSong** (970-586-4666; romanticriversong.com), 1765 Lower Broadview Rd. Ten guest rooms, named after wildflowers, on 27 wooded acres. Fireside candlelight dinners. Rooms $165–350.

    Sonnenhof Bed & Breakfast (970-577-7528; sonnenhofestespark.com), 650 Lakewood Ct. Three suites, all with Jacuzzi, fireplace, and private patio or deck. Rooms $150–195.

    Allenspark Lodge Bed & Breakfast (303-747-2552; allensparklodge.com), 184 Main CO 7, Allenspark. Built in 1933, this rustic three-story lodge has hand-peeled pine logs and lots of character. The lodge has 12 rooms, 7 of which have private baths. There is also an apartment with full kitchen and bath. The most popular room is the Hideaway Room. Tucked into the back end of the third floor, this room has views on three sides and a clawfoot tub. Rooms $105–150.

CAMPGROUNDS ☀ **Estes Park Campground at East Portal** (970-586-4188; evrpd.com), 3420 Tunnel Rd. Open May–Sept. Close enough to RMNP that you can hike in from your campsite. There are 68 sites in all. Amenities include picnic tables and fire rings, and modern toilet facilities. There is also a place to purchase ice and firewood. Sites $30–45.

    (((ŋ))) **Estes Park KOA** (1-800-562-1887; koa.com/campgrounds/estes-park), 2051 Big Thompson Ave. Just east of downtown Estes Park, this KOA is a great spot for parking your RV or renting a Kamping Kabin (there are a ton of cabins here). Tents are also welcome, if you don't mind pitching a tent on Estes Park's main thoroughfare. Sites $53–76. Kabins about $100.

    ☀ **Estes Park Campground at Mary's Lake** (970-577-1026; evrpd.com), 2120 Mary's Lake Rd. There are 90 RV sites here that accommodate double slide-outs. There's a full selection of hookups, including cable television. Tent campers

have a spacious site, and there are pop-up campers for rent. People fish on Mary's Lake—the camp store has everything you need from licenses and bait, to firewood and ice. A swimming pool and game room round out the extras. Sites $30–45.

CABINS & COTTAGES **Castle Mountain Lodge** (970-586-3664 or 1-800-852-7463; castlemountainlodge.com), 1520 Fall River Rd. This place offers a combination of multi-room cabins and motel-style rooms. It's an easy one to find, just west of downtown, because of its grand log-covered bridge. We've stayed here for Christmas a couple of times with a large family group, and it's always been a pleasant stay. The staff go above and beyond with guest service. Walk down by the river, watch the elk and turkeys wander the lawn. Summer rates: Rooms $75–155; private spas $140–395; cottages $195–500.

    (((ŋ))) **Glacier Lodge** (970-586-4401 or 1-800-523-3920; glacierlodge.com), 2166 CO 66. Glacier Lodge offers more than just its 28 cabins. It has a list of activities that rival local dude ranches. There are several lodging options, from one-bedroom units ($125–170) to full home-style ones that can have up to eight bedrooms ($300–1,000). Rates vary dramatically by size and season. Four-night minimum stay in summer.

    Streamside on Fall River (970-586-6464 or 1-800-321-3303; streamsideon fallriver.com), 1260 Fall River Rd. (CO 34). One mile west of Estes Park, Streamside has cabins that creep right to the edge of Fall River. Cabin decks overlook the river, and they all have fireplaces for cool evenings. Close to town and RMNP. Rates $110–340.

✳ Where to Eat

DINING OUT ♿ **Twin Owls Steakhouse** (970-586-9344; twinowls.net), 800 MacGregor Ave., at the Black Canyon Inn. Open daily for dinner at 5. Rustic mountain lodge, rough-hewn logs, moss rock fireplace, and so on. Twin Owls serves steak from organic grass-fed beef. Reservations are recommended. Entrées $23–45.

The Fawn Brook Inn (303-747-2556; fawnbrookinn.com), CO 7, Business Loop 357, Allenspark. For years, people have been making the drive out to The Fawn Brook Inn for the elegant continental dining experience. The restaurant has been described glowingly as a classic German inn. The menu features dishes such as beef Wellington. Entrées $42–64.

EATING OUT & **Dunraven Inn** (970-586-6409; dunraveninn.com), 2470 CO 66. The more than 13,000 one-dollar bills wallpapering the bar are autographed tips left by grateful diners for owner Dale Hatcher. (As he runs out of space, the money goes to local charities.) The inn has a definite local feel, and the Italian menu is supplemented with seafood and steak. Try the chicken Parmesan; it nearly overflows with cheesy goodness. Reservations recommended. Pasta dishes $16–30, pricier entrées up to $36.

& **Ed's Cantina & Grill** (970-586-2919; edscantina.com), 390 E. Elkhorn Ave. Open daily 11–close. Breakfast served Fri., Sat., and Sun. in summer; just Sat. and Sun. in winter. Ed's serves burgers and burritos, and this is a great place for a quick bite to eat. When weather permits, there's patio seating by the river. Breakfast under $8 and lunch and dinner $8–15.

& **Mama Rose's** (970-586-3330; mamarosesrestaurant.com), 338 E. Elkhorn Ave. Located in Barlow Plaza along the Riverwalk. Open daily in the summer for dinner 4–9; winter, daily 4–8. Closed in Jan. and the first week of Feb. Diners come to Mama Rose's for the service, the outdoor seating along the river, and, of course, for the decent Italian fare. Reasonably priced, the restaurant is busy in the summer, but lines move quickly. Perfect for eating out with the whole family. Dishes $9–20.

& **Penelope's World Famous Hamburgers and Fries** (970-586-2277; penelopesburgers.com), 229 W. Elkhorn Ave. Open daily at 11, Penelope's closes when there are no more customers. Right downtown, Penelope's is regularly voted best hamburger in Estes Park—and the handmade fries alone are worth a visit. Lunch is under $12.

🍴 **Wapiti Bar & Grill** (970-586-5056; thewapitipub.com), 247 W. Elkhorn Ave. Open year-round, daily 8–9. Wapiti is the Shawnee word for "elk." People return to the restaurant year after year for the food and kid-friendly environment. There is seating indoors and out. For variety, you can order a burger made of beef, elk, buffalo, or veggies. The fish tacos are outstanding, and quite a surprise this far east of Baja. Dishes run from under $10 for burgers or the fantastic fish and chips to $22 for the signature entrées.

BAKERIES & COFFEE SHOPS & (((•)))
Notchtop Bakery & Café (970-586-0272; thenotchtop.com), 459 E. Wonderview Dr., #4. More than just a coffee shop and bakery, Notchtop serves breakfast, lunch, and dinner as well. Healthy ingredients, great bread, and coffee. Breakfast is highly rated.

BARS, TAVERNS & BREW PUBS &
Estes Park Brewery (970-586-5421; epbrewery.com), 470 Prospect Dr. After a long day of hiking in RMNP, Estes Park Brewery is a great place to relax, get a little food, and enjoy some great beer. Try the Stinger Wild Honey Wheat or the Bear Lake Blueberry Wheat, both favorites with regulars.

SNACKS & **Flavor of the Rockies** (970-586-4374; flavoroftherockies.com), 101 W. Elkhorn Ave. Open daily 10–10. If you loved visiting Grandma's Mountain Cookies in Estes Park, you may grieve to hear they closed up shop a few years ago. The cookies are still being baked, but now in Loveland, but you buy them here at Flavor of the Rockies. The perfect place for a snack, FOTR has fudge, ice cream, caramel apples, and a great selection of chocolate treats.

✳ Entertainment

Estes Park Music Festival (970-577-9900 or 1-800-443-7837; estesparkmusic festival.org), The Stanley Hotel. Winter concerts are held on Sunday afternoons at 2, Nov.–April, at The Stanley Hotel. The summer series of concerts is held at various locations throughout Estes Park. See website for schedule.

✳ Selective Shopping

Earthwood Artisans (970-586-2151; earthwoodgalleries.com/earthwood-artisans), 360 E. Elkhorn Ave., and **Earthwood Collections** (970-577-8100; earthwoodgalleries.com/earthwood-collections), 141 E. Elkhorn Ave. Open year-round. Summer hours 10-9. These two galleries represent more than 230 local and regional artists (as well as numerous national artists). They carry a huge collection of oil paintings, watercolors, ceramics, and sculpture—much of it celebrating Colorado and the Rocky Mountains.

MacDonald Bookshop (970-586-3450; macdonaldbookshop.com), 152 E. Elkhorn Ave. Open daily in the summer 8–9:30; winter 8–6. This bookstore has been in business for more than 80 years. There is a photo that shows the MacDonald and Son General Merchandise shop at this location in 1928. The bookstore has an excellent local interest section covering Estes Park and a great selection of books on Colorado history.

Wynbrier Ltd. Wildlife Gallery (970-586-4074; wynbrier.com), 238 E. Elkhorn Ave. There are plenty of shops in Colorado selling wildlife art. Wynbrier Gallery is the oldest such shop in Estes Park, and it has a huge selection—everything from obsidian knives to art prints.

✳ Special Events

May: **Estes Park Jazz Fest and Art Walk** (visitestespark.com/events-calendar/special-events/jazz-fest-and-art-walk). Just like the name suggests, this festival brings together a series of jazz performances and an art walk for two days every year in May.

July: **Rooftop Rodeo** (970-586-6104; rooftoprodeo.com), Stanley Park Fairgrounds. The rodeo comes to Estes Park every July for six days.

September: **Longs Peak Scottish-Irish Highlands Festival** (970-586-6308; scotfest.com), Stanley Park Baseball Fields & Rodeo Grounds. Always held the weekend after Labor Day, the festival is the largest of its kind. It features a heavy armor jousting competition, Irish and Highland dancing, and medieval games competitions.

NORTHWEST COLORADO

■

BRECKENRIDGE & SUMMIT COUNTY

VAIL & EAGLE COUNTY

WINTER PARK & GRAND COUNTY

STEAMBOAT SPRINGS & THE YAMPA VALLEY

ASPEN & SNOWMASS

GLENWOOD SPRINGS

GRAND JUNCTION & COLORADO'S WESTERN SLOPE

BRECKENRIDGE & SUMMIT COUNTY

Breckenridge (a.k.a. "Breck"), which has nearly 9,000 permanent residents, is one of the most popular ski destinations in the state. Breckenridge hotels, lodges, and B&Bs can accommodate 25,000 during peak seasons. Just driving through town, it's hard to imagine that there are more than 100 restaurants and dozens of bars and saloons. One of the most charming aspects of Breckenridge is that so much of the town's history remains intact. With nearly 250 structures, the town is the largest historical district in Colorado. These structures have been restored and preserved to tell the story of the town's past.

As with most Colorado mountain towns, the story of Breckenridge began with the promise of gold. In 1859, gold was discovered near the Blue River. The mining camp that sprang up in the valley was officially established later that year. It was named in honor of President James Buchanan's vice president, John Cabell Breckinridge. During the Civil War, however, John Breckinridge sided with the South, and the town that bore his name quietly altered the spelling to Breckenridge.

By 1861, Breckenridge was a thriving little community. There were soon a few stores, hotels, and saloons. The U.S. post office came to town, and Breckenridge was the county seat of Summit County. By the 1880s, the railroad had come to town, and the population was nearly 2,000. Breckenridge became a trading center, supplying local miners and everyone else trying to make a living in Summit County. The town's growth, however, was primarily tied to the discoveries of gold, then silver, then zinc and lead. As these resources were discovered and subsequently mined out, the local economy rose and fell.

During these early years, Father John L. Dyer, a Methodist minister, lived in Breckenridge. Dyer came to town in 1862 to take over the Blue River Mission in Summit County. His circuit grew to include towns as far away as Leadville and Fairplay. At 50 years old, he took to his calling with a passion. Strapping a pair of "Norwegian snowshoes" (i.e., skis) to his feet, he trudged the mountains, hiking regularly over 13,188-foot Mosquito Pass, to care for his flock. His devotion earned him the nickname "the Snowshoe Itinerant," and in 1977 he was inducted into the Colorado Ski and Snowboard Hall of Fame.

By the turn of the century, hard-rock and placer mining had all but died out, and local companies were literally scraping by, using dredging boats to scour the local river bottoms for gold and other metals. In the years leading up to World War II, the town would be so desperate to keep people employed that it allowed the dredge boats down the Blue River through town, destroying most of the town's original buildings on the west side of the river.

When the Country Boy Mine was flooded and subsequently closed in 1945, it meant the end of mining in Breckenridge. As people moved on to find work, the town's population plummeted below 400. For 15 years, people struggled to stay on. Then in 1961, the Rounds and Porter Lumber Company out of Wichita got a permit to build a ski area. And beginning with one lift up Peak 8, Breckenridge's fortunes turned.

Today, 1.5 million visitors come through every year. They come to ski not only the Breckenridge ski area, but Keystone, Copper Mountain, and Arapaho Basin as well.

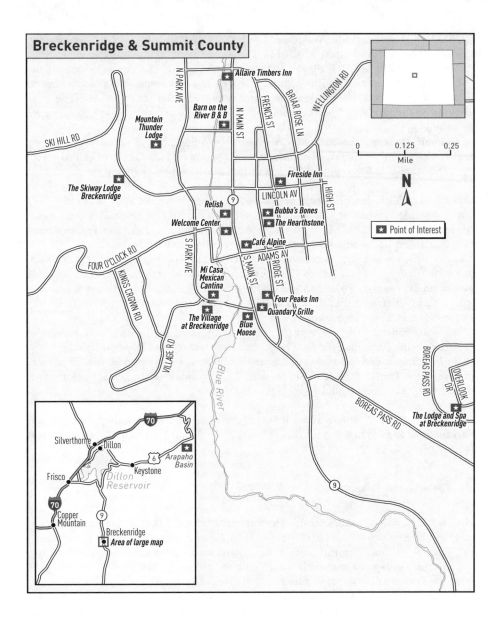

In the summers, people come to hike and bike and to celebrate during any one of the town's great summer festivals. While you're in the area, be sure to visit the neighbors: Frisco and Dillon have great recreational facilities—and a lake in the mountains is a great place to spend a hot day.

Most of the attractions, lodgings, and restaurants listed here are open year-round. However, many hours reduce significantly for about six weeks in the spring and fall. Be sure to call ahead during these two off-seasons. Unless otherwise indicated, all addresses are in Breckenridge.

GUIDANCE **Breckenridge Welcome Center** (1-877-864-0868; gobreck.com/what-to-do/breck-welcome-center), 203 S. Main St., is operated by the Breckenridge Resort Chamber (970-453-2913 or 1-800-221-1091; gobreck.com). The center is open daily 9–6. It is located in the Blue River Plaza. The building that houses the welcome center includes a 19th-century log cabin that was discovered when construction crews were working on the property. The cabin was left intact and is now the center's interpretive museum.

Summit County Chamber of Commerce (970-668-2051; summitchamber.org), Frisco. The chamber operates two information centers off I-70. One is in Frisco at exit 203. The other is in Silverton off CO 9 N. Information centers open daily 9–5.

GETTING THERE *By car:* Breckenridge is very accessible from I-70. Take either exit 201 or 203 into Frisco and follow CO 9 south 9 miles to Breckenridge. If you are heading to Copper Mountain, the ski area is right off the interstate at exit 195. For Keystone, take exit 205 at US 6 and follow that east about 8 miles to the ski area.

By air: The closest airport is **Denver International Airport** (303-342-2000 or 1-800-247-2336; flydenver.com), which is about 100 miles east of Breckenridge. **Colorado Mountain Express** (970-926-9800 or 1-800-525-6363; coloradomountainexpress.com) runs a shuttle between the DIA and Breckenridge. They will also bring you to nearby Keystone and Copper Mountain.

By train: **Amtrak** (1-800-872-7245; amtrak.com) offers its Thruway bus service in Frisco, meeting passengers at the Frisco Transfer Center (1010 Meadow Dr.).

By bus: **Greyhound** (1-800-231-2222; greyhound.com) picks up and drops off passengers at Frisco Transfer Center (1010 Meadow Dr.). Tickets must be bought beforehand, online, or by calling the number above.

GETTING AROUND *By bus:* **Summit Stage** (970-668-0999; summitstage.com), **Breckenridge Free Ride** (970-547-3140; breckfreeride.com), and **Shuttle at Keystone Resort** (970-496-4200).

✻ To See & Do

HISTORICAL SITES & MUSEUMS The **Summit Historical Society** (summithistorical .org) has an extensive list of historical sites in Summit County, including old mining projects, log cabins, Victorian homes, barns, and so on. Hours for the following sites change from season to season. It would be good to call before making plans. Aside from the Country Boy Mine, all these sites are free—donations are appreciated.

Barney Ford House Museum (1-800-980-1859; breckheritage.com/barney-ford-victorian-home), 111 E. Washington Ave. Open year-round; check for seasonal hours. Barney Ford was born into slavery in 1822. He escaped and headed west, eventually settling in Colorado, where he made and lost several fortunes in various entrepreneurial enterprises. Barney Ford and his wife, Julia, were considered prominent citizens in both Breckenridge and Denver. His house in Breckenridge is open to the public. Free; suggested donation $5.

Breckenridge Historic District (970-453-9767; breckheritage.com), 309 N. Main St. With 249 structures, Breckenridge has the largest historical district in Colorado. It offers all sorts of tours, from guided historic walking tours, a haunted tour of Breckenridge, and cemetery and gold mine tours, to self-guided tours and pedicab tours (for those who want to skip the walking altogether).

GROVE OF ASPENS

Edwin Carter Museum (1-800-980-1859; breckheritage.com/edwin-carter-discovery-center), 111 N. Ridge St. Open year-round; check for seasonal hours. Edwin Carter came to Breckenridge in 1860 as a prospector but was dismayed by the impact mining was having on the environment and wildlife in the region. He set about collecting specimens of Rocky Mountain mammals and raptors so there would be a record of the creatures for future generations. Free; suggested donation $5.

Dillon Schoolhouse Museum (970-468-2207; summithistorical.org/site_details.php?site=dillon_schoolhouse), 403 LaBonte St., Dillon. Open in summer Tue.–Fri. 11–3. From 1883 to 1910, this building was a one-room schoolhouse. It later served as a church. It's been restored to the way it would have looked at the turn of the century.

Frisco Historic Park & Museum (970-668-3428; townoffrisco.com/activities/historic-park-museum), 120 Main St., Frisco. Open in the summer Tue.–Sat. 9–5 and Sun. 9–3; winter, Tue.–Sat. 10–4 and Sun. 10–2. What began with a schoolhouse in 1983 has grown to include nine more historic structures—including an old jail, a ranch house, and a log chapel—all of which are used as exhibition space to share the history of Frisco with guests. As you roam through Frisco, you will notice numbers associated with various historic buildings. For information on these sites, call 970-281-3001 on your mobile phone and type in the number.

MINES ✎ **Country Boy Mine** (970-453-4405; countryboymine.com), 0542 French Gulch Rd. Open daily in the summer, 9:30–5:15. In the fall, Mon.–Fri. 10:30–2:15. Tours on the hour. See website for hours and winter schedule. The privately owned Country Boy Mine was once one of the region's biggest gold and silver producers. Today, guests can tour the mine and see what it was like 100 years ago. The tour is 45 minutes long

FRISCO HISTORIC PARK & MUSEUM

and takes you 1,000 feet underground. Afterward, visitors pan for gold or take a ride down the 55-foot ore chute. Adult admission $29.95, children (4–12) $23.95, and children under 4 free; gold-panning $15.95.

Lomax Placer Gulch (1-800-980-1859; breckheritage.com), 301 Ski Hill Rd. Summer tours Tue.–Sat. at 10 and 2 and Sun. at 10. A unique look at mining history, the Lomax Placer Mine was a hydraulic mine, using water at high pressure to push loose earth into the mine's ore recovery equipment. Gold panning is $10. Admission is free; suggested donation $5.

Washington Gold and Silver Mine (1-800-980-1859; breckheritage.com), in Illinois Gulch south of Breckenridge off Boreas Pass Rd. Summer tours Tue.–Sat. at 10 and 2 and Sun. at 10. At one time, this was one of the largest hard-rock mining operations in the area. The tour lets you explore a shaft house and mining cabin. Adults $15, children (12 and under) $10.

SCENIC DRIVES **Hoosier Pass.** The road south out of Breckenridge, CO 9, takes you over Hoosier Pass (elevation 11,539 feet) and through Alma, the highest incorporated town in the United States, on its way to Fairplay. Fantastic scenery in both directions.

❉ Outdoor Activities

ALPINE SKIING & SNOWBOARDING **Arapahoe Basin Ski Area** (970-468-0718 or 1-888-272-7246; arapahoebasin.com), 28194 US 6, Keystone. The ski area is open daily 9–4. The summit of Arapahoe Basin (known lovingly as A-Basin) is 13,050 feet above sea level. With a vertical drop of 2,257 feet to the base, this is the highest ski area in the country. Most of the runs start above timberline, and even without snowmaking equipment, the ski season at Arapahoe lasts into June (and sometimes July). Most of the trails at Arapahoe are appropriate for intermediate and advanced skiers. In the summer of 2007, the ski area added a quad lift that opened access to Montezuma Bowl, increasing the terrain by 80 percent to 900 skiable acres. The ski area also has two terrain parks, one for beginners and the other for more advanced snowboarders. There are few amenities at Arapahoe Basin, but there is a lot of fun. In March, the ski area's Early Riser parking lot becomes "the Beach." Imagine a skier's tailgate party, and you won't be far off.

Breckenridge Ski Resort (970-453-5000 or 1-800-789-7669; breckenridge.com), P.O. Box 1058, Breckenridge, CO 80424. The season runs November into April, depending on snow. The ski area is open daily 8:30–4. Skiing in Breckenridge is found on four mountains along the Ten Mile Range: Peaks 7, 8, 9, and 10. Twenty-nine lifts service the ski area's 2,358 acres. The highest chairlift in North America ascends Peak 8, bringing skiers up to 12,840 feet. With such a variety of terrain, there are runs here for everyone. Most of the beginner runs are on the lower sections of Peaks 8 and 9. Intermediate skiing is mostly found on Peaks 7 and 9. Black-diamond runs are concentrated on Peaks 8 and 10. Overall, more than half of the trails are rated for advanced and expert skiers and a third for intermediate. A classic descent for intermediate skiers is to take the Four O'Clock Trail 3.5 miles from the Vista Haus warming hut into town.

Copper Mountain (1-866-841-2481; coppercolorado.com), 209 Ten Mile Cir., Copper Mountain. Open daily 9–4 (and as early as 8:30 on weekends). With 2,433 acres of skiable terrain, including high alpine bowls and the Catalyst Terrain Park, Copper Mountain has something for everyone. There are plenty of long beginner and intermediate runs. For advanced skiers, there's free snowcat access to Tucker Mountain.

Snowboarders come for the Superpipe and the Catalyst Terrain Park—for younger beginners, there's the Kidz Terrain Park.

Keystone (970-496-2316 or 1-877-625-1556; keystoneresort.com), P.O. Box 38, Keystone, CO 80435. Lifts run 9–4 (later for night skiing). Three mountains—Keystone Mountain, North Peak, and the Outback—make up the Keystone Ski Area. This is a great spot for beginner and intermediate skiers (although half of the ski area is advanced/expert terrain). The longest trail, the 3.5-mile Schoolmarm, is an easy run that's great for getting a feel for the mountain. Keystone has one of the state's biggest night-skiing operations. On certain nights, the beginner slope, Dercum Mountain, and the A51 Terrain Park are kept lighted until 9 PM.

BICYCLING The name of the Ten Mile Recreation Pathway is a bit misleading. Named after the Ten Mile Range, the pathway offers more than 50 miles of paved path connecting Breckenridge to Frisco, Dillon, Copper Mountain, and Keystone. Several loops are possible for a variety of bike rides. Stop by any visitor or welcome center for a map. (See "Mountain Biking.")

CROSS-COUNTRY SKIING & SNOWSHOEING **Breckenridge Nordic Center** (970-453-6855; breckenridgenordic.com), 1200 Ski Hill Rd. The Nordic ski area at Breckenridge maintains more than 32 kilometers of groomed trails for cross-country skiers, and another 16 for snowshoeing. The ski area was recently expanded in the White River National Forest. Adult day pass $20, seniors and youths (7–17) $15. (70+) $5, and children under 7 free.

Frisco Nordic Center (970-668-0866; breckenridgenordic.com), 18484 CO 9, Frisco. Located in the Peninsula Recreation Area in Frisco, the Frisco Nordic Center offers nearly 40 kilometers of cross-country and snowshoeing trails, as well as lessons and equipment rental. Adult day pass $20, seniors and youths (7–17) $15. (70+) $5, and children under 7 free.

Gold Run Nordic Center (970-547-7889; breckenridgerecreation.com/locations /gold-run-nordic-center), 200 Clubhouse Dr. Based at the Breckenridge Golf Club, the Nordic Center has 20 kilometers of groomed cross-country skiing, more than 7 miles of snowshoe trails, and access to the backcountry. Adult day pass $20, seniors and youths (7–17) $15. (70+) $5, and children under 7 free.

The Summit Huts Association (970-453-8583; summithuts.org), 524 Wellington Rd., manages backcountry huts in Summit County. To reserve cabins, or to see a map of cabins on a network of trails, contact the 10th Mountain Division Hut Association (970-925-5775; huts.org).

DOGSLEDDING **Good Times Adventures** (970-453-7604 or 1-800-477-0144; goodtimesadventures.com), 6061 Tiger Rd. This is a great opportunity to really experience dogsledding. This outfitter takes guests out on a 6-mile relay, where they alternate between mushing and riding as passengers on the sled. The tour takes about an hour. Adult price $90 and children (4–8) $50. This activity is not recommended for kids under 4.

GOLF **Breckenridge Golf Club** (970-453-9104; breckenridgegolfclub.com), 200 Clubhouse Dr. The Elk, the Beaver, and the Bear are the three nine-hole courses that make up this 27-hole golf course designed by Jack Nicklaus. The Elk/Beaver combination is rated the second most challenging course in the state. Greens fees for 18 holes $67–117.

Copper Creek Golf Club (970-968-3333; coppercolorado.com/golf), 104 Wheeler Pl., Copper Mountain. Set against the Ten Mile Range, the front nine at Copper Creek

PLAYING IN THE BLUE RIVER

wind through alpine terrain with towering trees, lakes, and streams. The back nine cuts through the forest and the remains of an old mining town. Greens fees $60–99.

Raven Golf Club at Three Peaks (970-262-3636; ravenatthreepeaks.com), 2929 N. Golden Eagle Rd., Silverthorne. Raven Golf Clubs, wherever they are found around the country, strive to offer the best golfing experience possible. Three Peaks is no exception. The always "tournament ready" course takes full advantage of the quintessentially Colorado setting, winding its way through tall pine and aspen groves, surrounded by snowy mountain peaks. Greens fees $55–169.

HIKING There are more than 50 hiking trails in Summit County. One of the most popular is the 5-mile trek to Willow Falls, which takes you through meadows that are full of wildflowers in the summer. Along the way, hikers climb nearly 1,000 feet in elevation.

HORSEBACK RIDING **Breckenridge Stables** (970-453-4438; breckstables.com), Village Rd. The stables can be found off Village Road. From the Beaver Run Resort parking area, continue to the opposite end of the parking lot, turn right, and follow the dirt road up the mountain. Just follow the signs for Ten Mile Station until you see Breckenridge Stables. The stables offer 90-minute trail rides in the Ten Mile Range above Breckenridge. They also have breakfast and dinner rides. Trail rides $70; children (under 40 pounds who ride with an adult) $35.

MOUNTAIN BIKING **Peaks Trail** is a great mountain bike ride. Park your car in Frisco and take the bus to Breckenridge. The trailhead is just past the ski area on Ski Hill Rd. The route takes you on a rolling singletrack path, over mountain streams, and through thick forest. The final descent into Frisco is a knee-burner.

Lone Star Sports (970-453-2003; skilonestar.com), 110 S. Park Ave. In the winter, you can rent skis; in the summer you can rent full-suspension and hard-tail mountain bikes, as well as town cruisers. Full-day, full-suspension rental $52, path bike $32.

PADDLING & RAFTING **Breckenridge Whitewater Park** (970-453-1734), 880 Airport Rd. Behind the Recreation Center on the Blue River, the whitewater park is 1,800 feet long, making it the longest in Colorado. Free to use, the park has 15 features to challenge kayakers with varying degrees of experience.

AVA (1-800-370-0581; coloradorafting.net). This outfitter leads rafting trips all over Colorado. The Blue River flows out of Lake Dillon and offers the closest rafting to the Lake Dillon/Breckenridge area. Look for the "Blue River Express." The one-third day trip is $64 for adults.

✴ Green Space

Lake Dillon (a.k.a. the Dillon Reservoir) is a great place to get outside to relax or play. Located between Dillon and Frisco, the lake is surrounded by four parks: the Peninsula, Swan Mountain, Dillon Reservoir, and Lowry Air Force Recreation areas. There are plenty of paths and trails, Frisbee, golf courses, and picnic areas—and 27 miles of shoreline. This is the highest deep-water marina in the world. To get out on the water, consider renting a boat at the **Lake Dillon Marina** (970-468-5100; dillonmarina.com), 150 Marina Dr., Dillon.

✴ Lodging

HOTELS ♿ ☀ ((ᵖ)) **The Lodge at Breckenridge** (1-800-736-1607; thelodgeatbreckenridge.com), 112 Overlook Dr. Sitting high above Breckenridge, the lodge offers guests great views of town with the ski mountain as a backdrop. Most rooms have large picture windows to facilitate the appreciation of the fantastic scenery. The décor is western, and amenities include the onsite spa and athletic club. Rooms $79–508.

♿ **Mountain Thunder Lodge** (970-547-5650 or 1-888-400-9590; breckresorts .com/lodging/mountain-thunder-lodge), 50 Mountain Thunder Dr. The stone-and-timber exterior of Mountain Thunder Lodge is reflected in the hotel's mountain-lodge décor. The rooms are luxuriously appointed, with every unit having a rock fireplace, a slate floor in the bathroom, and granite countertops. Guests enjoy the heated outdoor pool, deck, and hot tubs. Close to the Skiway Skyway, the lodge offers ski-in, gondola-out

accommodations. Lodgings start at $289 during ski season.

♿ ☀ ((ᵖ)) **The Village at Breckenridge** (970-547-5725 or 1-800-379-6517; breckresorts.com/lodging/the-village-at-breckenridge), 535 S. Park Ave. Located at the base of the mountain, just steps away from downtown Breck, the Village is a sprawling hotel that offers true ski-in, ski-out accommodations. The nearby pedestrian plaza has shopping and dining. Amenities include onsite bar and dining, indoor and outdoor pools and hot tubs, and heated underground parking. Lodgings start at $149 during ski season.

☀ **Hotel Frisco** (970-668-5009 or 1-800-262-1002; hotelfrisco.com), 308 Main St., Frisco. For more affordable lodgings outside Breckenridge, consider staying in Frisco. The hotel is close to the free regional shuttle, so it's just a quick shot to the slopes. The rooms have all the amenities you would expect from a hotel, but they have the feel of a homey inn. Rooms $59–299.

BED & BREAKFASTS (((ẏ))) **Fireside Inn**
(970-453-6456; firesideinn.com), 114 N.
French St. Fireside Inn is a B&B *and* hostel. The original house was built in 1879,
and several additions give it plenty of
character. The inn has suites, private
rooms with bath, and dormitory-style
accommodations with shared bathrooms.
The rooms are decorated with antiques,
and beds are covered in quilts. A full
breakfast is available to all guests for an
extra charge. Rooms $80–206, dormitory
$35–55/person.

Skiway Lodge (970-453-7573; skiway
lodge.com), 275 Ski Hill Rd. The Skiway
Lodge (previously known as the Hunt
Placer Inn) has been consistently recommended as a great spot for a romantic
getaway. The inn has four guest rooms
and five mini-suites. All have private
baths, king-size beds, and 37-inch TVs.
Most have private balconies. The mini-suites have gas fireplaces, and guests
have use of the inn's outdoor hot tub. A
continental breakfast is available daily.
Rooms $99–290.

✳ Where to Eat

DINING OUT ♿ **Hearthstone Restaurant** (970-453-1148; hearthstonebreck
.com), 130 S. Ridge St. Open for dinner
daily at 4. Housed in a 120-year-old Victorian with fantastic views of the mountains, the Hearthstone features hand-cut
steaks, seafood, and wild game. Entrées
include dishes such as ginger sea scallops and blackberry elk. The wine list has
consistently received *Wine Spectator*'s
Award of Excellence. Entrées $25–44.

Le Petit Paris (970-547-5335;
lepetitparisbistro.com), 161 E. Adams
Ave. Open Tue.–Sat. for dinner at 5:30.
This is the only French restaurant in
Summit County. Guests rave about the
food as much as they do about the service. Steak and frites, French onion soup,
and even escargot and frog legs. Truly
one of the best places in Breck for dinner.
Entrées $31–48.

♿ ♆ **Relish** (970-453-0989; relish
breckenridge.com), 137 S. Main St. Open

HEARTHSTONE RESTAURANT

CRÊPES Á LA CART

daily 5–9; closed during the spring and fall shoulder seasons. Chef-owner Matt Fackler opened Relish in 2006 in what was formerly Pierre's Riverwalk Café. The new restaurant boasts Colorado-inspired cuisine with a menu that includes entrées such as pan-fried Colorado leg of lamb and balsamic-grilled buffalo tenderloin. The second-floor dining room is spacious but feels very intimate. Entrées $20–35.

EATING OUT ᕀ **Blue Moose** (970-453-4859), 540 S. Main St. Open daily for breakfast 7–1 (closes at noon in the slow season). The often lengthy wait for breakfast is a sign of just how good this place is. Nothing terribly fancy here, just traditional breakfast fare such as steak and eggs, buttermilk pancakes, and omelets. Breakfast dishes less than $12.

ᕀ **Giampietro Pasta & Pizzeria** (970-453-3838; giampietropizza.com), 100 N. Main St. Open daily 11–10. Over and over, this cozy Italian eatery wins awards for its outstanding pizza. Giampietro serves both New York–style thin crust

and Sicilian deep-dish pizza. The anti-pasti plate is a great appetizer. Classic pasta dishes and a nice wine list balance out the menu. Be sure to order an espresso or cappuccino with dessert. Pizzas $16–33 and other entrées under $15.

ᕀ **Mi Casa Mexican Cantina** (970-453-2071; micasabreck.com), 600 S. Park Ave. Open daily 11:30–9. Often recommended as the best Mexican restaurant in town, Mi Casa serves an exciting menu with daring dishes such as shrimp diablo (shrimp sautéed in a spicy guajillo chile sauce) and mango duck quesadillas. Window seats offer a great dining experience with a view of the Blue River. Dishes $15–20.

ᕀ **Quandary Grille** (970-547-5969; quandarygrille.com), 505 S. Main St. Open Mon.–Fri. 11:30–9, Sat. 11–10, and Sun. 10–9. Located at the Main Street Station, guests have a great view of the mountain. In the summer there is patio seating. The Quandary serves a classic burgers and burritos menu. Dinner entrées such as steaks, fish tacos, and ribs make for great eating. The proximity to the ski area has made the bar a popular spot with the après-ski crowd. Dinner entrées $17–29.

& **Log Cabin Cafe** (970-668-3947; logcabincafe.co), 121 Main St., Frisco. Open for breakfast and lunch daily 7–3. Located on the main drag in Frisco in a building that's not entirely unlike a log cabin, this humble restaurant is perhaps one of the best breakfast spots around. The portions are huge, even if you don't order the pork chop breakfast. The menu has both American and Mexican dishes. If you like huevos rancheros, be sure to try them here. Breakfast dishes $7–9. Most lunch dishes under $10.

& **Sunshine Cafe** (970-468-6663, sunshine-cafe.com), 250 Summit Place Shopping Center, Silverthorne. Open for breakfast and lunch daily 7–3. Stop by the Sunshine Cafe any time of year, and you will find the place packed with locals and tourists alike. This is the place for breakfast. It was here that I learned that huevos rancheros, when done right, can be amazing. Breakfast dishes around $10–12.

BAKERIES & COFFEE SHOPS & **Cool River Coffeehouse and Bakery** (970-453-1716), 325 S. Main St. Open daily 8–2. Cool River has a great menu, affordable prices, and patio seating. Its breakfast wraps and bagel sandwiches are popular, as are its gourmet lunch sandwiches. The espresso bar has a full drink menu with espressos, lattes, mochas, and smoothies. Breakfast $5 and lunch $5–6.

BARS, TAVERNS, & BREW PUBS & ¥ **Breckenridge Brewery & Pub** (970-453-1550; breckbrewpub.com), 600 S. Main St. Open daily 11–close. Breckenridge Brewery first opened its doors in 1990 and is the only brew pub in town. The brewery serves its own microbrews, such as Avalanche Ale and Oatmeal Stout, and for especially discerning drinkers it has small-batch brews on hand. It also serves some great pub food.

& ¥ **Downstairs at Eric's** (970-453-1401; downstairsaterics.com), 111 S. Main St. Open daily 11–midnight. The quintessential hangout, Downstairs at Eric's has an arcade, 29 flat-screen televisions, and more than 80 different beers. The perfect spot to watch the game. It's also a great place to grab a bite with the family. There is excellent pizza and the kind of appetizers you love to feel guilty about, such as the cheddar skins that can come topped with bacon, chili, or broccoli. The kitchen serves from the menu until close.

SNACKS **Crêpes á la Cart** (970-453-4022; crepesalacarts.com), 307 S. Main St. Open Mon.–Thu. 10–9, Fri. and Sat. 9–10, and Sun. 9–9. This semipermanent food cart near Kenosha Steakhouse serves crepes both savory and sweet. The Philly cheese steak crepe is excellent, and the s'mores crepe deserves its status as the most popular crepe on the menu.

❋ Entertainment

Backstage Theatre (970-453-0199; backstagetheatre.org), 121 S. Ridge St. Backstage Theatre has been bringing live performances to Breckenridge since 1974.

❋ Selective Shopping

Shops and restaurants line Main Street in Breckenridge from end to end, with a humbler selection on Ridge Street, two blocks to the east. The town is perfect for an afternoon walk, stopping at art galleries and clothing stores along the way.

Breckenridge Gallery (970-453-2592; breckenridge-gallery.com), 124 S. Main St. As any tourist with a point-and-shoot Kodak knows, it's seemingly impossible to capture the grandeur and beauty of the Rockies in two dimensions. Artists, however, have a way of doing just that. Breckenridge Gallery shows the work of the region's best painters and sculptors. Not a place for "arts and crafts," but a true gallery that's worth a stop even if you're not in the market for an oil to hang above the mantel.

❋ Special Events

January: **International Snow Sculpture Championships**. The best snow artist teams in the world compete in this annual event. Spectators can watch them create art from 12-foot-tall, 20-ton blocks of snow. Contact the Breckenridge Resort Chamber (970-453-2913 or 1-800-221-1091; gobreck.com) for more information.

Late July or early August: **Dillon Open** (dillonopen.com), Dillon. The sailing event of the year, the Dillon Open is the highlight of the Dillon Yacht Club's regatta season.

August: **Genuine Jazz & Wine** (970-418-2121; genuinejazz.com). Throughout the festival, jazz of all kinds is performed on two stages in town, including the floating stage on Maggie's Pond, and at various nightclubs. Saturday afternoon of this long weekend features wine tasting.

VAIL & EAGLE COUNTY

Vail is unique among Colorado's ski towns. Skiing isn't something the town added later—the skiing was first and the town grew from that. Fifty years ago, if you were driving along I-70 through the Vail Valley, nothing in particular would have grabbed your attention. During World War II, the U.S. Army's 10th Mountain Division trained at nearby Camp Hale. The camp was south of the Vail Valley and comprised a large swath of mountain terrain—its boundary included portions of five counties. Pete Seibert was one of the men who trained and subsequently fought with that original group of men. When he returned from World War II, he had a dream of coming to Colorado to start a ski area. Together with some partners, he did just that.

In 1962, work began on Vail Mountain. Over the years, the ski area grew, and today it is the largest ski area in the country. Not only are there more than 5,000 acres for skiing, but the mountain tallies up more than a million "skier days" each year. The town itself began humbly enough—a couple of hotels near the base of the mountain that tried to look as if they could be found in a quaint Bavarian village. Over the years, the town grew exponentially, expanding north and south along a long swath of I-70. Today it is divided into unofficial villages—West and East Vail, Vail Village, and Lionshead. Farther west are Avon and Edwards and the Beaver Creek ski area.

Because the town wasn't restricted by existing infrastructure, it could grow as it saw fit. Instead of being centered on a formal 19th-century downtown, with retail outlets split by the traditional Main Street, the heart of Vail is Vail Village, an outdoor pedestrian mall with winding stone streets and bridges over nearby Gore Creek. The village is right at the base of the mountain, with immediate access to the two major lifts.

The success of Vail as a ski resort and town was not guaranteed. One of the town's greatest promoters was the late president Gerald Ford. When he was still just a lowly congressman from Michigan, Ford bought property here. Later, when he became vice president and then suddenly president, the media began to take notice. During his presidency, he was photographed skiing Vail, and that gave the ski area a certain amount of prestige. Even after his presidency, Ford and his wife remained devoted cheerleaders for the town, lending their names to the city's auditorium and the botanic gardens.

Because the town doesn't have dozens of historic properties to restore or a mining culture to preserve, the focus remains on skiing. And Vail has some of the best skiing around. From the road, the mountain may not look that impressive. The front side has nice technical runs, but nothing to make it stand out among the state's other ski areas. But behind that humble exterior you find the coveted Back Bowls—these seven huge bowls stretch across 6 miles of terrain. And beyond that is the Blue Sky Basin with its backcountry mystique.

In any season, the town is a great place for roaming around, shopping, and dining. In the summer, you can take advantage of the somewhat cheaper rates for lodging and dining and come up for a vacation of fishing, hiking, or mountain biking.

GUIDANCE **Vail Valley Partnership: Chamber & Tourism Bureau** (970-476-1000; visitvailvalley.com). In the summer, the Vail Village Information Center (970-476-4790),

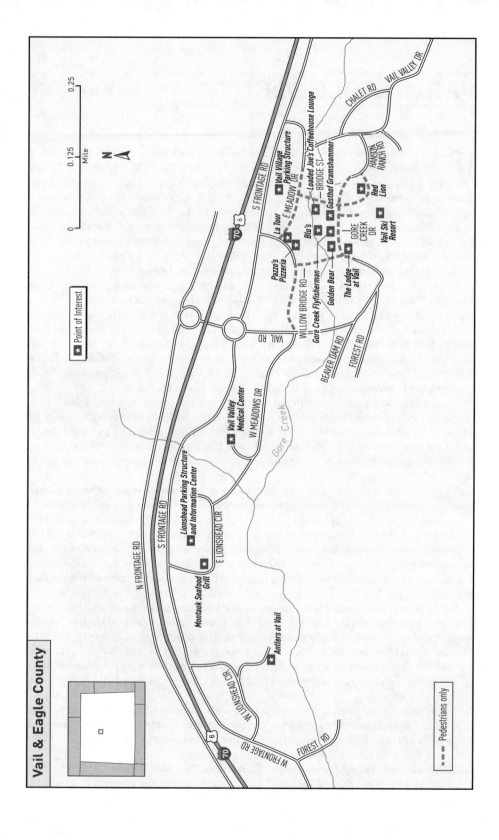

Vail & Eagle County

★ Point of Interest

- - - Pedestrians only

N

0   0.125   0.25
Mile

Points of Interest:
- Antlers at Vail
- Montauk Seafood Grill
- Lionshead Parking Structure and Information Center
- Vail Valley Medical Center
- Pazzo's Pizzeria
- La Tour
- Vail Village Parking Structure
- Loaded Joe's Coffeehouse Lounge
- Gasthof Gramshammer
- Blu's
- Gore Creek Flyfisherman
- Golden Bear
- The Lodge at Vail
- Vail Ski Resort
- Red Lion

Roads:
- N FRONTAGE RD
- S FRONTAGE RD
- W FRONTAGE RD
- E LIONSHEAD CIR
- W LIONSHEAD CIR
- FOREST RD
- W MEADOWS DR
- VAIL RD
- WILLOW BRIDGE RD
- BEAVER DAM RD
- E MEADOW DR
- BRIDGE ST
- GORE CREEK DR
- CHALET RD
- VAIL VALLEY DR
- HANSON RANCH RD

Gore Creek

next to the Village parking structure, is open daily 9–2. The Lionshead Information Center (970-476-4941), next to the Lionshead parking structure, is open noon–5. In the winter, both are open daily 9–5.

Also visit vail.net.

GETTING THERE *By car:* Located right on I-70, Vail is 96 miles west of Denver (little more than a 90-minute drive). Travelers from the south may want to cut over on US 50 in Pueblo and follow the Arkansas Valley north (US 285 to US 24) to I-70. Although more scenic, this route is only 7 miles shorter than taking I-25 north to I-70 west.

By air: From **Eagle County Regional Airport** (970-524-9490; flyvail.com) in Hayden, American, Delta, Continental, and United operate daily flights connecting the Vail Valley with Denver and several other cities around the country. If you are flying into **Denver International Airport** (1-800-247-2336; flydenver.com), it is about 120 miles east of Vail. **Colorado Mountain Express** (970-926-9800 or 1-800-525-6363; colorado mountainexpress.com) will bring you from the DIA to Vail and Beaver Creek.

By bus: **Greyhound** operates regular service to and from Vail from the **Vail Greyhound Transportation Center** (970-476-5137 or 1-800-231-2222; greyhound.com), 241 S. Frontage Rd. E.

GETTING AROUND *By bus:* **The Vail Transportation Center** (970-479-2178; vailgov .com/transportation-services) operates a free bus connecting all of Vail. **Eagle County Regional Transportation** (970-328-3520; eaglecounty.us/Transit), or ECO, offers bus service connecting Vail with other communities in the Vail Valley and Leadville. Check its website for route info.

❋ To See & Do

Betty Ford Alpine Gardens (970-476-0103; bettyfordalpinegardens.org), 522 S. Frontage Rd. (Ford Park, east of Vail). Open in the summer from snowmelt to snowfall, daily dawn to dusk. At 8,200 feet, this is the world's highest botanical garden. These beautifully landscaped gardens feature high-altitude plants. This is the perfect spot for a summer stroll. There are more than 2,000 varieties of plants here, all native to the Rocky Mountains. Free admission.

& ❦ **Colorado Ski Museum–Ski & Snowboard Hall of Fame** (970-476-1876; skimuseum .net), 231 S. Frontage Rd. E. Open in the winter daily 10–7:30; open daily in the summer 10–5:30. This fine museum might be of special interest to anyone involved in winter sports. It traces the history of skiing in Colorado for well over a century. Exhibitions include the first primitive skis used by miners and a display that tells the story of snowboarding. For 10th Mountain Division buffs, there's an entire room here telling the story of the men trained here in the Rockies in ski warfare. Free admission, although there is a suggested donation of $3 for adults.

❋ Outdoor Activities

ALPINE SKIING & SNOWBOARDING **Vail Mountain** (1-800-805-2457; vail.com). Far and away, Vail is the largest and busiest ski area in the country. The resort comprises 5,289 acres of skiable terrain, made up of 7 bowls and 4 terrain parks, serviced by 34 lifts. Every year the mountain sees more than a million "skier days." Vail is composed of three main sections—the Front Side, the Back Bowls, and Blue Sky Basin. The Front

Side is what you see from the village. This is where you find all the beginner runs and terrain parks (although there are slopes here for all level of skiers). Behind the Front Side are seven huge bowls. The Back Bowls span 6 miles and offer terrain for intermediate and expert skiers. Dr. Ruth Westheimer, who skis Vail regularly, loves the China Bowl. Even farther back is the Blue Sky Basin, with backcountry-style terrain serviced by four high-speed quad lifts. Belle's Camp atop the basin offers food concessions and an outdoor grilling area for those who bring their own grub. For freeskiers and snowboarders, Vail has four terrain parks, two pipes, and a superpipe with 18-foot walls. For folks looking for a change of pace, there's a mountain playground of sorts called **Adventure Ridge at Eagle's Nest** (1-877-570-8892; vailspa.com/adventure-ridge). This section of the ski area is set aside for ski biking, tubing, snowmobiling for the kids, ice skating, and all sorts of other activities. Adventure Ridge is lighted and open 2–9.

Beaver Creek (970-754-4636 or 1-80-842-8062; beavercreek.com). Folks looking for an experience that is more intimate than Vail often head a little farther down the road to Beaver Creek. This ski area has a reasonable 1,805 acres of skiable terrain, and an impressive 4,040 vertical drop. With 148 trails for skiing, and three terrain parks and a half pipe for snowboarding, visitors can spend a week here without feeling a need to venture out to other mountains. The Birds of Prey Downhill Course at Beaver Creek is the site of an annual World Cup competition. As such, it's a popular run for those out to test their skills on a classic double-black-diamond trail. For beginners, the Cinch Trail, which begins high up on the slope, offers a long easy glide to the bottom of the mountain.

THE MOUNTAINS AROUND VAIL

THE 10TH MOUNTAIN DIVISION

In 1939, Finnish troops on cross-country skis repelled an invading Soviet army of superior size and firepower. As the United States was confronted with entering World War II, it considered the success of the Finnish troops and questioned its own military preparedness for winter warfare. So in 1940, the American Alpine Club began working with the War Department to determine which kind of training and equipment would be necessary. They were soon joined in this endeavor by the chair of the National Ski Patrol Committee of the National Ski Association. Together they determined that a special unit of alpine soldiers needed to be formed.

In 1942, Camp Hale was established in the Rocky Mountains, north of Leadville. Staffed with volunteers who had previous experience in mountaineering and skiing, the division trained in the mountains throughout the winter of 1943/44. They were deployed to Italy toward the end of the war in 1945. Their efforts there routed the Germans from seemingly impenetrable strongholds in the Alps. During the Italian campaign, the 10th Mountain Division suffered 4,888 casualties, and 978 men lost their lives in action.

Many of the men who trained here returned to the Rocky Mountains. Their contribution to the war effort is memorialized by monuments at Camp Hale and at the summit of Tennessee Pass.

BICYCLING **Vail Bike Tech** (970-476-5995; vailbiketech.com), 555 E. Lionshead Cir. This biking outfitter has a shuttle to take riders up to Vail Pass for a thrilling ride back into Lionshead. This tour costs $41 (a little more with a guide). Vail Bike Tech can also hook you up for the ride to Frisco or Glenwood Springs. (See also "Mountain Biking," page 115).

CROSS-COUNTRY SKIING & SNOWSHOEING **Vail Nordic Center** (970-476-8366; vailnordiccenter.com), 1778 Vail Valley Dr. In the winter in Colorado, many golf courses open their property up for cross-country skiers. This Nordic center operates at the Vail Golf Course. There are 17 kilometers of ski trails and 10 kilometers set aside for snowshoeing. The center offers equipment rental and lessons. A day pass to the trails is only $10.

Beaver Creek's Nordic Sports Center & McCoy Park (970-754-5313; beavercreek .com), Beaver Creek. Located at the top of the Strawberry Park lift at Beaver Creek, the Nordic Sports Center maintains more than 30 kilometers of groomed and rustic trails for cross-country skiing and snowshoeing in McCoy Park. The center offers group lessons, private instruction, and a nature tour.

10th Mountain Division Hut Association (970-925-5775; huts.org). For backcountry skiing, huts make it possible for skiers to make multiday trips in the wilderness with the promise of comfortable, reliable shelter and a warm bed at night. The 10th Mountain Division Hut System comprises 29 backcountry huts connected by a network of trails (350 miles of suggested routes). Check the website for route information, hut availability, and rates.

DOGSLEDDING **Mountain Musher** (970-653-7877; mountainmusher.com), 16973 CO 131, Bond. The two dogsled tours Mountain Musher leads every day are on a private trail on the 10,000-acre Diamond Star Ranch. Twelve huskies pull the sled along a route that goes up and down the mountain. Guests can even drive the team themselves for part of the trip. For $200, guests get transportation to and from their hotel and everything they need for a comfortable tour (wool blankets, pillows, and a snack).

MEADOW MOUNTAIN TRAIL TO LINE SHACK TRAIL

Quite a few years ago now, my wife, Kim, rode in a shuttle van from Denver to Vail with Dr. Ruth Westheimer (better known simply as Dr. Ruth). As Kim remembers it, the good doctor recommended a nearby trail, and Kim took her advice, coming home with tales of acres of wildflowers spread out in all directions. Unfortunately, she forgot where to find the trailhead, and we spent years following faintly remembered clues before we found it again.

Just a few exits west of Vail, on the way to Minturn, you will find the Ranger Station for the Holy Cross Wilderness. From a neighboring parking lot is the trailhead for the Meadow Mountain Trail to Line Shack Trail. The trail is 4.5 miles, one way, and climbs a little over 2,000 feet. Along the way, hikers pass through miles of wildflowers. The latter half of July might be the best time for seeing the flowers in all their glory.

FISHING **Gore Creek** runs right through the middle of Vail and empties into the **Eagle River** west of town near Minturn. These are the two main waters for anglers in the Vail Valley. (The **Colorado River** is within easy driving distance if you are so motivated.) **Nottingham Lake** in Avon is also a good spot. It is stocked by the Colorado Division of Wildlife.

Fly Fishing Outfitters (970-845-8090; flyfishingoutfitters.net), 1060 W. Beaver Creek Blvd., Avon. This outfitter offers Orvis-endorsed guide services. Most of the outfitter's wade and float trips take anglers out on the Eagle, Colorado, and Roaring Fork rivers. A half-day wade trip for one person is $295 (two people $185 each). A half-day float trip for one person is $375 (two people $225 each).

Gore Creek Flyfisherman (970-476-3296; gorecreekflyfisherman.com), 193 E. Gore Creek Dr. This outfitter has been guiding anglers in Vail Valley for more than 20 years. Its guides will take you out on Eagle River, Gore Creek, and the Colorado. If the Vail location is not convenient, the company has four other shops in the area; check the website for a full list. A half-day wade trip for one person is $275 (two people $350). Float trips charged per boat—each accommodates one or two guests—and prices depend on the river.

GOLF The Vail Valley is home to more than 18 golf courses. Theoretically, because of the altitude, the ball should sail farther here. Most of these courses have a dress code of some sort—stay away from denim, make sure there's a collar on your shirt, and check with each course beforehand to see its own particulars.

Vail Golf Club (970-479-2260 or 1-888-709-3939; vailgolfclub.net), 1778 Vail Valley Dr. This 18-hole public course is just minutes from the Village. Greens fees $45–90.

Eagle Ranch Golf Club (970-328-2882; eagleranchgolf.com), 50 Lime Park Dr., Eagle. Located in the gently rolling Eagle Valley, this course is an Arnold Palmer Signature Design. Greens fees vary, but a walking golfer teeing off in the peak season will pay $99.

HIKING There are numerous places for day hiking and backpacking in and around Eagle County. One of the most popular hikes in Vail is the 3,100-foot ascent to **Booth Lake**. Beginning at the end of Booth Falls Rd. (exit 180 on I-70), the 6-mile hike takes you by Booth Creek Falls and then above the tree line to the pristine alpine lake. For an easier hike, turn around at the falls, which are about 2 miles in.

Vail Mountain (vail.com). Vail is so huge, there are plenty of trails for summer hiking. One of the benefits of hiking a ski mountain is that you can knock out some heavy climbing early on with the chairlifts. Eagle's loop offers an easygoing 1-mile trek with views of Holy Cross Mountain. A summer lift ticket (without bike haul) runs $22.

Beaver Creek Hiking Center (970-845-5373; beavercreek.com), located at the Beaver Creek ticket office. In the summer, the ski resort offers several guided hikes. The hikes start at $45 per person (that's the Rise and Shine cardio hike) to $185 to summit a Colorado 13er or 14er.

Paragon Guides (970-926-5299 or 1-877-926-5299; paragonguides.com), 198 Edwards Village Blvd, Edwards. For a hiking trip where you don't have to bust your hump carrying gear, consider llama trekking. Paragon Guides leads half-day trips, full-day trips, and peak ascents all summer. They also offer multiday backpacking trips throughout the central Rockies.

HORSEBACK RIDING **Beaver Creek Stables** (970-845-7770; beavercreekstables .com), P.O. Box 556, Avon, CO 81620. Operating on the Beaver Creek ski mountain, the stable has one- and two-hour trail rides that take you into the mountains, through aspen groves and meadows full with wildflowers. To make the ride more of an event, consider the picnic ride—the same route as the two-hour trip, but you are treated to a catered deli lunch in a mountain meadow midway.

MOUNTAIN BIKING **Vail Mountain** (vail.com). For an afternoon of downhill mountain biking, Vail has four trails on the Front Side. The Old Nine Line is plenty steep and technical—downhill gear (helmets and pads) are necessary. For $40, riders get a one-day lift ticket and bike haul.

Beaver Creek Sports (970-845-6221; beavercreeksports.com) rents mountain bikes for visitors wanting to pedal the Beaver Creek Ski Area. Unlimited rides on the chairlift with bike haul is $85 for adults, $70 for children.

✴ Green Space

Vail Nature Center (970-479-2291; vailrec.com/nature.cfm), 601 Vail Valley Dr. Located in the heart of Vail, the staff at the nature center lead visitors on guided nature hikes through alpine meadow and creek-side forest. Wildflowers, birds, and picturesque beaver dams are all part of nature's display. Guided hikes will cost you a couple of bucks (it was just $3/person last time we checked), and the center has more involved programs as well.

The **Eagles Nest Wilderness** east of Vail is part of the White River and Arapahoe National Forests. With more than 180 miles of trails constructed throughout the wilderness, there are seemingly endless opportunities to enjoy the park.

✴ Lodging

HOTELS ♿ (ᵖ) **Hotel Gasthof Gramshammer** (970-476-5626 or 1-800-610-7374; pepis.com), 231 E. Gore Creek Dr. Right in the heart of Vail Village sits the distinctive safety-yellow Bavarian-styled chalet that is Hotel Gasthof Gramshammer. Owned and operated by Pepi Gramshammer, former international ski racer, and his wife, Sheika, the hotel was one of the first in the valley after the ski resort opened. This European-style guest house offers tastefully decorated spacious rooms at affordable rates. Rooms, suites, and apartments $281–815 (winter), $145–725 (summer).

♿ (ᵖ) **The Lodge at Vail** (970-476-5011 or 1-800-367-7625; lodgeatvail .rockresorts.com), 174 E. Gore Creek Dr. This luxurious award-winning hotel has earned a reputation for rustic elegance and attentive personal service. Located at the base of Vail Mountain, the hotel has four hot tubs—two inside the spa and two outside—a sauna, and a heated outdoor pool. Rooms $300–4,000. More for condos and chalets.

Minturn Inn (970-827-9647 or 1-800-646-8876; minturninn.com), 442 Main St., Minturn. With the intimate atmosphere of a B&B and the attention to customer care of a boutique hotel, this log home from 1903 has been entirely refurbished and now offers luxury accommodations. It's the perfect alternative to the "hustle and bustle" of Vail Village. Some rooms have Jacuzzis for two. A full

HOTEL GASTHOF GRAMSHAMMER

breakfast with hot entrée is served daily. Rooms from $129.

☀ 🏨 ♿ **Ritz-Carlton Bachelor Gulch** (970-748-6200; ritzcarlton.com/en /hotels/colorado/bachelor-gulch), 0130 Daybreak Ridge, Avon. With heavy western accents, the Ritz-Carlton Bachelor Gulch epitomizes the ski-town mountain lodge. Catering to almost every need imaginable, the hotel even has a resident yellow Lab, Bachelor, to take with you on hikes in the mountains. Want to take a bath? Call the bath butler to draw you the perfect, fragrant steeping tub for your weary bones. The amenities here are really quite beyond all expectations. The rooms are luxuriously appointed with mountain and valley views and Frette linens on the beds. Rooms $179–2,549.

♿ **Sonnenalp Hotel** (970-476-5656; sonnenalp.com), 20 Vail Rd. Perennial reviewers of fine travel, *Condé Nast Traveler* recently published their Reader's Choice Awards, and Sonnenalp once again rates very high, not just in Colorado (where it was #2 in the state), but it also made the Top Ten in the United States. This is hardly an anomaly, as it often seems the hotel and resort bounces around the top of this list and others like it every year. The hotel offers rooms and suites and three rental residences. The amenities and service are all aimed at making guests comfortable, and a stay memorable. In addition to lodging, resort benefits include access to the spa facilities, use of resort vehicles, and nice touches like Mountain Top Picnics and yoga classes. The onsite restaurant, Ludwig's, is worth a visit, even if you're not a guest. Rooms and suites $192–3,000.

☀ ♿ **Vail Mountain Lodge & Spa** (970-476-0700; vailmountainlodge.com), 352 E. Meadow Dr. Positioned along Gore Creek, this stunning lodge is close to the heart of Vail Village and a short walk to the ski lifts. Although the hotel gives off a cozy, intimate vibe, it has the complete cadre of amenities you expect from the best of spas—sauna and steam rooms, access to the Vail Athletic Club equipment and classes, and free storage for your ski gear at the base of the mountain at Gondola One. Rooms $400–2,000.

BED & BREAKFASTS **Alpine Creek Bed and Breakfast** (402-476-1780; alpinecreek .net), 1850 S. Frontage Rd. W., #3. Located next to Gore Creek on Frontage Road, this B&B offers easy access to Vail 2.5 miles to the east. The inn has two rooms for guests, each with a private bath and walk-out deck. There is also a shared sitting room, where you can read or watch TV. Rooms $155–245.

CONDOS This is ski country, and you will find condos nearly everywhere. Many of these units are privately owned but rented out to guests when their owners are not in town. As with anything else, you get what you pay for—and the pricier units will repay the expense with more contemporary furnishings, newer carpet, and so on.

♿ ☀ (📶) **Antlers at Vail** (970-476-2471; antlersvail.com), 680 W. Lionshead Pl. Close to the gondola and the Lionshead Mall, Antlers rents condos—from studios with one bath to full-on condos with four bedrooms and four baths. Condos feature full kitchens, balconies, wide-screen TVs, and gas fireplaces. Pets are allowed in some rooms. Condos $240–2,695.

✳ Where to Eat

DINING OUT Be sure to call and make reservations for these restaurants, especially during ski season.

♿ **La Tour** (970-476-4403; latour-vail .com), 122 E. Meadow Dr. Open daily for lunch 11:30–3 and nightly for dinner 5–9:30. Chef-owner Paul Ferzacca has a motto of sorts: "Simplicity is the mother of beauty." This helps define the menu at La Tour, which features contemporary French cuisine. Dishes are rich and flavorful, but not so much that they confuse the palate. The dining room is warm and unpretentious. Entrées $29–36.

ANTLERS AT VAIL

Ludwig's (970-479-5429; sonnenalp
.com/dining/ludwigs), 20 Vail Rd. Breakfast is served daily from 7–11 (until noon
on Sundays). Dinner Wed.–Sun. 5:30–10.
Sonnenalp offers several dining options.
Ludwig's serves fine European cuisine
in an elegantly rustic dining room. Seafood—Chilean sea bass, soft-shell crab,
ahi tuna—features prominently on the
menu, as does Colorado venison and
lamb. It is interesting to note that the
entire menu at Ludwig's is gluten free.
Dinner entrées $29–52.

& **Montauk Seafood Grill** (970-476-
2601; montaukseafoodgrill.com), 549 E.
Lionshead Cir. Open nightly for dinner at
5:30. For seafood, there really is no better
restaurant than Montauk in the valley.
Fresh fish is flown in daily. Its signature
dish is the Hawaiian ahi, seared rare.
Like many restaurants in Vail, Montauk
offers huge discounts in the off-season.
Entrées $18–28.

Beano's Cabin (970-754-3463;
beanoscabinbeavercreek.com), Larkspur
Bowl, Beaver Creek. Open for dinner,

Thu.–Sun. in the summer. Open nightly
in the winter (Dec.–April) 5–10. The only
way to get to Beano's Cabin on Beaver
Creek Mountain in the winter is by sleigh
or on horseback. Colorado cuisine is the
theme of this innovative menu, which
features dishes such as "Duck Trap
River," smoked salmon quesadilla, and
the gingerbread-encrusted Colorado
rack of lamb. Chef Steven Topple's reputation goes beyond Colorado. He was
recently invited to prepare a five-course
dinner at the James Beard House in New
York. Prix fixe starts around $90. Reser-
vations required. Five-course meal (with
live music) runs $86 for guests arriving
by van. Wagon and horses bring it up to
$96.

Grouse Mountain Grill (970-949-
0600; grousemountaingrill.com), 141
Scott Hill Rd. at the Beaver Creek
Resort, Avon. Open daily for dinner 4–11.
Housed in Beaver Creek's Pines Lodge,
the dining room at Grouse Mountain
Grill features floor-to-ceiling windows
that look out over the Beaver Creek ski

slopes. The food is described as contemporary American cuisine. Special attention is paid to gathering the best ingredients, and Chef David Gutowski keeps summer garden plots that supply some of the kitchen's fresh produce in season. Dinner entrées $35–47.

    ᵔ **Mirabelle** (970-949-7728; mirabelle1 .com), 55 Village Rd., Beaver Creek. Open nightly for dinner at 6 (closed Sunday). Located at the entrance of Beaver Creek, the restaurant has made itself at home in a restored Victorian that once was a family farmhouse. Warm colors and white linens create a comfortable environment in which to enjoy Chef Daniel Joly's menu of French-influenced European cuisine. Four-course tasting menu $80. Entrées $29–48.

    Splendido at the Chateau (970-845-8808; splendidorestaurant.com), 17 Chateau Ln., Beaver Creek. Open for dinner Tue.–Sun. 6–10. Splendido excels at serving New American cuisine, prepared with the finest ingredients (locally sourced whenever possible). This results in a menu that changes with the seasons, making each visit a bit of an adventure. Recent exciting dishes included the Iowa Rabbit "Coq au Vin" and Colorado Lamb. Dinner entrées $38–67.

EATING OUT Aside from a few fast-food joints, there are really no chain restaurants in Vail. This is bad news for those who rely on Applebee's for a sense of continuity on the road. For everyone else, however, it means taking a chance on local grub—a scary prospect for some, but there's so much good food here, it makes the risk worthwhile.

    Pazzo's Pizzeria (970-476-9026; pazzos pizza.com), 122 E. Meadow Dr. A classic pizza joint, you will find that Pazzo's is conveniently located across from the village parking structure. Decent pizza and a host of other Italian dishes on the menu (calzones, lasagna, spaghetti . . . nothing too fancy) make this a safe bet for family dining. Pizzas $12–24, sandwiches and entrées $9–15.

    ᵔ **The Gashouse** (970-926-3613; gashouse-restaurant.com), 34185 US 6, Edwards. Open daily 11–10. For some, the dining room's numerous mounted animal heads might be a bit distracting. For others, it's all part and parcel of this quirky restaurant's fun atmosphere. The Gashouse is housed in a rustic log cabin that was originally built as a Conoco gas station in the 1940s, and that history is played up in the décor that includes license plate accents. In many ways, The Gashouse is still a filling station: The menu offers classic comfort food, such as fried chicken and ribs, as well as some upscale entrées, such as the quail or the elk tenderloin. Entrées $16–49.

    ᵔ **Minturn Saloon** (970-827-5954; minturnsaloon.com), 146 Main St., Minturn. Dining room opens nightly at 5:30 (winter) and 5 (summer). From the outside, this joint looks like an Old West saloon—in part because it is. Built in 1901, the saloon's 1830 bar comes from Missouri. While the atmosphere is western, the food is all Mexican (with some surprisingly classy dishes, such as the quail appetizer). To get here from the slopes, take the Minturn Mile off Vail Mountain and ski the 3.5 miles of backcountry right up to the saloon. Dishes $18–30.

BAKERIES & COFFEE SHOPS **Loaded Joe's Coffeehouse Lounge** (970-479-2883; loadedjoes.com), 227 Bridge St. Open daily at 7 until "at least midnight." Situated next to a covered bridge in Vail, this coffeehouse serves more than a great cup of joe—it is a gourmet coffeehouse with a split personality. When the sun goes down, it morphs into a hip lounge that screens independent movies and hosts dance nights with a DJ and cheap beer. The menu has grown to far beyond the usual coffee shop fare and now includes full breakfasts, burgers, etc.

BARS, TAVERNS, & BREW PUBS **The Red Lion** (970-476-7676; theredlion.com),

304 Bridge St. The Red Lion is a favorite après-ski hangout. For 25 years, Phil Long, one of Vail's most popular entertainers, performed here. These days the nightclub hosts a variety of performers. (Long, who is still a part-owner of The Red Lion, now performs down the street at the Shakedown Bar.)

Gore Range Brewery (970-926-2739; gorerangebrewery.com), 0105 Edwards Village Blvd., Edwards. Gore Range Brewery is a little hard to pin down. It's a great place to enjoy a beer and maybe catch a game on TV. It's also a great family restaurant that serves burgers and pizza. If you're looking for something a little more interesting, the brewery's specialties include fish and chips, ribs, and sautéed trout. A basket of beers are brewed on site, and there's the usual domestics available by the bottle.

✳ Entertainment

The Bravo! Vail Valley Music Festival (1-877-812-5700; vailmusicfestival.org) runs concerts in Vail for about six weeks every summer. It also schedules a short series of concerts in the winter, so check the website for current happenings.

Vail Valley Foundation (vvf.org) works to promote athletic, cultural, and educational endeavors in the Vail Valley. As such, it is a great resource for finding cultural events in the area. Check the online calendar for a list of concerts, performances, and talks throughout the valley.

✳ Selective Shopping

The Golden Bear (970-476-4082; thegolden bear.com), 183 E. Gore Creek Dr. This

BRIDGE STREET

FOOTWEAR AT KEMO SABE

iconic jewelry shop moved up the street to the Sitzmark in 2011. It still carries the must-have remembrance of time spent in Vail, the Golden Bear pendant. The line of Golden Bear merchandise is being expanded, so you'll continue to have more ways to tell people, "Hey, I went to Vail."

Kemo Sabe (970-479-7474; kemosabe .com), 230 Bridge St. There are two of these "cowboy stores" in Colorado—one in Aspen and the other here in Vail. For western wear, it's the only place to shop. You won't find a lot of cowboys shopping here, but Kemo Sabe works with you to bring out your own "inner cowboy." With Stetson hats, classic boots, and personal shoppers, there's no other western retailer like it. Go online and select a personal shopper, or just let the staff know you're coming and have a cold beer waiting for you when you visit.

✳ Special Events

April: **Spring Back to Vail** (springback tovail.com). The most recent headliner at Spring Back to Vail was Train. For two weeks in the spring, bars all over town help celebrate the end of the season with après-ski parties, and the town gathers together for the annual World Pond-Skimming Championships (how far will momentum carry you across a pool of water?).

Taste of Vail (970-926-5665; taste ofvail.com). Like the Taste of Colorado in Denver, this festival celebrates the culinary achievements of local restaurants and wineries. Plenty of concessions for the most discriminating foodie.

WINTER PARK &
GRAND COUNTY

Before 1928, the only "direct" way to the Fraser Valley was to climb a treacherous road over Berthoud Pass in the south or take a six-hour train ride over Rollins Pass that may or may not be delayed by avalanches and rockslides. In February 1928, the Moffat Tunnel opened a new route for the train, cutting a 6-mile path under the Continental Divide. The tunnel opened the Fraser Valley to logging operations; it also had an effect on the small local communities. In 1940, Denver installed a ski tow at its 90-acre mountain park and opened a ski area with three runs and two jumps. Thus, Winter Park was born. The nearby communities of Old Town and Hideaway Park eventually became "Winter Park" when the town was formally established in 1978.

For many years Winter Park was used primarily for day-skiing. The Ski Train dropped you off in the morning and took you back to Denver at night. The Ski Train has been replaced by the Winter Park Express, which shuttles skiers only on weekends.

The Winter Park ski area is really two or three interconnected ski areas (depending on whom you talk to). Winter Park and Mary Jane both have their own base areas, and there's also Vasquez Ridge. There are plenty of trails, from easy runs to backcountry steeps to the moguls on Mary Jane, which have a great reputation for shaking your teeth loose. Because Denverites often see Winter Park as their own personal ski park, the mountain gets lots of traffic—more than a million "skier days" each year.

As such, the sprawl of resorts and restaurants you find in other ski towns are surprisingly absent. Within the last five or six years, however, the city of Denver has brokered a deal with a ski-resort developer. The plan is to pump a ton of money into Winter Park, upgrade the facilities, and see if it can't be made into a more traditional resort town. The jury is out on whether or not the plan is working.

But skiing isn't all there is to Grand County. The Fraser River winds its way north through Fraser, Tabernash, and Granby to empty into the Colorado, which continues on to Hot Sulphur Springs and Kremmling. This region of the state is a paradise for hunting and fishing. In the winter, it's popular with snowmobilers.

The county also has several impressive lakes. In the northeast, there's a chain of lakes—Grand Lake, Shadow Mountain Lake, and Lake Granby. Nestled in the pines along the north shore of Grand Lake is a town of the same name. Grand Lake can be a bit touristy. It seems to fancy itself an Old West saloon town—a wide main street, wooden sidewalks, and western façades complete the effect. But beyond the cheesy trappings, Grand Lake offers unique opportunities to experience Colorado's natural beauty. Nearby marinas rent boats for getting out on the water, and the western portal of Rocky Mountain National Park is just a mile or so from town.

Most of the attractions, lodgings, and restaurants listed below are open year-round. Many, however, reduce hours significantly for about six weeks in the spring and fall. Be sure to call ahead during these two off-seasons. Unless otherwise indicated, all addresses are in Winter Park.

GUIDANCE **Winter Park–Fraser Valley Chamber of Commerce** (970-726-4118 or 1-800-903-7275; playwinterpark.com). Open daily 8–5, the chamber's visitor center is located east of town on US 40.

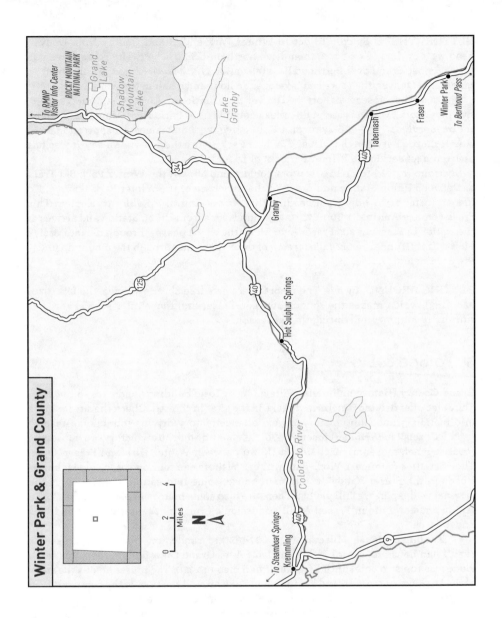

Granby Chamber of Commerce (970-887-2311 or 1-800-325-1661; granbychamber .com), 365 E. Agate Ave., Ste. B. The visitors can get tourist information in Granby Mon.–Fri. 9–5.

Grand Lake Area Chamber of Commerce (970-627-3402 or 1-800-531-1019; grandlakechamber.com). The chamber's visitor information center is located on US 34, right as you turn to head into town. Open daily in the summer 9–5.

Kremmling Area Chamber of Commerce (970-724-3472 or 1-877-573-6654; kremmlingchamber.com), 203 Park Ave. Visitor center is open Mon. 11:30–5:30, Tue.–Fri. 8:30–5:30 (closes at 3 on Wed.), and Sat. 10–4. The visitor center in Kremmling has clean restrooms and plenty of information on local activities.

GETTING THERE *By car:* To get to Winter Park and Grand County from Denver, head west on I-70 to exit 232, then drive north on US 40. The twisty route takes you up switchbacks and over Berthoud Pass (elevation 11,314 feet). Although only about 70 miles from Denver, the route can take over an hour and a half in the winter.

By air: The closest airport is **Denver International Airport** (1-800-247-2336; flydenver.com), which is about 68 miles east of Winter Park. **Home James Transportation Services** (970-726-4730 or 1-800-359-7503; homejamestransportation.com) runs a shuttle between the DIA and Winter Park—more than 20 runs a day. It also has chartered jet service to Winter Park out of DIA.

By train: It used to be that visitors could climb aboard the **Winter Park Ski Train** at Denver's Union Station and ride it to the very base of the Winter Park ski area. No longer. Instead, the only train heading that way is Amtrak's California Zephyr. This cross-country **Amtrak** (1-800-872-7245) train leaves from Union Station and arrives at the station in Fraser at 205 Fraser Ave. Along the way it passes through the impressive Moffat Train Tunnel—a 6.2-mile stretch of track that runs through the mountain under the Continental Divide.

GETTING AROUND *By bus:* The resort operates a free shuttle service, the **Lift** (970-726-4163), which makes the rounds between Fraser and the Winter Park ski area. It runs in the summer and during the ski season.

❋ To See & Do

Grand County History maintains quite a few historic buildings and sites in the area. They also offer driving itineraries to take in the sites in context. Check the site for more information: grandcountyhistory.org/experience-history/driving-tours-homesteads.

&. ⚲ **Cozen Ranch House Museum** (970-725-5488; grandcountyhistory.org/museums /cozens-ranch-museum), east side of US 40 between Winter Park and Fraser. Open Thu.–Sat. 10–4 (summer), Wed.–Sat. (winter). Visitors can tour one of the oldest homesteads in the Fraser Valley. In the main house, some interesting items, such as the original wallpaper, are still visible. There are also some historical photos of the Cozen family and early life in Fraser. Adult admission $5, seniors $4, students $3, and kids under 6 free.

⚲ **Kauffman House Museum** (970-627-9644; grandcountyhistory.org/museums /kauffman-house-museum), Pitkin and Lake Ave., Grand Lake. Built in 1892, this small lodge was run as a hotel until Ezra Kauffman died in 1920. The museum tells the story of the business of tourism and life in Grand Lake around the turn of the century. Open daily in the summer 11–5. Admission $5. Kids 12 and under free.

&. ⚲ **Pioneer Village** (970-725-3939; grandcountyhistory.org/museums/pioneer-village-museum), east end of Hot Sulphur Springs on US 40. Open Wed.–Sat. 10–4. Housed in the historic Hot Sulphur Springs school, the museum tells the story of Grand County. Included is an exhibition on early skiing in Colorado. Adult admission $5, seniors $4, students $3, and kids under 6 free.

❋ Outdoor Activities

ALPINE SKIING & SNOWBOARDING **Winter Park Resort** (970-726-1564; winterparkresort.com), 239 Winter Park Dr. This ski area began as one of Denver's mountain parks. In 1940, when the first ski tow was installed, there were only three formal trails.

KAUFFMAN HOUSE MUSEUM IN GRAND LAKE

Today Winter Park is known for incredible moguls; long, easy runs; and great terrain parks. The ski area is really two interconnected ski areas—Winter Park and Mary Jane, each of which has its own base area. Winter Park remains the most accessible for beginners and intermediate skiers. For more technically advanced skiing, Mary Jane has advanced and expert runs. The ski area's Vasquez Cirque is home to the park's extreme skiing areas. Overall, Winter Park has a 3,060-foot vertical drop and 2,886 acres of skiable terrain, and receives an incredible 370 inches of snow annually.

Ski Granby Ranch (970-877-5123 or 1-800-405-7669; granbyranch.com), 1000 Village Rd., Granby. The smaller Granby Ranch ski area has 287 skiable acres on two interconnected mountains. The East Mountain is best suited for beginner and intermediate skiers. The West Mountain has little for beginners but plenty of trails for intermediate and advanced skiers. The ski area has a terrain park and half-pipe. There's also a separate learn-to-ski park.

ALPINE SLIDE **Alpine Slide** (1-800-979-0332; winterparkresort.com). Accessed from the Arrow chairlift, the alpine slide at Winter Park is the state's longest. It runs 3,030 feet and has 26 turns. Riders control their speed. There are two parallel tracks—for slower and faster riders.

BOATING **Beacon Landing** (970-627-3671; beaconlanding.com), 1026 CR 64, Granby. Located on the largest of the county's lakes, Lake Granby, the Beacon Landing Marina rents pontoons and fishing gear—everything you need for a day on the water.

Trail Ridge Marina (970-627-3586; trailridgemarina.com), 12634 US 34, Grand Lake. Situated on Shadow Mountain Lake, the marina has fishing boats, pleasure

TRAIL RIDGE MARINA ON SHADOW MOUNTAIN LAKE

boats, and pontoons for rent. If you've brought along your own vessel, the marina has slip and dock rentals.

CROSS-COUNTRY SKIING & SNOWSHOEING **Devil's Thumb Cross-Country Center** (970-726-8231 or 1-800-933-4339; devilsthumbranch.com), 3530 CR 83, Tabernash. With 125 kilometers of groomed trails on 4,000 acres, this is one the best spots for cross-country skiing and snowshoeing in the Fraser Valley. Eight kilometers of trails are reserved for skijoring (a sport where skiers are pulled by a dog), and there are some lighted trails for night skiing. Skis and snowshoes are available for rent, and the ranch offers lessons and tours.

Winter Park Tour Center (1-800-729-7907; winterparkresort.com). The resort gives snowshoe tours that depart from the base of the mountain. Call for more information.

YMCA Nordic Center at Snow Mountain Ranch (970-887-2152; ymcarockies.org), US 40 between Winter Park and Grand Lake. With 100 kilometers of groomed trails, the Nordic center has routes for skiers and snowshoers of all abilities. The ranch offers equipment rental and instruction packages. In addition to ski facilities, guests can ice skate, enjoy a sleigh ride, and tube down a great sledding hill.

DOGSLEDDING **Dog Sled Rides of Winter Park** (970-726-8326; dogsledrides.com /winterpark), Kings Crossing Rd. A 45-minute dogsled tour through the forests of Winter Park covers 4 to 5 miles. Once guests are comfortable with the experience, they can try their hand at mushing. Reservations by phone are required.

FISHING **Grand County Fishing Company** (970-726-5231; grandflyfishing.com), 234 CR 803, Fraser. For fishing on the Fraser River, this outfitter has access to 4 miles of private water. Staff also take guests out on the Colorado, Green, and upper South Platte rivers. A half-day wade trip will cost $225—but the per person rate decreases for each person you add to the party (up to four).

Mo Henry's Trout Shop (970-531-8213; mohenrys.com), 78902 US 40. Since 2004, these two brothers have been sharing their passion for fly fishing with everyone who walks through the door of their shop. For fishing information only locals know, be sure to check out Mo Henry's first. The shop is located inside Winter Park Trading Company.

GOLF **Grand Elk Ranch & Club** (970-887-9122; grandelk.com), 1300 Ten Mile Dr., Granby. This nice 18-hole course blends into the surrounding Fraser Valley. With plenty of wild grass, this is more of a target-oriented course than others in the area. Greens fees $25–95.

Pole Creek Golf Club (970-887-9195; polecreekgolf.com), 6827 CR 51, Tabernash. Three nine-hole courses—Meadow, Ranch, and Ridge—make up Pole Creek. The beautifully wooded mountain surroundings make a pleasant backdrop to this links-style course. Greens fees $58–99.

HORSEBACK RIDING **Sombrero Ranch** (970-627-3514; sombrero.com), 1471 CR 491, Grand Lake. Located in Grand Lake, with access to nearby Rocky Mountain National Park, Sombrero Ranch offers trail rides to fit any schedule. There are breakfast rides and steak-fry rides as well. The two-hour ride runs $60 (less for kids).

MOUNTAIN BIKING **Trestle Bike Park at Winter Park Resort** (1-800-729-7907; trestlebikepark.com). In the summer, the Winter Park ski area opens its trails for mountain bike use. Fifty miles of trails connect with 600 miles of trails in Fraser

FLY FISHING ON THE COLORADO

Valley. Recently, the ski area has added 10 new trails for cyclists of varying ability. Thirty-three miles of trail are accessible by chairlift. You can buy a one-trip lift ticket or purchase unlimited rides for the day. Your best bet might be to start with the one-trip ticket and then upgrade to unlimited if you need more downhill fun. Bikes are available for rent at the base of the ski area at the **Trestle Park Bike Shop**. For very advanced riders, the Banana Peel elevated course is restricted to those with the skills needed to avoid catastrophic injury.

SNOWMOBILING **Grand Adventures** (970-726-9247; grandadventures.com), CR 50. Snowmobiling is a big activity in Grand County, from Kremmling over to Grand Lake. This outfitter leads guided trips and rents machines for unguided rides.

✳ Green Space

Rocky Mountain National Park is truly one of Colorado's great natural treasures. Grand Lake is the park's western portal. On US 34, heading east, visitors first come upon the **Kawuneeche Visitor Center** (970-627-3471; nps.gov/romo), the best place to get started exploring. (See the coverage of the RMNP in the chapter on Estes Park for more information.)

✳ Lodging

HOTELS ♿ 📶 **Devil's Thumb Ranch**
(970-726-8231 or 1-800-933-4339;
devilsthumbranch.com), 3530 CR 83,
Tabernash. The buildings at Devil's
Thumb Ranch are something to behold.
All of the stone exteriors were sourced
from a local landslide. The same stone
graces the onsite restaurant, Heck's,
where it features prominently in the central fireplace. The centerpiece of High
Lonesome Lodge is a 19th-century barn
moved from Ohio. There are several
options for lodging at the ranch: the
Main Lodge, High Lonesome Lodge, and
the Bunkhouse. There are also cabins.
The ranch has opportunities for Nordic
skiing in the winter and mountain biking
in the summer. There's a geothermally
heated indoor-outdoor pool open to
guests all year-round. Rooms run $200–
400. Call ranch for cabin rates, and the
budget-conscious should check out the
Bunkhouse.

♿ 📶 **Iron Horse Resort** (970-726-8851
or 1-877-541-0012; ironhorse-resort.com),
101 Iron Horse Way. This was one of Winter Park's first ski-in, ski-out lodges; from
the resort you can ski right to a lift line.
The resort rents condo units, from deluxe
studios to lodging with two bedrooms
and three baths. Condos in the summer
run $89–289, more in the winter.

♿ 🏨 📶 **The Vintage Hotel** (970-726-
8801 or 1-800-472-7017; vintagehotel
.com), 100 Winter Park Dr. Just seconds
from the Mary Jane base area, the Vintage offers both traditional hotel rooms
as well as suites with kitchenettes, fireplaces, and whirlpool tubs. Most of the
rooms provide fabulous views of the
surrounding mountains. There are ski
lockers and gear rental on-site. Rooms
and suites $99–370.

♿ 🏨 **Zephyr Mountain Lodge**
(970-726-8400 or 1-877-754-8400;
zephyrmountainlodge.com), 201 Zephyr
Way. Within the Winter Park Resort, this
is the only true ski-in, ski-out lodge. It's
at the base of the mountain, and rooms
come with excellent views. The spacious
condo-style rooms have full kitchens and
gas fireplaces. There are four outdoor
hot tubs, and the hotel has a free shuttle
to ferry guests into town. While many
of the hotels and lodges in the area have
dated décor, Zephyr Mountain Lodge has
a contemporary, hip western feel. Rooms
$50–1,500.

🐾 ♿ 🏨 📶 **Snow Mountain Ranch–
YMCA of the Rockies** (1-888-613-9622;
ymcarockies.org), 1101 CR 53, Granby.
(See *Front Range* for the Estes Park
portion of YMCA of the Rockies.) The
ranch offers a wide variety of programs
for families and groups. In addition to
a swimming pool, ropes course, and
horseback riding, there are opportunities
for mountain biking in the summer and
Nordic skiing in the winter. Snow Mountain Ranch offers visitors lodge rooms,
cabins, and campsites. Check out the Y's
website for a complete list of rates.

BED & BREAKFASTS 🏨 📶 **Wild Horse
Inn** (970-726-0456; wildhorseinn.com),
1536 CR 83, Fraser. From *Travel & Leisure* magazine to the inn's many guests,
everyone agrees this is the best B&B in
the valley. The main building, a log and
stone structure reminiscent of a classic
mountain lodge, is tucked back in the
woods, just off the road that leads to
Devil's Thumb Ranch. The inn offers
seven rooms and three log cabins—the
Mariposa, the Meadowcreek, and the
Saddleblanket. Each cabin has a kitchenette, fireplace, and a tub for two. The
décor throughout the inn could be
called rustically elegant—nothing over-
blown, every detail tasteful. A full gourmet breakfast is served every morning.
On-site massage is available (arrange
in advance). Rooms $135–260 and cab-
ins $195–275.

CAMPGROUNDS **Elk Creek Campground** (970-627-8502 or 1-800-355-2733;
elkcreekcamp.com), 143 CR 48, Grand
Lake. Open April–Oct. Just outside

Grand Lake, near Rocky Mountain National Park, Elk Creek Campground has wooded sites and many opportunities to view wildlife. It's not uncommon to catch sight of elk and moose. Tent sites $32 and RV sites (depending on hookups) $49.

CABINS & COTTAGES **Shadow Mountain Guest Ranch** (970-887-9524 or 1-800-647-4236; shadowmtnranch.com), 5043 CO 125, Granby. Northwest of Granby, Shadow Mountain Guest Ranch has five log cabins, each with plenty of character. A big ranch-cooked breakfast comes with all cabin rentals. Cabins $155–325.

✳ Where to Eat

DINING OUT ♈ **The Lodge at Sunspot** (970-726-1446 or 1-800-510-8025; winter parkresort.com/things-to-do/dining/ the-lodge-at-sunspot), Winter Park Resort. For a special mountain dining experience, take the Zephyr Express Lift for seven minutes to 10,700 feet. There you will find The Lodge at Sunspot, a large stone-and-log structure that offers panoramic views of the mountains. Inside, there are two dining options: the Provisioner (a classy food court) and the Dining Room (the more formal eatery, serving five-course meals and the like). The Dining Room is open for lunch and dinner during ski season. Reservations required for special dinners, and highly recommended otherwise. Five-course fine dining $79 for adults, $49 for children.

♿ ♈ **Ranch House Restaurant at Devil's Thumb Ranch** (970-726-5633 or 1-800-933-4339; devilsthumbranch.com), 3530 CR 83, Tabernash. Hours vary by season—please call for current hours and to make reservations (highly recommended). Located on Devil's Thumb Ranch, the Ranch House offers a fine menu prepared with organically grown, local produce and meats. Although the menu changes regularly, you can expect to find dishes such as elk, antelope, and bison as well as steak and seafood. The intimate dining room has exposed beams and fits easily in the ranch environment. Dinner entrées $32–46.

♿ ♈ **Back Street Steakhouse** (970-627-8144; davenhavenlodge.com), 604 Marina Dr., Grand Lake, at the Daven Haven Lodge. Open daily for dinner. Closed in shoulder seasons. Featured in *Bon Appétit,* this steakhouse has a reputation for fine dining. In keeping with the surroundings, there is nothing pretentious about the restaurant; just great food in a casual atmosphere. As you might suspect, the restaurant serves fantastic steaks, from prime rib to premium-cut Angus beef. The Jack Daniel's pork chops are a house specialty. Dinner entrées $20–36.

EATING OUT ♿ ♈ **Deno's Mountain Bistro** (970-726-5332; denosmountainbistro .com), 78911 US 40. Open for lunch and dinner at 11:30 and 5, respectively. The building that Deno's calls home has been in Winter Park for decades. At one time it housed a pharmacy and barbershop. As the Village Inn, there was a restaurant, bar, gas station, and stables. Today, the bistro serves lunch and dinner. The lunch menu is full of sandwiches and burgers, as well as some unexpected items, such as the baked goat cheese fondue and penne pomodoro. For dinner the menu is a bit more upscale, with steak, seafood, and chicken. There is also a great wine list. Dinner $20–39 and lunch $10–12; pizzas $14–20.

♿ **Hernando's Pizza Pub** (970-726-5409; hernandospizzapub.com), 78199 US 40. Open for dinner 4–10 during ski season; open fewer hours in the off-season. Since 1967, Hernando's has been dishing out pizzas in Winter Park. The dining room is especially comfortable with stained-glass windows and several fireplaces. There are other items on the menu besides pizza, such as pasta and Italian sandwiches, but don't do yourself a disservice—try the pizza. Pizzas $12–22 and pasta around $10.

♿ **Sagebrush BBQ & Grill** (970-627-1404 or 1-866-900-1404; sagebrushbbq.com), 1101 Grand Ave., Grand Lake. Open daily 7–10. Located at the corner of Grand Avenue and Pitkin Street, the Sagebrush is an oddity in a tourist town—this is exceptional family dining. Known especially for outstanding barbecue, Sagebrush also serves up one of the best bean burritos in Colorado. The breakfast menu isn't too shabby, either. Lunch and dinner entrées $12–22 (more for crab and steaks and the barbecue combo platter).

BAKERIES & COFFEE SHOPS ♿ **Rocky Mountain Roastery** (970-726-4400; rockymountainroastery.com), 543 Zerex, Fraser. Open daily 6–6. Boasting its "high mountain roasting process," this coffee shop offers several signature blends at two locations. The Original Roastery in Fraser has been in town since 1993. Out at the Winter Park ski resort, be sure to check out RMR Too (970-726-6838).

BARS, TAVERNS, & BREW PUBS ♿ **Hideaway Park Brewery** (970-363-7312; hideawayparkbrewery.com), 78927 US 40. These guys take beer making seriously. For their TOADally Fresh Pale Ale, they have driven out to Palisade to help harvest hops and then rushed back to use them right away. The atmosphere is laid back, perfect for a cool drink after a day of skiing or hiking.

Special Events

July: **Grand Lake Regatta and Lipton Cup Races** (contact Chamber of Commerce at 970-627-3402 for more information). This annual race brings sailors into the mountains—fantastic photo ops with full sails set against the Rocky Mountains.

STEAMBOAT SPRINGS & THE YAMPA VALLEY

Steamboat Springs is known for its unique western character. Images of Steamboat always include one of cowboys skiing. Much of that is due to the town's most famous ski personality, Billy Kidd, who won the silver medal in the slalom in 1964. He's the director of skiing at Steamboat, and he can often be seen coming down the mountain in his signature cowboy hat. He also invited rodeo stars to town back in 1975 to compete in what has become an annual ski competition.

It's this western, blue-collar vibe that gives Steamboat its personality. This is not a town of pampered lifties "doing Steamboat." The residents are hard-working farmers and ranch hands who happen to live in a town with ski bums (and some pampered lifties). As such, there's no shortage of affordable dining and lodging, because this is a place where people live. Driving in from the south, the entrance into downtown is marked by the giant neon sign in front of the Rabbit Ears Motel. This historic landmark has been greeting drivers for more than 50 years.

The town of Steamboat Springs has been around since the late 19th century. In 1865, three French trappers heard an unexpected sound as they worked the Yampa Valley. It was a chugging noise that they at first mistook for the sound of a steam-powered paddleboat coming down the Yampa River. It turned out to be the bubbling of the region's hot springs. This is how the town got its name. Several years later, in 1874, James Harvey Crawford came upon the Yampa Valley and staked a claim.

Unlike most ski towns in Colorado, Steamboat did not spring to life as a mining town. Instead, it began as, and to some extent remains, a town rooted in ranching and farming. It did not explode onto the scene like Aspen or Breckenridge, but instead grew slowly over the years.

In 1912, a Norwegian skier moved into town. Carl Howelsen was passionate about skiing—mainly cross-country and jumping—and his passion was contagious. By 1913, Steamboat had a ski jump, and Howelsen was teaching local youths how to compete in this new sport. Howelsen is credited with kicking off skiing as a sport in Colorado. Considering the impact skiing has had across the state, that's not an insignificant contribution. During the 1930s, alpine skiing started to become popular all over, and it soon replaced ski jumping in Steamboat. In 1961, the Steamboat ski area opened. Soon there were several lifts, and the resort took off from there.

Over the years, Steamboat has sent more athletes to the Winter Olympics than has any other town in the country, earning it the nickname Ski Town, USA. The town gets 331 inches of snow annually. Called Champagne Powder, the snow is the fluffiest and driest you can find anywhere, and when there's fresh powder, skiers are followed down the mountain by arcing plumes of the stuff. Many skiers dismiss Steamboat Springs, saying it lacks the extreme steeps found at other ski areas. Steamboat, however, has a great reputation for its easygoing long glides and stunningly beautiful wooded runs.

GUIDANCE **Steamboat Springs Chamber Resort Association** (970-879-0880; steamboatchamber.com), 125 Anglers Dr. The association operates the Steamboat Springs Visitor Center, which is open year-round Mon.–Fri. 8–5. During ski season, it's open on Sat. as well, 10–3. Summers Mon.–Sat. 10–6, Sun. 10–4.

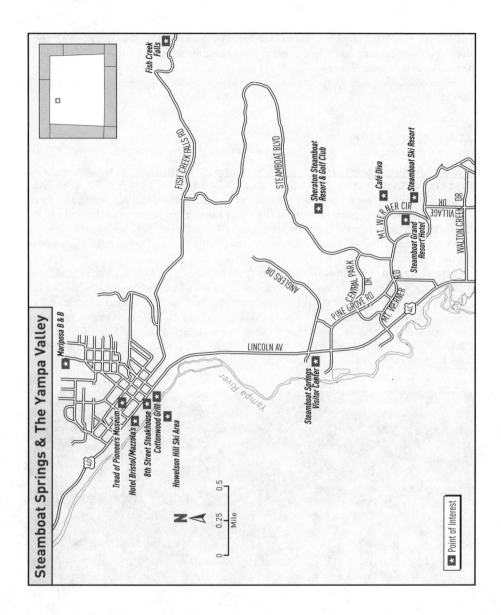

Steamboat Springs & The Yampa Valley

Points of Interest: Fish Creek Falls, Mariposa B & B, Tread of Pioneers Museum, Hotel Bristol/Mazzola's, 8th Street Steakhouse, Cottonwood Grill, Howelson Hill Ski Area, Steamboat Springs Visitor Center, Sheraton Steamboat Resort & Golf Club, Café Diva, Steamboat Ski Resort, Steamboat Grand Resort Hotel

N

0   0.25   0.5
        Mile

★ Point of Interest

GETTING THERE *By car:* Steamboat is a bit off the beaten track—about 155 miles from Denver (a three-hour drive). The best route is I-70 west to Silverthorne, then CO 9 north to Kremmling. Then turn left on US 40 and follow the road northwest over Rabbit Ears Pass (elevation 9,426) and into Steamboat Springs; US 40 continues west into Utah.

By air: From **Yampa Valley Airport** (970-276-5001; yampavalleyregionalairport .com) in Hayden, Delta and United operate daily flights connecting Steamboat Springs with Salt Lake City and Denver. If you are flying into **Denver International Airport** (1-800-247-2336; flydenver.com), it is about 180 miles east of Steamboat. The **Alpine Taxi** (970-879-2800 or 1-800-343-7433; alpinetaxi.com) operates a shuttle service that will pick up guests at the DIA or Yampa Valley Airport and bring them to Steamboat.

GETTING AROUND *By bus:* **Steamboat Springs Transit** (970-879-3717) is a "free to user" bus system that provides service between downtown and the ski resort base area. It operates year-round.

By taxi: **Alpine Taxi** (970-879-8294 or 970-879-2800; alpinetaxicom) operates a local taxi service.

✳ To See & Do

Fish Creek Falls. A short hike takes you to an overlook with a view of the 283-foot Fish Creek Falls. Another tad-more-difficult trail leads down to the creek itself. During the summer, families put on their bathing suits and suntan lotion and play on the rocks by and in the creek. The parking lots for the short hike to the falls are at the end of Fish Creek Rd. (CR 32). To get there from town, take Third Street one block north and turn right, and then follow this road 4.5 miles to the parking area. There are two lots—head for the second unless it's already full. $5 parking fee.

Strawberry Park Natural Hot Springs (970-879-0342; strawberryhotsprings.com), Strawberry Park Rd. Open Sun.–Thu. 10–10:30 and Fri. and Sat. 10–midnight. The hot springs water hits the mountain air at around 150 degrees F and cools as it flows into the successive stone pools. While you soak, enjoy views of the steep canyon walls and nearby creek. Tent sites, cabins, and other lodgings are available for a longer stay. Clothing is optional after dark. Adult soak $15, teens (3–17) $8, and children under 3 free. No one under 18 allowed after dark.

THE VIEW OF STEAMBOAT SKI AREA FROM TOWN

 ♿ ↟ **Tread of Pioneers Museum** (970-879-2214; treadofpioneers.org), Eighth and Oak Sts. Open Tue.–Sat. 11–5. Housed in a 1908 Queen Anne–style Victorian, the museum tells the story of pioneer life in Routt County. There are exhibitions on Native American life, and the museum has an impressive firearms collection. Of interest to many coming to Steamboat is the exhibition on the history of skiing. Adult admission $6, seniors $5, and children 6–12 $2.

✳ Outdoor Activities

ALPINE SKIING & SNOWBOARDING **Steamboat Ski Resort** (970-879-6111 or 1-877-237-2628; steamboat.com), 2305 Mt. Werner Cir. Steamboat is really an entire mountain range, adding up to 165 trails on 2,965 skiable acres. From summit to base, skiers enjoy an overall 3,668-foot vertical drop. The regulars who ski these slopes every year come back for the ski area's easygoing descents; more than half of the terrain is for intermediate skiers. They also come for the phenomenal snow. Steamboat gets 331 inches of the stuff annually—not just any snow, but the area's trademarked Champagne Powder, purportedly the fluffiest and driest snow you can find anywhere. For freeskiers and snowboarders, Steamboat has four terrain parks and the much-touted Mavericks Superpipe.

    Howelsen Hill Ski Area (970-879-8499; steamboatsprings.net/ski), 137 10th St. In 1912, the Norwegian skier Carl Howelsen brought the sport of skiing to Steamboat and soon was organizing the Steamboat Springs Winter Sports Club, training youth to compete in cross-country skiing and ski jumping. The hill that bears his name was used primarily for ski jumping until the popular rise of alpine skiing in the early 1930s. Today, the ski area is on the Colorado Register of Historic Places and stands as the oldest ski area still open in Colorado. The hill has a vertical drop of only 440 feet, and only 15 trails, but there are runs for every ability. There is also a small terrain park, runs for tubing, and trails for Nordic skiing.

    Ski Haus (970-879-0385; skihaussteamboat.com), 1457 Pine Grove Rd. Open daily in winter 9–6. For affordable rental gear, Ski Haus has all the skis and snowboards you need.

    Steamboat Powder Cats (970-879-5188 or 1-800-288-0543; steamboatpowdercats .com), 1724 Mount Werner Cir. This snowcat outfit takes skiers up to Buffalo Pass. On a good snow day, you can expect to make 10–16 runs. A full day of skiing runs $600.

BOATING **Steamboat Lake Marina** (970-879-7019; steamboatlakemarina.com), 61450 CR 62, Clark. To get out onto the water at Steamboat Lake State Park, check out the marina, where you can rent pontoons, fishing boats, canoes, paddleboats, and kayaks.

CROSS-COUNTRY SKIING & SNOWSHOEING **Steamboat Ski Touring Center** (970-879-8180; nordicski.net), P.O. Box 775401, Steamboat. With 30 kilometers of trails groomed for both classic and skate skiing, the Ski Touring Center is the most extensive and convenient cross-country location to the Steamboat ski area. An additional 10 kilometers have been set aside for snowshoeing. The center also rents equipment, offers instruction, and leads ski tours. Adult day pass $20 and seniors and children (12 and under) $13.

    The Nordic Center at Vista Verde Guest Ranch (970-879-3858 or 1-800-526-7433; vistaverde.com), P.O. Box 465, Steamboat. There are 30 kilometers of groomed ski trails on this 500-acre ranch. Lessons, guided tours, and equipment rental are available. Your trail pass also includes lunch.

FISH CREEK FALLS

Ski Haus (970-879-0385; skihaussteamboat.com), 1457 Pine Grove Rd. Open daily 9–6. For affordable rental gear, Ski Haus has equipment for all winter sports—alpine skis and snowboards, as well as a full selection of touring, Nordic, and telemark packages. It even has snowshoes.

DOGSLEDDING **Grizzle-T Dog Sled Tours** (970-870-1782; steamboatdogsledding .com), HC 66 Box 39. Ride through 12.5 miles of Steamboat's backcountry on a sled pulled by Alaskan huskies. During the peak season, following Thanksgiving until the snow runs out, the company runs a couple of tours every day, one early and one in the afternoon. They also offer a complimentary shuttle from and to your hotel.

FISHING **Steamboat Flyfisher** (970-879-6552; steamboatflyfisher.com), 35 Fifth St. Open daily 7:30–7:30. With so many options for fishing around Steamboat, a guided fishing outing might be the best way to get the lay of the land (so to speak). The guides at Steamboat Flyfisher customize trips to meet each angler's expectations. Multiday trips give you a chance to experience more of what the Yampa Valley has to offer.

GOLF **Haymaker** (970-870-1846; haymakergolf.com), 34855 US 40 E. In 2011, Haymaker earned *Golf Digest*'s four-star rating. With the tagline, "Golf as it was intended to be," the course promotes itself as a course for golfers. There are no residential developments crowding the course's 233 acres, just beautiful views of nearby Mt. Werner and 18 holes of golf. Greens fees $129 during the peak summer season.
 Rollingstone Ranch Golf Club (970-879-1391; rollingstoneranchgolf.com), 2200 Village Inn Ct. This mountain course takes advantage of its natural surroundings, incorporating rollicking streams and elevation changes. From the course you can see the ski area above the trees. Greens fees $45–159.

HIKING With **Medicine Bow/Routt National Forest** (fs.usda.gov/mbr), the **Flat Tops Wilderness**, and four state parks, the mountains around Steamboat are full of trails for hiking. One exhilarating trail in the Flat Tops Wilderness takes hikers across the Devil's Causeway, a narrow rocky spine that splits two valleys. At times the trail is only 3 feet wide and drops hundreds of feet on either side.

HORSEBACK RIDING **Del's Triangle 3 Ranch** (970-879-3495; steamboathorses.com), 55675 CR 62, Clark. The ranch runs summer and winter trail rides. In the winter, guests can meet the ranch shuttle at the gondola. Winter rides last two hours and cost $80. Summer rides begin at one hour ($55) to full day ($350, includes lunch). This is a fantastic way to see the mountains.

MOUNTAIN BIKING There are some great mountain bike trails around Steamboat. For example, more than 25 miles of singletrack can be accessed from **Rabbit Ears Pass** in the Routt National Forest.
 Steamboat Ski Resort (970-879-0740 or 1-877-237-2628; steamboat.com), 2305 Mt. Werner Cir. For mountain biking in a ski town, start with the ski mountain. With a $30 lift ticket (that's $20 for you and $10 for the bike), you can take your bike up the mountain and enjoy 50 miles of trails with a lot of exciting descents.
 Ski Haus (970-879-0385; skihaussteamboat.com), 1457 Pine Grove Rd. Open daily 9–6. In the summer, this purveyor of ski equipment rents mountain bikes. A full-suspension ride runs $64/day.

RAFTING **Bucking Rainbow Outfitters** (970-879-8747 or 1-888-810-8747; bucking rainbow.com), 730 Lincoln Ave. The Yampa River runs right through Steamboat Springs. The rapids here are gentle class II and III, but a rafting trip down the Yampa is a nice way to spend a warm summer afternoon. Bucking Rainbow also leads trips on other rivers farther afield, such as the Colorado, Elk, and Eagle. For hardcore whitewater fans, the full-day Cross Mountain Canyon trip is all class IV and V. Trips down the Yampa, however, are $50 for adults, $45 for kids.

SNOWMOBILING **Steamboat Snowmobile Tours** (970-879-6500 or 1-877-879-6500; steamboatsnowmobile.com), located between mile markers 151 and 152 on US 40 east of Steamboat. Open daily 8–8. Fly across the snow on Rabbit Ears Pass, driving your own snowmobile. These folks lead several snowmobile tours, from a short two-hour affair to a full day. They also have lunch tours and the Rocky Mountain Sunset Dinner tour. Two-hour tour, $129–149 for each driver. Lunch tour $199 for each driver. (The tours are a bit cheaper for passengers.)

✳ Green Space

Steamboat Lake State Park (970-879-3922; cpw.state.co.us/placestogo/Parks /SteamboatLake), north on CO 129 to Hahns Peak Village. Overlooking the park are Sand Mountain and the impressive Hahns Peak. The Steamboat Lake reservoir is perfect for boating and fishing. There's a swim beach at the Dutch Hill area, but even in late summer, the water does not get warmer than the low 70s. In the winter there's cross-country skiing and snowshoeing. Daily vehicle pass $7.

    Yampa River State Park (970-276-2061; cpw.state.co.us/placestogo/parks/Yampa River), 6185 US 40, Hayden. This unique state park encloses a 134-mile stretch of the river that reaches from Hayden to Dinosaur National Monument. The main park headquarters is in Hayden and has a campground and visitor center. Daily park pass $7.

✳ Lodging

HOTELS ((y)) **Hotel Bristol** (970-879-3083 or 1-800-851-0872; steamboathotelbristol .com), 917 Lincoln Ave. Built in 1948, Hotel Bristol has become a landmark in downtown Steamboat Springs. For years it served as a B&B, but reopened in 1997 as a 24-room hotel. The rooms are tastefully decorated with a subdued western theme, blending the historic charm of the building with modern comforts. Downstairs is Mazzola's, one of the best restaurants in town. Hotel rooms $109–169.

& ((y)) **Steamboat Grand Resort Hotel** (1-877-269-2628; steamboatgrand.com), 2300 Mt. Werner Cir. The hotel's 327 rooms and suites are located near the base of the ski area, walking distance to the gondola. Rooms are clean and tastefully decorated, if a little small. The deluxe king room comes with a Jacuzzi for two. The hotel also has studios, condos, and penthouses available for larger parties. Accommodations $124–2,400, which includes everything from a standard studio with a queen-size bed to a five-room penthouse that sleeps 12.

BED & BREAKFASTS **Mariposa** (970-879-1467 or 1-800-578-1467;

steamboatmariposa.com), 855 N. Grand St. The décor at Mariposa (Spanish for "butterfly") could be described as southwestern. There's more than a hint of Santa Fe, from the lodgepole furnishings, stucco walls, and exposed-beam ceilings. The rooms are comfortable with handmade quilts on each bed. The sunroom overlooks the nearby Soda Creek. The innkeepers, Bob and Cindy Maddox, live next door, which allows guests to avoid the feeling that they are intruding (if they want to stretch out on a couch for a nap, for example). In the morning, guests are taken care of with a full breakfast. Rooms $149–189.

CAMPGROUNDS **Yampa River State Park** (970-276-2061; cpw.state.co.us /placestogo/parks/YampaRiver), 6185 US 40, Hayden. Campground open in the summer only. The state park's Headquarters Campground has 50 sites. Thirty-five have electricity; the rest are walk-in tent sites. The campground has shower and laundry facilities. Tent sites $10–18, electric $24, and tipi $25.

CABINS & COTTAGES ♿ 🐾 **Columbine Cabins** (970-879-5522; historiccolumbine .com), P.O. Box 716, Clark. Located 29 miles north of Steamboat Springs on CO 129, Columbine Cabins is nestled under aspens and evergreens. Fifteen cabins are available with one to two bedrooms. Log walls, exposed beams, and woodstoves all add to the rustic charm of these lodgings. All have kitchens, and all but one have running water. The Caron House, the largest cabin, is the only one with a full bath. Bathrooms and shower facilities are located in the modern lodge. The lodge also offers laundry and a rec room with pool table and couches. Outside there's a wood-fired steam sauna. Cabins $80–180.

CONDOS **Torian Plum** (970-879-8811 or 1-866-599-9019; torianplum.com), 1855 Ski Time Square Dr. Operated by Resort-Quest, Torian Plum offers condos with ski-in, ski-out access to Steamboat. The accommodations range from 700-square-foot units with one bedroom and one bath to five-bed, six-bath apartments with 3,200 square feet of living space. Torian Plum has two sections: Plaza Tower and the newer Creekside. Units have full kitchens, fireplaces, and Jacuzzi tubs. Depending on the season and size, condos rent anywhere from $200 to more than $2,000.

❋ Where to Eat

DINING OUT During ski season, be sure to make reservations at any of the fine-dining restaurants you hope to visit.
 ❦ **Café Diva** (970-871-0508; cafediva .com), 1855 Ski Time Square Dr. Open nightly at 5:30. The menu changes seasonally at Café Diva, which is located in the Torian Plum Plaza, at the ski area base. Chef Kate Rench, who trained at the French Culinary Institute in New York, blends the classic flavors of world cuisine to create an innovative and highly praised menu. Entrées $24–45.

EATING OUT Steamboat Springs has plenty of options for eating out, including small regional chains such as Beau Jo's and The Egg & I. Because the town has nearly 10,000 year-round residents, and locals have to eat, Steamboat isn't top-heavy on fancy restaurants like other ski towns.
 ❦ **8th Street Steakhouse** (970-879-3131; 8thstreetsteakhouse.com), 50 Eighth St. Open daily for dinner 5–close. This classic western steakhouse in downtown Steamboat has a unique hook. You buy your meat and then grill it yourself on one of the two long grills. They supply spices and sauces, and a little direction on grilling the perfect cut of meat. For the kids, there are authentic saddle seats, and there are free s'mores for dessert. None of the steaks here will disappoint—and if they do, you only have yourself to blame—all the steaks are aged and cut onsite. Most

cuts $15–37, but with dishes such as Kobe steak, the menu tops out at $40.

&. **Backcountry Delicatessen** (970-879-3617; backcountry-deli.com), 635 Lincoln Ave. Open daily 7–7. Catering to Steamboat's recreational adventuring types, Backcountry Delicatessen provides hearty sandwiches made from the finest deli meats and cheeses. Eat in or take it with you for the trail. Sandwiches all less than $10.

&. **Mazzola's Majestic Italian Diner** (970-879-2405; mazzolas.com), 917 Lincoln Ave. Open nightly 5–10. Mazzola's has been through several hands since the Mazzola family first opened the joint back in 1970. Today, the restaurant continues the tradition of serving a classic, made-from-scratch Italian menu. The restaurant prides itself on its family-dining affordability. From the red-and-white-checkered tablecloths to the incredible food, Mazzola's is not to be missed. Entrées $16–24 and pizzas $13–19.

&. **The Mountain** (970-879-5800; eatatthemountain.com), 2500 Village Dr. Open Tue.–Sun. 3–11. For 34 years, guests came to La Montana for classic Mexican and southwestern cuisine. The owners of that establishment retired, and the new owner remodeled and launched an entirely new experience. The Mountain serves classic American comfort food—perfect after a day in the snow. Entrées $14–24.

&. **Rex's American Grill & Bar** (970-870-0438; rexsgrill.com), 3190 S. Lincoln Ave. Open daily for breakfast, lunch, and dinner 6:30–11. Owned by the same folks who own Mazzola's downtown, this new eatery impresses locals with its affordable, classic American menu. It's where you go if you are looking for delicious half-pound burgers and great comfort food, such as buttermilk fried chicken and mac & cheese. There are some creative upscale items on the menu as well—the shrimp and elk sausage, for example, is a great take on the traditional surf and turf. Dinner entrées $11–24 (fish tacos and the mac & cheese dinners come in

at $12–17) and lunch burgers and sandwiches $9–12.

&. **The Tap House Sports Grill** (970-879-2431; thetaphouse.com), 729 Lincoln Ave. Open Mon.–Thu. 4:30 PM–midnight, Fri. 11:30–midnight, and Sat.–Sun. 10–midnight. This sports bar's large dining room serves a traditional bar menu that won't empty your wallet. Excellent burgers and fries, plates of onion rings, and nachos piled high keep bringing people back. The Tap House has a small video arcade and 40 televisions, including some seriously wide screens. With the satellite connection, every game you can imagine is shown. To get in on some of the local action, come on Tuesday for Wing Day—half-priced wings all day. Sandwiches and burgers around $12–14, steaks under $20.

BAKERIES & COFFEE SHOPS &. **Gondola Joe's Café** (970-871-5150), Gondola Sq. Open daily in the winter 7–5. There's always time to grab a cup of coffee and a bagel sandwich in the morning, especially at Gondola Joe's, right next to the gondola at the Steamboat Springs base area. While you're there, you can buy a boxed lunch for later in the day.

BARS, TAVERNS, & BREW PUBS &. **Slopeside Grill** (970-879-2916; slopesidegrill.com), 1855 Ski Time Square Dr. Known as much for its pasta dishes and brick-oven pizza as the succulent baby back ribs, Slopeside Grill is also a great place for an après-ski drink. Late night happy hour, 10–midnight (9–11 in the summer), has great pizzas and cheap pints.

✳ Entertainment

Strings in the Mountains Music Festival (970-879-5056; stringsmusicfestival.com), 900 Strings Rd. at the corner of Mt. Werner and Pine Grove roads. More than 85 performances are produced every summer in Steamboat Springs. Concerts celebrate many musical traditions, including chamber music, jazz, rock, country, and bluegrass.

✳ Selective Shopping

F. M. Light & Sons (1-800-530-8908; fmlight.com), 860 Lincoln Ave., has been serving Steamboat Springs since 1905, beginning as a men's clothier outfitting local ranchers and farmers. The shop is your best shot for getting authentic western duds, including Stetson hats and cowboy boots. Run by the same family for more than 100 years and five generations, F. M. Light & Sons is living history.

✳ Special Events

January: **Cowboy Downhill** (970-879-6111; steamboatchamber.com/things-to-do/events/cowboy-downhill). This annual ski rodeo is one of those events that epitomize a town. Steamboat Springs prides itself on its great ski hills and western cowboy heritage. Both of these come together when the cowboys take to the slopes—many of them for the first time—to compete on skis. The tradition began in 1975, when the city invited some professional rodeo cowboys competing in Denver to enjoy the state's other sport. They had so much fun they keep coming back.

February: **Steamboat Springs Winter Carnival** (970-879-0880; steamboatchamber.com/signature-events/winter-carnival). Since 1914, the folks in Steamboat have been fighting off cabin fever with a celebration of winter. The carnival includes strange seasonal activities that include children being pulled through the streets on skis while being pulled by horses, a donkey jump, and an adult snow shovel race.

July: **Cowboys' Roundup Days** (970-879-0880; steamboatchamber.com/signature-events/july-4th-celebration). Every year the Steamboat Springs Chamber puts on a "salute to the West" festival culminating on the Fourth of July. There are fireworks, tours of local working ranches, and an old-time cattle drive through the middle of town.

September: **Steamboat OktoberWest** (steamboatoktoberwest.com). Colorado brewers, plenty of food, and lots of family activities make for a festive three-day weekend in mid-September.

F.M. LIGHT & SONS CLOTHIERS

ASPEN & SNOWMASS

Aspen has an international reputation as a glamorous retreat for the nation's rich and famous, with expensive restaurants, dozens of art galleries, and boutiques that sell $300 jeans. This is the side of Aspen that most people hear about—the celebrity stories that make headlines and sell newspapers. But Aspen is much more than a ritzy getaway.

As a ski town, it offers what many consider the best and most varied terrain in Colorado. Recreational activities are available year-round. Thousands come in the summer for mountain biking, hiking around the Maroon Bells, and fishing the area's rivers and mountain streams. Surrounding the town of Aspen are nearly 2 million acres of the White River National Forest. The Roaring Fork River barrels through Aspen and the valley that bears its name, on its way north to meet up with the Colorado. Encircling peaks reach above 14,000 feet—mountaintops that remain snowcapped nearly year-round. In 1972, John Denver recorded "Rocky Mountain High," a song that celebrates his passion for these mountains. (The song became one of Colorado's two official state songs in 2007.) It is this aspect of Aspen that continues to draw visitors, even when the town itself may seem too pricey or ostentatious.

Aspen's roots go back to 1879, when miners from Leadville crossed over Independence Pass into the Roaring Fork Valley. These gentlemen found the silver they were looking for, and within a year three mining camps had sprung up and were subsequently organized into the town of Aspen. Several years later, Jerome B. Wheeler (one-time president of Macy's in New York) came to Aspen. He bought some mining claims and began investing in the community.

From the time the railroad came to town in 1887 to the repeal of the Sherman Silver Purchase Act in 1893, Aspen was the richest silver mining region in the country. The town grew to 12,000 people and supported six newspapers, two banks, and a telephone service. Wheeler built the hotel and the opera house that bear his name. The change that came in 1893 was radical. With the government no longer buying silver, the market plummeted overnight, and those who had made their fortune in this metal, such as Jerome Wheeler, were left bankrupt. The town began to die, and by 1930, there were only 700 people left.

Little by little, skiing came to Aspen. During the Depression, the WPA built a boat tow on Aspen Mountain. There were thoughts of bringing a full-fledged resort to the area, but World War II stalled any plans that were being considered. However, in 1945, Walter Paepcke and his wife, Elizabeth, moved to Aspen. Paepcke was an industrialist, and he had a dream of transforming Aspen into a resort community with a world-class ski area.

Paepcke was not just envisioning a pampered retreat for the wealthy—his desire was to create a cultural center, a place where artists and intellectuals could flourish. The town today owes much of its character to the efforts of the Paepcke family.

By the 1970s, Aspen's reputation as a ski town had been established. Big names came to ski the town's four ski areas—Aspen Mountain, Aspen Highlands, Buttermilk, and Snowmass. Throughout the 1970s and '80s, the celebrities began to make Aspen their own.

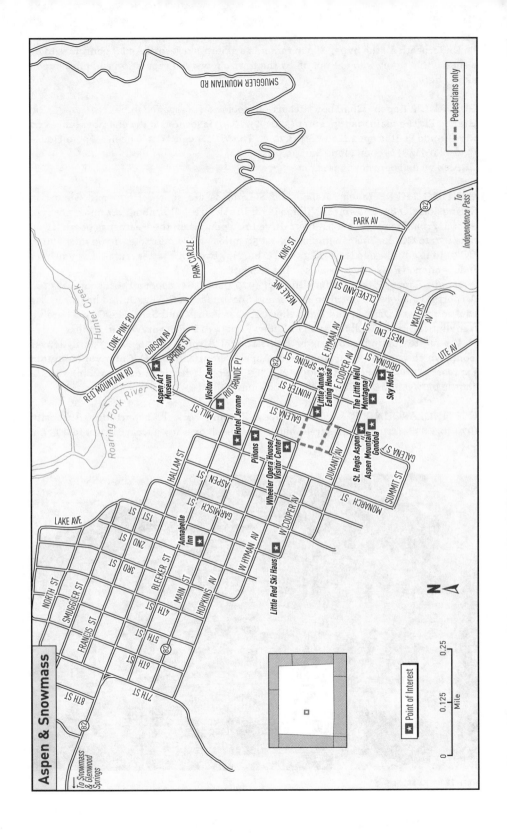

Aspen & Snowmass

SMUGGLER MOUNTAIN RD

Pedestrians only

To Independence Pass

PARK AV

82

KING ST

PARK CIRCLE

NEALE AVE

CLEVELAND ST

WATERS AV

WEST END ST

UTE AV

Hunter Creek

LONE PINE RD

GIBSON AV

SPRING ST

RED MOUNTAIN RD

Aspen Art Museum

Visitor Center

RIO GRANDE PL

E HYMAN AV

E COOPER AV

ORIGINAL ST

Roaring Fork River

MILL ST

Hotel Jerome

SPRING ST

HUNTER ST

GALENA ST

82

Little Annie's Eating House

The Little Nell

Montagna

Sky Hotel

Piñons

Wheeler Opera House / Visitor Center

DURANT AV

St. Regis Aspen

Aspen Mountain Gondola

GALENA ST

HALLAM ST

ASPEN ST

MONARCH ST

SUMMIT ST

LAKE AVE

1ST ST

GARMISCH ST

W COOPER AV

NORTH ST

SMUGGLER ST

2ND ST

Annabelle Inn

BLEEKER ST

MAIN ST

HOPKINS AV

W HYMAN AV

Little Red Ski Haus

FRANCIS ST

3RD ST

4TH ST

5TH ST

6TH ST

7TH ST

8TH ST

82

To Snowmass & Glenwood Springs

N

Point of Interest

0   0.125   0.25
Mile

Underneath all the hype, Aspen remains a skiers' ski resort. And it continues to be a shame that many who are put off by the town's moneyed reputation will miss out on skiing here.

GUIDANCE **Aspen Chamber Resort Association** (aspenchamber.org), 425 Rio Grande Pl. The main visitor center (970-925-1940) is located at the chamber offices on Rio Grande Pl. It is open Mon.–Fri. 8:30–5. The visitor center at Wheeler Opera House (970-920-7148) is open Mon.–Sun. 10–6.

Also visit aspensnowmass.com.

GETTING THERE *By car:* Aspen and Snowmass are south of I-70 and Glenwood Springs on CO 82. Snowmass Village is off Brush Creek Rd., about 4.7 miles north of Aspen. From Denver, it's a 3.5-hour drive to Aspen, when the weather is good, if you take I-70 to CO 82. You can knock almost 50 miles off the odometer if you take I-70 to CO 91 to Leadville, and then US 24 to CO 82. However, this latter route takes you over Independence Pass, which is closed in the winter.

By air: **Aspen/Pitkin County Airport** (970-920-5384; aspenairport.com), 0233 E. Airport Rd., is located between Aspen and Snowmass on CO 82. United has a regular shuttle route to Denver, and Delta flies between Aspen and Salt Lake City. There's a free shuttle bus that will take you to Rubey Park (430 E. Durant Ave.) in Aspen.

If you are coming into **Denver International Airport** (1-800-247-2336; flydenver .com), which is a four-hour drive from Aspen (about 220 miles), **Colorado Mountain Express** (970-926-9800 or 1-800-525-6363; coloradomountainexpress.com) runs a shuttle between the DIA and Aspen/Snowmass.

GETTING AROUND *By shuttle:* Aspen's **Roaring Fork Transportation Authority** (970-925-8484; rfta.com) has free shuttle service all over town from 6:30 AM to 2:15 AM.

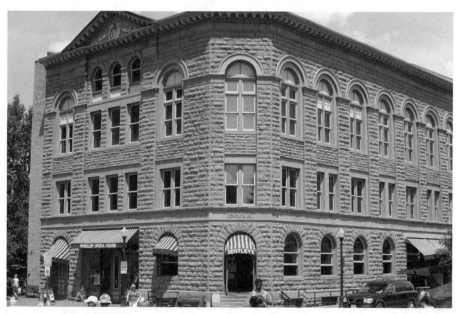

WHEELER OPERA HOUSE

The hub is at Rubey Park, 430 E. Durant Ave. There is also shuttle service to all the ski areas, Maroon Bells, and Glenwood Springs.

By taxi: **The Ultimate Taxi** (970-925-6361; ultimatetaxi.com) driven by Jon Barnes, offers the best ride in town—transportation and a floor show, complete with live music and special effects. A 45-minute ride costs $200 (per group). Check out the site for photos of celebrity passengers.

✽ To See & Do

Maroon Bells. It is said that the Maroon Bells are North America's most photographed peaks. It's hard to imagine a more perfect alignment of natural features—the two 14,000-foot peaks tower over the lush valley with wildflowers, meadow, and a lake. It's simply breathtaking. A short hike from the parking lot goes out and around the lake. There are other, longer trails if you want to make a day of hiking the Bells. Because the U.S. Forest Service, the caretakers of the Maroon Bells Scenic Area, wants to control the traffic to and from the Bells, visitors must come by bus (or nonmotorized transportation). To catch the bus, park at Aspen Highlands and purchase bus tickets at Four Mountain Sports inside. The bus picks you up outside. Adult ticket $8, seniors and children (6–16) $6, and children under 6 free.

↑ ♿ **Aspen Art Museum** (970-925-8050; aspenartmuseum.org), 590 N. Mill St. Open Tue.–Sun. 10–6. Aspen Art Museum is a noncollecting institution that promotes contemporary art with an ever-changing rotation of shows and exhibitions. Admission to the museum is free, thanks to a generous donor.

↑ **Holden/Marolt Mining and Ranching Museum** (970-925-3721; heritageaspen .org/hm.html), 40180 CO 82. Call to schedule a tour. The area's mining and ranching history is preserved at this museum, located on the site of the Holden Lixiviation Mill (1891). Adult tour $10, seniors $8, and children under 12 free. Admission also gets you into Wheeler/Stallard Museum.

↑ **Wheeler/Stallard Museum** (970-925-3721; aspenhistory.org/tours-sites/wheeler-stallard-museum), 620 W. Bleeker St. Open Tue.–Sat. 1–5. The museum resides in a Queen Anne home from 1888. The first floor has been restored to what it would have looked like in the 19th century. The second floor is a gallery with different shows exhibited regularly. Adult tour $10, seniors $8, and children under 12 free. Admission also gets you into Holden/Marolt Museum.

Independence Pass to Twin Lakes. The drive over to Twin Lakes crosses the Continental Divide and takes you over Independence Pass. It's one of the most scenic routes in the area. The pass is the highest paved path in North America at 12,095 feet. The road, CO 82, is closed in the winter.

✽ Outdoor Activities

ALPINE SKIING & SNOWBOARDING Aspen is home to four ski areas, each with its own distinct personality. Aspen and Snowmass see 300 inches of annual snowfall, and all the ski areas have impressive vertical drops.

The town of Aspen sits at the base of **Aspen Mountain**. Littered with black-diamond runs, most of this 673-acre ski area is for advanced skiers; the rest is for intermediate. There are no runs for beginners at Aspen Mountain. The overall vertical drop is 3,267 feet. The gondola in town takes passengers right to the top of the ski area.

MAROON BELLS

Aspen Highlands is just out of town on Maroon Creek Rd. The ski area is 1,010 acres with a 3,635-foot vertical drop. Half of the runs are for advanced skiers (they love the 50-degree drop into Highland Bowl), a third for intermediate, and a measly fifth for beginners.

The largest of Aspen's four ski areas, **Snowmass** has 3,128 skiable acres with 4,406 vertical feet of drop. There are plenty of long runs and steep descents. Only 6 percent of the terrain is for beginners. The mountain is accessed by 23 lifts. Snowmass is 10 miles from Aspen and has its own resort village.

Buttermilk is the smallest of Aspen's ski areas at 435 acres, with nine lifts. There's a 2,030-foot vertical drop, and there are an even number of trails for skiers of varying abilities. A great destination for snowboarders, Buttermilk has terrain parks and a superpipe. The Winter X Games are held here annually.

One lift ticket to **Aspen/Snowmass** (aspensnowmass.com) buys you access to all four of Aspen's ski areas. The day rate decreases with multiday tickets.

Aspen Mountain Powder Tours (970-920-0720 or 1-800-525-6200 ext. 3720; stayaspen snowmass.com). For snowcat access to backcountry slopes, consider a Powder Tour. Skiers will experience 10,000 vertical feet of ungroomed descents. The cost includes lunch and snacks.

BICYCLING **Maroon Creek Road** is one of the area's most scenic bike rides. The paved road steadily climbs a gentle grade for nearly 10 miles from CO 82 to where it ends at the Maroon Bells and Pacific Peak. You will have to pay a $5 fee at the ranger station. **Independence Pass**, on the other hand, has nothing gentle about it. The road climbs 4,000 feet in 17 miles on its way to Twin Lakes. From Aspen to Twin Lakes is about a 37-mile trip, just 21 miles to the pass. Steep and twisty, the route makes you pay for the fantastic panoramic views of the Collegiate Peaks.

CROSS-COUNTRY SKIING & SNOWSHOEING **Ashcroft Ski Touring** (970-925-1971; pinecreekcookhouse.com/ashcroft/ashcroft-winte), 11 miles up to the end of Castle Creek Rd. at the Cabin Nordic Center. Nearly 22 miles of groomed trails on 600 acres, the Nordic center also rents out ski and snowshoe equipment. Adult day pass $25, seniors and children under 12 $15.

Aspen/Snowmass Nordic Trail System (970-429-2039; aspenpitkin.com/Departments /Cross-Country-Skiing). A network of cross-country ski trails in Aspen and Snowmass are connected by the Owl Creek Trail. Snowshoers are welcome to use the trails—just don't walk on the groomed tracks. See website for complete trail information. These 60 miles of trails are open to the public. Although the trails are free, donation boxes can be found at the trailheads and the ski centers in Aspen and Snowmass.

10th Mountain Division Hut Association (970-925-5775; huts.org). For backcountry skiing, huts make it possible for skiers to make multiday trips in the wilderness with the promise of comfortable, reliable shelter and a warm bed at night. The 10th Mountain Division Hut System comprises 29 backcountry huts connected by a network of trails (350 miles of suggested routes). Check website for route information, hut availability, and rates.

FISHING **Aspen Flyfishing** (970-920-6886; aspenflyfishing.com), 601 E. Dean St. For fly-fishing trips, the guides at Aspen Flyfishing take anglers wading on the Roaring Fork and lower Frying Pan rivers. For float-fishing, they head out to the Roaring Fork or go north to the Colorado. The outfitter also has access to a private lake stocked with trout, and there are trips available just for kids. Half-day wade trip for one $275; three guests $475. Half-day float trip for one or two $425.

Taylor Creek Fly Shops (970-927-4374; taylorcreek.com), 183 Basalt Center Cir., Basalt. From gear to guides to fishing reports, Taylor Creek Fly Shops is one of the oldest in Colorado. It has an impressive roster of guides with decades of experience fishing this part of Colorado.

GOLF **Aspen Golf and Tennis** (970-544-1772; aspenrecreation.com), 39551 CO 82. As part of the Aspen Recreation Center, the golf course prides itself on offering a great course with reasonable fees. Greens fees for 18 holes $30–160.

River Valley Ranch Golf Club (970-963-3625; rvrgolf.com), 303 River Valley Ranch Dr., Carbondale. About 45 minutes away in Carbondale, River Valley Ranch sits at the base of Mt. Sopris, incorporating the valley's Crystal River into the course design. Greens fees $50–90.

Snowmass Club (970-923-9155 or 1-800-525-0710; snowmassclub.com), 239 Snowmass Club Cir. This semiprivate course in Snowmass Village charges upward of $175 for 18 holes, including a cart. Members only until one o'clock.

HIKING There are plenty of hikes in the mountains around Aspen. One of the most popular is the hike from Aspen to Crested Butte via West Maroon Pass (mountain bikers like the longer Pearl Pass route). **Dolly's Mountain Shuttle** (970-349-2620; crestedbutteshuttle.com) can drive you back to Aspen for only $60/person.

Aspen Alpine Guides (970-925-6618; aspenalpine.com), P.O. Box 659, Aspen. Throughout the summer, hikers take guided trips into the mountains around Aspen, led by the good folks at Aspen Alpine Guides. Tours include day hikes and fitness hikes, as well as rock climbing and backpacking. You can climb Area 14ers or make the trek to Crested Butte. In the winter, trips include cross-country skiing and snowshoeing.

HORSEBACK RIDING & CARRIAGE/SLEIGH RIDES **Aspen Carriage and Sleigh** (970-925-3394; aspencarriage.com), P.O. Box 38, Aspen. It's kind of classy to take the family out on a carriage or sleigh ride. A 20-minute tour through town costs $20 for adults, kids $10 (with a $50 minimum). In the winter the company offers sleigh rides. The carriages can also be reserved to serve as a unique taxi service.

Aspen Wilderness Outfitters (970-928-0723; aspenwilderness.com), 554 CR 110. Guided horseback rides can be taken all over the Aspen region, including to the Maroon Bells. Aspen Wilderness Outfitters leads trail rides and pack rides (overnighters). They also run Snowmass Stables, which offers shorter rides around Snowmass and Buttermilk. Reservations required. Two-hour rides with lunch $80.

Maroon Bells Lodge and Outfitters (970-920-4679; maroonbellsaspen.com), 3125 Maroon Creek Rd. On the ride up to the Maroon Bells, you can't miss the Maroon Bells Lodge—it's the large log lodge with the red roof on your right heading toward the Maroon Bells Scenic Area. Located on the T Lazy 7 Ranch, the outfitters offer guided trail rides and pack rides, as well as wagon and sleigh rides. Several ride-and-dine packages are available—all include a gourmet meal. Rides around Buttermilk start at $75 and go up to $235 for the all-day ride with the cowboy dinner. Ride packages change every now and then, so check the website for the most up-to-date adventures.

MOUNTAIN BIKING **Government Trail** is one of Aspen's most classic rides. It begins at the Snowmass Ski Area, and on the way to Aspen follows some of the state's best singletrack—much of the way through aspen groves.

Aspen Sports (970-925-6331; aspensports.com), 408 E. Cooper Ave. A great selection of rental bikes—mostly the town cruiser types. Since this company has a location

CREEK NEAR MAROON BELLS

in Snowmass, you can ride one way and drop the bike off there. It also rents out of the St. Regis Hotel.

Timberline Bike Tours (970-274-6076; timberlinebike.com), 730 E. Cooper, located at Johnny McGuire's Deli. These folks lead hut-to-hut mountain bike tours, as well as day trips on the area's best singletrack. Check out the website for a complete list of trips. Day trips $85, which includes lunch.

PARAGLIDING **Aspen Paragliding** (970-925-6975 or 970-379-6975; aspenparagliding .com), 426 S. Spring St. For a unique adventure in Aspen, try soaring above the valley on a parachute. No experience is necessary; guests fly tandem with a guide. The take-off is a few running steps down a gentle slope (no freediving off the mountain), and the entire activity takes about two hours. The flight will last about 15 minutes, but if conditions are good it could be longer. Tandem flights $275.

PADDLING & RAFTING **Blazing Adventures** (970-923-4544 or 1-800-282-7238; blazingadventures.com), 48 Upper Village Mall, Snowmass. In addition to providing biking and Jeep tours, this outfitter leads half-day trips down the upper and lower Roaring Fork and the Colorado rivers. Certain trips include class IV rapids. Pirate trips promise extra fun for families. Half-day trips start around $114 for adults.

✳ Green Space

White River National Forest (fs.usda.gov/whiteriver). Aspen is surrounded by green space. The White River National Forest has eight wilderness areas. Within the Aspen/ Sopris Ranger District, there are eight 14ers, hundreds of miles of trails for mountain biking and hiking, and eight campgrounds. This is, in fact, the most visited national forest in the country. The Aspen office (970-925-3445) is at 806 W. Hallam St.

✳ Lodging

HOTELS ♿ (ᵂⁱᶠⁱ) **Annabelle Inn** (970-925-3822 or 1-877-266-2466; annabelleinn.com), 232 W. Main St. Since 1948, Annabelle Inn (which went by the moniker "the Christmas Inn" until 2005) has been an Aspen lodging mainstay. The inn's 35 rooms are all uniquely decorated and include flat-panel TVs with cable and Internet access. Premium rooms have a balcony, a mountain view, and a fireplace. Ski movies are shown nightly next to one of the inn's two hot tubs—perfect for soaking after a chilly day on the slopes. A buffet breakfast is served every morning. Rooms $119–429.

♿ ✿ **Hotel Jerome** (970-920-1000 or 1-855-331-7213; hoteljerome.aubergeresorts.com), 330 E. Main St. In 1889, town founder Jerome Wheeler built Hotel Jerome, which he hoped would rival elegant lodgings in Europe and New York. The hotel has served Aspen for well over 100 years, offering guests top-of-the-line accommodations in an historic setting. Digital TVs, 24-hour room service, and an efficient concierge desk are just some of the accommodations you can expect. Rooms $199–1,499.

♿ ✿ (ᵂⁱᶠⁱ) **The Little Nell** (970-920-4600 or 1-855-920-4600; thelittlenell.com), 675 E. Durant Ave. Located right at the base of the Silver Queen Gondola, The Little Nell has 15 rooms and 77 suites. The hotel's outdoor pool is heated for year-round use, allowing guests to sit in the pool (or Jacuzzi) at the base of Aspen Mountain. Internet service is available, and pets are allowed (always on a leash). The hotel prides itself on exceptional customer service, including a ski concierge for slope-side amenities. Rooms and suites $400–4,800.

♿ (ᵂⁱᶠⁱ) **The Little Red** (970-925-7123; thelittlered.com), 118 E. Cooper Ave. Back when Aspen was a hard-working mining town, it is believed this adorable cottage on Cooper Avenue was a brothel. For a time it was certainly used as a boarding house, and then it was turned into The Little Red Ski Haus, providing dorm-style lodging for budget-conscious skiers. In the past decade it became a private home/vacation rental, but is now back as an inn. The house has 9 rooms and 13½ bathrooms. Contact for rates and reservations.

♿ ✿ (ᵂⁱᶠⁱ) **St. Regis Aspen** (970-920-3300 or 1-888-454-9005; stregisaspen.com), 315 E. Dean St. This five-star hotel is strategically located at the base of Aspen Mountain, close to the gondola and two popular ski lifts. The property is exquisitely decorated with bronze sculptures and classic oils. The hotel is known for exceptional concierge service, and the staff cater to every whim of their guests—people who come with high expectations for being pampered. Rooms and suites $379–3,300.

♿ ✿ (ᵂⁱᶠⁱ) **Sky Hotel** (970-925-6760 or 1-800-882-2582; theskyhotel.com), 709 E. Durant Ave. Strategically located at the base of Aspen Mountain, Sky Hotel is, hands down, Aspen's swankest hotel. Amenities include a heated outdoor pool and spa and a great lounge, 39 Degrees. Rooms $199–869.

CAMPGROUNDS (ᵂⁱᶠⁱ) **Aspen-Basalt Campground** (970-927-3405), 20640 CO 82, Basalt, just south of mile marker 20, between Glenwood Springs and Aspen. The new bikeway to Aspen runs just behind this campground, and the Roaring Fork River flows behind it as well, providing easy fishing access. All of the 75 sites have either electric and water or full hookups. Hot showers available year-round. Sites $47.

Silver Bar, **Silver Bell**, and **Silver Queen Campgrounds**, White River National Forest. Located along Maroon Creek Rd., these three campgrounds have potable water and vault toilets. In addition to camping fees (around $15), campers have to purchase a $5, five-day vehicle permit to enter the park. Reservations can be made by calling

1-877-444-6777 or visiting the website, recreation.gov.

CABINS & COTTAGES 🐾 📶 **Avalanche Ranch** (970-963-2846; avalancheranch .com), 12863 CO 133, Carbondale. With Mt. Sopris above and the Crystal River below, Avalanche Ranch is right in the middle of some beautiful scenery. The ranch is an hour from Aspen. There are 14 cabins, a loft, a ranch house, and a shepherd's wagon. Cabins have bathrooms with tubs or showers and kitchens. Cabins $120–395. The three wagons sleep two, but cost $85 night.

Taylor Creek Cabins (970-927-9927; rent-cabins-colorado.com), Basalt. The cabins can be found outside of Basalt on Frying Pan Road (call or visit website for directions). These cozy cabins are situated across from the Frying Pan River and are owned and operated by Frying Pan Anglers. A quick glance might suggest they are rustic, but inside the accommodations are all modern. Guests enjoy access to this private stretch of the river. A three-night minimum stay is required. Cabins $160–200.

✳ Where to Eat

DINING OUT Getting a table in Aspen's nicer dining rooms will require reservations—especially during peak months in the summer and winter.

  ♿ **Element 47** (970-920-6330; the littlenell.com/dining/element-47), 675 E. Durant Ave. Open for breakfast, lunch, and dinner. Located in The Little Nell at the base of the gondola, Element 47 was named for silver, the precious metal that got Aspen its auspicious start. The restaurant has an extensive cellar, featuring more than 20,000 wines. The tiered dining area is comfortable, and the food is meticulously prepared. As much as possible, everything at Element 47 is created in-house, and classic dishes are reinvented and brought up a notch. Dinner entrées $27–65.

♿ **Matsuhisa** (970-544-6628; nobumatsuhisa.com), 303 E. Main St. Hours change seasonally. In 1998, Nobu Matsuhisa brought his signature style of Japanese cuisine to Aspen. Seafood tops the menu, with dishes such as Chilean sea bass topped with truffles and baby abalone with light garlic sauce. A sushi bar is available in the lounge. Dishes $13–32 (up to current market price on many entrées).

  ♿ **Pine Creek Cookhouse** (970-925-1044; pinecreekcookhouse.com), 11399 Castle Creek Rd. Open daily for lunch noon–2 and dinner 6–8:30. The dining experience at Pine Creek begins with just getting there. In the winter, guests have to cross-country ski, snowshoe, or come by sleigh. The cookhouse itself is the picture of rustic elegance, contributing to an overall memorable evening. Dinner for two, including the sleigh ride, can cost $260. For a more affordable option, ask about the summer hikers' buffet.

  ♿ **Piñons** (970-920-2021; pinons.net), 105 S. Mill St. Open for dinner nightly at 5:30. Closed during the shoulder seasons. This restaurant remains a local favorite, and reservations are a must here. The western-themed menu features dishes such as pan-roasted pork tenderloin and macadamia nut ahi. The chocolate peanut butter pie is a great dessert. Dishes $25–50.

EATING OUT ♿ **Little Annie's Eating House** (970-925-1098; littleannies.com), 517 E. Hyman Ave. Open daily 11–10. Locals love this laid-back restaurant with its red-and-white-checked tablecloths and homestyle eating. They named the burger here Aspen's best. Comfort food tops the menu—ribs, burgers, chili, thick soups, and latkes are all favorites. Dinner entrées $12–28, burgers and sandwiches $12.

  ♿ **The Big Wrap** (970-544-1700), 520 E. Durant Ave. Open Mon.–Sat. 10–6. Nothing beats a wrap for a quick and possibly healthy lunch. This could be the most affordable meal option in Aspen, and this restaurant delivers. Wraps around $7.

 ♿ **Woody Creek Tavern** (970-923-4585; woodycreektavern.com), 2 Woody Creek Plz., 2858 Upper River Road, Woody Creek. Open daily 11–10. Great down-home cooking and great mountain hospitality define this quirky tavern just a few miles out of Aspen. Back in the day, Hunter S. Thompson used to hang out here. Lunch dishes around $15, dinner entrées $21–28.

BARS, TAVERNS, & BREW PUBS ♿ **The J-Bar** (970-920-1000; hoteljerome.com), 330 E. Main St. Open daily from 11:30 AM–1 AM. Located in Hotel Jerome, the J-Bar has been serving Aspenites since 1889. For a while during Prohibition, the bar became a soda fountain. Later it was a soda fountain/bar. It's no wonder then that the J-Bar's signature drink is the Aspen Crud (French vanilla ice cream and bourbon).

✳ Entertainment

Aspen District Theater (1-866-449-0464), 235 High School Rd. The theater is home to the Aspen Santa Fe Ballet (970-925-7175; aspensantafeballet.com). The ballet performs a regular season of world-class dance.

Belly Up (970-544-9800; bellyupaspen.com), 450 S. Galena St. This all-ages club has a regular schedule of live music. Everybody from G. Love to Lucinda Williams to Method Man and Redman have played here. Check out the website for coming performances.

Wheeler Opera House (970-920-5770; wheeleroperahouse.com), 320 E. Hyman Ave. The opera house has been entertaining patrons since 1889. Today, both live performances and movies fill the calendar.

THE FOUNTAIN AT SOUTH MILL STREET MALL

✳ Selective Shopping

Elliott Yeary Gallery (970-429-1111; elliottyeary.com), 419 E. Hyman Ave. This fine art gallery specializes in exhibiting contemporary work and caters to both collectors and first-time art buyers.

Huntsman Gallery of Fine Art (970-963-0703; huntsmangallery.com), 1180 Heritage Dr., Carbondale. This gallery carries the sculptures of Don Huntsman as well as dozens of others. Artists working in oils seem to dominate the space.

Ute Mountaineer (970-925-2849; utemountaineer.com), 210 S. Galena St. From snowshoes to carabiners to GPS units, Ute Mountaineer can supply all your outdoor gear needs.

Vintage Ski World (970-963-9025 and 1-800-332-6323; vintageskiworld .com), 1521 Panorama Dr., Carbondale. This shop specializes in vintage ski equipment as well as classic and antique ski posters and prints. For those who celebrate ski culture, there's no better shop in town.

✳ Special Events

January: **Winter X Games** (970-925-1220; stayaspensnowmass.com). This is the biggest annual event in winter action sports. Athletes from around the world come to compete on snowboards and skis, snowmobiles, and motorcycles.

July: **Aspen Ideas Festival** (970-544-7955; aifestival.org). The Aspen Ideas Institute sponsors this event annually to bring together leaders from around the world to participate in programs, seminars, and discussions on some of the most relevant and important issues of our time.

September: **Aspen Filmfest** (970-925-6882; aspenfilm.org). The festival, which has been held annually since 1979, features independent films and documentaries.

Jazz Aspen Snowmass (970-920-4996; jazzaspen.com). The four-day jazz festival during Labor Day weekend concludes a summer full of free and paid concerts, as well as a festival in June.

October: **John Denver Celebration** (johndenvercelebration.com). This weeklong festival celebrates the life and music of John Denver.

GLENWOOD SPRINGS

Glenwood Springs sits at the confluence of the Roaring Fork and Colorado rivers, at the end of Roaring Fork Valley. Many travelers pass through Glenwood Springs on their way south to Aspen. Although not a particularly popular ski destination, the town does have its faithful corps of regular visitors, and the number of attractions in Glenwood Springs seems to increase every year.

Historically, the thing that has brought visitors to Glenwood Springs over the years has been the great hot springs pool. Early on, the Ute came to bathe in the pool and to rest in the nearby vapor caves. They saw the springs as a gift from Manitou and named the place Yampah, meaning "big medicine." In 1860, Capt. Richard Sopris led an expedition into the area and became the first white man to see the massive hot springs pool. In 1879, James Landis settled in the area and became the first owner of the hot springs property. Not long after that, a tent city was born on the site and named Defiance. A few years later, the region's Ute population was moved to reservations in Utah, and the whole western part of the state was opened to settlers. When the town was incorporated in 1885, the name was changed to Glenwood.

In the 1880s, the Glenwood Hot Springs Pool was built and soon was attracting highfalutin guests from around the world. Before skiing was a recreational sport in the United States, back when Aspen was a mining town, Glenwood Springs was one of the world's premier travel destinations. The "grand dame" Hotel Colorado was built in 1893 and hosted guests such as Presidents Taft and Roosevelt, and the "unsinkable" Molly Brown. While filming in the area, the great western screen star Tom Mix even stayed there.

As the resort town grew, attractions were added. In 1897, the Glenwood Caverns and Fairy Caves were opened to the public and were proclaimed in advertisements as the "Eighth Wonder of the World."

Travelers today come for the hot springs, but also to enjoy the region's recreational opportunities. There's rafting on the Colorado River, hiking up to Hanging Lake, and biking through Glenwood Canyon. The Glenwood Caverns and Adventure Park can keep a family entertained all day with a new mountain roller coaster and zip line course, and the town has numerous places for both fine dining and gathering the family around the trough.

GUIDANCE **Glenwood Springs Chamber Resort Association** (970-945-6589 or 1-888-4GLENWOOD; glenwoodchamber.com) 1102 Grand Ave. The visitor center is open in the summer (Memorial Day to Labor Day) Mon.–Fri. 9–5 and weekends 10–3; winter, Mon.–Fri. 9–5. Outside there's a 24-hour, unmanned information kiosk that has brochures covering lodging, dining, and attractions in Glenwood Springs.

See also visitglenwood.com.

GETTING THERE *By car:* Glenwood Springs is right on I-70 at exits 114 and 116. It's about 180 miles (three hours, give or take) west of Denver and 117 miles east of the Utah border.

By air: **Aspen/Pitkin County Airport** (970-920-5384; aspenairport.com), 0233 E. Airport Rd., is about 37 miles south of Glenwood Springs on CO 82. Both United and

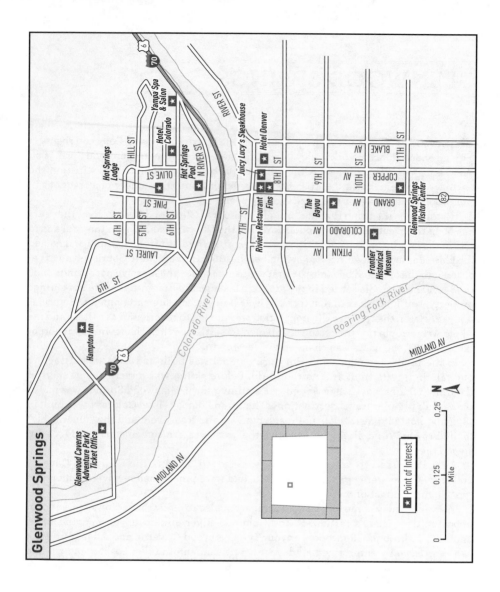

Glenwood Springs

Delta fly into this airport. **Denver International Airport** (1-800-247-2336; flydenver .com) is about 180 miles east of Glenwood Springs. It's a three-hour drive, but **Colorado Mountain Express** (970-926-9800 or 1-800-525-6363; coloradomountainexpress.com) does operate a shuttle from the DIA to Glenwood Springs.

By train: **Amtrak** (1-800-872-7245; amtrak.com) offers train service from its station at 413 Seventh St. The station is open daily 9:30–5.

By bus: **Greyhound** (970-945-8501 or 1-800-231-2222; greyhound.com) operates regular service to and from Glenwood Springs from its station at the Phillips 66 Station (51171 US 6). Open daily 4 AM–midnight.

GETTING AROUND *By bus:* **Ride Glenwood Springs** provides transportation around Glenwood Springs. This service is managed by the **Roaring Fork Transportation**

GLENWOOD CANYON

T he spectacular Glenwood Canyon is the largest canyon on the upper Colorado River. It's a beautiful 13-mile stretch of scenery—the walls rise 2,000 feet above the canyon floor. As far back as the 1880s, pioneers used the canyon as a throughway. The first travelers brought wagons along a rough path beside the river, and by 1902 the Taylor State Road connected Denver and Grand Junction. When the interstate highway system was first conceived, there were no plans to connect Denver with Utah, but by the 1960s it became clear that I-70 would need to be extended west.

The Glenwood Canyon section of the highway became one of the most difficult engineering feats of its day. To preserve the canyon's fragile environment, special care was taken to avoid unnecessary blasting. Huge retaining walls, tunnels, and complex bridges had to be created. Construction on the road began in 1964 and was finally completed in 1993.

There are four rest stops accessible from both the highway and the paved path that runs east from Glenwood Springs to Dotsero. A favorite stop for exploring the canyon is the parking lot for the Hanging Lake Trail (see "Hiking").

Authority (970-925-8484; rfta.com), which provides shuttle service to all of Aspen's ski areas, the Maroon Bells, and Glenwood Springs.

✳ To See & Do

&. **Hot Springs Pool** (970-945-6571 or 1-800-537-7946; hotspringspool.com), 401 N. River St. Open daily during peak season 7:30–10, off peak 9–10. A visit to Glenwood Springs must include a day, or at least a few hours, of soaking and swimming in the town's legendary Hot Springs Pool. The sandstone lodge and bathing pools were built in the 1880s. The first guests to "take the waters" in Glenwood stayed across the street at Hotel Colorado. (The Hot Springs Lodge was built in 1986.) The spring expels 3.5 million gallons of mineral-rich spring water every day. This water is channeled into two pools—the smaller hot pool, which stays about 104 degrees F, and the large main pool where the water is a more tolerable 90 degrees F. In the summer, there's a Kiddie Pool with fountains for young children, plus two waterslides for kids of all ages. Adult pool $15.75–23.25, and children (3–12) $10.75–14.25. Additional fees for waterslide, mini-golf, and towel and suit rental.

&. ☂ **Yampah Spa & Salon** (970-945-0667; yampahspa.com), 709 E. Sixth St. Open daily 9–9. Another way to enjoy the region's geothermic qualities is to spend some time in the natural vapor caves at Yampah Spa & Salon. Hot mineral water flows through the floor of the cave's three main chambers, creating a natural steam bath. Vapor cave pass $15.

Glenwood Caverns Adventure Park (1-800-530-1635; glenwoodcaverns.com), 51000 Two Rivers Plaza Rd. Open year-round, daily in the summer 9–8. Reduced hours in the fall and spring, and only open Thu.–Sun. in the winter. Glenwood Caverns began as a cave tour. Thousands have come to explore the caverns and the historic Fairy Caves. Guests today can take the 70-minute walking tour or gear up for a more strenuous exploration of the caverns. The Adventure Tour and Wild Tour offer guests a chance to see parts of the caves not accessible without getting a little dirty. In addition to the caverns, the park has several attractions such as the Tramway, a climbing wall, and horseback riding. There are also rides like the Cliffhanger Roller Coaster and the Alpine Coaster. The former is a typical roller coaster in a mountain setting. The latter

HOT SPRINGS POOL

is like an alpine slide, but its track system allows for more dips, jumps, and hairpin turns. For a zip-line experience, try the Soaring Eagle Zip Ride, which takes you whizzing through the trees as you descend the 650 vertical feet to the end of the ride. Adult park entrance, tram ride, cave tour, and other attractions $40; children (3–12) $35.

⛄ **Frontier Historical Museum** (970-945-4448; glenwoodhistory.com), 1001 Colorado Ave. May–Sept., open Mon.–Sat. 11–4; Oct.–April, open Mon. and Thu.–Sat. 1–4. The museum documents the history of Glenwood Springs and Garfield County, from the first expedition by Captain James Sopris to the establishment and growth of Glenwood as a resort destination. Adults $5, seniors $4, kids free.

Doc Holliday's Grave. In 1887, Doc Holliday came to Glenwood Springs hoping to recoup somewhat from his tuberculosis. He died there on Nov. 8 of that year. Many speculate that the sulfur from the springs did his lungs more harm than good. He was buried in the Linwood Cemetery overlooking the town. The short hike to his grave begins at Bennett and E. 12th Street. There is a sign and a bench. It's a moderate climb with a great view of town at the top.

Ruedi Reservoir (basaltchamber.org/recreation/ruedi-reservoir). For a scenic drive, head south on US 82, turning east in Basalt on Frying Pan Rd. The windy drive up to Ruedi Reservoir is often a bit congested with cyclists. The route takes you along the Frying Pan River. At the end you are rewarded with a stop at the 1,000-acre Ruedi Reservoir.

✳ Outdoor Activities

ALPINE SKIING & SNOWBOARDING **Sunlight Mountain Resort** (970-945-7491 or 1-800-445-7931; sunlightmtn.com), 10901 CR 117. Lifts open 9–4. This intimate ski area has 470 skiable acres, with 67 runs and a 2,010-foot vertical drop. The majority of terrain is rated for intermediate skiers, with advanced skiers and beginners splitting the remainder. The terrain park has plenty of new jib park features with jumps, fun boxes, and rails.

Sunlight Mountain Ski & Bike Shop (970-945-9425; sunlightmtn.com), 309 Ninth St. You can rent ski equipment on the mountain or in town at the resort's ski and bike shop. This is also a great place to rent skis for those staying in Glenwood but skiing in Aspen.

BICYCLING **Glenwood Canyon Bike Path.** A 17-mile paved path runs along the Colorado River, through Glenwood Canyon, from Glenwood Springs to Dotsero. There is little elevation gain along the scenic route, making for an enjoyable ride in either direction.

Sunlight Mountain Ski & Bike Shop (970-945-9425; sunlightmtn.com), 309 Ninth St. For a nice day trip, the shop offers bike rental and shuttle ride packages. For $25 (kids $20), you get a bike and a drop-off anywhere along the Glenwood Canyon Bike Path.

CROSS-COUNTRY SKIING & SNOWSHOEING **Sunlight's Cross-Country Skiing and Snowshoeing** (970-945-7491 or 1-800-445-7931; sunlightmtn.com), 10901 CR 117. Sunlight Mountain Resort has 18 miles of groomed ski and snowshoe trails. Equipment can be rented at Sunlight Mountain Ski & Bike Shop in town (309 Ninth St.) or at the mountain. There is no fee for use of the trails.

FISHING **Roaring Fork Anglers** (970-945-0180 or 1-800-781-8120; alpineangling .com), 2205 Grand Ave. This outfitter has been serving anglers for more than 25 years. Its guides will take you out on the Roaring Fork, Colorado, Frying Pan, and Crystal rivers. With hundreds of miles of great trout water in the region, these folks can get you to the sweet spots. Half-day wading trip $250 (cheaper per person when you bring friends). Half-day float trip $400.

GOLF **Glenwood Springs Golf Club** (970-945-7086; glenwoodgolf.com), 193 Sunny Acres Rd. Since 1952, golfers have been enjoying this nine-hole course in northwest Glenwood Springs. Greens fees $40.

Rifle Creek Golf Club (970-625-1093 or 1-888-247-0370; riflecreekgc.com), 3004 CO 325, Rifle. This course was designed in 1960 to take advantage of the area's natural beauty. Following the terrain led the back nine to be a more target-oriented course than the more traditional front nine. Greens fees $43.

TRAM TO GLENWOOD CAVERNS

HANGING LAKE

HIKING **Hanging Lake Trail,** just off I-70 in the heart of Glenwood Canyon. To find the trailhead, you must travel east on the interstate. If you're heading west, turn around at the Grizzly Creek rest area. This trail is several miles west of the Shoshone exit. From the trailhead, it's 1 mile to the lake, but a steep mile. At the top, hikers are rewarded with a beautiful mountain lake, fed by several waterfalls cascading from the wooded cliff above. With more than 80,000 hikers making the trek up to Hanging Lake every year, it is important that everyone follow the three basic rules that have been put in place to protect the trail and the lake: (1) leave no trace, (2) no dogs on the trail, and (3) no swimming in the lake.

PADDLING & RAFTING **Colorado Whitewater Rafting** (970-945-8477 or 1-800-993-7238; coloradowhitewaterrafting.com), 2000 Devereux Rd. This rafting outfitter is a local favorite. It has full- and half-day trips, but the most popular is the three-hour tour through Glenwood Canyon on the Colorado River. Adult half-day trip $52 and youth (under 13) $42.

    Rock Gardens Adventures (970-945-6737 or 1-800-958-6737; rockgardens.com), 1308 CR 129. The Shoshone Half-Day trip is RGA's most popular. It's a float down the Colorado River through Glenwood Canyon. Adults $52 and youths $42.

✳ Lodging

HOTELS There are several chains in Glenwood Springs. Hampton Inn is one of the nicer of those next to the highway, but for lodging with a local flavor, try some of these.

 ♿ ♨ (𝕨)) **Hotel Colorado** (970-945-6511 or 1-800-544-3998; hotelcolorado.com), 526 Pine St. Hotel Colorado was built in 1893 to offer first-class accommodations for wealthy travelers who were making their way to Glenwood Springs to take the waters. Over the years, many presidents have stayed here, including Teddy Roosevelt, who made several visits. He once stayed for three weeks in 1905 while hunting bear. The tradition of elegance continues today at this five-star hotel. The hotel has several eateries, including a fantastic restaurant, Baron's, and a courtyard café in the summer. Rooms $129–499.

♿ ♨ (𝕨)) **Hotel Denver** (970-945-6565 or 1-800-826-8820; thehoteldenver.com), 402 Seventh St. This historic hotel has all the conveniences modern travelers have come to expect but with the charm and comfort of an intimate lodge. The rooms are tastefully decorated with thick quilts and antiques. Hardwood floors, four-poster and sleigh beds, and great views of the springs are found in many rooms. The hotel's largest suite, the Cupola, has a kitchenette, three televisions, and a private rooftop hot tub. Rooms $119–399.

♿ (𝕨)) **Hot Springs Lodge** (970-945-6571 or 1-800-537-7946; hotspringspool.com), 415 E. Sixth St., across the street from the springs and next to Hotel Colorado. One of the best amenities is that guests get free access to the Hot Springs Pool—on the day they check in through the day they check out. Otherwise, the accommodations are pretty standard. Rooms $139–378.

BED & BREAKFASTS (𝕨)) **The B&B on Mitchell Creek** (970-945-4002; mitchell creekbb.com), 1686 Mitchell Creek Rd.

Overlooking Mitchell Creek, this secluded B&B offers two rooms with king-size beds and a private entrance. Each room has its own deck and fire pit for campfires along the creek. A full breakfast is served every day. Rooms $145.

Four Mile Creek (970-945-4004; four milecreek.com), 6471 CR 117. This B&B is part of the Four Mile Ranch, originally homesteaded in 1885. Two rooms are available in the historic log home, and there are two log cabins that sleep up to four guests. A full breakfast is served every morning in the main dining room. Rooms $95 and cabins $145–155.

HISTORIC HOTEL COLORADO

CAMPGROUNDS ♿ **Glenwood Canyon Resort** (970-945-6737 or 1-800-958-6737; glenwoodcanyonresort.com), 1308 CR 129. Open year-round. Located just west of Glenwood Springs, the resort is right off exit 119 (the same as the No Name rest area). There are sites for RVs and tents, and the resort rents out cabins. The campground is well shaded and there are fantastic tent sites right along the Colorado River. Warm showers and coin-operated laundry are available. And the resort has ready access to the Glenwood Canyon Bike Path and fishing on the Colorado River. Tent sites $28 ($46 for sites by the river), RV $60, and camper cabins start at $45, up to $199.

Where to Eat

DINING OUT ♿ 🍸 **Rivers** (970-928-8813; theriversrestaurant.com), 2525 S. Grand Ave. Open daily for dinner at 4:30. Overlooking the Roaring Fork River, Rivers Restaurant serves innovative American cuisine. The outdoor deck is open when weather permits. Start with an appetizer, such as the grilled elk quesadilla, and continue with the fantastic warmed spinach salad with smoked bacon and toasted walnuts. Dinner entrées include steak and fresh seafood as well as duck and game. Entrées $16–30.

♿ 🍸 **Riviera Restaurant** (970-945-7692; rivieraglenwood.com), 702 Grand Ave. Open daily for dinner at 4:30. The Riviera Supper Club sign that hangs out front remains because it is a Glenwood Springs landmark. The restaurant inside, however, is a completely new venture. The open dining room, now full of natural light, was transformed with contemporary décor. The eclectic menu features classic dishes such as prime rib and porterhouse steak as well as the more daring Riviera duck and seafood risotto. Guests are entertained by live piano music. Entrées $13–28.

JUICY LUCY'S STEAKHOUSE

EATING OUT **Daily Bread** (970-945-6253), 729 Grand Ave. Open daily for breakfast and lunch. This café and bakery serves breakfast and lunch. The menu is full of hearty and affordable food. All the baked goods are made on the premises. A regular favorite is the cinnamon roll French toast. Dishes $4–10.

🍸 **Italian Underground** (970-945-6422), 715 Grand Ave. Open daily for dinner 5–10. With red-and-white-checkered tablecloths, brick walls, and a dining room filled with antiques, this out-of-the way Italian eatery has tons of charm. It also could very well be the best Italian place in town. It serves everything from pizza to chicken cacciatore and there's a full bar. Dishes $13–15.

♿ 🍸 **Juicy Lucy's Steakhouse** (970-945-4619; juicylucyssteakhouse.com), 308 Seventh St. Open daily. Sun.–Thu. 11–9:30. Fri.–Sat. 11–10. This family steakhouse serves only prime graded beef that is hand cut and aged on the premises. It also serves chicken, fish, lamb, and elk. Just underneath the bridge, with the right seat, you can enjoy the nearby river from the window. Most entrées $12–20; filet mignon and king crab legs push the high end up to $40.

BAKERIES & COFFEE SHOPS ☐ ((ͻ))
Sacred Grounds (970-928-8804; sacredgrounds.biz), 725 Grand Ave. Open daily at 7. In addition to a full coffee menu of espresso, cappuccino, and mocha, Sacred Grounds has deli sandwiches and fantastic baked goods. Be sure to try a brownie if you get a chance. Or grab a boxed lunch for the trail.

BARS, TAVERNS, & BREW PUBS ☐ ☐
Glenwood Canyon Brewing Company (970-945-1276; glenwoodcanyonbrewpub.com), 402 Seventh St. Open daily for lunch and dinner 11–10. Located on the first floor of The Hotel Denver, this brew pub has a full bar and wine menu, and serves lunch and dinner daily. Eight of its handcrafted beers are on tap, and each goes great with a game of pool in the billiard room.

✳ Selective Shopping

Book Grove (970-384-0992 or 1-800-303-7290; bookgrove.com), 801 Blake Ave. Open Wed.–Sat. 10–5:30. This bookstore sells used and out-of-print books, including first editions and many autographed books.

✳ Special Events

June: **Strawberry Days** (970-945-6589; glenwoodchamber.com/strawberry-days-festival.html). The three-day Strawberry Festival kicks off with a parade, led by a vintage car show. There's live entertainment for the whole family, an artisan fair, and free strawberries and ice cream.

GRAND JUNCTION & COLORADO'S WESTERN SLOPE

Colorado's Western Slope is often overlooked as a tourist destination. This is a shame. The region has two of the state's most stunning national monuments—the Colorado National Monument and Dinosaur National Monument. There are also a number of beautiful state parks, one of which features a long stretch of the Colorado River. Towns along the Western Slope run on the small side. As such, they are home to friendly, hardworking people who understand hospitality. Even Grand Junction, the Mesa County seat with 140,000 residents, has a certain small-town charm.

The little tourism there is centers on Grand Junction. In recent years, there has been a surge of interest in the region. Interest in small independent wineries has been growing for more than a decade along Colorado's Front Range. As these wineries seek to educate their customers on Colorado wines, they inevitably point west toward the vineyards that produce their grapes. As an agricultural center, Grand Junction and Palisade have been producing fruit—especially peaches, apricots, and grapes—since the 19th century. As these new wine tourists have learned about the state's wine industry, their curiosity has been peaked, and more and more people are coming out to tour the wineries and vineyards of western Colorado.

There also have been an increasing number of recreational tourists. Fruita (pronounced froo-ta) has become known for its mountain biking trails. Miles and miles of technical singletrack and the ever-prized slickrock draw thousands of riders annually.

Grand Junction and the Grand Valley also have become prized for the region's natural beauty. The nearby Grand Mesa rises 10,000 feet above the valley floor, making it the tallest mesa (or flat-topped mountain) in the world. To the north, you see the eastern section of the Bookcliffs, which continue west nearly 200 miles into Utah.

This boom in tourism has allowed Grand Junction to offer more resources for travelers. The town offers everything from hotel chains along the highway to several exceptional B&Bs. More than a dozen restaurants can be found in Grand Junction's downtown area. As the town becomes savvier about catering to visitors, be sure to stop by the local visitor centers to see what's new.

GUIDANCE **Grand Junction Visitor and Convention Bureau** (970-244-1480 or 1-800-962-2547; visitgrandjunction.com), 740 Horizon Dr., Grand Junction. Open in the summer Mon.–Sat. 8:30–6, Sun. 9–6; winter, Mon.–Sat. 8:30–5, Sun. 9–5.

Colorado Welcome Center at Dinosaur (970-374-2205; colorado.com/colorado-official-state-welcome-center/colorado-welcome-center-dinosaur), 101 E. Stegosaurus Dr., at the corner of US 40 and CO 64 in Dinosaur. Open daily in the summer 8–6. Open 9–5 the rest of the year. Closed Dec.–Feb.

Colorado Welcome Center at Fruita (970-858-9335; colorado.com/colorado-official-state-welcome-center/colorado-welcome-center-fruita), 340 CO 340, Fruita (exit 19 on I-70). Open daily in the summer 8–6. Open 8–5 the rest of the year. Complimentary maps and untold hundreds of brochures covering all of Colorado.

Grand Junction & The Western Slope

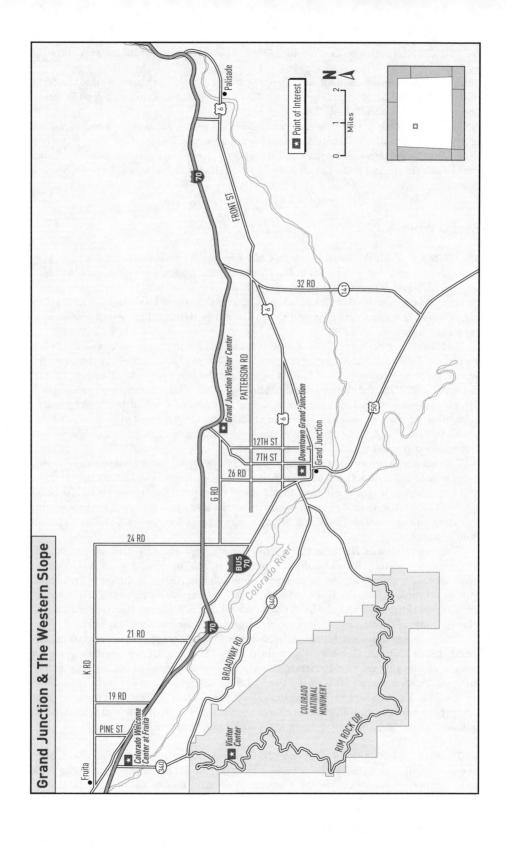

GETTING THERE *By car:* The Western Slope is easily accessed from the east and west by I-70.

By air: **Grand Junction Regional Airport** (970-244-9100; gjairport.com) is located 1 mile north of I-70 off Horizon Dr. (exit 31). The airport serves airlines such as Frontier, Southwest, Delta, and United.

By train: **Amtrak** (1-800-872-7245; amtrak.com) offers train service from its station at 339 S. First St., Grand Junction. The station is open daily 10–6.

By bus: **Greyhound** (970-242-6012 or 1-800-231-2222; greyhound.com) operates regular service to and from Grand Junction from its station at 230 S. Fifth St. Station closed daily 4:30 PM–10:30 PM.

✳ To See & Do

MUSEUMS ♿ ♈ **Museums of Western Colorado** (museumofwesternco.com) has several museum and historical sites in the Grand Junction area, each exploring different aspects of the region's history. Admission can be purchased for each attraction or you can purchase a combination ticket that gets you into the three following sites: Museum of the West, Dinosaur Journey, and Cross Orchards Historic Site. Adult combo $12, seniors $10, and children $8.

♈ **Museum of the West** (970-242-0971; museumofwesternco.com/museum-of-the-west), 462 Ute Ave., Grand Junction. Open Mon.–Sat. 9–5, Sun. noon–4, in the summer. Rest of the year Mon.–Sat. 10–4. This museum tells the story not just of Colorado, but of the American West. Exhibitions are designed for interaction—not merely rows of glass displays where you look but can't touch. The museum has one of the finest firearm collections around, as well as an excellent exhibition of Southwest pottery. They even have a full-sized WAAIME uranium mine. Adult admission $7, seniors $6, children $4, and family groups $20.

♈ **Dinosaur Journey** (970-858-7282; museumofwesternco.com/dinosaur-journey), 550 Jurassic Ct., Fruita. Open daily in the summer 9–5. Rest of the year Mon.–Sat. 10–4 and Sun. noon–4. Step back in time to the age of dinosaurs. Exhibits include full-sized models that "come to life" and demonstrations that show how it must have looked and felt when dinosaurs roamed the earth. Adult admission $9, seniors $7, children $5, and family groups $25.

♈ **Cross Orchards Historic Site** (970-434-9814; museumofwesternco.com/cross-orchards), 3073 F Rd., Grand Junction. Open May–Oct., Thu.–Sat. 9–4. Cross Orchards gives guests a glimpse back into Grand Junction's agricultural history. Costumed guides introduce life as it was in the early part of the 20th century. The orchards' barn and packing shed and the bunkhouse are all on the National Register of Historic Places. Adult admission $5, seniors $4, children $3.50, and family groups $11.

♈ ♿ **Gateway Canyons Automobile Museum** (970-931-2895; gatewayautomuseum .com), 43224 CO 141, Gateway. Open daily 10–5. This 30,000-square-foot museum houses 40 classic cars that illustrate the historic development of automobile design and performance during the past 100 years. The prize of the collection is the 1954 Oldsmobile F-88. This concept car was designed by the legendary Harley Earl but never went into production. All the vehicles here have been preserved in or restored to showroom quality. Adult admission $15, seniors $10, youth 12 and under free.

NATIONAL MONUMENTS **Colorado National Monument** (970-858-3617, ext. 360; nps.gov/colm). The park can be accessed from Grand Junction and Fruita. The park visitor center is open daily in the summer (Memorial Day to Labor Day) from 8–6.

COLORADO NATIONAL MONUMENT

Open the rest of the year 9–5 (except Dec. and Jan. when it's 9–4). To get there, take exit 19 on I-70 in Fruita and follow CO 340 south until you see the turn for the park. The visitor center is about 4.5 miles into the park on the left.

In 1906, a man named John Otto came to Grand Junction and was awed by the beauty of the nearby canyons. Most locals believed the canyon lands to be inaccessible, but Otto settled down there and began building trails. He was convinced that the region should be preserved as a national park and set about making that happen. In 1911, President Taft created Colorado National Monument, and Otto was paid a symbolic $1/month salary to stay as the park's first caretaker (he remained until 1927).

The beauty of the park is undeniable. The Uncompahgre Plateau rises over 2,000 feet above the Grand Valley, south of Grand Junction and Fruita. It is part of the greater Colorado Plateau, which includes geological wonders such as the Grand Canyon and the Arches (of Arches National Park in Utah). Thousands of years of erosion have dug deep canyons in the plateau and have created numerous rock formations. Independence Monument, for example, was once part of a canyon wall, but now stands alone, 450 feet above the canyon floor. Other rock structures, such as the Coke Ovens and the ever-popular Window Rock, draw more than a quarter of a million visitors a year.

The best introduction to Colorado National Monument is to simply drive the length of Rim Rock Drive from either end of the park, stopping at the overlooks to take in the scenery. Coming from the east, the rock formations get increasingly dramatic. From the west, the visitor center offers a nice orientation to the park. It can give you information on camping and backcountry hikes as well as the geological history of the plateau and canyons.

Once you've driven the main road and gazed over a number of overlooks, consider taking a short hike. The hike from the visitor center out to Window Rock, for example, is a level 1.5-mile round-trip. Another trail on the east end of Rim Rock Drive is the Serpents Trail, which follows an older section of the main road. This 1.75-mile hike (one way) has more than 50 switchbacks as it climbs the plateau. Park admission $10/vehicle and individuals (hikers and cyclists and such) $5; good for 7 days.

Dinosaur National Monument (970-374-3000 or 435-781-7700; nps.gov/dino), 4545 E. US 40, Dinosaur. The temporary visitor center near Jensen, Utah, is open daily in the summer (Memorial Day to Labor Day) 8:30–5:30, and the rest of the year 8:30–4:30. The Canyon Area Visitor Center near Dinosaur, CO, is open daily in the summer (Memorial Day to Labor Day) from 9–4. In the spring and fall, the center is closed on Monday and Tuesday. It's also closed in the winter, Nov.–Feb.

The big attraction at Dinosaur National Monument was the chance to see and touch fossils at the Dinosaur Quarry Visitor Center. The two-story building surrounded a wall of dinosaur fossils, still embedded in the rock, allowing visitors to see them up close in a sheltered and air-conditioned environment. Built in 1957 on expansive soils, the foundation of the Quarry Visitor Center has deteriorated over the years. In the summer of 2006, the building was determined to be a serious hazard and was closed. In October 2011, the new Quarry Visitor Center and Quarry Exhibit Hall were opened to the public.

Throughout the summer, ranger-guided tours take visitors on a Fossil Discovery Hike to see fossils in an ancient riverbed. There are also two auto tours that explore other aspects of the park—brochures available at all visitor centers. The Tour of the Tilted Rocks takes visitors 11 miles from the Quarry out on Cub Creek Road to the historic Josie Morris Cabin. Along the way you'll pass a prehistoric petroglyph site and some nature trails. While out at Josie's cabin, you might want to take a little hike on the Box Canyon Trail, an easy walk with some great shade from the summer heat.

The Journey through Time tour begins at the visitor center near Dinosaur. This 62-mile round-trip introduces visitors to the natural aspects of the park—not so much here about dinosaurs. It highlights the park's ecosystems and its geological beauty.

For a river-rafting trip through the park, contact **Adrift Adventures** (435-789-3600 or 1-800-824-0150; adrift.com) about one-day and multiday trips down the Yampa River. For multiday trips, you should also consider **Adventure Bound** (1-800-423-4668; raft-colorado.com).

Park admission for noncommercial, private vehicles $20, motorcycles $15, individuals hiking or biking into the park $10; good for 7 days.

WINERIES ♿ **Carlson Vineyards** (970-464-5554 or 1-888-464-5554; carlsonvineyards.com), 461 35 Rd., Palisade. Open daily 10–5:45 for tasting and tours. Carlson Vineyards Winery has been producing wine since 1988, and it has become a required stop on all regional winery tours. If Parker or Mary Carlson are around (and they are, more often than not), be sure to take a moment to chat about their wines and perhaps ask for a tour of the winery.

♿ **Plum Creek Winery** (970-464-7586; plumcreekwinery.com), 3708 G Rd., Palisade. Tasting room is open daily 10–5. Plum Creek holds Colorado winery license #10—no other winery in the state has one that's older. Doug and Sue Phillips began growing grapes in 1980 and opened the winery in 1984 using only Colorado grapes. When visiting the tasting room, ask about getting a tour of the winery (but call ahead if you have a large group).

♿ **Two Rivers Chateau and Winery** (970-255-1471 or 1-866-312-9463; tworiverswinery.com), 2087 Broadway. The tasting room and winery at Two Rivers are surrounded by 15 acres of vineyard. The property is relatively new—before 1999, it was a vacant lot—but

TWO RIVERS CHATEAU AND WINERY

the owners have clearly worked hard to create an Old World feel. When you visit the tasting room, be sure to ask about a tour of the winery.

✳ Outdoor Activities

ALPINE SKIING & SNOWBOARDING **Powderhorn Resort** (970-268-5700; powder horn.com), 48338 Powderhorn Rd., Mesa. Lifts run 9–4 in-season. Half of the trails at Powderhorn are designated intermediate and 20 percent are beginner. The ski area has 600 skiable acres and gives skiers an overall 1,650-foot vertical drop. The resort gets 250 inches of snow annually, meaning the resort doesn't often have to rely on snow-making equipment. The two terrain parks, Pepsi Tyro Park and Mt. Dew Junction Park, offer many features to tackle that get more and more difficult as you improve your skills (although there are no pipes—half, super, or otherwise).

GOLF **Redlands Mesa Golf Course** (970-263-9270; redlandsmesa.com), 2325 West Ridges Blvd. A couple of years back, *Golf Digest* magazine named this course the Best New Affordable Golf Course in the U.S. The course blends into the desert landscape, keeping native features intact wherever possible—including many elevation changes. Greens fees $55–65.

MOUNTAIN BIKING In Fruita, you can find some of the best singletrack in the country. Much of the effort was spearheaded by Troy Rarick, the owner over at Over the Edge Sports. To get acquainted with the local trails, check in at Over the Edge and start asking questions. **Kokopelli's Loop Trail System** offers a number of rides. You can piece together loops to fill the day with as much riding as you like. Try Mary's Loop for a technical ride with some slickrock. Kokopelli's Trail takes riders 142 miles from Loma to Moab. Campsites along the way are strategically placed for riders making the multiday trip. The trail is a combination of singletrack, dirt roads, and some pavement.

Over the Edge Sports (970-858-7220; otesports.com), 202 E. Aspen Ave., Fruita. OTE rents a fleet of full-suspension mountain bikes. Day rates $90.

✳ Green Space

James M. Robb–Colorado River State Park (970-434-3388; cpw.state.co.us/places togo/parks/JamesMRobbColoradoRiver), Clifton, on both sides of the Colorado River from Fruita in the west to Island Acres east of Palisade. Open daily 5–10 for day use. The park has some nice hiking trails and provides access to the Colorado River for boating and fishing. Daily park pass $7.

✳ Lodging

HOTELS ☂ ☀ (ᵠ) **Gateway Canyons Resort** (970-263-9270; gatewaycanyons .com), 43200 CO 141, Gateway. The resort has several lodging options. Kayenta Lodge features rooms and suites. The rooms are decorated in a subtle southwestern style, complementing the resort's adobe exterior. Casitas offers condos with full kitchens, two bedrooms, and one bath. These condos can sleep six, and pets are welcome. Finally, Kiva Lodge has 38 luxury rooms and suites that open out to the resort's pool area. Rooms $300–2,050, more for premium rooms and suites.

BED & BREAKFASTS (ᵠ) **The Bookcliffs** (970-261-3938 or 970-434-5974; thebook cliffsbnb.com), 3153 F Rd. Located at the east end of town, south of I-70 and close to the I-70 Business Loop, this modest B&B is accessible to all of Grand Junction. The inn's three bedrooms are all on the main floor, warmly decorated with Tuscan accents. Each room has a private bath, and the innkeepers serve a really great breakfast. Rooms $155–150.

☂ (ᵠ) **Castle Creek** (970-241-9105; castlecreekbandb.com), 638 Horizon Dr. The innkeepers at Castle Creek designed their bed and breakfast from the ground up with the idea that both men and women should feel at home when they stay at a B&B. The four rooms at the inn are large, with huge bathrooms. Amenities include king-size beds, jetted tubs for two, cable TV, and wireless Internet. All the rooms are tastefully decorated. The large deck off the back of the house offers guests a place to rest with an overlooking view of the nearby creek. Full breakfast served on weekends—continental breakfast on weekdays. Rooms $115–155.

(ᵠ) **Los Altos** (970-256-0964; losaltos grandjunction.com), 375 Hillview Dr. From its own lofty hilltop, Los Altos offers guests stunning views of Grand Mesa and Colorado National Monument. The inn has seven rooms, each with a private bath and French doors that open out to the wraparound balcony. Try the top-floor Vista Suite, with its private captain's walk, for the best views in the house. A full gourmet breakfast is served every morning. Rooms $129–215.

(ᵠ) **Willow Pond** (970-243-4958; willowpondbnb.com), 662 26 Rd. This fabulously remodeled 1916 farmhouse on its wooded lot is close to downtown Grand Junction but seems a world away. The hosts are known for their hospitality. Breakfast is prepared for guests each morning. Rooms $120–165.

CAMPGROUNDS **James M. Robb–Colorado River State Park** (970-434-3388;

cpw.state.co.us/placestogo/parks/JamesMRobbColoradoRiver), Clifton. There's camping in the Fruita Section of the Colorado River State Park. Forty-four sites for RV and tent camping sit next to the Colorado River. The nearby lake has a swimming beach and offers opportunities for fishing. Although the campground is open year-round, coin-operated laundry and showers are closed in the winter. Tent sites $18 and RV sites $24–28.

✳ Where to Eat

DINING OUT ♿ ⏦ **Le Rouge Restaurant & Piano Bar** (970-257-1777; lerougerestaurant.com), 317 Main St. Open for dinner daily at 5. Open for lunch seasonally. Once called Rendez Vous, and then Moulin Rouge, with the addition of a wine bar and live jazz piano, it is now simply "Le Rouge." The menu offers outstanding French cuisine and live music on Fridays and Saturday. Entrées $22–47.

♿ ⏦ **626 on Rood** (970-257-7663; 626onrood.com), 626 Rood Ave. Open Mon.–Sat. 11–11 and Sun. 4–10. One of Grand Junction's finest restaurants, this eatery has a wine bar and touts itself as *the* place of modern American cuisine. Black-bean burgers and cherry-wood smoked duck salad have featured on the lunch menu. Steak and fresh seafood are prepared nightly for dinner. If you get a chance, be sure to try one of the many dishes that feature local meat and produce. Entrées $20–35 ($140 for the 40-ounce Wagyu ribeye).

EATING OUT ♿ **Main Street Cafe** (mainstreetcafegj.com), 504 Main St. Open daily 7–4 (except Sun. when they close at 3). This 1950s restaurant on Main Street in the heart of Grand Junction serves classic diner food for breakfast and lunch. The mashed potatoes are made from scratch, and there's always a blue-plate special. This is the perfect place for a hearty yet cheap breakfast. For the full experience, order an

MAIN STREET CAFÉ

FRUIT STAND IN PALISADE

old-fashioned fountain drink. Entrées run about $10.

 ♿ **Nepal Restaurant** (970-242-2233; nepalgj.com), 356 Main St. Downtown Grand Junction has a bit of everything, including great Nepali and Indian food. In true Indian restaurant style, there's a lunch buffet with tandoori chicken and fresh naan. Dinner $9–15 and lunch buffet $8.95.

BAKERIES & COFFEE SHOPS ♿ (((•)))

Main Street Bagel (gjmainstreetbagels .com), 559 Main St. This is where you go in Grand Junction for great coffee and fresh bagels. Right outside is a fountain with some patio seating—a nice option when there's live music downtown. Be sure to try the artisan breads.

✳ Special Events

April/May: **Fruita Fat Tire Festival** (970-858-7220; fruitafattirefestival.com), Fruita. Celebrate mountain biking with a ride on the best singletrack around—later, grab a beer and listen to some live music.

August: **Palisade Peach Festival** (palisadepeachfest.com), Palisade. For nearly five decades, the good folks of Palisade have been celebrating their peaches. The festival features live music, lots of great food, and artists hawking their goods. And of course, there are the peaches.

September: **Colorado Mountain Winefest** (coloradowinefest.com), Palisade. The other agricultural gem of the Western Slope is the grape. And good grapes mean wine. Wine tasting, grape stomping, and live music make for a very festive weekend.

SOUTH-CENTRAL COLORADO

■

COLORADO SPRINGS

CAÑON CITY & THE GOLD RANGE

UPPER ARKANSAS VALLEY

SAN LUIS VALLEY

COLORADO SPRINGS

A mild climate and stunning scenery, as well as endless recreational opportunities in the nearby mountains, make Colorado Springs a great place to live. It's also a great place to visit, at least judging by the city's 6 million annual visitors. There are more than 50 attractions—museums, springs, parks, caves, the zoo—not to mention Pikes Peak.

Colorado Springs started out as a tourist town. In 1871, General William Palmer, builder of the Denver & Rio Grande Railroad, decided to start a resort community and purchased 10,000 acres east of what is now Old Colorado City. Palmer was a masterful town planner. The city he built had wide, tree-lined boulevards. In an attempt to set Colorado Springs apart from its rowdy neighbors in Colorado City and Manitou Springs, the making, selling, and drinking of alcohol was prohibited (not to be repealed until the end of Prohibition in 1933). In 1883, Palmer built The Antlers hotel. To market his new endeavor, he named the town Colorado Springs and latched onto the bubbling waters in nearby Manitou Springs as a central theme in his advertising. He even enlisted the services of a doctor whose job it was to promote the "taking of the waters" as a healthy, invigorating activity.

In the 1890s, Spencer Penrose moved to Colorado. He made a fortune when gold was found in Cripple Creek. In turn he invested heavily in Colorado Springs. He built The Broadmoor hotel, Cheyenne Mountain Zoo, and Pikes Peak Highway. He continues to contribute to the well-being of all Coloradoans through El Pomar Foundation—an organization that gives $20 million to nonprofits throughout the state each year.

Today, Colorado Springs has a population of over 400,000, and the greater metro area is closing in on 575,000. With Fort Carson, Peterson, and Schriever air force bases, the Air Force Academy, and NORAD, the military has a significant presence in the Springs and remains the city's largest employer. In 1991, Focus on the Family, a Christian organization that offers advice on marriage relationships and child-rearing, moved its headquarters from California to Colorado Springs. This significantly bolstered the community's conservative image.

Visitors who come to Colorado Springs have all the conveniences and resources of a major metropolitan—restaurants, malls and shopping centers, dozens of hotels, museums, and art galleries. The historic towns of Old Colorado City and Manitou Springs offer quaint shopping districts. Visitors also can take advantage of the great outdoors just beyond their hotel room, as the Garden of the Gods, Cave of the Winds, and, of course, Pikes Peak, are just moments away.

GUIDANCE (ꜛ) **Colorado Springs Convention and Visitors Bureau** (1-877-745-3773; visitcos.com), 515 S. Cascade Ave. The bureau is home to the Pikes Peak Visitors Center. Open summers Mon.–Fri. 8:30–5 and Sat. and Sun. 9–5. Other seasons open Mon.–Fri. 8:30–5. The bureau has information on all local attractions. The staff are well informed and can help guests arrange lodging, find places to eat, and choose fun stuff to do and see.

Manitou Springs Visitors Bureau (719-685-5089 or 1-800-642-2567; manitou springs.org), 354 Manitou Ave. As you come into town from Colorado Springs and US 24, the visitor center is located on the right side of the road, just before you hit the main

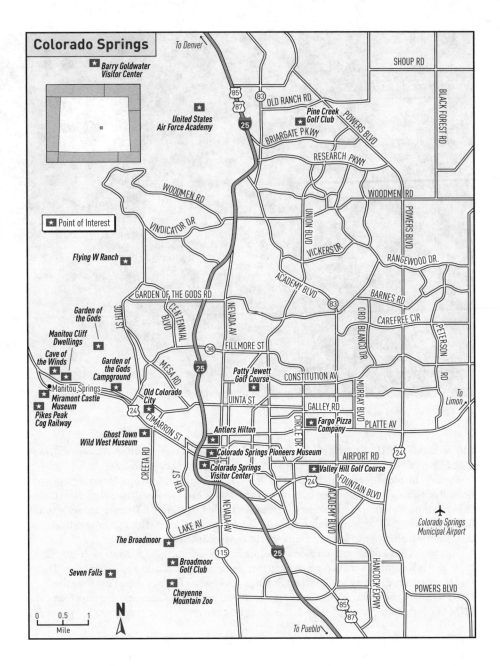

drag. The maps here show where all of Manitou's historic springs can be found. There are even cups for those who want to drink from each spring as they go.

More websites:

pikes-peak.com

GETTING THERE *By car:* Interstate 25 runs right through the heart of Colorado Springs and is your main route from the north and south. Coming in from eastern

ONE OF MANITOU'S MANY SPRINGS

Colorado on I-70, US 24 cuts off in Limon and makes a straight path southwest to Colorado Springs. From the west, the main routes are I-70 and US 50 to I-25.

By air: The most accessible airport is, of course, **Colorado Springs Airport** (719-550-1972; flycos.com), 7770 Milton E. Proby Pkwy. Many cities have direct flights to Colorado Springs. Be sure to also check prices for flights to Denver. **Denver International Airport** (1-800-247-2336; flydenver.com) is about 100 miles north of Colorado Springs, and it's often cheaper to land in Denver and rent a car there.

By train: There is no rail service to Colorado Springs, although **Amtrak** (1-800-872-7245; amtrak.com) has train terminals in Denver to the north, and you can take its Thruway bus service directly to Colorado Springs (see below for bus depot information).

By bus: **Greyhound** operates regular service to and from Colorado Springs from the TNM&O Terminal (719-635-1505 or 1-800-231-2222; greyhound.com), 120 S. Weber St.

GETTING AROUND *By car:* Getting around Colorado Springs is a pretty simple proposition. The city stretches out north to west along I-25, and that's the best bet for getting from one side of town to the other. Academy Boulevard is the other north–south corridor, and it meets up with I-25 at both ends of town. It is much slower going. Parking is plentiful in and around town.

By bus: The city operates the Metro, a complete public transportation system of buses. See the city website, springsgov.com, for a complete schedule. Adult fares $1.75 for a one-way pass or if using it for a few days you can purchase a 20-ride ticket for $32.

✳ To See & Do

Air Force Academy (www.usafa.af.mil). This sprawling 18,000-acre campus receives a million visitors every year. It's no wonder. Located at the base of the Rampart Range, the property has several hiking trails, a lake for fishing, and picnic areas. The academy itself is an attraction. A self-guided tour begins at the **Barry Goldwater Visitor Center** (719-333-2025), 2346 Academy Dr., # 102. The visitor center is open daily 9–5. The academy is open daily to visitors 8–6. Ask for the "Follow the Falcon" brochure, which will take you on a self-guided tour.

Many visitors will want to see the Cadet Chapel up close. The 17-spired chapel makes quite an impression rising above the trees and surrounding buildings. It is open for tours Mon.–Sat. 9–5, Sun. 1–5. The Air Force Academy and chapel tours are all free to the public.

🐾 ♿ **Cheyenne Mountain Zoo** (719-633-9925; cmzoo.org), 4250 Cheyenne Mountain Zoo Rd. Open daily 9–5. Cheyenne Mountain in southwest Colorado Springs is home to the only mountain zoo in the United States. As zoos go, it's pretty small—only 70 acres of the 146-acre site have been developed—but what it lacks in size is made up for with unique animal exhibitions and an unparalleled setting. Kids can feed and pet giraffes from a platform in the African Rift Valley or watch gorillas and orangutans in Primate World. In 2008, the zoo unveiled Rocky Mountain Wild, featuring grizzly bears, mountain lions, and moose. Adult admission $19.75, seniors $17.75, children (3–11) $14.75, and children under 3 75¢. Admission to the zoo allows you free access to the **Will Rogers Shrine of the Sun** (719-578-5367; cmzoo.org/index.php/about-the-zoo/history/will-rogers-shrine), 4250 Cheyenne Mountain Zoo Rd. Open daily at 9;

GIRAFFES AT CHEYENNE MOUNTAIN ZOO

closes an hour before the zoo. Built in 1937, the 80-foot observation tower affords views of the entire Colorado Springs area.

& ⸷ **Colorado Springs Fine Arts Center** (719-634-5583; csfineartscenter.org), 30 W. Dale St. Open daily 10–5. The FAC recently unveiled a 48,000-square-foot, two-story expansion. This is a significant addition for an art museum that is bringing in more visitors every year. The museum has an outstanding collection of Native American and Spanish colonial art. The traveling exhibitions are always interesting and worth a visit. Adult admission $15, children 12 and under free.

& ⸷ **Colorado Springs Pioneers Museum** (719-385-5990; cspm.org), 215 S. Tejon St. Open Tue.–Sat. 10–5. Located in the restored El Paso County Courthouse, the Pioneers Museum celebrates the history of Colorado Springs and the Pikes Peak region. The museum features a restored courtroom circa 1903 and a portion of Helen Hunt's cabin. The museum attracts thousands every year and is a great introduction to the history of the land and the people who have lived here. Admission is free.

Garden of the Gods (719-634-6666; gardenofgods.com), 1805 N. 30th St. The park grounds are open daily in the summer 5–11; winter 5–9. Maps are available at the **Garden of the Gods Visitor & Nature Center** (open daily in the summer 8–7; winter 8–5). The Garden of the Gods is an impressive park full of red sandstone formations known as hogbacks, which jut into the sky at an angle. The tallest is 320 feet high. Some of the juniper growing on the rocks are 1,000 years old. Tourists seem to especially enjoy climbing around Balanced Rock. There are 15 miles of trails here, many paved.

Dedicated in 1909, the land that is now the Garden of the Gods was given to the city with the understanding that it would always be open to the public, that no alcohol would be sold there, and that no building would be constructed except those necessary for the public use of the park. These rules still stand and continue to guide the decisions made by park officials. Admission is free.

& ⸷ **Ghost Town Wild West Museum** (719-634-0696; ghosttownmuseum.com), 400 S. 21st St. Open summer Mon.–Sat. 9–6 and Sun. 10–6; winter, daily 10–5. More tourist trap than museum, Ghost Town tries to re-create an Old West town circa 1880. In addition to the indoor Old Main Street with shooting galleries and old carriages, the museum has a petrified sequoia tree trunk that was discovered in the Florissant Fossil Beds and a bedroom suite that once belonged to President Chester A. Arthur. There is also a trough to try your hand at gold panning. Adult admission $7.50, children (6–16) $5, and children under 6 free.

⸷ **McAllister House Museum** (719-635-7925; mcallisterhouse.org), 423 N. Cascade Ave. Open summer Tue.–Sat. 10–4; winter, Thu.–Sat. 10–4. Closed the month of January. Built in 1873, the McAllister House preserves the charm and elegance of Colorado Springs in the 19th century. Guided tours offered daily. Adult admission $5, seniors $4, and children (6–12) $3. Children under 6 free.

⸷ **ProRodeo Hall of Fame** (719-528-4764; prorodeohalloffame.com), 101 ProRodeo Dr. Open daily in the summer 9–5; winter, Wed.–Sun. 9–5. For die-hard rodeo fans, there is no better attraction in town. This is the only museum in the world dedicated to the history and promotion of rodeo. Adult admission $8, seniors $7, military $6, children (6–12) $5, and kids under 6 free.

& **Seven Falls** (719-632-0765; broadmoor.com/broadmoor-adventures/seven-falls), 2850 S. Cheyenne Canyon Rd. Check the website for a complete listing of hours. The South Cheyenne Creek falls majestically 181 feet to the floor of a box canyon. The falls—the creek forms seven of them on its way down—can be viewed from above and below. A steep staircase climbs to the observation deck, but there's also an elevator for those who don't want to hike up the stairs. Along the top of the canyon, two hiking trails offer views of Colorado Springs or another attraction, Midnight Falls. At night, the Seven Falls are lighted for dramatic effect. The falls were owned by the Hall family for 70 years. The 2013 floods devastated the falls, and the attraction was closed for a time. The Broadmoor eventually purchased the property and set about restoring the falls, the facilities, and adding a fine dining establishment, Restaurant 1858. Adult day admission $14, children (2–12) $8.

↑ **Van Briggle Art Pottery Factory and Showroom** (719-633-7729; vanbriggle.com), 1024 South Tejon St. Van Briggle Pottery Co. was founded in 1901 and is one of the country's oldest art potteries. The pieces created here have a strong art nouveau sensibility and feature colors common to Chinese ceramics. Today, visitors can tour the factory and see how clay is transformed into art. Open Mon.–Sat. 9–5. Admission is free.

& ↑ **Western Museum of Mining and Industry** (719-488-0880 or 1-800-752-6558; wmmi.org), 225 North Gate Blvd. Open Mon.–Sat. 9–4 (until 5 in summer). The history of mining is the theme of this museum, and the focus is on the technology that has contributed to the history of mining and the people who have been a part of mining in the American West. Guided tours are offered twice daily at 10 and 1. Adult admission $9, seniors and students $7, children (4–12) $5, children under 3 free.

IN MANITOU SPRINGS

✇ ↑ **Arcade Amusements** (719-685-9815), 930 Block Manitou Ave., Manitou Springs. Open in the summer 10–10. Located right behind Patsy's, this alley is full of video games, from vintage to modern. World Famous Penny Arcade has classic 1980s favorites and some old classics. The Arcade Derby next door has an old horse racing game. If you like arcades, bring your pennies, dimes, and quarters and prepare to spend a couple of hours in heaven.

↑ **Cave of the Winds** (719-685-5444; caveofthewinds.com), 100 Cave of the Winds Rd. (exit 41 off US 24), Manitou Springs. Open every day but Christmas; 9–9 in summer and 10–5 in winter. The cave was discovered by two boys on a church outing in

VINTAGE PINBALL IN MANITOU SPRINGS

Williams Canyon near Manitou Springs in the spring of 1880. It soon opened to the public for tours and has been attracting the adventurous for over a century. The popular Discovery Tour takes guests on a quarter-mile walk through the cave. The 45-minute tour isn't overly strenuous, but you must climb 200 steps as you move through the caverns. The Lantern Tour takes guests underground with only handheld lanterns to light the path—much as visitors would have experienced the cave 100 years ago. Discovery Tour: adult admission $20, children (6–12) $12, children under 6 free. Lantern Tour: adult admission $30, children (ages 6–11) $15, not open to kids under 6.

Gold Camp Road. Before the Short Line Railway was dismantled and the rail bed was converted to a road, Theodore Roosevelt took the ride from Colorado Springs to Victor by train and declared that the beauty of the route bankrupted the English language. This 40-mile route is truly spectacular. A collapsed tunnel closed an eastern portion of the road; that section is now a popular hiking and biking trail that can be picked up off N. Cheyenne Boulevard. To get to the rest of Gold Camp Road, take Old Stage Road 5.5 miles to where it hits Gold Camp.

Manitou Cliff Dwellings Museum (719-685-5242 or 1-800-354-9971; cliffdwellings museum.com), just off US 24 on 10 Cliff Dwellings Rd. in Manitou Springs. Open daily in summer 9–6, winter 10–4, and spring and fall 9–5; closed Thanksgiving and Christmas. Around the turn of the century, material from cliff dwellings in the Mesa Verde area were used to reconstruct these cliff dwellings near Manitou Springs. Tourists

MANITOU SPRINGS CLIFF DWELLINGS

MIRAMONT CASTLE MUSEUM

benefit by being able to climb inside these dwellings—and the attraction is close to town with plenty of parking. Native dancers perform traditional dances, and there is an extensive gift shop and museum lodged in a 100-year-old pueblo building. Adult admission $9.50, seniors $8.50, children (7–11) $7.50, and kids under 7 free.

    ᴛ **Miramont Castle Museum** (719-685-1011; miramontcastle.org), 9 Capitol Hill Ave., Manitou Springs. Open daily 9–5 in the summer; in the winter Tue.–Sun. 10–4. Miramont Castle was built in 1895 by the French-born priest Jean Baptiste Francolon. It was later converted into a sanitarium by the Sisters of Mercy. The museum tries to capture Victorian life in Manitou Springs. There is a miniatures museum on the bottom level and a doll collection on the top. The museum also has a Tea Room that serves high tea as well as lunch items. Adult admission $9, seniors $8, children (6–12) $5, children under 6 free.

    North Pole: Home of Santa's Workshop (719-684-9432; santas-colo.com), 5050 Pikes Peak Hwy., Cascade. Open daily in the summer; closed Wed. and Thu. in the spring and fall, closed Thu. in the winter. Standard hours 10–5, but call for seasonal variations. Kids can ride down the peppermint slide on a potato sack, feed animals, ride a just-their-size Candy Cane Coaster, and get a picture with Santa in his house. Not just for Christmas, the North Pole drums up holiday cheer all year long. Built in 1955, when theme parks were a more local affair, the park still draws crowds of excited children. General admission $22, seniors and children under 2 free.

✳ Outdoor Activities

CROSS-COUNTRY SKIING & SNOWSHOEING **Mueller State Park and the Crags** (719-687-2366; cpw.state.co.us/placestogo/Parks/Mueller), 21045 CO 67 (3.5 miles south of Divide). Around the back of Pikes Peak, this park offers 50 miles of ungroomed trails for cross-country skiing and snowshoeing. Daily pass $7.

PIKES PEAK

In 1806, Zebulon Pike and his party arrived at the confluence of the Arkansas River and Fountain Creek, near present-day Pueblo, and set up camp. In the distance he saw what he described as a small blue cloud. It was later determined to be the summit of a surprisingly high mountain, and Pike decided to take a side trip and see if he couldn't reach the top. For several days he attempted the summit, but was eventually turned back by waist-deep snow and waning provisions. He boldly predicted that no one would ever be able to conquer this mountain and returned to camp.

Today, over half a million people summit Pikes Peak every year, making it the most visited peak in North America. Rising 14,110 feet above sea level, it is the easternmost of the 14ers. Millions have been inspired by the mountain's grandeur. As a landmark, it was celebrated by the prospectors who came west during the 1859 gold rush with the slogan "Pikes Peak or Bust."

In the summer of 1893, Katharine Lee Bates and fellow teachers from Colorado College climbed Pikes Peak by wagon and mule. So enthralled was she by the view from the summit that she was moved to write the poem "America the Beautiful."

Summiting Pikes Peak is almost a requirement of tourists making their way to Colorado Springs. You can make your own way to the top by car, train, or by hoofing it.

Barr Trail. The trail was constructed by Fred Barr from 1914 to 1921 and is the most direct hike up to Pikes Peak. The trailhead is located in Manitou Springs. There is a dedicated trailhead parking area just beyond the Cog Railway parking area, on Ruxton Avenue. The trail is 12.6 miles long and climbs 7,300 feet to the summit. Along the way, you walk through three ecological life zones. Drinking water may not be available until you reach the Barr Camp (about halfway), and you will need to treat any water you pull from streams. The weather at the bottom of the trail can be dramatically different from the top (last time I was there it was 75°F in Manitou Springs and 32°F on the summit), so dress accordingly. A round-trip can take experienced hikers 16 hours, so you might want to have someone pick you up at the top.

Crags Trail Hike. See "Hiking" under Outdoor Activities.

Pikes Peak Cog Railway (719-685-5401; cograilway.com), Ruxton Ave. (depot). Open year-round. In the summer, the train leaves the station every 80 minutes from 8 to 5:20. Check the schedule on the website for other times of the year. The Cog Railway is one of the easiest and most scenic ways to get to the top of Pikes Peak. The unique design of the cog system allows the train to climb very steep terrain, including two 25 percent grades. It is 8.9 miles to the summit from the station, and the round-trip takes 3 hours and 10 minutes—giving you 30–40 minutes to grab a bite to eat, use the restrooms, and take in the panoramic views. Keep in mind that there are no bathrooms on the train, and it's a 75-minute trip to the top. Rates vary by season. In the summer, adult tickets $38, children (3–12) $20.50, and children under 3 free (if held on lap).

Mountain Chalet (719-633-0732; mtnchalet.com), 226 North Tejon St. This mountaineering store rents and sells snowshoes and Nordic gear. The shop also has telemark equipment for sale and for rent.

BICYCLING **Challenge Unlimited** (719-633-6399 or 1-800-798-5954; bikithikit.com), 204 S. 24th St., near Old Colorado City. There are plenty of great spots to ride in Colorado Springs. Two of the most spectacular are the trail down from Pikes Peak and Gold Camp Road. Challenge Unlimited offers tours (guided and not) of these and other routes around the state. There are also guided bike trips overseas.

Criterium Bike Shop (719-599-0149; criterium.com), 6150 Corporate Center Dr. Open Mon.–Sat. 8–8 and Sun. 10–6. A lot of shops will skimp on the bikes they send

Pikes Peak Highway (719-385-7325 or 1-800-318-9505; coloradosprings.gov/ppam), P.O. Box 1575-MC060 Colorado Springs. The 19-mile highway is accessed west of town off US 24. It is paved part of the way and stays open year-round (weather permitting). There are 156 curves as the highway ascends to the 14,110-foot summit of Pikes Peak. The views above and below tree line are breathtaking, and there are ample turnouts for motorists to pull off, rest their engine, and take in the mountain. The toll is $40 per car or $12 per adult and $5 per child.

THE PIKES PEAK COG RAILWAY AT THE SUMMIT

out as rentals. Criterium, however, has a great mountain bike lineup—Rockhoppers for the more casual rider and full-suspension Stumpjumpers and Epics for more serious riders. The staff know a bit about the local riding scene, too, if you need some inside info to get started. Same-day rentals $30–60.

Pikes Peak Mountain Bike Tours (719-337-5311 or 1-888-593-3062; bikepikespeak .com), 302 S. 25th St. Open May–Oct. If you are the type who gets to the top of Pikes Peak and asks, "I wonder what it would be like to barrel down this mountain on a bike?" then you need to call these guys. The tour begins at the summit of Pikes Peak via van or cog railway (depending on the tour). The rest is all up to gravity. Tours go on all summer and into September. Depending on your group size, the Pikes Peak tour is $90–120 (depending on the number in your group) and the Ride-n-Rail $140/person ($125 if you can get three or more).

FISHING **Eleven Mile Canyon and Reservoir** is located in Eleven Mile State Park (719-748-3401; cpw.state.co.us/placestogo/Parks/ElevenMile), 4229 CR 92, Lake George. Located up in the mountains 32 miles west of Woodland Park and open 24 hours. Trout are the prize catch out at this reservoir—cutthroat, brown, and rainbow. There are northern pike in there are well. The park hosts regular fishing tournaments, and there are plenty of boat ramps. Daily park pass $7.

Manitou Park Lake is 7.8 miles north of Woodland Park on CO 67. In addition to fishing for the lake's rainbow trout, there are hiking trails, a picnic area, and restrooms at the lake.

Rampart Reservoir. Boat ramp and parking, open daily 7–7. The Rampart Reservoir Recreation Area is located 4.2 miles east of Woodland Park. The 500-acre reservoir is home to lake, cutthroat, brown, and rainbow trout. It is stocked by the Colorado Division of Wildlife. Day-use fee $5.

GOLF **Broadmoor Golf Club** (719-577-5790; broadmoor.com), 1 Lake Ave. The three 18-hole courses at the Broadmoor are highly rated. The Mountain Course, for example, has wide fairways and beautiful scenery. The greens fees at Broadmoor are a bit steep at $140–280 (depending on the season), but if golf is your game, these courses will not disappoint. Broadmoor also offers club rentals for $74.

Patty Jewett Golf Course (719-385-6950; pattyjewettgolfshop.com), 900 E. Española St. This is the third-oldest course west of the Mississippi. The 18-hole golf course has the sense of the classic about it—from the rich wrought-iron gate to the 100-year-old trees that line the drive up to the clubhouse. There is also a separate nine-hole course. Greens fees: 18 holes $29–31, 9 holes $15–16.

Pine Creek Golf Club (719-594-9999; pinecreekgc.com), 9850 Divot Trail. Designed by Richard Phelps, this 18-hole course has great views of Pikes Peak and the Colorado Springs skyline. In sync with the surrounding landscape, the course challenges golfers with a 376-foot change in elevation, meandering creek beds, and other natural obstacles. Greens fees $40–67.

Valley Hi Golf Course (719-385-6917; pattyjewettgolfshop.com), 610 S. Chelton Rd. This newer public course was bought by the city in 1975. The 18-hole course has views of Pikes Peak and Cheyenne Mountain. The Learn-to-Golf program is a great introduction to the sport for beginners. Greens fees: 18 holes $29–31; 9 holes $15–16.

HIKING Hikers in Colorado Springs are just a short drive away from **Pike National Forest**, **Mueller State Park**, and **Cheyenne Mountain State Park**. All offer exceptional trails for hikers of all levels. **Garden of the Gods** has paved trails that are great for walking, running, and biking. Following are some trails that deserve special mention.

Colorado Front Range Trail is a moderate, 5-mile, out-and-back hike with little elevation gain. The Front Range Trail is a work in progress. The final product will be a 900-mile trail that stretches from Wyoming into New Mexico, connecting the communities along the eastern edge of the Rocky Mountains. Throughout the state, many sections have been completed. In Colorado Springs, there's a trailhead, about a quarter of a mile west of I-25 on Woodmen Road. Parking is on the north side of the road. The trail heads north along Monument Creek and passes through the Air Force Academy. About 2.5 miles in, there's a little lake and a picnic area. It has great views of the mountains.

Columbine Trail in **North Cheyenne Cañon Park** begins at the **Starsmore Discovery Center** (719-385-6086), 2120 S. Cheyenne Cañon Rd. It follows the North Cheyenne

Creek for some time on its way to Helen Hunt Falls and the falls visitor center. The canyon is gorgeous, and the trail wanders through patches of shady trees and over exposed rock. Along the 4-mile route you gain nearly 1,000 feet in elevation.

Crags Trail Hike is a moderate hike that begins on the other side of Pikes Peak. The trailhead is just south of Mueller State Park on CO 67, south of Divide. The 4-mile round-trip gains about 640 feet in elevation. The "crags" are a geological feature of the area and provide interesting scenery for hiking. For a more challenging hike from the same trailhead, hikers can connect with a trail that will take them to the Pikes Peak summit. The trail to the summit begins about 200 feet down the Crags Trail, on the right. This hike is a nearly 12-mile round trip and is a bit more grueling (although less so than Barr Trail—see sidebar on Pikes Peak).

HORSEBACK RIDING **Academy Riding Stables** (719-633-5667 or 1-888-700-0410; arsriding.com), 4 El Paso Blvd. This stable offers guests a chance to ride horses through the Garden of the Gods. As you meander the trails, a guide will point out interesting features of the park. One-hour ride $49.25, two-hour $71.25.

Riding Stables at The Broadmoor (719-448-0371; comtnadventure.com), Old Stage Rd. To get to the stables, get off I-25 at exit 138 and take Lake Avenue west. Once you reach The Broadmoor, follow signs around to Cheyenne Mountain Zoo. Before you get to the zoo, turn right on Old Stage Road and go 5.8 miles to the stables. Guides will take you on one- or two-hour horseback rides through the mountains. They have pony rides for younger kids and plenty of animals for petting. One-hour ride $49, two-hour $76, and 20-minute children's ride $25 (ages 4 and older).

✳ Lodging

HOTELS ♿ ((ɪ)) **The Antlers, A Wyndham Hotel** (719-473-5600; antlers.com), 4 S. Cascade Ave. The Antlers was built by Gen. William Palmer shortly after he founded the city of Colorado Springs. The hotel was the centerpiece of what he hoped would be a resort community. The first Antlers hotel was opened in 1883. The hotel is on its third incarnation—it's a much more modern facility with all the amenities of high-end lodging. The hotel has 285 rooms and 7 suites. Rooms $100–250.

♿ ☗ **The Broadmoor** (719-577-5775 or 1-866-837-9520; broadmoor.com), 1 Lake Ave. More than just a hotel, The Broadmoor is a luxury resort with three golf courses, a tennis club, a spa, and several excellent restaurants. The resort sits at the base of Cheyenne Mountain on 3,000 acres. The first hotel on the property was built in 1918 by Spencer Penrose. Even if you are not staying at The Broadmoor, it's worth a visit. The public can tour the fabulously landscaped grounds, grab a bite to eat at any of the many cafés, do some shopping, and even tour the resort's carriage museum. Rooms $200–800 and suites $420–1,500.

♿ ☗ ((ɪ)) **Cheyenne Mountain Resort** (719-538-4000 or 1-800-588-0250; cheyennemountain.com), 3225 Broadmoor Valley Rd. Found a few short miles from The Broadmoor, Cheyenne Mountain Resort has 316 rooms and sits on 218 acres at the base of Cheyenne Mountain. The resort is home to the Country Club of Colorado—the club golf course wraps around a 35-acre recreational lake that is used for sailing and fishing. There are four swimming pools and indoor and outdoor tennis courts. Near the Pro Shop, guests can dine at the Pineview Dining Room and Pub. Each room at the resort has its own private balcony with views of the mountains or the Country Club. Of special interest to business travelers, study areas in the rooms have two desks set up to be used as computer workstations. Rooms and suites $209–799.

& (((•))) **The Cliff House** (719-785-1000 or 1-888-212-7000; thecliffhouse.com), 306 Cañon Ave., Manitou Springs. Located in the heart of Manitou Springs, The Cliff House was built in 1873. The site was originally a stagecoach stop on the route to Leadville. The hotel now boasts 55 guest rooms and suites, each decorated in the style of the late 1800s but with a modern flare. Rooms $109–199 and suites $199–475.

BED & BREAKFASTS & (((•))) **Old Town Guesthouse** (719-632-9194 or 1-888-375-4210; oldtown-guesthouse.com), 115 S. 26th St. Voted the best bed & breakfast in Colorado Springs, Old Town Guesthouse was built in 1997. Just a block from Old Colorado City, the inn has eight rooms—each named after a flower. Rooms have TVs and DVD players as well as refrigerators and coffee machines. The amenities are great for business travelers. All the inn's floors can be reached by elevator. Rooms $175–275.

(((•))) **Victoria's Keep** (719-685-5354 or 1-800-905-5337; victoriaskeep.com), 202 Ruxton Ave., Manitou Springs. Victoria's Keep sits right at the corner of Ruxton and Capitol Hill avenues (the latter road leads to the Miramont Castle)—walking distance to downtown Manitou Springs. The wooded lot is fronted by a fast-moving creek. The bed & breakfast has six rooms, each with a tub for two, fireplace, and private bath. The house has a wraparound porch where you can sit and listen to the creek. A full gourmet breakfast is served each morning, promptly at 9. Rooms $90–165.

🐾 **Pikes Peak Paradise** (719-687-6656 or 1-800-728-8282; pikespeakparadise .com), 236 Pinecrest Rd., Woodland Park. Two suites, two deluxe suites, and two rooms. Amenities include in-room hot tubs, fireplaces, and private decks. Rooms have HD flat-screen TVs and DVD players. Decorated in a contemporary style, the beds have luxurious linens and the baths feature Egyptian cotton towels. Guests enjoy spectacular

views of Pikes Peak and the Front Range. Every morning, the inn serves a gourmet breakfast. Rooms and suites $180–250.

CAMPGROUNDS **Garden of the Gods Campground** (719-475-9450; rvcoutdoors .com/garden-of-the-gods), 3704 W. Colorado Ave. Open May 1–Sept. 30. This campground has several accommodation options. There are sites for tent camping and RV sites with a variety of hookup configurations. Cabins are rustic with a bunk bed and double bed (bring your own linens). The bunkhouses are like the cabins, but they have indoor plumbing. The deluxe bunkhouse even has a kitchenette. Pets are welcome at tent and RV sites. The campground has two heated pools, a game room, and plenty of shower and laundry facilities. Tent sites $26-35, RV sites $43-62. The campground also has "escape cottages" and "tiny houses" if you prefer being indoors. In the off-season, only tent and RV site available (at a cheaper rate).

Pike National Forest has numerous campgrounds in the Pikes Peak region. Reservations can be made online at recreation.gov, where you can also get a complete list of available sites at all federally run campgrounds. **South Meadows** (719-686-8816) is located 5 miles north of Woodland Park on CO 67. This rustic campground has 64 sites, a limited potable water supply, and pit toilets. There are also miles of nearby hiking and biking trails. **Thunder Ridge** (719-636-1602) is east of Woodland Park, about 4 miles from the Rampart Reservoir entrance on Rampart Range Rd. The campground has 24 sites. It is shady, and amenities include pit toilets, firewood, and a dumpster. There are trails for hiking and biking, and boaters can push off onto the nearby reservoir.

❋ Where to Eat

DINING OUT & 🍸 **The Broadmoor** (719-577-5775 or 1-800-634-7711; broadmoor

.com/dining), 1 Lake Ave., has several restaurants of outstanding quality. **Ristorante del Lago** is The Broadmoor's take on Italian dining. The dining room evokes a sense of relaxed Old World elegance. The menu, inspired by several regions of Italy, does the same. Dishes $16–36. The **Penrose Room** is open for dinner Mon.–Sat. The restaurant prides itself on providing fine Continental dining in an elegant atmosphere. Live music and dancing complete the experience. Three- and four-course meals cost $87 and $98, respectively. **La Taverne** is open for lunch and dinner, serving steak and seafood. There is a live orchestra with live music and dancing in the evening, Wed.–Sun. Dinner $19–72. Check the website for dress code requirements at each.

♿ **MacKenzie's Chop House Downtown** (719-635-3536; mackenzieschophouse.com), 128 S. Tejon St. Open for lunch Mon.–Fri. 11–3 and dinner Mon.–Thu. 5–10, Fri.–Sat. 5–11, and Sun. 5–9. There are a number of great steakhouses in Colorado Springs, and MacKenzie's may be the best. It serves classic steaks, such as porterhouse, New York strip, and filet mignon, and there are a host of elegant seafood favorites such as Alaskan king crab and almond-encrusted salmon. MacKenzie's offers patio dining and allows cigar smoking in the lounge. Dinner entrées $25–30.

EATING OUT ♿ **Amanda's Fonda** (719-227-1975), 3625 W. Colorado Ave. Open Sun.–Thu. 11–9 and Fri. and Sat. 11–10. The product of a family that has spent generations in the restaurant business, many of the dishes at Amanda's come from the late owner's mother and grandmother—and from recipes they developed while living in Guadalajara. It is often cited as the best Mexican food in town. The eatery is known for excellent *arroz con pollo* and an outstanding *mole*. Patio seating by the creek is a favorite with the margarita crowd.

♿ **Bird Dog BBQ** (719-596-4900; birddogbbq.com), 5984 Stetson Hills Blvd. Open Mon.–Sat. 11–9 and Sun 11–8. There are several barbecue joints in the Springs, but Bird Dog stands out from the pack. Slow cooked and oak smoked, the meat here drips with flavor. Bird Dog has the best prime rib brisket in town. All the dishes can be ordered on a bun for an easy lunch. Combo plates offer a sampling of meats—try the turkey for something different. (There is also a second restaurant at 1645 Briargate Pkwy.) Plates $12–14 and sandwiches $4.25–11.

♿ **Edelweiss** (719-633-2220; edelweissrest.com), 34 E. Ramona Ave. Open daily 11:30–9 and until 9:30 on Fri. and Sat. This German restaurant first opened in 1967. Its 100-year-old building was first used as a schoolhouse. Edelweiss is authentically Bavarian, with hearty dishes such as bratwurst and sauerkraut. There's a *Biergarten* in the summer and live music on the weekends. Dinners $18–22, more for steak.

☯ ♿ **Fargo's Pizza Company** (719-473-5540; fargospizza.com), 2910 E. Platte Ave. Open Sun.–Thu. 11–9 and Fri. and Sat. 11–11. A bit of a dining novelty, Fargo's is a Victorian pizza parlor, laid out like an old-timey gambling hall. The women wear long dresses, and the men, garters on their sleeves. There is a wraparound balcony, and two mannequins sit at one end in full period dress. Guests order and pay for pizza at the window (then order and pay for drinks at the bar), find a seat, and wait until their number is called up on one of the mirrors around the restaurant. The pizza is pretty good, as is the salad bar. After eating, kids can head to the arcade to play video games. Bring cash—Fargo's doesn't take checks or credit cards. Large pizza $12–18.

King's Chef Diner (719-634-9135; kingschefdiner.com), 110 E. Costilla St. Open for breakfast and lunch Mon.–Fri. 8–2ish. The distinctive clown-castle look of King's Chef may put off some people, but this little diner has quite a loyal following. Big breakfast dishes such as the Grump (a heaping stack of hash browns, meat, eggs, cheese, and country gravy), have kept them coming in since 1956. The diner may be best known for the green chili that smothers everything from breakfast burritos to cheeseburgers. Breakfast and lunch dishes $5–10.

    ᣜ **Panino's Restaurant** (719-635-7452; paninos.com), 604 N. Tejon St. Open Mon.–Thu. 11–9 and Fri. and Sat. 11–10. A panino is traditionally a toasted sandwich made from a small loaf of bread. At Panino's in Colorado Springs, the sandwich is rolled in a flatbread, not unlike a thin, toppingless pizza crust. There are panini for all sorts of appetites, such as the Spaghetti Pie with noodles, meat, and cheese smothered in marinara, and the classic Reuben with corned beef and sauerkraut. Panini under $10.

    Stagecoach Inn (719-685-9114; stagecoachinn.com), 702 Manitou Ave., Manitou Springs. Open Fri.–Sun. 11–9, Mon.–Thu. 11–8. A red stagecoach sits prominently on the front lawn of Stagecoach Inn, located right on the main street in downtown Manitou Springs. The story goes that there was a stage stop here, and that the main dining area was once an electric company that used a large water wheel in Fountain Creek to bring electricity to Manitou Springs. Today, the restaurant serves classic American fare with renowned western hospitality. There is seating on two decks that overlook the creek. Dinner entrées $12–30, lunch dishes around $10.

BAKERIES & COFFEE SHOPS ᣜ **Pikes Perk Coffee & Tea House** (719-522-1432; theperkdowntown.com), 5965 N. Academy Blvd. #203. There are Pikes Perk locations all over the Springs, but Academy Boulevard was the first. Playing on the shop name, its tagline is, "Coffee with an Altitude." Fresh ground coffee and gourmet-quality ingredients make for a great coffeehouse. There are also 101 flavors of milk shakes.

BARS, TAVERNS, & BREW PUBS ᣜ **The Golden Bee (at The Broadmoor),** (719-577-5733 or 1-800-634-7711; broadmoor .com/dining/golden-bee), 1 Lake Ave. Open daily 11:30–1:30 AM. This pub at The Broadmoor is really cool. Completely authentic, the entire pub was brought from London. It has a piano player who leads the bar in singing.

    ᣜ **Jack Quinn's Irish Ale House and Pub** (719-385-0766; jackquinnspub.com), 21 S. Tejon St. Open daily 11–late, brunch on Sat. and Sun. 11–3. This is a classic Irish pub with live music nearly every night.

    ᣜ **Phantom Canyon Brewing Company** (719-635-2800; phantomcanyon .com), 2 E. Pikes Peak Ave. Open daily from 11 AM–last call. This brewery/ restaurant serves fresh ale, unfiltered and unpasteurized. There's also a full lunch and dinner menu of classic pub food. Lunch $11–14 and dinner $11–21.

SNACKS ᣜ **Josh & John's** (719-632-0299; joshandjohns.com), 111 E. Pikes Peak Ave. A lot of folks agree that this is the best ice-cream place in town. All the ice cream at Josh & John's is made right there in the shop, using Colorado dairy goods. Starting with a wide selection of flavors, banana splits, sundaes, and floats round out the menu.

✳ Entertainment

🔊 ᣜ **Flying W Ranch** (719-598-4000 or 1-800-232-3599; flyingw.com), 3330 Chuckwagon Rd. For generations, this was a must-see attraction in Colorado Springs. Folks came in droves for a night of western cooking and good old cowboy music by the Flying W Wranglers. (The Wranglers are an exceptional bunch of musicians. From guitar and upright bass to fiddle and mandolin, this group is a favorite among cowboy music aficionados.) Before guests would gather for the chuck wagon supper and concert, they usually roamed around the ranch's

Western Village and toured the gift shops, or let the kids take the mine ride, or toured the property's historic buildings. This all ended when disaster struck in the form of the 2012 Waldo Canyon Fire. The ranch was devastated. It's taken a lot of work, but the ranch should be welcoming guests once again in the summer of 2017. As I write, there are no firm times or prices, but keep an eye on the Flying W website for current details.

Loonees Comedy Corner (719-591-0707; loonees.com), 1305 N. Academy Blvd. Open nightly Thu.–Sat. Loonees keeps a good flow of comics coming through the Springs. See its website for a list of upcoming headliners. Admission is $6 on Thu., $10 Fri. and Sat. There's a two-item minimum.

⚓ **The Iron Springs Chateau Melodrama Dinner Theater** (719-685-5104; ironspringschateau.com), 444 Ruxton Ave., Manitou Springs. Shows performed year-round, with a limited schedule fall to spring. For a night of full-on entertainment, consider taking the family to dinner and a show. At the Melodrama Dinner Theater, the audience is encouraged to participate in the performance with boos and hisses for the villain and cheers for the hero. Shows are usually engaging and highly comical. Couple that with a family-style dinner of oven-fried chicken and barbeque beef, and you have a night of fun. The evening concludes with an old-time vaudeville olio—a miscellaneous collection of songs, jokes, and sing-alongs. Adult dinner-and-show ticket $31, seniors $29, and children (under 12) $16.50. You can also get tickets for just the show or just the dinner.

✳ Selective Shopping

Old Colorado City (shopoldcolorado city.com), centers on W. Colorado Ave. between S. 21st and 30th streets. This is the raucous town that inspired General

FLYING W RANCH, AS IT WAS

DOWNTOWN MANITOU SPRINGS

William Palmer to start a more chaste city of his own, Colorado Springs, down the road. For a time it was the territorial headquarters. In the park you can visit the log cabin where the territorial legislature convened for business. Today the town is a quaint section of storefronts with an abundance of shops and restaurants.

Manitou Springs (manitousprings .org) is located west of Colorado Springs just off US 24. The historic part of town is a fantastic place for a walk. There are numerous art galleries and antiques shops.

Commonwheel Artists Co-Op (719-685-1008; commonwheel.com), 102 Cañon Ave., is one of them. It may be the town's best gallery. There are a lot of pieces here by amazingly talented local artists. Open daily 10–6.

Garden of the Gods Trading Post (719-685-9045 or 1-800-874-4515; gardenofthegodstradingpost.com) is located just past the Balanced Rock as you enter the park from the south. Open daily 8:30–5. If you simply must have a Garden of the Gods T-shirt, a plastic bow and arrow set, and a couple of souvenir shot glasses, do not miss the Trading Post. No other tourist shop in the Springs has this much inventory.

✳ Special Events

July: Every year, drivers compete in the **Pikes Peak International Hill Climb** (719-634-7333 ext. 1012; ppihc.com), a race to the top of Pikes Peak.

Pikes Peak or Bust Rodeo (pikespeak orbust.org). Sanctioned by the Professional Rodeo Cowboys Association, this rodeo showcases competitors on their way to the yearly championships.

August: **Pikes Peak Ascent and Marathon** (pikespeakmarathon.org). On the first day of the race, the Ascent, runners race to the top of Pikes Peak. The next, they race to the top and back again.

September: During the **Colorado Springs Labor Day Lift Off** (719-471-4833; coloradospringslabordayliftoff .com) the sky above Colorado Springs is filled with nearly 100 hot-air balloons. Great photo opportunities.

CAÑON CITY &
THE GOLD RANGE

Most of the tourist activities in Cañon City are centered on the Royal Gorge. Folks are traveling up the gorge on the popular Royal Gorge Route train, paddling through the gorge down the Arkansas River, or driving out to the Royal Gorge Bridge to appreciate the 1,000-foot walls from a higher perspective. The tourists you find in town seem to be either on their way to or from one of these activities, or they're just passing through.

Cañon City came into its own as a result of gold being discovered in Cripple Creek. Between 1899 and 1910, most of the downtown was built with the money of wealthy miners who set up house in town. With three railroads serving Cañon City, it was natural that the town would become a regional transportation hub, attracting the wealth of the nearby Gold Range. With the end of mining in the mountains, the town's fortunes waned. Today, the town's main industry is incarceration. There are nine prisons in town, and nearby Florence has another four. And, in fact, the town's most interesting museum is the Colorado Territorial Prison Museum.

The gold that was once found in Cripple Creek made a few people rich, but the boom was over in a few short years. Back in the 1890s, the promise of striking it rich drew many a poor man into the mountains—gold fever they called it. Today, Cripple Creek draws people with a different kind of gold fever, gambling. The Old West mining town has been transformed, just as quickly as it was first built. Casinos have taken over the entire downtown. Unlike the glitzy light of Vegas, however, the casinos in Cripple Creek have maintained the town's Old West look and feel. This is definitely gambling, Colorado style.

The town of Victor is just up the road from Cripple Creek. Gold Camp Road, which heads into the mountains west of Colorado Springs, ends up in Victor. This small struggling town has plenty of recreational activities available in the nearby mountains. A number of trails will take you back to old mining sites, and there are plenty of old roads and railroad grades for mountain biking.

GUIDANCE **Cañon City Chamber of Commerce** (719-275-2331 or 1-800-876-7922; canoncity.com), 403 Royal Gorge Blvd. The visitors center is located in the historic Peabody House. The house was built in 1880 and was once the home of James Peabody, the 13th governor of Colorado.

Cripple Creek Welcome Center (1-877-858-4653; visitcripplecreek.com), 501 E. Bennett Ave. Located right next to the train depot on the east end of town.

More websites:

canoncitycolorado.com

victorcolorado.com

GETTING THERE *By car:* The best way to get to Cañon City and the towns of Cripple Creek and Victor is by car. Parking in Cañon City is easy enough. If you are not in town visiting a casino, you will have to park a couple of blocks from downtown in Cripple Creek.

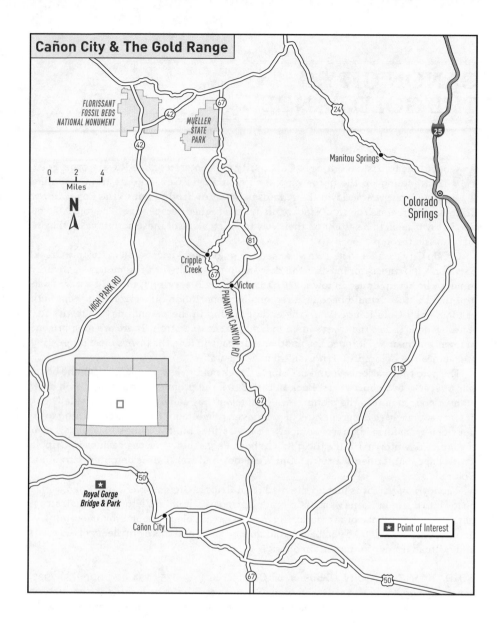

Cañon City & The Gold Range

FLORISSANT FOSSIL BEDS NATIONAL MONUMENT

MUELLER STATE PARK

42

67

24

25

Manitou Springs

Colorado Springs

0 2 4
Miles

N

HIGH PARK RD

Cripple Creek

81

67

Victor

PHANTOM CANYON RD

115

67

50

★
Royal Gorge
Bridge & Park

Cañon City

67

50

★ Point of Interest

✳ To See & Do

Royal Gorge Bridge & Park (719-275-7507 or 1-888-333-5597; royalgorgebridge.com), 4218 Fremont CR 3A, Cañon City. Open year-round; see website for seasonal hours. Some locals may call it the "highest suspension bridge in the world to nowhere," but for the 300,000 visitors who come each year to gaze down into the Royal Gorge from a height of 1,053 feet, it's worth the visit. The bridge is an impressive feat of engineering. Built in 1929, it's the highest suspension bridge in the world. And although it's true that the bridge is not a throughway for any traffic, the bridge and the park offer unique ways to experience the Royal Gorge. (Many of the facilities around the

ROYAL GORGE BRIDGE

bridge were damaged in the 2013 wildfires, and since then the whole park has been rebuilt.) The Aerial Tram, the longest of its kind in the world, carries guests 1,100 feet above the canyon floor. It offers outstanding views of the gorge and the bridge. Or to explore the gorge from below, you can get to the canyon floor via the park's Incline Railroad. For the kids, there's a mile-long ride on the Silver Rock Railway. In all, there are 21 rides and attractions, including a regular schedule of live entertainment. Adult admission $23, seniors $19, and children (4–11) $17. In the off-season, adults $22, seniors $19, and children $17.

Royal Gorge Dinosaur Experience (1-800-209-0062; dinoxp.com), 44895 W. US 50, Cañon City. Open daily (except for Christmas Day) 10–5. The only way to get to the Royal Gorge is to follow US 50 to CR 3A. As such, the intersection has attracted a cluster of businesses intended to appeal to tourists. There are helicopter tours of the gorge, a river rafting outfitter, a small campground, zip-line tours, and another rock shop. The newest attraction is somewhat unique and continues, in its way, the legacy of the now-closed Dinosaur Depot Museum in Cañon City. The museum portion of the Royal Gorge Dinosaur Experience features interactive exhibitions, life-size dinosaur models, and fossil casts. Outside, the dinos come to life, animatronically at least, for the Dinosaur Wild Walk. Adjacent to the main building is a ropes course, built between four tall steel towers. General admission: adults $12, kids up to 12 $8. Another $10/$6 for adults and children, respectively, for "add-ons," which would be the ropes course or the Dinosaur Wild Walk.

GAMBLING Cripple Creek has made quite a name for itself as a popular gaming destination. Unlike Blackhawk and Central City, which combined have become a mini-Vegas with all the lights and glam, Cripple Creek has maintained an Old West feel. Storefronts have been preserved so that even when a casino stretches a city block,

Bennett Avenue still has the charm of a small mountain town. In a sense, the casinos moved like a hermit crab into the shell of Cripple Creek, and with 17 casinos there are plenty of opportunities here for folks to play away their cash.

& **Bronco Billy's Sports Bar and Casino** (719-689-2142 or 1-877-989-2142; bronco billyscasino.com), 233 E. Bennett Ave., Cripple Creek. Bronco Billy's boasts of being a true Colorado-style casino. It has more video poker games than any casino in town. They also have a number of top-notch eateries.

& **Double Eagle Hotel and Casino** (719-689-5000; decasino.com), 442 E. Bennett Ave., Cripple Creek. The largest casino in town, the Double Eagle has plenty of parking, dining, and gaming.

HISTORIC SITES & MUSEUMS & ⚓ **Cañon City Municipal Museum** (719-269-9018), 612 Royal Gorge Blvd. Open in the summer Tue.–Sun. 10–4. The museum looks at the lives of the area's first residents. The complex includes a few buildings, such as the 1860 log cabin of Anson Rudd. Admission is free.

& ⚓ **Colorado Territorial Prison Museum** (719-269-3015 or 1-877-269-3015; prison museum.org), 201 N. 1st St. Open daily in the summer 10–6; winter Wed.–Sun. 10–5; and spring and fall daily 10–5. Rarely will you get a chance to tour a 19th-century prison. This facility began housing prisoners in 1871. Thirty-two cells are open to the public. The museum offers MP3 and CD tours for individuals looking for a structured approach to the history of the prison. Exhibitions include the noose from the last execution by hanging in Colorado, weapons confiscated from inmates, and a gallery of inmate art. Adult admission $7, seniors $6, and youths (6–12) $5.

Florissant Fossil Beds National Monument (719-748-3253; nps.gov/flfo), 15807 Teller County 1, Florissant. The visitor center is 2 miles south of Florissant on Teller County 1. Open daily 9–5. Tens of thousands of fossils have been found at the Florissant Fossil Beds. The park protects those yet to be found and helps visitors put the known finds in context. The only known fossilized sequoia trunks are found here, as are the fossilized remains of thousands of plants and insects. The park has nature trails, and

BENNETT AVENUE IN CRIPPLE CREEK

COLORADO TERRITORIAL PRISON MUSEUM

the park service offers guided tours and interpretive talks. The schedule of tours and talks depends on availability of rangers on any particular day, so call for more information. Admission $5 for adults (16 or older). The park accepts only cash and checks.

🚲 🚂 **Mollie Kathleen Gold Mine** (719-689-2466 or 1-888-291-5689; goldminetours .com). Located 1 mile north of Cripple Creek at 9388 CO 67. Open daily in the summer 9–6; Mar., open Wed.–Sun. 9–5; and April and Oct., open daily 9–5. Closed in the winter. Tours leave every 10 minutes during the busy season and last about an hour. The last tour leaves one hour before close. To enter the Mollie Kathleen Gold Mine, guests descend 1,000 feet into the earth in a man-skip elevator. The mine tour takes you back to the turn of the century, where you can see how hard-rock miners worked. The tour includes a train ride through the mine. Adult admission $20, children (3–12) $12, and children under 3 free.

🚂 **Old Homestead House Museum** (719-689-9090; oldhomesteadhouse.com), 353 Myers Ave. Open daily in the summer 11–5; open weekends until Christmas. This former brothel was the most famous in Cripple Creek. Built in 1896 by madam Pearl DeVere, the house was reputed to have the most beautiful women in town—and the most expensive. The house has been restored and is full of the Victorian touches that were found inside more than 100 years ago. The tour includes the history of Cripple Creek and the Red Light District. Tour $5.

RAILROADS **Royal Gorge Route** (719-276-4000 or 1-888-724-5748; royalgorgeroute .com), 401 Water St., Cañon City. The railroad operates late May–early Oct. The train leaves daily at 9:30, 12:30, 3:30, and 7. Few train rides compare with the trip from Cañon City into the Royal Gorge on the Royal Gorge Route Railroad. The scenery is breathtaking. If you want more than just a ride, the railroad has Dinner Trains, Lunch Trains, and Murder Mystery trips. Coach tickets are the most affordable. If you need more of a view, coach passengers can try the open-air observation car. The Vista Dome cars have a curved glass ceiling for unobstructed views. The Lunch Train comes with

HOMESTEAD NEAR FLORISSANT FOSSIL BEDS NATIONAL MONUMENT

a three-course gourmet lunch in the vintage dining cars. Adult coach $44 and children (3–12) $34. Adult Vista Dome $69 and children (3–12) $59. Adult Lunch Train $79–99.

Cripple Creek & Victor Narrow-Gauge Railroad (719-689-2640; cripplecreekrail road.com), 5th St. and Bennett Ave., Cripple Creek. The railroad runs mid-May– mid-October. There's no better way to get a feel for gold-mining country than to see it being pulled behind a steam locomotive on a narrow-gauge railway. This is how it was done back in the day. The Cripple Creek & Victor Narrow-Gauge Railroad leaves every 40 minutes for a 45-minute, 4-mile round-trip. Adult ticket $15, seniors $14, and children (3–12) $10.

SCENIC DRIVES **Cripple Creek to Victor**. The route to Victor is just 5 miles—head south of town on CO 67. The road is well maintained and pretty wide. It's a short ride with pleasant scenery. Once you get to Victor, there are a couple of shops and a restaurant or two where you can grab a bite to eat.

Gold Belt Tour (goldbeltbyway.com). This is a Scenic and Historic Byway drive— quite beautiful, although some portions require four-wheel drive (and others a serious dose of fortitude). The byway begins in Florissant and splits into three routes, each eventually terminating in Cañon City. The most laid back, with little gain in elevation, is **High Park Road**. Follow CO 11 south to US 50 and head east to Cañon City. The other two routes take you into Cripple Creek. **Shelf Road** begins a little south of town off CO 67. Following the road will take you straight to Cañon City, but sections of the road are single lane and four-wheel drive is recommended. CO 67 becomes **Phantom Canyon Road** right past Victor. The road is passable, but it's dirt most of the way. The road takes you to Florence where you can head west on CO 115 back to Cañon City.

✱ Outdoor Activities

HIKING, FISHING, & RAFTING **Echo Canyon River Expeditions** (1-800-755-3246; raftecho.com), 45000 US 50 West. Take a trip down through the Royal Gorge or other sections of the Arkansas River. There are half- and full-day trips, as well as trips that combine rafting with a horseback ride or a ride on the Royal Gorge Railway. Half-day trips through the Royal Gorge run $79.

Skaguay Reservoir is east of Victor. There's a trail to the lake, and the reservoir is a nice spot for some fishing. To get to Skaguay, take Phantom Canyon Road east of Victor to the first fork. Skaguay Road is on the left and will take you to the reservoir and the parking area. The trail is north of the parking area.

Tunnel Drive Trail is just west of Cañon City off US 50 and Tunnel Drive. The 2-mile trail follows the Arkansas River. Hikers can enjoy passing views of the Royal Gorge Railroad, kayakers and rafters, and occasional wildlife.

✱ Green Space

Ten miles north of Cañon City is **Red Canyon Park**. This 600-acre park has trails for hiking and biking, as well as picnic areas. The park's unique rock formations are a big draw. To get there, head north on Field Avenue, which turns into Red Canyon Road (CR 9). The park is almost exactly 10 miles north of US 50.

THE ROYAL GORGE PARK HAS COLORADO'S ONLY WATER CLOCK

✳ Lodging

HOTELS Cañon City has several hotels and motels. Chains include Holiday Inn Express, Best Western, and Comfort Inn. In Cripple Creek, the **Double Eagle**, **Gold Rush**, and **Imperial** casinos all have hotel lodging.

 ♿ ✿ ☎ **Quality Inn and Suites of Cañon City** (719-275-8676 or 1-800-525-7727; qualityinncanoncity.com), 3075 E. US 50. You won't find mention of many chains in this book, but this Quality Inn has a unique history. Over the years, a lot of movies have been filmed in and around Cañon City, and the hotel has hosted many celebrities. If the rooms are available, guests can sleep in the same rooms that were once used by the likes of John Wayne, Jane Fonda, and Goldie Hawn, to list just a few. See website for a complete list with room numbers.

BED & BREAKFASTS ☎ **Jewel of the Canyons** (719-275-0378 or 1-866-875-0378; jewelofthecanyons.com), 429 Greenwood Ave., Cañon City. This beautifully restored 1890s Queen Anne has hardwood floors throughout, and the rooms have been tastefully decorated with antique furniture. The B&B has one room and two suites. All have a private bath (although the room's bath is down the hall a bit). Rooms $139.

Carr Manor (719-689-3709; carrmanor.com), 350 E. Carr Ave., Cripple Creek. The town's old high school, built in 1897 and 1905, has been converted into this lovely boutique hotel that operates as a B&B. The inn has 14 rooms and suites. They are all attractively decorated—many of the rooms still have the original chalkboards. Amenities include fireplaces, cable TV, and private baths with showers and tubs. Rooms $100–400.

The Last Dollar Inn (719-689-9113 or 1-888-429-6700; lastdollarinn.com), 315 E. Carr St., Cripple Creek. This brownstone structure was originally built in 1898. The inn has six rooms, each with a full private bath. Throughout, the house has been decorated to give guests a sense of the turn of the century, with some rooms more frilly than others. A full country gourmet breakfast is served every morning.

CAMPGROUNDS ✿ **Royal Gorge KOA Kampground** (719-275-6116 or 1-800-562-5689; koa.com/campgrounds/royal-gorge), 559 CR 3A, Cañon City. Open April 15–Oct. 1. There are tent sites in the campground's Wilderness Tenting area, a shady lot toward the back of the property. There are also sites for RVs and KOA Kamping Kabins. But that's not all in terms of activities, this campground has mini-golf, go-karts, a giant slide, a Dairy Queen, and a swimming pool. Sites and cabins $36–61.

✿ ☎ **Royal View Campground** (719-275-1900; royalviewcampground.com), 9 miles west of Cañon City on US 50, 1 mile past the entrance to the bridge. The campground has hot showers, laundry facilities, and a swimming pool. There are sites for tents and RVs, and the campground has small cabins as well. Sites and cabins $26–65.

✿ **Lost Burro** (719-689-2345 or 1-877-689-2345; lostburro.com), 4023 CR 1, Cripple Creek. This campground has 48 tent sites, 28 sites with electricity, and another 6 with full hookups. The sites at Lost Burro have plenty of tree cover for shade. There are also hot showers and a dump station. Sites $25–42.

✳ Where to Eat

DINING OUT ♿ **Le Petit Chablis** (719-269-3333; lepetitchablis.com), 512 Royal Gorge Blvd., Cañon City. Open for lunch Tue.–Fri. 11:30–1:30; dinner Tue.–Sat. 5:30–8:30 (until 9:30 on Fri. and Sat.). If you are suddenly hit with a craving for coq au vin or beef daube, head out to Cañon City. For fine French cuisine, you cannot do much better than Le Petit Chablis, located on Royal Gorge Boulevard in an old home. The menu changes daily at this upscale French restaurant, and is written on a chalkboard every day—in French. (You will have to ask what it says if you don't know the language.) Entrées $20–30.

&. **Winfield's** (719-689-5034; decasino.com/dining/winfield-s), 442 E. Bennett Ave., Cripple Creek. Open Fri. and Sat. for dinner 5–10. This upscale restaurant in located in Double Eagle Casino. The menu is primarily French cuisine and includes steak, lobster, chicken, and lamb. Be sure to call for reservations. Entrées $19–33.

EATING OUT &. **The Owl Cigar Store** (719-275-9946), 626 Main St., Cañon City. Open daily 9–7. Not only does the Owl serve the best burgers in town, it may just be the cheapest. Last time we stopped in, hamburgers and cheeseburgers were around $2.

&. **Waffle Wagon** (719-269-3428), 1310 Royal Gorge Blvd., Cañon City. Open daily for breakfast and lunch 6–1. It doesn't look like much from the outside, but this classic diner consistently serves up a delicious breakfast. The menu features the usual suspects—eggs, pancakes, bacon and sausage, and omelettes. They also do a couple of local favorites, such as the Lester Special that puts country-fried steak on an English muffin, topped with eggs, hash browns, cheese, and gravy. For lunch, there are burgers and a host of hot sandwiches. Meals $4–6.

BAKERIES & COFFEE SHOPS &. **16th Street Café** (719-275-5211), 302A N. 16th St., Cañon City. Open Mon.–Sat. 7:30–3. This bakery and espresso bar serves breakfast and lunch daily. It has fantastic muffins. For lunch, there are French baguette sandwiches and pizza.

✳ Entertainment

Thin Air Theatre at the Butte Opera House (719-689-6402; buttetheater.com), 139 E. Bennett Ave., Cripple Creek, puts on melodrama Wed.–Sun. every week in the summer. The show begins with a sing-along and ends with an olio (a hodgepodge of vaudeville-style singing, dancing, and comedy). The melodrama is always engaging and the cast welcomes the audience's participation. Boos, hisses, cheers, and commentary are all part of the fun. Shows are held at the Butte Opera House. Tickets all safely under $20. Call ahead for reservations because performances often sell out.

✳ Special Events

May: **Cañon City Music and Blossom Festival** (719-275-7234; ccblossomfestival.com), Cañon City. Held the first weekend in May, the festival features a parade, plenty of food vendors, and lots of great music.

June: **Donkey Derby Days** (719-689-3315 or 1-877-858-4653), Cripple Creek. This weekend-long event includes a parade, a donkey race, and the "Gold Stroll" and 1890s-style barn dance.

July: **Gold Rush Days** (719-689-0468; victorcolorado.com/goldrushdays.htm), Victor. This three-day festival is held the third weekend of July. A lot of musicians come to play, and others come to compete in the Battle of the Bands.

September/October: **Aspen Tours** (719-689-2169), Cripple Creek. For three weeks, folks can come up to Cripple Creek to celebrate fall. The town offers free Jeep rides into the mountains to see the aspens change color.

UPPER ARKANSAS VALLEY

Way back in August 2004, *Outside* magazine included Salida, Colorado, on its list of "20 Dream Towns." And it's only gotten better since then. Salida is a recreational paradise. The Arkansas River, which cuts through the middle of the valley, is where Colorado's whitewater enthusiasts come to play. All summer, the river is full of rafts, kayaks, and duckies tackling everything from class I to V rapids. Whereas the mountain towns (e.g., Crested Butte) stay cold into June and slickrock country (e.g., Fruita) is unbearably hot all summer, mountain bikers boast that Salida's mild climate means there is comfortable riding here year-round. For hikers, not only are there fifteen 14ers to conquer and hundreds of miles of trails, but the epic Colorado Trail is right here, winding through the Collegiate Peaks (including Mounts Harvard, Yale, and Princeton) along the valley's western boundary.

This recreational spirit extends north to the towns of Buena Vista and Leadville. The town of Buena Vista serves as a kicking-off point for many folks recreating in the valley. One of the most popular rafting trips in the country begins in Buena Vista and heads through Browns Canyon before it hits Salida. Buena Vista is also a place for relaxation and contemplation. It's a small town with a few nice options for staying the night and several exceptional restaurants. Nearby are two hot springs where guests can soak and relax.

Farther north is the town of Leadville. Sitting at 10,430 feet, it is the highest incorporated city in North America. At one time, it was the second-largest city in Colorado. During the Silver Boom, fortunes were made in Leadville. It was during this time that the landmark Tabor Opera House and Delaware Hotel were built downtown. Today, just a shadow of the town's former glory remains. Walking up and down Leadville's side streets, you will find many historic Victorian homes. Nearby you can explore the remains of the town's mining industry. While no longer the bustling city it once was, Leadville has several nice restaurants, plenty of lodging, museums galore, and a nice little ski area to the south.

GUIDANCE **Buena Vista Chamber of Commerce** (719-395-6612; buenavistacolorado .org), 343 US 24 S. Open year-round Mon.–Fri. 9–5. In the summer, open on weekends. The chamber offices and visitor center are located right on US 24 in an old church, which was originally built in 1879.

Heart of the Rockies Chamber of Commerce (719-539-2068 or 1-877-772-5432; salidachamber.org), 406 W. CO 50, Salida. The visitor center is open daily in the summer 9–5.

Leadville/Lake County Chamber of Commerce (719-486-3900 or 1-888-532-3845; leadvilleusa.com), 809 Harrison Ave. Open daily in the summer 9–4. The chamber runs a visitor center at this address.

More websites:
leadville.com

GETTING THERE *By car:* Coming from the west on I-70, get off at US 24 in Minturn (exit 171) and head south. From the east, take CO 91 south at Wheeler Junction (exit 195). Both roads meet in Leadville, at the top of the Upper Arkansas River Valley. Buena

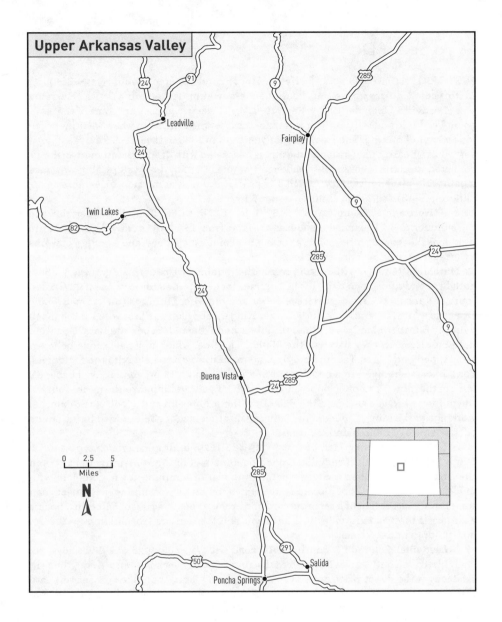

Upper Arkansas Valley

Vista and Salida are farther south along the Arkansas River. From Denver, US 285 is a straight shot to Buena Vista. From the southeast, in the area of Pueblo, the best route is US 50 west to Salida.

By air: **Eagle County Regional Airport** (970-328-2680; eaglecounty.us/airport), 219 Eldin Wilson Dr., in Gypsum is the closest commercial airport. Six major airlines have regular flights in and out of Eagle County Regional Airport.

GETTING AROUND *By car:* A car is your best bet in the Arkansas Valley. If you rent a high-clearance, four-wheel-drive vehicle, more of the mountain roads will be open to exploration.

✳ To See & Do

HISTORIC ATTRACTIONS ⚲ **Healy House and Dexter Cabin** (719-486-0487; historycolorado.org/museums/healy-house-museum-dexter-cabin), 912 Harrison Ave., Leadville. Open daily May–Sept. 10–4:30. These two houses are some of the earliest in Leadville and tell a little of what life was like when the town was a wealthy, populous center of mining. The Healy House was built in 1878 in the Greek Revival style. It served as a boardinghouse for a time and is decorated with grand Victorian furnishings collected from the area. As the residence of James Dexter, the Dexter Cabin was once a gathering place for the town's rich and powerful. Adult admission $6, seniors $5.50, children (6–16) $4.50, and children under 6 free.

    ♿ ⚲ **Heritage Museum** (719-486-1878), 102 E. Ninth St., Leadville. Open daily in the summer 10–4. The museum houses artifacts from Leadville's early days. There are dioramas illustrating mining life, a scale model of the Ice Palace, and a gallery of works by local artists. Small admission fee.

    Matchless Mine (719-486-3900; mininghalloffame.org/page/history), 414 W. Seventh St., Leadville. Open daily in the summer for self-guided tours noon–4:45. Guided tours at 1 and 3. The story of Horace Tabor and his wife, Elizabeth (nicknamed "Baby Doe"), is a local legend. One of the Silver Kings, Tabor left his first wife for the much younger Elizabeth McCourt. When the silver boom busted, Tabor and Baby Doe were left penniless. All they had was the Matchless Mine, which most everyone believed was tapped out. When Tabor was dying, he told Elizabeth to hold onto the Matchless. For 36 years she lived in a shack near the mine, hoping to prove that her husband's faith in the mine was not in vain. She eventually died watching over the mine. Tours of the property include a peek in the Baby Doe Tabor Museum and a look at the external workings of the mine. Guided tours: adults $12, students $10. Self-guided tours: adults $8, students 6. Children under 6 free.

    ♿ ⚲ **National Mining Hall of Fame** (719-486-1229; mininghalloffame.org), 120 W. Ninth St., P.O. Box 981, Leadville. Open Tue.-Sun. 9–5 in the winter and daily 9–5 in the summer. Exhibitions include a detailed model of a mining town, complete with model railroad. A series of dioramas illustrates the history of mining, and guests can walk through a section of a reproduction hard-rock mine. The Hall of Fame also boasts a large gift shop and art gallery. Adult admission $12, seniors $10, children (6–12) $10, and children under 6 free.

    ♿ **Leadville, Colorado & Southern Railroad Co.** (719-486-3936 or 1-866-386-3936; leadville-train.com), 326 E. Seventh St. During the busy season (June–Aug.), the railroad leaves the depot twice daily at 10 and 2. The 2.5-hour tour takes passengers into the nearby mountains with views of the Arkansas River valley and the Continental Divide. Adult admission $37, children (4–12) $20, and children under 4 free.

    ⚲ **Buena Vista Heritage Museum** (719-395-8458; buenavistaheritage.org/Heritage-Museum), 506 E. Main St., Buena Vista. Open in the summer, Memorial Day weekend through Labor Day weekend, Mon.–Sat. 10–5 and Sun. noon–5. Located in the Old Chaffee County Courthouse (completed in 1882), the Heritage Museum houses artifacts from the early years of Buena Vista's history. Adult admission $5, youth (6–18) $1.

HOT SPRINGS The mountains around the Upper Arkansas Valley are home to several hot springs that have been developed and channeled into pools and soaking tubs. Unlike many springs you might find elsewhere in Colorado, the mineral water emanating from the springs in this region is odorless.

THE VIEW OF MT. MASSIVE FROM LEADVILLE

 ♿ **Cottonwood Hot Springs Inn & Spa** (719-395-2102; cottonwood-hot-springs.com), 18999 CR 306, Buena Vista. Located 5.5 miles west of town. These lithium hot springs are open daily 9–midnight. In addition to the spa's large natural stone soaking pools, private hot tubs are available for an additional fee. Adult admission $20 and children (under 17) $15 on weekends; on weekdays the adult price drops to $18.

    Mt. Princeton Hot Springs Resort (719-395-2447 or 1-888-395-7799; mtprinceton .com), 15870 CR 162, Nathrop. Pools are open Sun.–Thu. 9–9 and Fri. and Sat. 9–11. Following Chalk Creek south of Mt. Princeton, the Hot Springs Resort sits nicely between the creek and road. There are three pools—a soaking pool, a cooler lap pool, and an even cooler fun pool with a 300-foot waterslide. The fee is $18 per day for adults, $12 for children and seniors.

 ♿ ☂ **Salida Hot Springs Aquatic Center** (719-539-6738; salidapool.com), 410 W. Rainbow Blvd., Salida. Check the website for a current pool schedule. This naturally hot mineral water is pumped 5 miles from its source in the mountains to the aquatic center in Salida. The indoor facility is open year-round and features a pool with lanes for swimming laps and a recreational pool. Adult admission $11, seniors $9, children (6–17) $5, and children (under 6) $3. Towels, suits, lockers, and showers are all available for an additional fee.

SCENIC DRIVES **Independence Pass** connects Twin Lakes with Aspen, crossing the Continental Divide along the way. It's one of the most scenic routes in the area. The pass is the highest paved path in North America at 12,095 feet. The road, CO 82, is closed in the winter.

    Route of the Silver Kings is the title of a map offered at the Leadville Chamber of Commerce. The map leads you on a self-guided driving tour of Leadville's mining district. Along the way, it tells a little history of each mine. Most roads do not require a four-wheel-drive vehicle.

LEADVILLE'S MOST FAMOUS COUPLE

In 1956, a new opera by composer Douglas Moore and librettist John Latouche premiered at the Central City Opera in Colorado. The work was entitled *The Ballad of Baby Doe*, and it retold the tragic story of Leadville's most famous couple.

Horace Tabor moved to Colorado in 1859 with his wife and son. They came after hearing of gold in the mountains. Tabor was an ambitious man. He was soon running the general store and post office in Leadville. He played an active role in the community and served for a short time as the town's mayor. In 1878, he agreed to provision two prospectors in return for a portion of whatever profits they might make. Within two months, Tabor's original investment of $17 in equipment and supplies returned to him $10,000, which he quickly invested in other mining endeavors. He soon bought the Matchless Mine, which for a time was the most productive in Leadville.

In 1880, a beautiful young woman of Irish stock came to Leadville. Elizabeth Bonduel McCourt Doe, or "Baby Doe" as she was called, had recently divorced her first husband. Not long after, Baby Doe and Tabor struck up a relationship—an affair, if you will. It seems Tabor and Baby Doe were very much in love, and after divorcing his wife he married Baby Doe officially in 1882. With money in his pocket and an adoring wife, he was able to follow his political ambitions with a vengeance, serving as lieutenant governor of Colorado and as U.S. senator—all the while building opera houses and other monuments to his wealth.

In 1893, with the repeal of the Sherman Silver Purchase Act, Tabor suddenly found himself penniless. Bankrupt, but not without friends, he was appointed to the job of postmaster of Denver. Tabor and Baby Doe's misfortune, however, was not yet over. In 1899, he got appendicitis and died. On his deathbed he made a final request. He asked Baby Doe to hold on to the Matchless Mine, telling her that when silver returned, the mine would restore her fortunes.

Baby Doe took his words to heart and returned to Leadville. She lived in an old storage shack beside the matchless mine for 36 years, always believing her beloved Horace was right. She became a recluse, and many folks believed she was a touch insane. She was found, in 1935, frozen to death in her shed.

✳ Outdoor Activities

ALPINE SKIING & SNOWBOARDING **Ski Cooper** (719-486-2277 or 1-800-707-6114; skicooper.com), 232 CR 29. Not to be confused with Copper Mountain, Ski Cooper is 10 miles north of Leadville on US 24 (on Tennessee Pass). The ski hill offers 1,200 vertical feet from the base to the summit. There are 26 trails, the longest 1.4 miles. Four hundred skiable acres are served by three lifts. There are another 2,400 acres accessible by snowcat. The ski area has a ski school with instruction for all levels and ages.

Monarch Ski and Snowboard Area (719-530-50000; skimonarch.com), 23715 W. Hwy 50, Monarch. Located a little more than 21 miles west of Salida on US 50. The chairlifts run 9–4 daily during the ski season. There are no snowmakers here, so the ski area's 54 trails are covered in natural snow. From the summit to the base is a 1,170-foot vertical drop. There are 800 skiable acres here; another 900 are available by snowcat. The terrain parks are separated for snowboarders of varying abilities.

Bill's Ski Rentals (719-486-0739; www.billsrentals.com), 225 Harrison Ave., Leadville. Located at the south end of town, the rental shop is the sister store for Bill's Sport Shop downtown. Bill's rents skis and snowboards, and sells discounted lift passes to Ski Cooper.

CROSS-COUNTRY SKIING **Piney Creek Nordic Center** (719-486-1750; tennessee pass.com/nordic-center), at the base of the Ski Cooper ski area, 10 miles north of Leadville on US 24. Open daily 9–4:30. Miles of groomed cross-country skiing trails are available with a $15 pass (seniors and children $10). There are routes for all abilities, and the center offers ski rental and private ski instruction as well.

FISHING The **Arkansas River** offers some of the best fly fishing in Colorado. **Halfmoon Creek** and **Chalk Creek** are also popular spots to float a fly. Additionally, several lakes make for a good day out on the water. **Twin Lakes Reservoir** is south of Leadville in the town of Twin Lakes; there is also **Turquoise Lake**. The mountain setting alone makes this lake worth a visit. It's just west of Leadville.

ArkAnglers (719-539-4223; arkanglers.com), 7500 W. US 50, Salida. This full-service fly shop offers guided tours, fishing gear, and intimate knowledge of local fishing conditions and locations. It also has a shop in Buena Vista (719-395-1796) at 517 US 24 S.

FOUR-WHEELING **Weston Pass** and **Mosquito Pass** were once the main routes to Leadville. Mosquito Pass is the highest auto pass in the United States at 13,986 feet. Both routes have sections that require four-wheel drive.

Buena Vista Jeep Rental (719-395-4418; bvjeeps.com), 212 US 24 S., Buena Vista. To get over some of the more remote passes, such as Mosquito or Hagerman Pass, you need a four-wheel-drive vehicle. Rent a Jeep Wrangler or Cherokee and see the mountains without a guide for $180/day and week rates.

High Country Jeep Tours (719-395-6111 or 1-866-458-6877; highcountryjeeptours .com), 410 US 24 S., Buena Vista. Guests will not need to rent a vehicle or consult a map when they take one of these Jeep tours. Tours include trips to St. Elmo and the Mary Murphy Mine, Mt. Princeton, and Mt. Antero. Adult full-day tour rate $135 and children under 13 $75; half-day adult $70 and children $48.

ST. ELMO, A GHOST TOWN

MONARCH RIDGE SOUTH

Monarch Ridge South offers not so much a hike but a nice meander at altitude. The Continental Divide, and thus the Continental Divide Trail, crosses US 50 at Monarch Pass. On the east side of the road, at 11,312 feet, is the Monarch Crest Scenic Tramway and Gift Shop (719-539-4091; monarchcrest.net; 24500 US 50, Salida). It's a great tourist stop, as those things go—a huge selection of T-shirts, some unique souvenirs, and a decent snack counter. The tramway, at the south end of the dirt parking lot, takes passengers up to Monarch Ridge South (elevation 11,898 feet). From the summit, a panorama of peaks (the southern end of the Sawatch Range) makes this one of the state's most stunning vistas. The tramway shed has a second level with an enclosed viewing area and a wrap-around deck, but everyone should walk along the ridge, examine the tiny high-altitude wildflowers, and explore a little before returning to the parking lot.

Interesting fact: In 2016, a 148-mph gust of wind was recorded by the weather station on Monarch Pass. This is the strongest wind gust recorded by the National Weather Service in Colorado.

GOLF **Mount Massive Golf Course** (719-486-2176; mtmassivegolf.com), 259 CR 5, Leadville. This nine-hole public course on the outskirts of Leadville is North America's highest golf course. Greens fees for 9 holes $24–31.

HIKING Upper Arkansas Valley, between the Collegiate Peaks and the Mosquito Range, has plenty of trails to get you into the mountains. The most noteworthy is the **Colorado Trail**. The trail stretches across the state from Durango to Denver. The section that passes through this region sticks to the west side of the valley. A nice 13-mile trek would be to begin at the trailhead at the west end of Turquoise Lake. Take the trail south until it crosses Halfmoon Road at Emerald Lake.

In Twin Lakes, the Colorado Trail passes along the southern shore of the lakes. Called here the **Interlaken Trail**, the 3-mile route begins at the dam and takes you around the lake to the historic resort town of Interlaken. There are paths here that lead up to Hope Pass, if you are looking for more adventure.

In addition to the network of trails, two 14ers near Leadville offer hikers a chance to put a couple of notches in their belts. **Mt. Elbert** and **Mt. Massive** can each be ascended in a day. Mt. Elbert is an especially juicy conquest because it is the tallest peak in Colorado (14,433 feet). The trailhead for Mt. Elbert is just north of Twin Lakes on CR 24, just past the Lakeview Campground. The route is an 8-mile round-trip from the end of the four-wheel-drive road. The trailhead for Mt. Massive is just beyond Elbert Creek Campground on Halfmoon Road, southwest of Leadville. The round trip is 13.75 miles.

The Trailhead (719-395-8001 or 1-866-595-8001; thetrailheadco.com), 707 US 24 N., Buena Vista. Open May–Sept. 8–8, and the rest of the year 9–5:30. The folks at the trailhead are an excellent resource for getting familiar with local trails and activities. They offer a full line of equipment for rent, including mountain bikes and camping gear in the summer. And in the winter they rent cross-country and backcountry skis and snowshoes.

MOUNTAIN BIKING Mountain biking is one way to tackle some of the area's tougher back roads. **Mosquito Pass** and **Weston Pass**, which climb the mountains east of US 24, are very popular routes, as is **Hagerman Pass**, west of Turquoise Lake. Speaking of the

KAYAKING THE ARKANSAS RIVER IN SALIDA

lake, the **Turquoise Lake Trail** runs from May Queen Campground to Sugarloaf Dam. The 6.4-mile route is a scenic stretch of trail that overlooks the lake.

The mountains around Salida also boast miles of great mountain biking. The **Monarch Crest Trail** is one of the area's best. There is talk that the government might restrict access, so check with a local shop before heading out. The **Colorado Trail**, another great trail for riding, parallels the Continental Divide from Leadville down to Buena Vista, a bit to the west from Salida. And for a more strenuous ride, try the **Rainbow Trail**, which skirts across the Sangre de Cristo Mountains. You can do a loop that begins and ends in town—ask the folks at Absolute Bikes for route information.

Absolute Bikes (719-539-9295; absolutebikes.com), 330 W. Sackett St. Few shops have as much local mountain biking knowledge as this one. Their website has up-to-date trail condition information. They also rent mountain bikes, town cruisers, and trailers for pulling the kids. Full-day trail bike rental $12 (for kids bike) to $75 (for the all-out trail bike).

PADDLING & RAFTING **Dvorak's Rafting & Kayak** (719-539-6851 or 1-800-824-3795; dvorakexpeditions.com), 17921 US 285, Nathrop. Dvorak's offers rafting trips down the Arkansas as well as other rivers in a five-state region—not including trips down the Rio Grande in Texas and those its guides lead overseas. And you don't have to travel far for multiday adventures. The Arkansas River has enough water to stretch a rafting trip out for several days. Half-day trips for adults run about $60 for adults.

Noah's Ark Whitewater Rafting Co. (719-395-2158; noahsark.com), 23910 US 285, Buena Vista. Noah's guides take rafters on several stretches of the Arkansas River—Royal Gorge, the Narrows, Browns Canyon. They also offer rafting and backpacking trips. Rates vary by the trip you schedule, but seem to run about $66 for half-day trips and $125 for full-day trips. Children's rates, of course, are a little less.

DELAWARE HOTEL IN LEADVILLE

CHALK CLIFFS SOUTHWEST OF BUENA VISTA

Twin Lakes Canoe & Kayak Adventures (719-251-9961; twinlakescanoeandkayak
.com), 6251 E. CO 82, Twin Lakes. For those yearning to get out on the water, but
looking for something different than whitewater rafting, Twin Lakes Canoe & Kayak
Adventures has canoes and kayaks for rent—perfect for exploring Twin Lakes or Turquoise Reservoir.

✳ Green Space

Arkansas Headwaters State Park (719-539-7289; cpw.state.co.us/placestogo/Parks
/ArkansasHeadwatersRecreationArea), 307 W. Sackett Ave., Salida. Open 24 hours a
day. This impressive park is unlike other state parks with a central office and visitor
center. The Arkansas Headwaters State Park runs along the Arkansas River from Leadville to Lake Pueblo, a distance of 150 miles. There are six campgrounds and numerous
boating access points along the river. Walk-in fee $3; daily vehicle pass $7.

✳ Lodging

HOTELS ((•)) **Delaware Hotel** (719-486-
1418 or 1-800-748-2004; delawarehotel
.com), 700 Harrison Ave., Leadville. The
Delaware is fashioned in full-out Victorian style. Each room is different and
decorated in antique furnishings. Every
available common space has antiques on
display—so much so that the hotel often
seems to be an antiques gallery. In a very
real sense, it is. All the antiques, even
those in the rooms, are for sale. All
rooms have cable TV. The hotel has no
elevator. There's a great restaurant
downstairs. Rooms $50–265.

BED & BREAKFASTS ((•)) **Liars' Lodge**
(719-395-3444or 1-888-542-7756;
liarslodge.com), 30000 CR 371, Buena
Vista. Liars' Lodge is a modern log cabin

with vaulted ceilings and panoramic windows overlooking the Arkansas River. The lodge offers five rooms and one cabin. Two of the rooms have a Jacuzzi for two. Others have a deck overlooking the river. (Children under 5 and pets may be allowed in the cabin, but guests must discuss that with the innkeepers ahead of their visit.) Rooms $88–178.

(ᵞᵖ) **Mountain River Inn** (719-395-8599; mountainriverinn.com) 30670 CR 371, Buena Vista. The rooms at Mountain River Inn highlight the rustic charm of the mountains. But don't let the knotty pine and colorful quilts fool you. The inn offers all the amenities necessary for a comfortable stay. There are heated slate floors in the private bathrooms; each room has a microwave and refrigerator; and one features a gas-fired log stove. You will want to linger in the well-appointed common areas, and the property's location on the Arkansas River offers opportunities to watch the water or gaze at nearby mountain peaks. Rooms $165–185.

& ❀ (ᵞᵖ) **Tudor Rose** (719-539-2002 or 1-800-379-0889; thetudorrose.com), 6720 CR 104, Salida. This B&B was built in 1979 as a private residence. It was converted to an inn in 1995. It sits on 37 acres of piñon pine, just 1.5 miles from Salida. The guest rooms are spacious and comfortable. The inn's one suite, the Henry Tudor Suite, has a raised hot tub for two and great views of the mountains. All rooms have TVs and CD players. Free wireless Internet is available in the chalet. A full breakfast is served every morning. Rooms $80–185.

CABINS **Merrifield Homestead Cabins and Hot Springs** (719-581-0282; coloradohotspringsresort.com), 19320 CR 306, Buena Vista. Two cabins. The smaller was built in the 1800s and can sleep six. It is fully updated with modern amenities. The larger was originally built in the 1920s and can accommodate up to eight

guests. Both have a hot springs pool. Cabins start at $350 and $550 per night.

CAMPGROUNDS **Sugar Loafin' Campground** (719-486-1031; leadville.com /sugarloafin), 2665 CR 4, Leadville. This shady campground is located just east of Turquoise Lake. In addition to tent and RV sites, the campground rents out cabins as well. Tent sites $34.05 and RV sites $35–45 and cabins for $130.

✳ Where to Eat

DINING OUT **Tennessee Pass Cookhouse** (719-486-8114; tennesseepass.com /cookhouse.htm), Leadville. Serving lunch on Sat. and Sun. at noon or 1:30. Dinner by reservation. Groups meet at the base of the Ski Cooper Ski Area (10 miles north of Leadville on US 24) at 5:30 for dinner. As a group they then hike, bike, or Jeep the 1 mile to the cookhouse's remote location in the mountains. In the winter guests hike, snowshoe, or cross-country ski to the cookhouse. Dinner is an elegant, four-course affair. The menu offers a few selections that must be made ahead of time (when you make reservations). Because of the rustic nature of the cookhouse (there is no electricity or running water), the only light is candlelight and heat comes from a woodstove. Dinner $85. Lunch is from the menu, entrées $14–18.

& ❢ **Amícas** (719-539-5219; amicas salida.com), 127 F St., Salida. Open Thu.–Sun. 7–9-ish and Mon.–Wed. 11–9-ish. Casual Italian fare in Salida. Wood-oven baked pizza and microbrews are what make this pizzeria/microbrewery the place for dinner on a Friday night (or any night). They have a beer sampler for newcomers looking to find their favorite brew, and both the pizzas and beer can be taken to go. Now serving in the morning, guests can dig into breakfast tacos or a breakfast pie (i.e., pizza). Pizzas $14.

EATING OUT   & ♈ **Grill Bar and Cafe**
(719-486-9930; grillbarcafe.com), 715
Elm St., Leadville. All the locals will tell
you this is the best Mexican food in
Leadville. The restaurant started as a
boardinghouse. The food was so popular
that eventually the boarders were kicked
out to make room for diners. The green
chili is pretty darn good, and diners like
to talk about how much they enjoy the
margaritas. Dishes $10–20.

  & **Shallots** (719-559-4759; shallots-
salida.com), 137 E. First St., Salida.
Open daily 11–9, Sun. brunch 9–2. If
you remember First Street Café, seeing
this newcomer in its place might cause
a small frown. But don't be discouraged.
Shallots may be a little more upscale
(burger menu reveals Latin and Asian
influences), but it's still great food.
Burgers and sandwiches $12–14. Dinner
entrées $14–29.

Sweetie's Sandwich Shop (719-539-
4248; sweetiesinsalida.com), 124 F St.,
Salida. Open 10–4 every day but Sun.
There might be no better place in town
for a great lunch. The menu here is
expansive, offering a host of cold and hot
sandwiches, all in the $10 range.

BAKERIES & COFFEE SHOPS & **Sacred
Ground Coffee** (719-539-7500; mountain
phoenixcoffee.com), 216 W Rainbow
Blvd, Salida. Open daily 7–5 (closing at
noon on Sundays). A lot of coffeehouses
are about something else—ambiance,
baked goods, street cred. Sacred Ground
is about the coffee, but it has some of that
other stuff too.

✳ Selective Shopping

Fabulous Finds Emporium (719-530-
0544), 243 F St., Salida. Open daily in the
summer, Mon.–Sat. 10–6 and Sun. 1–5;
fall and winter closed a half hour early
during the week; during spring, closed
on Tuesday. This antiques mall has more
than 35 vendors and 7,500 square feet of
antiques.

✳ Special Events

June: **Blue Paddle FIBArk Whitewater
Festival** (fibark.com), Salida. FIBArk
stands for "First in Boating the Arkansas." The festival has all sorts of water
events—kayaking competitions and a
raft rodeo. There's also live music.

August: **Boom Days** (719-486-3900;
leadvilleboomdays.com), Leadville. The
first weekend in August, Leadville celebrates its mining history with a pancake
breakfast, parade, and pack burro race.
Other activities such as mining events
and live entertainment round out the
weekend.

Gold Rush Days (719-395-6612;
buenavistacolorado.org/buena-vista-
gold-rush-days), Buena Vista. Burro
races, a rubber duck race, and tons
of live entertainment punctuate this
annual festival. Performers include an
impressive array of musicians, as well as
storytellers, western dancers, and actors
presenting melodrama.

Leadville Trail 100 (719-219-9352;
leadvilleraceseries.com), Leadville. This
mountain bike race covers 100 miles of
technical mountain terrain. Riders will
climb more than 14,000 feet over the
course of the competition. There's also a
foot race later in the month.

SAN LUIS VALLEY

Driving west from Walsenburg along US 160, you cross the Sangre de Cristo Range and a wide valley opens up before you. It is 50 miles across the valley floor to the San Juan and La Garita ranges. From north to south, the valley stretches 125 miles. As such, the San Luis Valley is one of the largest valley basins in the country.

Hemmed in by stunning mountain peaks, yet with no peaks of its own, this region is often ignored by the tourists who come to Colorado for Rocky Mountain majesty. If they do come, they are likely here to see the area's biggest attraction, the Great Sand Dunes National Park. These massive dunes rest up against the Sangre de Cristos, northeast of Alamosa.

Because so few people have made the San Luis Valley a vacation destination, there is little tourist infrastructure. There are no boutique hotels, no historic shopping districts, no monthly art walks along the galleries of Main Street. There is no fine dining. This also means that there are no long lines, no crowded streets, no pretentious waiters, and no cheesy tourist trappings.

What the valley does have are a number of small towns that offer true hospitality. Here and there you will find decent small-town diners and restaurants. There are also a few quality B&Bs with innkeepers who really go all out for guests. And there are attractions such as the Cumbres & Toltec and the Rio Grande Scenic Railroads. For these reasons, the San Luis Valley is prime country for those who want to be near the mountains but enjoy peace and solitude.

The valley is also very popular with hunters and anglers. With several wide rivers and plenty of free-roaming game, it's the perfect spot for a sportsman's vacation.

GUIDANCE **Alamosa County Chamber of Commerce** (719-589-3681; alamosa.org), 610 State Ave., #1. Open Mon.–Sat. 8–5. Located in the yellow building that looks like an old train depot, the Alamosa Visitor Center shares an office with the chamber of commerce.

The **Monte Vista Chamber of Commerce** (719-852-2731; monte-vista.org) operates a visitor center that is open Mon.–Fri. 8–5. The center is located on Main Street next to the historic Monte Villa Inn.

GETTING THERE *By car:* The San Luis Valley is a large stretch of land. The region is cross-cut by US 160, which runs east and west, and US 285, which runs north and south. For some reason, US 285 makes a jog west of Alamosa, and travelers coming from the north will want to follow CO 17.

By bus: **Greyhound** (719-589-4948 or 1-800-231-2222; greyhound.com) operates regular service to and from Alamosa from the SLV Van Lines at 8480 Stockton.

✤ To See & Do

Great Sand Dunes National Park and Preserve (719-378-6300; nps.gov/grsa), 11500 CO 150, Mosca. Open year-round, 24 hours a day. The Great Sand Dunes are one of Colorado's most spectacular geological features—also one of the state's most unique

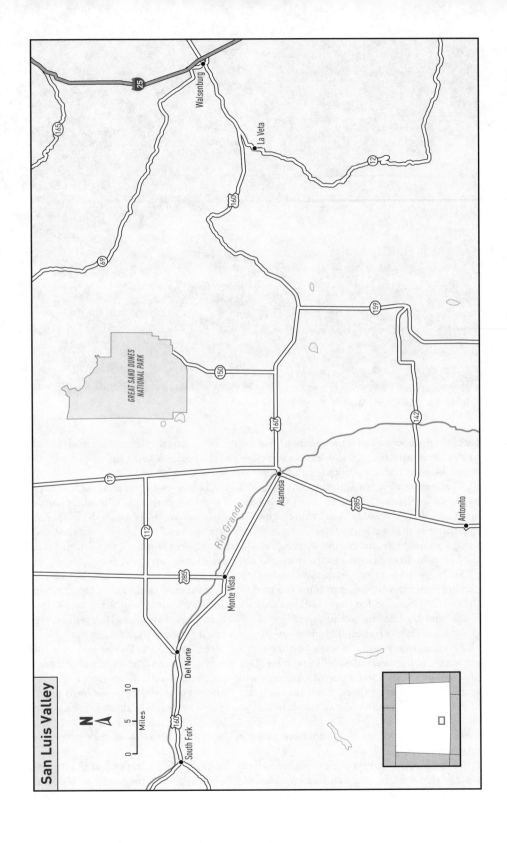

GREAT SAND DUNES NATIONAL PARK

natural attractions. The dunes seem to rise mystically from the plains. At first dwarfed by the mountains behind, the dunes soon overtake the horizon, towering over the landscape, leaving visitors gawky for a moment in sublime awe.

Thousands of years ago, the San Luis Valley was covered by a shallow lake; it's called Lake Alamosa by those who study and discuss such things. Climatic change and possible geological events caused the lake to shrink and eventually disappear. A sprawling sand sheet was left behind. Over the years, the sand was blown into a natural pocket against the mountains by the prevailing southwest winds. Storm winds from the opposite direction caused the dunes to rise—the highest up to 750 feet.

For more than 11,000 years, the area has attracted human visitors—from the ancient nomadic people who came to hunt the prehistoric bison and mammoths that grazed the nearby plains, to the eager park visitors who slather on sunscreen, strap on a CamelBak, and try hoofing to the top of the big dune. In 1932, President Hoover created Great Sand Dunes National Monument—it was made a national park in 2000.

After paying the entrance fee, begin your tour of the Great Sand Dunes at the visitor center. Exhibitions and displays illustrate the natural processes that led to the creation of the dunes. Throughout the day, rangers give informative talks, and there's a bookstore and small art gallery. After tackling the visitor center, most people head down to Medano Creek at the foot of the dunes. If you arrive before July, there will be water enough to cool your feet. This is a nice way to counter the hot sand. After July, the creek dries up until spring. From here, you can begin a walk up the dune or simply sit by the creek in the shade.

Several trails lead into the mountains from the park. With a high-clearance, four-wheel-drive vehicle, you can head up Medano Creek Trail and then hike to Medano Lake. But the best experience of the dunes has to be blazing your own trail to the top and taking in the view. (When Zebulon Pike climbed the one of the taller dunes in 1807, he could see the Rio Grande flowing nearly 30 miles to the southeast.) For those interested in camping on the dunes, a free permit from the visitor center is required. Entrance to the park is $15/vehicle. An annual pass only costs $30; it admits the pass holder and all family members in the vehicle into the park for one year.

Rio Grande Scenic Railroad (1-877-726-7245; coloradotrain.com), 610 State Ave., Alamosa. This rather new scenic railroad takes passengers on two routes. The main full-day trip, the San Luis Express, heads east over the mountains through La Veta Pass, and then stops in La Veta for two hours before heading back. The other trip, the Toltec Gorge Limited, heads south to Antonito, where passengers can connect with the Cumbres & Toltec Scenic Railroad. The train rides on standard gauge rails and uses steam locomotion to transport passengers. Round-trip tickets run $50–150; call for current pricing.

& **Cumbres & Toltec Scenic Railroad** (1-888-286-2737; cumbrestoltec.com), 5234 B US 285, Antonito. Trains depart daily from Antonito, Colorado, and Chama, New Mexico. The season runs mid-May–mid-Oct. This is the highest and longest narrow-gauge railroad in the country. The main route is a full-day round-trip to Osier that crosses the Colorado–New Mexico border several times as it winds over and through the mountains. Tickets $50–200, depending on level of service.

Los Caminos Antiguos Scenic and Historic Byway (codot.gov/travel/scenic-byways /south-central/los-caminos). This scenic byway takes travelers around the San Luis Valley. Beginning in Alamosa, the route travels north and then east by the Great Sand Dunes National Park. It then heads south to Fort Garland and San Luis, where it turns west to Cumbres Pass in the southern San Juan Mountains, passing Antonito en route. Along the way, you may see wildlife such as golden eagles and pronghorn antelope.

⬥ **San Luis Valley History Museum** (719-587-0667; museumtrail.org/SanLuis ValleyHistoryMuseum.asp), 401 Hunt Ave., Alamosa. Open Tue.–Sat. year-round 10–4. This museum strives to tell the story of the people who explored and settled the San Luis Valley. From the area's first inhabitants to today's ranchers and farmers, museum exhibitions illustrate the region's deep history. Adults $3, children $2, and kids under 5 free.

✳ Green Space

San Luis Lakes State Park (719-378-2020; cpw.state.co.us/placestogo/Parks/Sanluis), P.O. Box 150, Mosca. Open daily 5–10. The Sangre de Cristo Range serves as a majestic backdrop to the park's San Luis Lake and Head Lakes. The park offers 4 miles of trails. The landscape is flat and the trails are accordingly easygoing for both hiking and mountain biking. Visitors may also go boating or do some fishing. Daily vehicle pass $7.

✳ Lodging

HOTELS **Steam Train Hotel** (719-376-5300 or 1-888-686-7510; steamtrainhotel .com), 402 Main St., Antonio. There's not a lot by way of lodging in this part of Colorado. The Steam Train Hotel is likely the best place to stay within a several-hours' drive. Perfect for families making the trek out to ride the Cumbres & Toltec Scenic Railroad, the hotel is also close to the Indiana Jones Home (indianajonesbedandbreakfast.com), which was used for scenes from *Indiana Jones and the Last Crusade* with River Phoenix playing a younger Indy. (The home is now a B&B.) Rooms start at $109.

THE GREAT SAND DUNES

BED & BREAKFASTS **Indiana Jones Bed & Breakfast** (719-376-2278 or 1-800-497-5650; indianajonesbedandbreakfast.com), 502 Front St., Antonito. Featured in the movie *Indiana Jones and the Last Crusade*, this simple abode played the role of Indy's childhood home. The inn is located one block off Main Street in Antonito. Each of the four rooms is simply decorated; one has a private bath. This is a great stop for Spielberg fans. Rooms $129–140.

CAMPGROUNDS **San Luis Lakes State Park** (719-378-2020; cpw.state.co.us/placestogo/Parks/Sanluis), P.O. Box 150, Mosca. The campground has 51 sites. The park recently announced that campers need to bring their own potable water and ice, because it has become cost prohibitive to maintain the water system. Sites $24 (not including the $7 park vehicle pass).

✳ Where to Eat

EATING OUT ♿ **Calvillo's Mexican Restaurant** (719-587-5500; calvillos.com), 400 Main St., Alamosa. Open daily 8–10. Serving Mexican cuisine with roots all over Mexico and the Southwest, Calvillo's has quite a local following. Guests rave about the buffet (only $9.95), but even more so about the menu of fine dishes such as the *chiles rellenos*, or the *parrillada estilo Calvillo*, or the UFO enchiladas (this one is served up New Mexico style with two eggs on top). Dinner entrées $7–8.

SOUTHWEST COLORADO

■

DURANGO, SILVERTON,
& THE FOUR CORNERS

PAGOSA SPRINGS & THE
SOUTHERN SAN JUANS

TELLURIDE & OURAY

CRESTED BUTTE & GUNNISON

DURANGO, SILVERTON, & THE FOUR CORNERS

The story of Durango begins with the railroad. The town was founded in 1880 when Gen. William Palmer, owner of the Denver & Rio Grande Railroad, was refused a spot for his train depot in nearby Animas. By 1882, narrow-gauge rail service had been extended to Silverton, and soon the new town of Durango was busy smelting ores brought down from the mountains. As mining played out in the mountains, the railroad struggled to survive for a while, and then was closed. The Durango smelter remained busy with uranium for some time after World War II, but the rail line looked as though it might be abandoned altogether. A group of individuals lobbied hard for the preservation of the Durango & Silverton Railroad as a tourist attraction and won. It wasn't long before Hollywood took notice and featured the train in several movies.

Throughout its history, Durango has catered to tourists. The scenic value of the train ride to Silverton was touted to potential passengers from the beginning. When Mesa Verde National Park was established in 1906, it was yet another attraction that might draw tourists to southwest Colorado.

Today, Durango is established as the region's largest city and continues to flourish. The Animas Riverwalk has opened up the river to pedestrians. The Children's Museum is expanding, and in several years a new museum of wider scope, the Durango Discovery Museum, will be housed in a new complex that will include the town's old Power House. Durango is home to Fort Lewis College (the highest college in North America), Rocky Mountain Chocolate Factory, and the locally popular Zuberfizz soda company. The biggest industry in town, however, is tourism. Durango serves as a base camp for trips into the Four Corners region as well as a gateway to the mountains. Visitors pour into town to ride the Durango & Silverton Narrow-Gauge Railroad, which makes daily runs to and from Silverton throughout the summer. The Mesa Verde National Park cliff dwellings attract thousands each year. These archaeological sites of the ancient Pueblo have proven to be quite a draw for visitors, and more sites have been found throughout the Four Corners, in Hovenweep National Monument and Canyons of the Ancients National Monument.

Durango has also become a recreation center. Hundreds of miles of trails for hiking and mountain biking can be accessed right from town. The Colorado Trail, which begins in Denver, has its western terminus just north of town. And in the winter, Purgatory Resort has alpine skiing and snowboarding.

As you read through this chapter, be advised that all the addresses are in Durango unless otherwise indicated.

GUIDANCE **Durango Area Tourism Office** (1-800-525-8855; durango.org), 111 S. Camino del Rio. Just as you come into town from the east on US 160 (Camino del Rio), Santa Rita Park will be on your left, along the Animas River. The tourism office/visitor center is there in the park (1-800-463-8726).

Colorado Welcome Center at Cortez (970-565-4048 or 1-800-253-1616; mesaverdecountry.com), 928 E. Main St. Open daily in the summer 8–9 and in winter 8–5. The welcome center is operated by the Cortez Chamber of Commerce and the Colorado Tourism office. It provides extensive information for those visiting Colorado, and

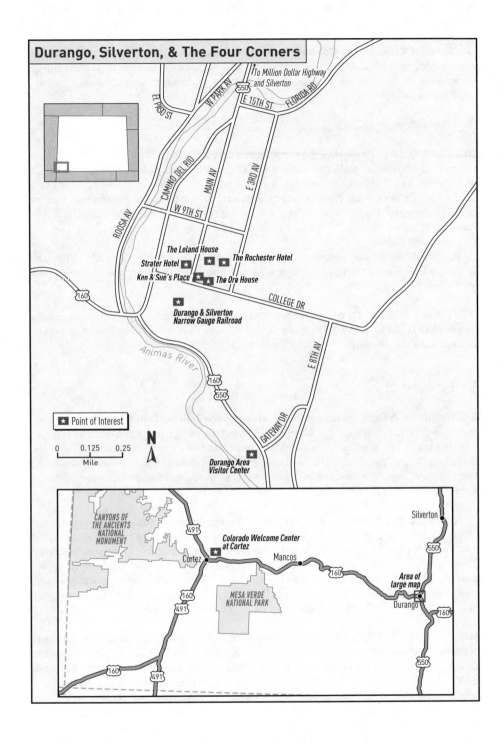

the staff are able to offer an insider's perspective on visiting Cortez and Mesa Verde National Park. There are walls and walls of brochures, a small bookstore, and clean restrooms.

Silverton Chamber of Commerce & Visitor Center (970-387-5654 or 1-800-752-4494; silvertoncolorado.com), located where US 550 and CO 110 meet at 414 Greene St. Open daily in the summer 9–6, spring and fall 9–5, and winter 10–4.

More websites:

durango.com

durangodowntown.com

GETTING THERE *By car:* US 160 runs east and west through Durango, terminating in the east in Walsenburg. US 550 runs north and south through town. To the north, US 550 connects with US 50 and continues on to I-70.

By air: **Durango–La Plata County Airport** (970-247-8143; flydurango.com or durangogov.org/airport), 1000 Airport Rd., hosts two major airlines—American Airlines and United Airlines. Together they provide daily service to and from Denver, Phoenix, and Dallas.

By bus: **Greyhound** operates regular service to and from Durango from the Durango Greyhound station (970-259-2755 or 1-800-231-2222; greyhound.com) at 250 W. Eighth St.

GETTING AROUND *By bus or trolley:* **Durango Transit** (970-375-4940; durangogov .org/transit) operates a system of buses and trolleys that cover all of Durango—many run late into the evening.

✳ To See & Do

EXCURSIONS ♿ **Durango & Silverton Narrow-Gauge Railroad** (1-888-872-4607; durango train.com), Durango Depot, 479 Main Ave. During the peak summer season the railroad has four trains leaving Durango daily. The train has been used in a number of movies, including *Butch Cassidy and the Sundance Kid*. The 45-mile trek to Silverton runs along the Animas River. The layover in Silverton gives passengers more than two hours to roam the town—plenty of time to grab a bite to eat and do some window shopping.

HOT SPRINGS **Trimble Spa & Natural Hot Springs** (970-247-0111; trimblehotsprings .com), 6475 CR 203. Hot Springs hours: Open daily (except Wed.) 11–8:45. Back in the day, both Marilyn Monroe and Clark Gable soaked in the Trimble Hot Springs. Today, Trimble offers a large swimming pool, hot pools, and a beautifully landscaped picnic area. For the full treatment, consider the spa services, which include several massage treatments. Hot Springs rates: $18 for all-day pass for adults, $12 for children (4–12), and $11 for seniors. Check the website or call for current spa rates.

MONUMENTS & PARKS OF SOUTHWEST COLORADO **Canyon of the Ancients National Monument** (www.blm.gov/co/st/en/nm/canm.html), west of Cortez. A visit to Canyon of the Ancients should begin at the **Anasazi Heritage Center** (970-882-5600; co.blm.gov/ahc), 27501 CO 184, Dolores. This museum is open daily in the summer 9–5 and in the winter 10–4. The museum offers visitors the perfect introduction to ancestral Pueblo culture and the canyon. Over 6,000 archaeological sites have been discovered at the park—many from the ancestral Pueblo, but also a number of more recent Navajo sites. These finds are not recognizable to the average visitor, and their locations are

DURANGO & SILVERTON NARROW-GAUGE RAILROAD

not publicized. For many visitors this makes for a frustrating tour, but those who like exploring and the joy of discovery will find it a fun place to visit. Museum admission $3 for adults (free Nov.–Feb.); kids under 17 are free.

Four Corners Monument (928-871-6647; navajonationparks.org/navajo-tribal-parks /four-corners-monument), southwest corner of the state, right on US 160. Open daily in the summer 7–8 and in winter 8–5. This is the only place in the United States where the boundaries of four states meet in one place. Such a fortuitous alignment cannot be ignored, so in 1912, a cement slab was laid down to mark the spot. Since then a regular granite and brass monument has been erected. Admission is $53 for all ages.

Hovenweep National Monument (970-562-4282 ext. 10; nps.gov/hove), McElmo Route, Cortez. The visitor center is open daily April–Sept. 8–6 and Oct.–March 8–5. Tucked inside Canyon of the Ancients, Hovenweep preserves a large number of ancestral Pueblo structures. The most accessible are part of the Square Tower Group—the largest collection of such sites in the park. A paved trail leads out to an overlook of the site. Continuing on, the path is unpaved and becomes moderately strenuous as it follows the canyon rim. Hikers are rewarded for their efforts with excellent views of all the ruins. No entrance fee.

Ute Mountain Tribal Park (970-565-9653; utemountaintribalpark.info), P.O. Box 109, Towaoc. On a reservation more than a half-million acres in size, the Ute tribe offers visitors a unique perspective on and experience of the region's cliff dwellings. Serving fewer visitors than pour into Mesa Verde, Native American Ute guides lead tours of the park's cliff dwellings, petroglyphs, and unique geological formations. All of this is interpreted through Ute eyes. The half-day tour (9–12:30) runs $29 per person. The full-day tour (9–4), which includes a 3-mile hike to explore cliff dwellings, costs $60.

MUSEUMS & HISTORIC SITES &♥ **Animas Museum** (970-259-2402; animasmuseum .org), 3065 W. Second Ave. Open in the summer Mon.–Sat. 10–5 and in winter Tue.– Sat. 10–4. Exhibitions and displayed artifacts tell the story of Durango and La Plata County. The museum itself is a bit of history; it's housed in a schoolhouse from 1904.

Inside, a classroom has been restored to 1908. The museum also preserves the oldest intact structure in Durango—a cabin built by blacksmith C. B. Joy back in the 1870s. Adult admission $4, seniors 65 and over $3, children (7–12) $2, and children under 7 free.

National Historic Districts, Durango. Downtown Durango, centered on Main Ave., is a registered historic district. Some of the more noteworthy buildings are the Palace and Statler hotels. A block away, Third Avenue has also been designated as a national historic district. On either side of the tree-lined boulevard you'll find historic homes—many from the Victorian period.

 ♧ **Old Hundred Mine** (970-387-5444 or 1-800-872-3009; minetour.com), 721 CR 4A P.O. Box 430, Silverton. The mine is located east of Silverton, so just head out of town on CR 2 and follow the blue-and-white signs. Open daily in the summer. Tours leave on the hour 10–4. The mine tour takes visitors 1,600 feet underground (it's below 50 degrees F in there, so dress accordingly). For 50 minutes, guides share the history of the mine and demonstrate mining techniques on actual equipment. After the tour, guests can head to the sluice box and pan for gold, silver, and precious stones. Adult admission $18.95, seniors $16.95, children (5–12) $9.95, and children under 5 free if held on lap.

⚟ **Mayflower Gold Mill Tour** (970-387-0294; sanjuancountyhistoricalsociety.org /mayflower-mill.html), Silverton; located 2 miles north of Silverton on CO 110, CR 2. Open daily in the summer for self-guided tours. Up until 1991, this facility was used to process precious metals. Guests can tour the mill and see the equipment demonstrated by former employees. The site is owned by the San Juan County Historical Society, which maintains a small gift shop and staffs the mill in the summer.

Galloping Goose Railroad Museum (970-882-7082; gallopinggoose5.com), 421 Railroad Ave., Dolores. Open daily in the summer 9–4. This museum celebrates the quirky period of railroad history when the Rio Grande Southern began using Galloping Geese. These unique vehicles were a hodgepodge combination of old buses and trucks fitted to run on train rails. They usually just pulled one car and were used to transport freight and passengers cheaply. Another museum for railroad buffs would be **Ridgway Railroad Museum** (ridgwayrailroadmuseum.org) at the Ouray County Fairgrounds in Ridgway—open on weekends in the summer.

SCENIC DRIVES **San Juan Skyway Byway** (codot.gov/travel/scenic-byways/south west/san-juan-skyway). Durango is a great place to begin one of Colorado's most scenic drives. The San Juan Skyway is a 230-mile loop that heads north from Durango to Ridgway on US 550. It then cuts west on CO 62 to Placerville, then south to Cortez on CO 145, and finally heads back to Durango on US 160. Along the way you'll see some of the state's most stunning scenery.

The stretch of road between Durango and Ouray is known as the Million Dollar Highway. It may have gotten its name from the idea that there was gold ore mixed in with the fill dirt or that it cost a million dollars a mile to build the road over several passes and a gorge. In either case, the trip up to Ouray is at times both breathtakingly beautiful and frighteningly harrowing. Even Colorado natives will admit to some fearful moments on this road, which has stunning drop-offs yet no guardrails.

Along the more westerly route back down to Cortez, the road is easier on the mind, with expansive views of green valleys and white peaks rising above wooded slopes. Part of the byway takes you on a side trip to Telluride.

✱ Outdoor Activities

ALPINE SKIING & SNOWBOARDING **Purgatory Resort** (970-247-9000; purgatory resort.com), US 550, 28 miles north of Durango. Open daily 9–4. Until 2000, it was called the Purgatory Ski Area, then it was branded Durango Mountain Resort, and now it's Purgatory Resort. Throughout all those changes, folks just called it "Purgatory." The ski area has a vertical drop of 2,029 feet with 1,200 skiable acres. The mountain gets nearly 300 inches of snow, and 250 acres are supplemented with snowmaking, with 85 runs in total, most in the intermediate range. There are a host of lessons for kids and adults, beginning and experienced skiers alike. For beginners, the Guaranteed to Green Package promises to get you comfortably skiing on a green run—if not, the next lesson is free.

In the summer, the ski area offers more than 50 miles of trails for mountain biking. A single lift up the mountain will cost you $15, but you can use the chairlift all day for $40. Purgatory also rents bikes.

San Juan Ski Co. (970-259-9671 or 1-800-208-1780; sanjuanuntracked.com), 1831 Lake Purgatory Dr. Based at Purgatory Resort, the San Juan Ski Co. gives skiers access to 35,000 acres of ungroomed backcountry powder. Guides take skiers out in snowcats and boast that their guests will ski down 8,000–12,000 vertical feet of untouched wilderness wonderland in a day. Food and beverages, as well as use of powder skis and avalanche gear, are included in the cost, which is $385 per person.

Silverton Mountain Ski Area (970-387-5706; silvertonmountain.com), 6226 CO 110, Silverton. Silverton Ski Area is the highest in North America. It's also the steepest. As such, only advanced and expert skiers are allowed. Guests must be comfortable skiing black-diamond slopes and hiking along a ridgeline for up to 20 minutes. They must also either bring or rent an avalanche beacon, shovel, and probe to be allowed to use the mountain. The ski area offers guided and unguided skiing. There is one chairlift, and with some hiking you can enjoy 3,000-foot vertical drops. They also offer heli-skiing, from single drops to all-day heli-skiing.

Cliffside Ski & Bike (970-385-1461; cliffsideski.com), 46825 US 550. This shop can be found about 2.5 miles south of Purgatory Resort. It rents equipment for skiers of all skill levels.

CROSS-COUNTRY SKIING & SNOWSHOEING Two hundred miles of groomed trails in the Durango area are open to cross-country skiers. Hillcrest Golf Course (970-247-1499; golfhillcrest.com), 2300 Rim Dr., is on a mesa overlooking Durango and has trails for skiing. **Vallecito Nordic Ski Area** at Pine River Valley (970-884-9782; vallecito nordic.org) is a bit farther afield, but open to the public. The trailhead can be found just east of the dam and then north a little ways on the gravel road. Use of the trails is free, but donations are appreciated.

Purgatory Nordic Center (970-385-2114; purgatoryresort.com/activities/purgatory-nordic-center) at Purgatory Resort (see "Alpine Skiing & Snowboarding") has more than 9 miles of groomed trails for cross-country skiing. The center offers instruction and ski rental.

FISHING Fishing is good in Durango and the surrounding area. The **Animas River** runs right through town, and there are plenty of creeks for fly fishing. To the west in Mancos is Mancos State Park, which has the **Jackson Gulch Reservoir**—another terrific spot to cast a line. A great way to get oriented to the Durango fishing scene is to take a trip with a local guide who can show the best the region has to offer.

MESA VERDE NATIONAL PARK

Mesa Verde National Park (970-529-4465; nps.gov/meve), park entrance 10 miles east of Cortez just off US 160. Driving east out of Cortez on the road to Durango, looking to the south, an impressive mesa rises 2,000 feet from the valley floor. The Spanish called it *Mesa Verde*, or "Green Table." At a glance, there is nothing about Mesa Verde that hints at the secrets the mesa holds.

For 700 years, from A.D. 600 to 1300, the mesa was inhabited by people who farmed its top, hunted its canyons, and over time built their shelters on the cliff walls, hundreds of feet above the canyon floor. The same overhanging cliffs that offered them shelter preserved their dwellings long after they left this place. Most visitors come to see the cliff dwellings, but there are more than 4,000 archaeological sites at Mesa Verde that tell the story of this ancient people.

When you get to Mesa Verde, head straight for the Far View Visitor Center. Certain cliff dwellings, such as Balcony House and Cliff Palace, are open to guests only on a ranger-guided

CLIFF PALACE AT MESA VERDE NATIONAL PARK

tour. The visitor center is the only place in the park that sells the tickets for the tours (and it's a long drive back to get tickets if you miss this step). The earlier you can start your day, the better; the tours fill up quickly in the summer. No matter when you get there, however, the rangers are very adept at helping guests create an itinerary based on tour availability. The park also maintains a nice bookstore here for more in-depth information on Mesa Verde.

Many cliff dwellings are visible only from a distance. These are indicated on the park map and by signs and parking areas along the road. There are also mesa-top sites—places where the ancestral Pueblo lived before moving down to the cliffs. Most people, however, come to Mesa Verde to tour the cliff dwellings—to get in and among the ancient walls.

The cliff dwellings open to the public are found on two of the park's mesas. Chapin Mesa is the closest, and it is where you find Cliff House, Balcony House, and Spruce Tree House. Chapin Mesa also has a museum and a snack bar that serves lunch. For this reason, most visitors spend their day on Chapin Mesa. Wetherill Mesa is to the west about 20 miles from Chapin by road, which can take up to an hour to drive. It is where you will find Step House and Long House. Visitors park their cars at the Wetherill Mesa information kiosk and take a tram around to the various sites.

Following is a quick summary of the largest and most-visited cliff dwellings:

Cliff Palace is the largest cliff dwelling at Mesa Verde. You will need to take a ranger-guided tour to view the site. Although you only walk a quarter-mile, you will climb five ladders to return to the top of the mesa (they are about 8–10 feet each).

Balcony House is probably the most strenuous of the ranger-led tours. You take the stairs to a ledge below the site and then climb a 32-foot ladder up into the dwelling. To exit the site, you crawl through a 12-foot tunnel that is 18 inches wide at its narrowest point. After that, there are two 10-foot ladders, and a harrowing climb across open rock to get back to the top and the parking lot.

Spruce Tree House is in some rights the best preserved of the dwellings, and it is unique in that the kiva roofs have been restored. However, a rock fall in 2015 led the park to close the site to the public. Further inspection raised more safety concerns. The dwelling will remain closed while the park determines the best plan for preserving the site and providing a safe experience for visitors.

Long House is the second largest cliff dwelling at Mesa Verde. Tours begin at the Wetherill information kiosk where you board the tram. The ranger-guided tour is 90 minutes and boasts of being the park's most in-depth tour. The three-quarter-mile hike will take you up two 15-foot ladders, and you will gain 130 feet in elevation on your way back to the tram.

Step House is just a short hike from the Wetherill information kiosk. The three-quarter-mile round-trip takes you down and back up 100 feet along a winding path. On this self-guided tour, you will get a chance to see a pit house and petroglyphs.

Another option for seeing the park is to sign up for a guided bus tour at Far View Lodge or Far View Terrace (or call 1-800-449-2288 to make a reservation). The tours, conducted by Aramark Leisure, cost $42–46 for adults and include the 700 Years Tour, the Classic Pueblo Tour, and the Far View Explorer Tour.

The national park requires a $15 vehicle pass for entry (drops to $10 Sept.–May). Ranger-led tours of the sites cost anywhere from $5 (for the most popular tours of Balcony House, Cliff Palace, or Long House) to $25 for the new 3-hour tour of Mug House on Wetherill Mesa. This last tour is a real treat, especially for those who have been to Mesa Verde before. Take note, however—it's a strenuous hike.

Animas Valley Anglers (970-259-0484; gottrout.com), 264 W. 22nd St. These guides can take you on both floating and wading trips on all the local rivers and creeks. One trip to consider begins with a ride on the Durango-Silverton Narrow-Gauge Railroad into San Juan National Forest, where anglers are dropped off for a day of fishing. The remote location means fewer people and more fish.

Duranglers (970-385-4081 or 1-888-347-4346; duranglers.com), 923 Main Ave. Duranglers offers guide services on all the local rivers—the Animas, Dolores, and Los Pinos. It also takes anglers out to the Piedra and San Juan in the east and Black Canyon of the Gunnison to the north. The shop gives lessons on all aspects of fly fishing, from building a rod and tying a fly to casting and landing a fish.

GOLF **Dalton Ranch Golf Course** (970-247-8774; daltonranch.com), 589 CR 252. This semiprivate course, 6 miles north of Durango, incorporates the Animas River into its design. Greens fees $75–120, including cart.

Hillcrest Golf Course (970-247-1499; golfhillcrest.com), 2300 Rim Dr. Hillcrest is located north of Fort Lewis College on the mesa overlooking Durango and the Animas Valley. Greens fees $39 for 18 holes or $55 with cart.

HIKING A local trails advocacy group, **Trails2000** (trails2000.org), publishes a free map of Durango-area trails. It is distributed through sporting goods shops around town, such as Mountain Bike Specialists and Gardenswartz Outdoors on Main Avenue.

The **Colorado Trail** is one of the most significant trails for hikers in the state. Durango is the western terminus of this trail, which stretches northeast to Denver. The trailhead is at the end of Junction Creek Road, west of Durango. Hikers looking for a longer trip can always tackle the entire Colorado Trail—it's only 482.9 miles to Denver.

Close to town, the **Animas Mountain Trail** is a 5-mile loop that climbs 2,000 feet. The hike offers great views of Durango and the Animas Valley. The trailhead and parking area is west off Main Avenue on 32nd Street. Turn north on Fourth Avenue and the parking lot is at the end of the road on the right (you'll have to ignore the one-way sign).

For a leisurely hike in town, follow the **Animas River Trail**, which as the name suggests runs along the Animas River. This paved path begins in Memorial Park at 32nd St. and continues 5 miles to the Mall on S. Camino del Rio (US 160).

Colorado Mountain Expeditions (970-759-8737 or 1-888-263-4453; coloradotrail hiking.com), 935 CR 125. There is no easier way to hike along the Colorado Trail. Colorado Mountain Expeditions offers five-day hiking vacations that include all of your meals, and even takes care of transporting your gear. All you carry is a day pack. The cost for such pampering is $1,250 per person for each section of the trail.

HORSEBACK RIDING **Buck's Livery** (970-385-2110; buckslivery.com), US 550 north at Purgatory Resort. There is a ride to suit your every inclination at Buck's—trail rides, dinner rides, and backcountry rides, as well as sleigh rides in the winter. Guides will even take you out hunting and fishing.

Seventy Seven Outfit (970-247-3231; 77outfit.com), 11374 US 550 S. The guides at Seventy Seven lead day rides and overnight camping trips. They also rent horses if you are looking to ride on your own. Rates vary by the number of people in your party. A two-person day ride is $180 each and a four-person day ride $140 each.

MOUNTAIN BIKING In 1990, the first professional UCI Mountain Bike & Trials World Championships were held in Durango. Seen as a mountain biking mecca of sorts, Durango has more than 2,000 miles of trails, hundreds of which are the ever-coveted singletrack. There are some great downhill sections at **Purgatory Resort** (see "Alpine Skiing & Snowboarding" for lift information).

A ride closer to town is the **Colorado Trail & Hoffheins Connection**. This 20-mile loop starts at the Colorado Trail trailhead at the end of Junction Creek Road, west out of Durango. Riding up the trail, Hoffheins Connection is just over 600 feet past Gudy's Rest (an overlook with a bench, placed in honor of Gudy Gaskill, who was a driving force behind the creation of the Colorado Trail). Hoffheins Connection Trail continues on to Lightner Creek Road and US 160, which takes you back to Durango.

Hermosa Creek Trail takes riders from Purgatory Resort down to the town of Hermosa—following Hermosa Creek much of the way. The 20-mile trek is smooth downhill singletrack. Although not overly technical, there are some tricky spots. The one-way ride begins 8 miles up Hermosa Park Road, behind Purgatory Resort.

To spend your entire vacation pedaling, the **San Juan Hut System** (970-626-3033; sanjuanhuts.com), P.O. Box 773, Ridgway, operates along a 214-mile route of backcountry roads from Durango to Moab. About every 35 miles, riders crash for the night at one of the huts. The trip takes seven days and six nights and costs $895 per person. In exchange, riders get a sleeping bag and a place to sleep, three meals a day, and trail descriptions and maps.

Pedal the Peaks (970-259-6880; durangobikeshop.com), 598B Main Ave. These guys rent full-suspension and hard-tail mountain bikes. They also know a lot about local trails.

Cliffside Ski & Bike (970-385-1461; cliffsideski.com), 46825 US 550. This shop can be found about 30 miles north of Durango. They rent full-suspension and hard-tail mountain bikes.

PADDLING & RAFTING **Durango Rivertrippers** (970-259-0289 or 1-800-292-2885; durangorivertrippers.com), 720 Main Ave. Durango Rivertrippers was the first river outfitter licensed by the state. It takes guests on rafting trips down the Animas River. With spring runoff, the river sees class IV rapids, which makes for an exciting ride. In the summer, the river levels off and sees rapids up to class III. There are two trips down the Animas: one is two hours and the other a half-day. You can also make the run in a rented inflatable kayak. If you can't get enough of rafting on one of the shorter trips, there are one-, three-, and six-day trips down the Dolores River, which takes you as far as the Colorado River in Utah. Adult half-day trip with lunch $57, children $47. Adult two-hour trip $36, children $31.

✳ Green Space

Mancos State Park (970-533-7065; cpw.state.co.us/placestogo/Parks/mancos), 42545 CR N, Mancos. Open 24 hours a day. Enclosing Jackson Gulch Reservoir, the park has camping and trails. The Chicken Creek Trail connects with the Colorado Trail north of Durango. There are other trails here that would make nice short nature walks, and 5 miles of in-park trails open to biking, hiking, cross-country skiing, and snowshoeing. The reservoir is great for boating and fishing. Daily vehicle pass $7.

San Juan Public Lands Center (970-247-4874; fs.fed.us/r2/sanjuan), 15 Burnett Ct. Open Mon.–Fri. 8–4:30. San Juan National Forest stretches from Dolores in the west all the way to south-central Colorado in the east. North of Durango, most every time you step out of your car, you're standing in the national forest. To learn more about these public lands, check out the bookstore at the Public Lands Center. It has an extensive collection of books and maps on all aspects of enjoying the public lands around Durango and in southwestern Colorado.

✳ Lodging

HOTELS ((ᵖ)) **The Strater Hotel** (970-247-4431 or 1-800-247-4431; strater.com), 699 Main Ave. In the hotel's early years, Durango residents would abandon their homes in the winter and stay at the Strater, which had wood-burning stoves in every room. Built in 1887 by an enterprising young pharmacist, the Strater has been a symbol of Durango's status throughout its history. When Durango saw tough times, the Strater saw tough times. In the 1920s, the hotel was restored to its former glory. As an historical site, the hotel's public spaces are used to display antiques and artifacts. The rooms have been modernized and are decorated with subtle Victorian touches. Rooms $139–302.

((ᵖ)) **The Lodge at Tamarron by Purgatory Resort** (970-259-2000, 1-800-982-6103, or 1-800-525-0892; purgatoryresort .com), 40292 US 550 N. (18 miles north of Durango). Part of Purgatory Resort, the Lodge at Tamarron is perfect for a ski vacation. The lodge has rooms, suites, studios, and lofts—many with kitchens and kitchenettes and beds for larger groups. Some of the accommodations are greater than 1,800 square feet. Rooms are comfortably contemporary. There are indoor and outdoor pools, Jacuzzis, and tennis courts. The lodge also offers a free shuttle to the ski area. Rooms from $99.

🐾 ((ᵖ)) **Wyman Hotel and Inn** (970-387-5372; thewyman.com), 1371 Greene St., Silverton. The Wyman was built in 1902 and is on the National Register of Historic Places. As such, it completely complements the Old West feel of Silverton. There are 15 rooms, including suites and various combinations of beds (double queen suites, single queen suites, rooms with king-size beds, etc.). All the rooms have private baths, several with whirlpool tubs. In addition to the rooms in the hotel, a caboose from the Southern Pacific Railroad has been converted into a honeymoon suite and sits in the neighboring courtyard. A full gourmet breakfast is served every morning, as is an afternoon wine-and-cheese social.

THE STRATER HOTEL

THE WYMAN IN SILVERTON

Rooms $145–240. The Candlelight Caboose goes for $225.

BED & BREAKFASTS ♿ (())) **Apple Orchard Inn** (970-247-0751 or 1-800-426-0751; appleorchardinn.com), 7758 CR 203. John and Celeste are your hosts at Apple Orchard Inn—one of the finest B&Bs in Colorado. Casually elegant, upscale, and romantic is how guests describe their stay at the Apple Orchard. There are four guest rooms in the main house and six cottages on the property's 4.5 acres. The yard is beautifully landscaped, complete with a meandering stream. Cottages each have private decks, and three have fireplaces. Cottages with whirlpool tubs and private hot tubs are also available. Celeste received culinary training in Europe and prepares a full gourmet breakfast every morning. Dinner is available if arranged in advance. Rooms $90–185 and cottages $110–250.

♿ 🐾 (())) **The Leland House** (970-385-1920; rochesterhotel.com), 721 E. Second Ave. The Leland House began as an apartment building. Since 1992, it has been a B&B with very spacious accommodations—five queen suites, four queen studios, and the Pittman Suite (essentially a two-bedroom apartment with a full kitchen).

Not long after opening The Leland House, the owners, the mother-and-son team of Diane Wildfang and Kirk Komick, looked across the street at the old Rochester. Built in 1892, the hotel had deteriorated over the years. Realizing that the rundown building could only hurt business for their side of the street, they decided to buy the hotel and make some renovations. Redesigning the interior, they took the building from a dilapidated hotel with 33 rooms to a comfortable inn with 15 rooms, each with its own bath. Soon **Rochester Hotel** (rochesterhotel.com), at 721 E. Second Ave., was open to the public. Decorated in contemporary cowboy style with Old West Victorian touches, the hotel also has a movie theme with posters and photos from films shot in and around Durango.

GUEST BIKE AT THE ROCHESTER HOTEL

The office for both buildings is in The Leland House, but the full gourmet breakfast is served at Rochester Hotel. So in tune are these two lodgings that if all the doors are open, you can stand at the back of Rochester Hotel and see clear through the hotel and across the street, through the hallway of The Leland House and out its back door. Suites and studios at The Leland House run $129–299, and rooms at Rochester Hotel are $129–299.

♿ **Blue Lake Ranch** (970-385-4537; bluelakeranch.com), 16919 CO 140, Hesperus. This B&B has 16 lodging options from the Cabin on the Lake to the Cottage in the Woods to the River House—some can accommodate up to eight guests. The tastefully appointed rooms are complemented by the ranch's natural setting. Like a classic B&B, an excellent gourmet breakfast is served daily. Suites and cabins $179–429.

✎ (((•))) **Willowtail Springs** (970-533-7592 or 1-800-698-0603; willowtail springs.com), 10451 Rd. 39, P.O. Box 89, Mancos. Willow Springs has three cabins nestled on 60 wooded acres. Depending on the cabin, they can accommodate 4–6 guests. The Bungalow overlooks the lake and features a clawfoot tub and fireplace. The Garden Cottage has views of the La Plata Mountains and the lake and features a fireplace. The Lakehouse has a 40-foot ceiling in the living room, sleeps

up to six, and has a TV with satellite and DVD player. All the cabins are homey yet luxuriously appointed with fresh flowers adorning the tables and lush garden landscaping. Wireless Internet is available in the office. Cabins from $249.

CAMPGROUNDS (((•))) **Lightner Creek Campground** (970-247-5406; camplightner creek.com), 1567 CR 207. This shady campground along Lightner Creek offers sites for tent campers and RVs. There are also camping cabins for rent as well as two rooms in the main lodge. There's a heated swimming pool, and the creek is open for fishing. This campground is far from the beaten path—a secluded and quiet retreat. Tent sites $33–38, sites with hookups $46–56, and camper cabins $47 up to $195 for housekeeping cabins.

Transfer Park Campground (Mancos-Delores Ranger District, 970-882-7296) is located north of US 160 on CR 243 east of Durango. Open Memorial Day–Labor Day. With just 25 sites along the Florida River and no showers, just vault toilets and drinking water, Transfer Park doesn't get a lot of traffic. This is a shame as the campground is set in a beautiful spot. This was once the place where horses were unloaded and their cargo transferred to mules for trips into the mountains. Sites $15.

Mancos State Park (970-533-7065; cpw.state.co.us/placestogo/parks /mancos), 42545 CR N, Mancos. The park has two campgrounds—32 sites in all. There are vault toilets and drinking water, but no showers. The park also maintains two yurts that are available year-round (heated in the winter). Sites $18 and yurts $80.

RESORTS ☀ (((•))) **Dunton Hot Springs** (970-882-4800 or 1-877-228-4674; dunton hotsprings.com), 52068 W. Fork Rd., #38, Dolores. Quite possibly the most elegant and most unique lodging in Colorado, Dunton Hot Springs began as a ghost town. Its old buildings have been converted into upscale accommodations.

There are 11 cabins on the property. Guests also have use of the Pony Express Stop, including its yoga and Pilates studios, fully stocked library, and bath house with steam showers and indoor hot springs. And in keeping with the fact that this was a town from the Old West, there's a saloon, which houses a dance hall and kitchen. Cabins range from $600–2,000 per night. A full menu of spa services is available. All spa treatments are $185 for 75 minutes.

✱ Where to Eat

DINING OUT ♿ **Cyprus Cafe** (970-385-6884; cypruscafe.com), 725 E. Second Ave. Open daily for lunch and dinner (hours change seasonally). Located next door to The Leland House in a century-old Victorian, Cyprus Cafe serves a delicious and innovative menu of Mediterranean cuisine. Guests can eat inside or, in the summer, take their meal on the garden patio. Salads are made of the freshest greens, and the menu includes entrées such as Colorado lamb, pork chop with pine nuts, and vegetarian dishes. Entrées $17–32 for dinner or $9–16 for lunch.

♿ **Ken and Sue's Place** (970-385-1810; kenandsues.com), 636 Main Ave. Open for lunch Mon.–Fri. 11–2:30. Dinner served Sun.–Thu. 5–9, Fri. and Sat. 5–10. The menu at Ken and Sue's features Southwest-style dishes with a contemporary flare. Asian influences can be seen in dishes such as the ginger-chicken pot stickers. Seafood is also a central theme seen even in salads and sandwiches, such as the ancho-dusted gulf shrimp salad and grilled tuna steak sandwich. Dishes $10–24.

♿ ♈ **Ore House** (970-247-5707; orehouserestaurant.com), 147 E. College Dr. Open nightly 5–11. Ore House has been Durango's premier steakhouse since it opened in 1972. Located just a block from the train depot, the interior has an old-timey historical feel. The menu includes top sirloin, New York strip, and filets. For seafood, there's everything from Colorado mountain trout to ahi tuna. During the busy season, Ore House can get a lot of tourist attention, but that hasn't kept it from becoming a local favorite. Dishes $25–73.

Sow's Ear (970-247-3527; sowsear durango.com), 48475 US 550 N., Purgatory Resort. Guests seated daily for dinner 5–9. This casual dining room has fantastic views of the West Needles Mountains. The menu has several fantastic steak options as well as seafood, chicken, pork chops, and lamb. Reservations recommended on weekends and holidays. Dinner entrées $20–36 and children's menu items $8.

EATING OUT ♿ **Derailed Pour House** (970-247-5440), 725 Main Ave. Open Tue.–Fri. 3–9, and Sat. and Sun. 11–9. Bar open late every night but Mon., when the restaurant is closed. This used to be the address for Farquahrts and Pizza Mia, the best place in town for pizza, beer, and live music. The new ownership has kept the live music and classed up the menu with an extensive selection of small plates and a long burger menu. Burgers and sandwiches $9–12.

Olde Schoolhouse Cafe (970-259-2257; oldeschoolhousesaloon.com), 46778 US 550 N. Located 2 miles south of Purgatory Resort. Call for seasonal hours. Open Mon.–Fri. 4–2 AM, Sat.–Sun. 11–2 AM. During the day, the Olde Schoolhouse is the perfect family restaurant. Not only does it have a full menu of gut-pleasers such as brats and chicken wings, it may just serve the best pizza in Colorado. After the kitchen closes, the bar takes on a life of its own and becomes a favorite après-ski hangout (or après-bike, après-rock climbing, whatever). Dishes $10–30.

BAKERIES & COFFEE SHOPS ♿ **Bedhead Coffee** (970-426-8712; bedheadcoffeehouse.com), 929A Hwy 3. Open Tue.–Sat. 7–3. Located south of town on CO 3, the owners of this coffee shop approach the task of producing a cup of coffee as an art, an artisanal endeavor, so to speak. There's no free WiFi, reinforcing the mindful atmosphere they are hoping to create. Great ambience, even better coffee.

BARS, TAVERNS, & BREW PUBS Ÿ

Lady Falconburgh's Barley Exchange (970-382-9664), 640 Main Ave. Open daily 11–"late night." This local pub proudly serves more than 140 beers, 38 on tap. Inside, the large four-sided bar allows for socialization. It also serves food—the usual pub grub with some Southwest-style dishes. It has been voted Durango's best pub and is a perennial favorite with locals.

Ÿ **Steamworks Brewing Co.** (970-259-9200; steamworksbrewing.com), 801 E. Second Ave. Open daily at 11. For locally handcrafted beer, this brew pub is the spot. It serves a nice pub menu that includes oven-fired pizza. When weather permits, there is seating on the patio.

✸ Entertainment

Bar D Chuckwagon Suppers (970-247-5753; bardchuckwagon.com), 8080 CR 250. Ticket booth opens at 5:30. Dinner served promptly at 7:30. The Bar D Ranch has plenty of activities for families before the dinner show. There are hay rides, a little train, and plenty of shops selling tourist kitsch and crafts. Beef or chicken $26 and steak $36. Children (4–10) $12.

✸ Selective Shopping

Maria's Bookshop (970-247-5916; marias bookshop.com), 960 Main Ave. Open daily 9–9. The bookstore is named after Maria Martinez, a potter of the San Ildefonso Pueblo, whose work inspired the shop logo. This local bookstore has a surprisingly large inventory. The staff are knowledgeable and open to offering reading suggestions.

Rocky Mountain Chocolate Factory (970-259-1408; rmcf.com), 561 Main Ave. You've seen this chocolate everywhere, from Maine to Oregon. Although you can now find this confectionary in nearly every mall in America, it all began here on Main in Durango. The factory is now located at 265 Turner Dr. Call and ask about taking a tour.

Toh-Atin Gallery (970-247-8277 or 1-800-525-0384; toh-atin.com), 145 W. Ninth St. Open Mon.–Sat. 9–5. Open longer hours and on Sun. in the summer. This gallery carries one of the finest selections of Southwest and Native American art in the state.

✸ Special Events

May: **Iron Horse Bicycle Classic** (970-259-4621; ironhorsebicycleclassic.com), 3777 Main Ave. This annual race pits cyclists against the Durango & Silverton Narrow-Gauge Railroad in a race to Silverton. The train has a shorter route, but it can only go so fast. Bikes can haul downhill, but they have farther to go. For 35 years, the race has been a coveted Memorial Day weekend event.

June: **Animas River Days** (970-259-3583; animasriverdays.com). The event involves a river parade and lots of fun on the water.

August: **Durango Cowboy Gathering** (970-749-2995; durangocowboygathering .org). Celebrating the "rich culture and heritage of the American cowboy," the gathering features cowboy poets, musicians, and storytellers. There's even a gun shoot at the Gun Club Range.

PAGOSA SPRINGS &
THE SOUTHERN SAN JUANS

For centuries, people have been making their way to this spot, west of the mountains along the San Juan River, to soak in the hot sulfur springs. The town's name, Pagosa Springs, comes from the Ute name for this place. *Pagosa* means "healing waters." The water's medicinal quality was confirmed back in the 19th century by U.S. Army physicians, who proclaimed them to be "the most wonderful and beneficial in medicinal effects that have ever been discovered."

There is a definite Southwest feel to Pagosa that you don't find elsewhere in Colorado. It's a laid-back town where people put a premium on enjoying the outdoors and taking time to soak it all in. For some that means literally soaking, whether in a hot tub or just floating in a tube down the San Juan River. For others it means taking advantage of the town's proximity to the mountains and the San Juan Valley, with all the region's opportunities for hiking, mountain biking, and horseback riding.

North and east of Pagosa Springs are the southern San Juan Mountains. In 1890, Nicholas Creede discovered silver in the area (near the Rio Grande River). The town that bears his name, Creede, is the only town in Mineral County. When silver was discovered, the town's population leapt up to 10,000. In a state full of rowdy mining towns, Creede was considered the rowdiest. Some of the Old West's most famous and infamous characters—the likes of Calamity Jane and Bat Masterson—passed through at one time or other.

Farther north is Lake City, which was founded in 1874 as a mining town. Lake City gets its name from nearby Lake San Cristobal, which was formed 800 years ago by the Slumgullion Earthflow—a portion of a nearby mountain sloughed off and blocked the Gunnison River, creating the lake. Today most of Lake City is a National Historic District, with more than 75 buildings from the 19th century. The town is forever remembered as the place where Alferd Packer and his six companions were stranded in the mountains during a harsh winter in 1874. When spring came, only Packer remained. The rest of the party was dead and had been eaten by Packer himself.

GUIDANCE **Pagosa Springs Chamber of Commerce & Visitor Center** (970-264-2360 or 1-800-252-2204; pagosaspringschamber.com), 402 San Juan St.

    Creede/Mineral Country Chamber of Commerce (719-658-2374; creede.com), 1207 N. Main St.

    Lake City Chamber of Commerce (970-944-2527 or 1-800-569-1874; lakecity.com), 800 Gunnison Ave.

    Also visit pagosa.com.

GETTING THERE *By car:* Pagosa Springs sits on US 160, which stretches east and west across the state. The town is also easily accessible to nearby Santa Fe (just 150 miles to the south) via US 84. Creede and Lake City are between US 50 and US 160 on CO 149. They are separated by 50 miles and the Continental Divide, but share this region of the San Juans.

By air: **Durango–La Plata County Airport** (970-247-8143; flydurango.com), 1000 Airport Rd., is only 60 miles to the west. Two major airlines provide daily service to and from Denver, Phoenix, and Dallas.

✻ To See & Do

Pagosa Hot Springs. One of the first impressions visitors have when coming to Pagosa for the first time is the smell. The town centers on the Pagosa Hot Springs, which are in fact hot sulfur springs. They have a strong odor, but it's not so unpleasant that you don't quickly get used to it. There are two places that offer ways to soak in the springs. The first is the **Springs Resort** (970-264-4168 or 1-800-225-0934; pagosahotsprings .com), 165 Hot Springs Blvd. The resort is open daily in the summer 7 AM–midnight. In the winter it's open 7–11. Water from the Great Pagosa Hot Spring, behind the hotel portion of the resort, is piped to the pool area. There are 18 different pools of varying temperatures for your soaking pleasure. The property is well maintained, and each pool has a distinct character of its own. River water mixes in the pools down by the river's edge—some relief if the springs have gotten you overheated. Adult admission $26, children (2–10) $14, and infants and toddlers free with an adult. Resort hotel guests soak for free.

Another option is the **Spa at Pagosa Springs** (970-264-5910 or 1-800-832-5523; pshotsprings.com), 317 Hot Springs Blvd. Open daily 8–10. More therapeutic in nature, the spa has an indoor bath, swimming pool, and a coed hot tub. Adult daily rate $11, seniors $8, and children (3–12) $7.

PAGOSA HOT SPRINGS

CHIMNEY ROCK

Chimney Rock Archaeological Area (970-883-5359; chimneyrockco.org), 3 miles south of US 160 on CO 151. Visitor center open daily mid-May–Sept. 9–4:30. The park offers several guided walking tours every day throughout the season. A thousand years ago, the unique geological features of this landscape attracted the attention of the ancestral Pueblo people, who came here and lived on the mountain. The archaeological site has more than 200 known structures. The Great House, the Great Kiva, and the Ridge House have been uncovered and reconstructed. The community was related to the people of Chaco Canyon in New Mexico, as well as Mesa Verde 100 miles to the west. In fact, it is believed that Chimney Rock was used as a natural observatory for tracking the sun and, most especially, the moon. Were the people here able to signal their counterparts from the summit of Chimney Rock? Take the two-and-a-half-hour tour and find out. Wear good walking shoes. Adult fee $12, children (5–12) $5, and children under 5 free.

North Clear Creek Falls. About halfway between Creede and Lake City is one of Colorado's most beautiful waterfalls. Easy access from the road, no doubt, plays into the fact that it's also one of the state's most photographed waterfalls. A short way up Forest Rd. 510, east off CO 149, you'll find spectacular views of North Clear Creek Falls as it tumbles into a box canyon.

⛏ **Underground Mining Museum** (719-658-0811; undergroundminingmuseum .com), 503 Forest Service Rd., #9, Creede. Open daily in the summer 10–4; fall and spring 9:30–3. This entire museum facility is underground—dug out of solid rock. Exhibitions show the tools and methods used throughout the history of mining. Adult admission $7, seniors $6, and children $5.

&. ⛏ **Creede Historic Museum** (719-658-2374; creedehistoricalsociety.com), 17 Main St. in the Rio Grande Railroad Depot (behind Basham Park), Creede. Open daily in the summer 10–4, except Sun. when it's open 1–4. Located in an historic rail depot, the museum houses a collection of artifacts from Creede and Mineral County. Adults $2, seniors $1, families $5, and children under 12 free.

Silver Thread Scenic Byway (codot.gov/travel/scenic-byways/south-central/silver-thread) is a 75-mile stretch of road between South Fork and Lake City, passing through Creede en route. Along the way, you will pass the Slumgullion Earthflow—a continuously moving mass of earth, 4 miles long, that slid down a mountain 700 years ago, damming the Lake Fork of the Gunnison River and creating Lake San Cristobal.

Alpine Loop Scenic Byway (codot.gov/travel/scenic-byways/southwest/alpine-loop) is a 63-mile scenic route through the mountains and passes west of Lake City that requires a four-wheel-drive vehicle. Begin on Alpine Loop Road up to Engineer Pass. The road turns south and crosses Cinnamon Pass on Cinnamon Pass Road heading east back to Lake City. The route also connects up with Ouray or Silverton. The loop will take you through the ghost towns of Sherman and Animas Forks.

✳ Outdoor Activities

ALPINE SKIING & SNOWBOARDING **Wolf Creek Ski Area** (970-264-5639 or 1-800-754-9653; wolfcreekski.com), located east of Pagosa Springs, just east of Wolf Creek Pass on US 160, P.O. Box 2800, Pagosa Springs. No ski area in Colorado gets as much snow as Wolf Creek. With 465 inches of the white stuff falling annually, there is no need for snowmaking equipment here. There's an overall 1,604-foot vertical drop, and the longest of the 77 trails stretches 2 miles. The ski area is serviced by seven lifts. Wolf Creek has no on-site lodging, but there are two concession stands and a cafeteria-style eatery. With an even number of runs for skiers of all abilities, Wolf Creek is good for groups.

HIKING Pagosa Springs and the San Juan Mountains have hundreds of miles of trails for hiking. For a thorough introduction to the area's vast recreational resources, stop by the Pagosa Springs Visitor Center. It has brochures that cover the best local trails.

Piedra Falls Trail is an easy hike to a spectacular waterfall. To get to the trailhead, take Piedra Road 17 miles north to Middle Fork Road. Turn right, drive 2 miles to the first road on your right, E. Toner Road. At the end of the road is where your path begins. Be advised, E. Toner becomes too dangerous to drive in wet weather. It's a short 15- to 30-minute walk to the falls, which you will hear from the start.

Williams Creek Trail offers a more strenuous hike. It's located about 25 miles north of Pagosa Springs—deep into the San Juan Mountains. Take Piedra Road north 22 miles to Williams Creek Road and turn right. The trailhead at the end of the road begins a 14-mile trek to the Continental Divide.

FISHING The San Juan and the Piedra provide miles of river for fly fishing. The **Piedra River** is an angler's dream, with 40 miles of canyon water full of wild brown and rainbow trout. In the Pagosa Springs area, there are **Echo Lake** and **Capote Lake**. Farther south is the **Navajo Reservoir** near the New Mexico border. And to the north in Lake City sits **Lake San Cristobal**.

Dan's Fly Shop (970-944-2281in summer and 970-252-9106 in winter; dansflyshop .com), 723 Gunnison Ave., Lake City. For nearly five decades Dan has been tying flies and introducing anglers to the best fishing in the San Juans. Through the fly shop, Lake City Angling Services leads guided fishing trips for all level of anglers. The shop has everything you need for a day out on the water, from custom rods to hand-tied flies.

ALFERD PACKER

In the winter of 1874, Alferd Packer and five other men left the town of Montrose for Gunnison. Although they were advised to wait until spring, the party was anxious to get to their final destination of Breckenridge to start prospecting for gold. Two months later, while people were starting to wonder whatever happened to the six prospectors, Packer emerged from the mountains . . . alone.

There are conflicting stories about exactly where and when Packer was first spotted. It is clear that sometime in April, he was found in the San Luis Valley, spending lots of money that he didn't have when he went into the mountains. His story, at first, was that one by one members of the party died. The remaining members had eaten the dead men to survive. The bodies (or at least what remained), he said, could be found along the trail where the men had died.

True or not, few people were buying his story. He was convicted of murder and cannibalism and jailed in Saguache, Colorado. It wasn't long, however, before the bodies of the prospectors were found. They were not strewn along the path as Packer had claimed. Instead, they were found all together on a plateau near Lake City, and it looked as if they had all met a violent end. When the authorities went to Saguache to confront Packer with this information, they found he had escaped.

It was nearly 10 years before the law caught up with Packer, who was living in Wyoming under an alias. This time he told another story—how he went out scouting and came back to find one of the party, Shannon Bell, roasting the flesh of the men he had killed with his hatchet. When Shannon Bell charged at him with the hatchet, Packer said he shot him in self-defense.

The new story did not convince anyone either, and Packer was eventually sentenced to 40 years. He was paroled in 1901 and lived the remainder of his life in Littleton, Colorado. He died in 1907, and because of his service during the Civil War, was buried in Littleton Cemetery with full military honors.

Now, more than 130 years since that fatal winter, questions about Packer's guilt or innocence still persist. Recent forensic investigations, which involved Packer's gun (found on Cannibal Plateau in Lake City) and the exhumation of Shannon Bell's body, reveal that Packer did indeed shoot Shannon Bell. The other victims had been killed with a hatchet. The evidence, at least, seems to support Packer's second confession.

Guilty or innocent of murder, Alferd Packer, the Colorado Cannibal, remains one of the more colorful characters in Colorado history, and his legend seems to be forever tied to Lake City and the San Juan Mountains.

Dan also keeps up a fly-fishing museum with vintage equipment and fishing supplies from the Lake City area. Trips should be reserved 4–8 weeks in advance if possible.

Let It Fly (970-264-3189; flyfishpagosa.com), 1507 W. US 160 #2, Pagosa Springs. This is a great source for local knowledge and gear, and the staff are happy to refer customers to reliable local guides.

GOLF **Pagosa Springs Golf Club** (970-731-4755; golfpagosa.com), 1 Pines Club Pl. Located 3 miles west of Pagosa Springs on US 160 at the base of the San Juan Mountains. This golf club has three nine-hole sections (Meadows, Piñon, and Ponderosa) that combine for three 18-hole courses. Greens fees for 18 holes $86 (from May–Oct.); off-season $40.

HORSEBACK RIDING **Astradle a Saddle** (970-731-5076; astraddleasaddle.com), 531 CR 139. Located 4 miles west of the Wyndham Resort at Pagosa on US 160. This outfitter offers scenic trail rides. Be sure to also ask about the barbecue dinners and winter sleigh rides. One-hour trail rides $40 and two-hour rides $65.

RIVER SPORTS **Pagosa Outside** (970-264-4202; pagosaoutside.com), 350 Pagosa St. This outfitter is a one-stop shop for outdoor recreation. Its staff lead rafting trips and mountain-biking tours, as well as guided fly-fishing trips through Backcountry Angler. There are several rafting options on the San Juan: half-day trips through Mesa and Montezuma canyons and a two-hour float through town. For a relaxing afternoon, consider renting an inflatable kayak or river tube. Once you float through town, you can jump on the shuttle van (small fee for the whole day) and run the river again. Adult Mesa Canyon trip $69 and children (under 11) $54.

✳ Green Space

Echo Canyon Lake State Wilderness Area (cpw.state.co.us/swa/Echo%20Canyon%20 Lake%20SWA), located 4 miles south of Pagosa Springs on US 84. Echo Canyon Reservoir was built in 1968 to provide a spot for the public to go fishing. The 211-acre lake is used for fishing, boating, hunting, and picnicking. There are often opportunities to view wildlife as well. From the park, you can see the San Juans resting picturesquely to the north.

    Navajo State Park (970-883-2208; cpw.state.co.us/placestogo/Parks/Navajo), 1526 CR 982, Arboles. Open 24 hours. The park is located near the New Mexico border along the western shore of Navajo Reservoir. To get there, follow CO 151 south of US 160. Navajo Reservoir has more than 15,000 surface acres and stretches 35 miles up the San Juan River. There are some short trails in the park, but the real attraction is the water. For more than a day trip, the park has three campgrounds and two areas set aside with primitive campsites. It also has three cabins for rent. Daily vehicle pass $7.

✳ Lodging

HOTELS & MOTELS ♿ ✹ **The Springs Resort** (970-264-4168 or 1-800-225-0934; pagosahotsprings.com), 165 Hot Springs Blvd., Pagosa Springs. The accommodations are clean and spacious, but the best feature of the resort is that guests get free access to the resort soaking pools. There is also a spa, salon, and boutique on the premises, which if taken advantage of can make for a very pampered stay. Rooms $199–619, which includes 24-hour access to the springs.

    ✹ ♿ **Matterhorn Mountain Motel** (970-944-2210; matterhornmotel.com), 409 Bluff St., Lake City. For a comfortable and affordable stay in Lake City, the Matterhorn is the place. This motel, built in the 1940s, has 12 rooms (6 with kitchens) and 2 cabins—all the accommodations have cable TV. Rooms from $119 in peak season. All rooms are non-smoking.

BED & BREAKFASTS ✹ (⬤) **Creede Firemen's Inn** (719-658-0212; theoldfire house.com), 123 N. Main St., Creede. The inn's three rooms and one suite all have a private bath, TV, and DSL Internet access. The rooms are simply decorated in a casually western style—the beds all have beautiful quilts. Not content to simply provide lodging, the inn is also a restaurant and ice-cream parlor. Depending on the season, breakfast is served off the menu in the inn's restaurant or is a continental affair provided in the B&B common area. Rooms $135–145 and suite $145–155.

CAMPGROUNDS ✹ **Bruce Spruce Ranch** (970-264-5374; brucespruceranch

.com), 231 West Fork Rd., Pagosa Springs. Nestled in the mountains, this wooded campground has 32 RV sites (most with full hookups), an open tent area, and a mess of cabins. Tent sites $28, RV sites $35, and cabins $66–397.

((ᵞ)) **Pagosa Riverside Campground and Camper Cabins** (970-264-5874 or 1-888-785-3234; pagosariverside.com), 2270 E. US 160, 1.3 miles east of US 84. Open April–Nov. This campground sits next to the San Juan River and has plenty of shady sites. For RVs, there are sites with full hookups, including cable TV and phone lines. Tent sites $25 and RV sites $42–47.

CABINS & COTTAGES ((ᵞ)) **Cabins at Hartland Ranch** (970-264-1111 or 1-866-377-1115; hartlandranch.com), 403 CR 200 (Snowball Rd.), Pagosa Springs. Hartland Ranch has five vacation cabins spread out on 85 acres, each with full kitchen, satellite TV, and Internet. The cabins have one to three bedrooms, and each bedroom has its own bath, fireplace, and TV. The high-ceilinged living rooms offer expansive views. Cabins $175–600.

♨ **L-Z Ranch Cabins** (970-264-5548 or 970-946-0402; lbarzcabins.com), 2244 E. US 160, Pagosa Springs. Two large log cabins, which easily sleep four people, come with full kitchen, bath, and living room area. The genuine rugged charm of these cabins is felt when you see exposed beams or a stone fireplace, but the rustic nature of the lodgings does not extend so far that you can't enjoy modern conveniences such as cable TV and kitchen appliances. Cabins $145–155 (for four people).

✳ Where to Eat

DINING OUT ♿ **Antler's Rio Grande Riverside Restaurant** (719-658-2423; antlerslodge.com), 26222 CO 149, Creede. Open in the summer daily for dinner at 5. Closed after Sept. Antler's Rio Grande Lodge is home to their Riverside Restaurant. The menu is known for gourmet appetizers, like hot smoked Pacific salmon rillettes, as well as steak and seafood entrées. Reservations highly recommended.

EATING OUT ♿ **Boss Hogg's Restaurant & Saloon** (970-731-2626), 157 Navajo Trails Dr., Pagosa Springs. Open daily 11–10. This barbecue joint is known as much for its disjointed decorating as it is for serving great steaks and ribs. The soup and salad bar is always fresh, and the portions are huge. Dinner and lunch dishes $6–30.

♿ ⲩ **Kip's Grill & San Juan Room** (719-658-0220; kipsgrill.com), 5th and Main St., Creede (and 970-264-3663, 12 Pagosa St. in Pagosa Springs). Open daily from May–Sept. 11–8. This little cantina serves Baja-style tacos, hamburgers, and hot dogs. Kip's also has good margaritas, Colorado microbrews on tap, and Mexican imports on hand. Dinner and lunch dishes $8–12.

✳ Entertainment

♿ **Creede Repertory Theatre** (719-658-2540; creederep.org), 124 N. Main St., Creede. In 1966, as the townsfolk of Creede watched the mining industry decline, it was decided that the town needed something to bring in business. They decided to create a theater and sent out a letter to several colleges and universities asking talented young theater majors to come to Creede. Twelve students from the University of Kansas answered the call, and the Creede Repertory Theatre was born. Every season, the ensemble cast performs a variety of plays. The quality of theater in Creede is highly praised locally and nationally. Hundreds audition every year to be part of the cast. Shows are performed in the Old Creede Opera House. The success of the summer season has led to the creation of an extended season that goes through September. Tickets $8–40.

TELLURIDE & OURAY

Touring Colorado's mountain towns, folks will notice a pattern to the terrain. In most cases, there are two ways in and out of town—the easy way (up the valley) and the hard way (over the mountain). Aspen, for example, is approached from the north by a wide four-lane highway. To the south is Independence Pass, the highest paved pass in North America. The highway that leads into Telluride is much as you'd expect, perhaps the walls are a bit steep, but the way out is nearly impassable. That doesn't mean there is no way out, but Black Bear Road, which leads west over Black Bear Pass, is so narrow and steep that traffic is only allowed in one direction—down.

The steep walls that surround Telluride add significantly to its scenic beauty, which is enhanced by its old mountain mining town charm. Strict rules have been established on which kinds of buildings can be built in Telluride. They must, it seems, complement the town's historic character and emulate the "old mining town" look. In recent years, this translates into either quaint Victorian cottages or larger mill-like structures with steel roofs and distressed plank exteriors. Interestingly, although Telluride would like to maintain the look of its mining heritage, recent efforts to open an actual small hard-rock mining operation in the nearby mountains have been thwarted on the grounds that the helicopters transporting gear to the mine would put off tourists.

Telluride's story is like that of many mining towns. The town began as a mining camp, when gold and silver was discovered in 1875. Although thousands came to join in the mining operations, the real boom didn't take off until 1890, when the railroad arrived. As remote mining towns often were, Telluride was rowdy, with plenty of saloons and a thriving red-light district. In 1889, Butch Cassidy robbed his first bank here.

In 1891, Telluride made history when Lucien Lucius Nunn called on George Westinghouse and the enigmatic Nikola Tesla to power his mines with electricity. South of Telluride, in the town of Ames, they constructed a high-voltage generator. In keeping with Tesla's ideas, the generator produced alternating current, and Telluride became the first town in the world to light its streetlamps with alternating current.

Skiing didn't come to Telluride until the 1970s. As an isolated ski town, Telluride was laid back, a haven for hippies who moved in to take advantage of the cheap property rates and fantastic natural surroundings. But money soon followed, and after the airport was built in the mid-1980s, Telluride took off. A gondola now carries people up and over the mountain to the ski resort. Mountain Village, on the other side, has become an official town and an entire resort community has risen out of thin air. Because of the region's naturally steep terrain, Telluride offers some hellacious descents. There are also long, gentle slopes, and the ski area has become a favorite with families.

East of Telluride, over the mountain, sits the little burg of Ouray, which was a mining town at one point. Today, people come to Ouray to get into the mountains. A couple of companies in town rent Jeeps and take passengers on Jeep tours of the region's spectacular mountain meadows and passes. In the summer, the flowers are fantastic. In the winter, ice climbers come to try their hand at Ouray's ice-climbing park.

Most of the attractions, lodgings, and restaurants listed here are open year-round. Many, however, reduce hours significantly for about six weeks in the spring and fall.

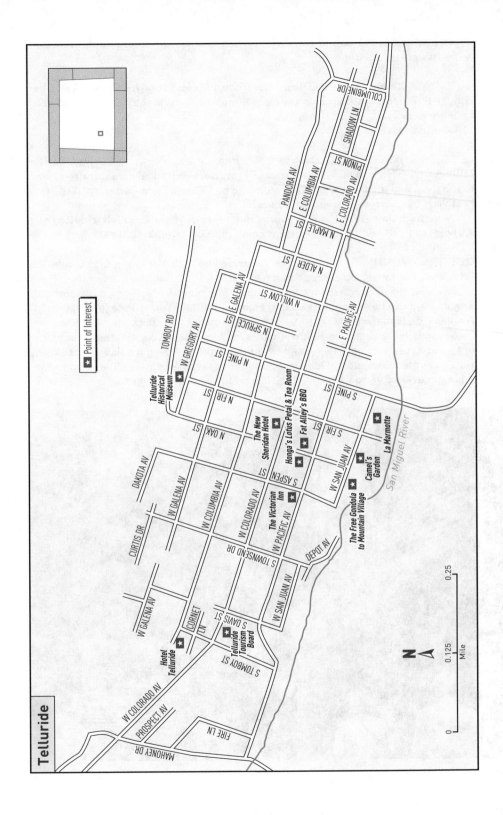

Telluride

Point of Interest

Tomboy Rd

COLUMBINE DR
SHADOW LN
PIÑON ST
E COLUMBIA AV
E COLORADO AV
PANDORA AV
N MAPLE ST
N ALDER ST
E GALENA AV
N WILLOW ST
E PACIFIC AV
N SPRUCE ST
W GREGORY AV
N PINE ST
S PINE ST
N FIR ST
S FIR ST
N OAK ST
S ASPEN ST
W SAN JUAN AV

Telluride Historical Museum

The New Sheridan Hotel

Honga's Lotus Petal & Tea Room

Fat Alley's BBQ

La Marmotte

Camel's Garden

The Victorian Inn

The Free Gondola to Mountain Village

San Miguel River

DAKOTA AV
W GALENA AV
W COLUMBIA AV
W COLORADO AV
W PACIFIC AV
W SAN JUAN AV
CURTIS DR
S TOWNSEND DR
DEPOT AV

W GALENA AV
CORNET LN
S DAVIS ST
S TOMBOY ST

Hotel Telluride

Telluride Tourism Board

W COLORADO AV
PROSPECT AV
MAHONEY DR
FIRE LN

N

0   0.125   0.25
Mile

Be sure to call ahead during these two off-seasons. Unless otherwise indicated, all addresses are in Telluride.

GUIDANCE **Telluride Tourism Board** (visittelluride.com), 700 W. Colorado Ave. Open daily 9–6. The tourism board has plenty of literature to guide your stay in Telluride.
More websites:
telluride.com

GETTING THERE *By car:* Getting to Ouray from the south requires a drive along the Million Dollar Highway up from Durango. From here, Telluride is a short drive north to Ridgway, and then west on CO 62 and south on CO 145. From Cortez, CO 145 heads northeast in a near-direct route to Telluride.
By air: Both United and Frontier Airlines offer service to and from **Telluride Regional Airport** (970-728-8600; tellurideairport.com), 1500 Last Dollar Rd. # 1.

GETTING AROUND *By bus:* The free **Telluride Bus** (970-728-5700), 1370 Black Bear Rd., runs an in-town loop every 20 minutes.
By dial-a-ride: For guests and residents of Mountain Village, free transportation around town can be arranged by calling **Mountain Village Dial-a-Ride** (970-728-8888). Available daily in the winter 6:30 AM–12:30 AM; summer 7 AM–12:30 AM.
By gondola: Getting from Telluride to nearby Mountain Village is simply the matter of taking a free gondola ride up and over the mountain. The **gondola** (970-728-0588) runs from the north end of Oak Street into the heart of Mountain Village from 7 AM–midnight every day from Nov. 17–April 8 and May 24–Oct. 21.

DOWNTOWN TELLURIDE

FREE GONDOLA TO MOUNTAIN VILLAGE

✱ To See & Do

&. ↑ **Telluride Historical Museum** (970-728-3344; telluridemuseum.com), 201 W. Gregory Ave. Open in the summer Mon.–Sat. 11–5 (until 7 on Thu.) and Sun. 1–5. In winter, Tue.–Sat. 11–5 (until 7 on Thu.). The local museum is housed in the Old Miner's Hospital Building. Since 1966, the museum has sought to preserve the region's history while providing educational opportunities for the public. The museum has many hands-on exhibitions that illustrate Telluride's colorful history—a history that begins with the Ute people who camped and hunted in the area and continues on in the rowdy stories of an Old West mining town. Of particular interest is the replica of the Tomboy Bride Cabin, which shines some light on the life of women around the turn of the century in the mountains of western Colorado. Adult admission $5, seniors and students (6–17) $3, and children under 6 free.

Box Canyon Falls and Park (970-325-7080; ci.ouray.co.us/staticpages/index.php?page=ParksRecreation). If you drive south out of Ouray on US 550, the entrance to Box Canyon is at the bend of the first switchback on CR 361. Open May–Oct. 8–8 and 10–10 the rest of the year. A short walk from the parking lot takes you into Box Canyon, across a steel platform, to a very impressive waterfall. The canyon is narrow, yet it seems the rock should not be able to hold in the rushing torrent as it drops 285 feet. So much power within such a tight space is truly sublime. From the steel platform, you can take the stairs to the bottom of the canyon for a different perspective on the falls. Another trail takes you to the top of the canyon, where there's an impressive bridge. Adult admission $4, seniors $3, and children (6–12) $2.

✆ **Bachelor-Syracuse Mine Tour** (970-325-0220; bachelorsyracusemine.com), 1222 CR 14, Ouray. Tours leave on the hour daily 9–4 May–June 15. From mid-June through Aug., the last tour is at 5. Closed July 4th. The hour-long tour at Bachelor-Syracuse Mine takes you deep into Gold Hill by train to see the workings of an actual gold and silver mine. Afterward, learn how to pan for gold in the stream that runs out of the mine. If you have time, come early in the day and enjoy the all-you-can-eat buffet at the mine's outdoor cafe. Adult tour $15 and children (4–11) $8.

 ♿ **Ouray Hot Springs Pool** (970-325-7073; ourayhotsprings.com), 1220 Main St., Ouray. Summer hours Mon.–Fri. noon–8:45 and Sat. and Sun. 11–8:45. Open year-round, this outdoor pool is fed by the local hot springs. It is divided into three temperature levels—the coolest is cool enough to swim laps. There's also a waterslide. The pool has been undergoing some major renovations, so call ahead to be sure it's open.

Orvis Hot Springs (970-626-5324; orvishotsprings.com), 1585 CR 3, Ridgway. Open daily 9–10. The facility has both indoor and outdoor soaking pools. Outside, is the Island Pond with a waterfall or the Lobster Pot that gets up to 114 degrees F. In addition to the indoor pool, a private soaking tub is available to whoever gets to it first. Adult all-day admission $16, children (4–12) $6, and children under 4 free.

Million Dollar Highway is what they call the 75-mile stretch of road between Durango and Ouray. No one is certain where the name came from. Some say it cost a million dollars to build each mile of the highway, which reaches 11,008 feet at Red Mountain Pass. Others say that the dirt used to build the road contained gold ore. Although the moniker is applied to that entire section of US 550, it is the 12 miles south of Ouray that have earned the road its white-knuckle reputation. Along the route old mining operations can be seen on the mountainsides. There are beautiful vistas at every sweeping, nail-biting turn.

San Juan Skyway Byway (codot.gov/travel/scenic-byways/southwest/san-juan-skyway). This 230-mile loop takes you around to Cortez, over to Durango, and back up to Ouray and then Telluride. (See *To See & Do* in *Durango* for more information.)

✳ Outdoor Activities

ALPINE SKIING & SNOWBOARDING **Telluride Ski Resort** (970-728-6900; telluride skiresort.com).565 Mountain Village Blvd. Lifts run daily during ski season 9–4. From Telluride, the mountain can look a little intimidating—a few lifts heading up from town and all black diamonds coming down. Over on the Mountain Village side, however, the perspective widens considerably. The ski area offers 1,700 skiable acres with an over-all vertical drop of 3,530 feet. The longest of the 84 runs is Galloping Goose, a gently sloping 4.6 miles. The number of trails for beginner, intermediate, and advanced skiers is pretty evenly distributed—as are the three terrain parks. In recent years, the resort opened eight runs of backcountry-style terrain in Black Iron Bowl. The new runs are accessible by a 10- to 30-minute hike along Prospect Ridge from the top of Lift 12.

Lee's Ski Hill, Ouray. Located east of town on Third Avenue, a free rope tow operates on weekends and during the week in the late afternoon. The short run only drops 75 vertical feet and provides a great opportunity for kids learning the basics of skiing. The hill opens once there's a 9-inch base.

Boot Doctor (970-728-8954 or 1-800-592-6883; bootdoctor.com), 650 Mountain Village Blvd. Open daily in the winter 8–7. Located in Mountain Village at the base of the gondola and Lift 4. Boot Doctor primarily makes custom ski boots. It also rents equipment.

CROSS-COUNTRY SKIING & SNOWSHOEING **Telluride Nordic Trails** (970-728-1144; telluridenordic.com), Telluride Town Park, 500 E. Colorado Ave. This organization grooms trails for cross-country skiing at Trout Lake, Priest Lake, and Faraway Ranch. It also provides ski lessons and an equipment swap, and organizes an annual Nordic ski race.

TopAten Nordic and Snowshoe Trails (970-728-7300; tellurideskiresort.com /the-mountain/terrain/nordic-skiing). Located at the top of Lift 10, the ski and snowshoe area has more than 6 miles of groomed trails. There is also a warming tipi and restrooms. If you don't already have a pass for skiing, you can purchase a passenger lift ticket for Lift 10—this allows you access to the facilities with Nordic gear and snowshoes. Snowshoe tours leave daily at 10 AM; check for pricing.

San Juan Hut System (970-626-3033; sanjuanhuts.com), P.O. Box 773, Ridgway. The hut system maintains five backcountry huts that connect Telluride, Ridgway, and Ouray along a route that skirts the Mt. Sneffels Wilderness. A stay at each hut will run $30. There's only room for eight in each hut, so reservations are a must.

Ouray Trail Group (970-325-0808; ouraytrails.org), P.O. Box 50, Ouray. The trail group publishes a map describing the trails in Ouray County. A branch of the trail group, the Ouray County Nordic Council, grooms several miles of trails in the Ouray area for cross-country skiing. Snowshoers are welcome to share the trail but must avoid tramping the set tracks.

FISHING **San Miguel Anglers** (970-728-4477; sanmiguelanglers.com), 150 W. Colorado Ave. The San Miguel River flows out from Telluride to the northwest, where it eventually flows into the Dolores. The guides at San Miguel Anglers lead full- and half-day fishing trips on the San Miguel. They also offer one-on-one fly-fishing instruction. A one-person, half-day trip runs $250, and a full-day trip $375. The per-person rate decreases with each additional guest.

RIGS Fly Shop & Guide Service (1-888-626-4460; fishrigs.com), 555 Sherman Hwy., Ridgway. The guides at RIGS offer several fly-fishing trips on private sections of the Uncompahgre River. They offer half- and full-day trips as well as fishing instruction. A one-person, half-day trip is $260.

FOUR-WHEELING One of Ouray's biggest activities is four-wheeling through the surrounding mountains. Old mining roads and railroad grades offer unprecedented

MOUNTAIN VILLAGE

access to stunning mountain views. In the middle of summer, folks go up to see the wildflowers blooming in the high mountain meadows. There are plenty of reasonably safe roads to take in the area; **Black Bear Road** is not one of them. For experienced, mountain-tested four-wheelers, the road is considered a challenge. The road begins at Red Mountain Pass on US 550 and heads up to Black Bear Pass. It then begins a treacherous descent to Telluride, down a mess of steep/narrow switchbacks.

Switzerland of America Tours (970-325-4484 or 1-866-990-5337; soajeep.com), 226 Seventh Ave., Ouray. For four-wheel tours, Switzerland of America will take you up into the mountains to explore ghost towns and discover old mining operations or simply gaze upon meadows of wildflowers and scenic waterfalls. Half- and full-day trips are available. For those interested in ditching the driver and taking the wheel themselves, the company also rents Jeep Wranglers. Half-day tours $60, full day $130, and Jeep rental $149–169.

HIKING Telluride is a great town for hikers. Many trails leave right from town. One of the most popular is the trail to **Bridal Veil Falls**. It's 2.2 miles to the top of the falls, and the hike is moderate to difficult. The trail begins a couple of miles east of town on CO 145, where the asphalt ends.

Telluride Adventures (970-728-4101; tellurideadventures.com), 300 S. Mahoney Ave. Among other things, the folks at Telluride Adventures lead guided hiking tours. They offer full- and half-day treks as well as multiday backpacking trips. Half-day hike $100 and full day $125.

HORSEBACK RIDING **Telluride Horseback Adventures** (970-728-9611; ridewith roudy.com), 242 Hawn Ln. Roudy Roudebush has a motto: "Gentle horses for gentle people, fast horses for fast people, and for people who don't like to ride, horses that don't like to be rode." Roudy offers trail rides year-round, and in the winter he takes guests on a sleigh ride around the Mountain Village Nordic Ski Area. Rides last from one hour up to a whole day. Call to make reservations.

ICE CLIMBING **Ouray Ice Park** (970-325-4288; ourayicepark.com), Uncompahgre Gorge, Ouray. The ice park is located south of town—take CO 361 toward Box Canyon, but stay left at the split. There's parking by the upper bridge. Every year, hundreds of climbers come to Ouray to climb the cliffs at the world's first park devoted solely to ice climbing. Uncompahgre Gorge was used for ice climbing in the past, but once water from nearby sources was redirected over the cliff walls, the gorge became a real-live attraction. There are 13 different climbing areas, including a Kid's Climbing Park. Because the park is entirely run by the generosity of those who give their time and money to the project, admission is free; however, donations are appreciated. As you would expect, the ice park is only open in winter.

MOUNTAIN BIKING For a gut-busting climb, try the 17-mile route from Telluride to Ouray over Imogene Pass (elevation 13,114 feet). The initial ascent climbs more than 4,300 feet. The route is popular with the four-wheel crowd—so if you are heading to the mountains to escape traffic, try another trail.

For a true mountain bike journey, the **San Juan Hut System** (970-626-3033; san juanhuts.com), P.O. Box 773, Ridgway, operates along a 215-mile route of backcountry roads from Telluride to Moab. About every 35 miles, riders crash for the night at one of the huts. The trip takes seven days and six nights and costs $850 per person. In exchange, riders get a sleeping bag and a place to sleep, three meals a day, and trail descriptions and maps.

Further Adventures (1-800-592-6883; furtheradventures.com), 650 Mountain Village Blvd., Mountain Village. This outfitter leads half-, full-, and multiday mountain bike trips all summer for riders of all experience. For beginners, there is the half-day Lizard Head to Galloping Goose ride, which begins with riders being shuttled up to a higher elevation by van and then riding a gentle grade back down to the valley. Prices vary by ride, but a half-day ride for one usually runs about $200. It gets cheaper per person when you add people to your group.

✳ Lodging

HOTELS ♿ 🏠 (•)) **Camel's Garden** (1-888-772-2635; camelsgarden.com), 250 W. San Juan Ave. Located kitty-corner to the gondola, Camel's Garden has 35 rooms, suites, and condos. From the outside, like most buildings in Telluride, the architecture pulls from the town's mining days. Inside, the hotel has a more modern feel. Rooms are furnished in a contemporary style, such as Italian marble bathrooms and cherry-oak furniture. Rooms have fireplaces, and most have balconies with a view of town or the mountain. A continental breakfast is served every morning. Accommodations (rooms, suites, condos) $200–1,300.

♿ 🏠 (•)) **The Hotel Telluride** (970-369-1188 or 1-866-468-3501 for reservations; thehoteltelluride.com), 199 N. Cornet St. The spacious rooms at The Hotel Telluride are tastefully decorated with southwestern mountain touches. Luxury is its angle, and guests are promised a wonderful night of rest on the "Incredible Bed," which features 250-thread-count sheets, feather bedding, and a down comforter. A full breakfast is served daily. Rooms $216–429.

♿ (•)) **New Sheridan Hotel** (970-728-4351 or 1-800-200-1891; newsheridan.com), 231 W. Colorado Ave. Located in the heart of Telluride, the original Sheridan opened its doors in 1891. Not long after, it burned to the ground, and the New Sheridan was built (in 1895). For well more than 100 years, the Sheridan has been welcoming guests to Telluride. Today, the hotel strives to maintain the building's historic character, and the Victorian style is preserved throughout the hotel. A full breakfast is served daily. The hotel also has a bar (the oldest in Telluride) and a restaurant, the New Sheridan Chop House. Rooms $228–348.

♿ (•)) **The Victorian Inn** (970-728-6601 or 1-800-611-9893; tellurideinn.com), 401 W. Pacific Ave. As Telluride continues to grow, finding affordable accommodations in town gets harder and harder. The Victorian Inn remains one of the most affordable stays in town. The rooms are spacious and clean. There is no air-conditioning in the summer, but the

NEW SHERIDAN HOTEL

rooms cool off plenty overnight. A continental breakfast is served every morning. Rooms $138–359.

  ♿ **Inn at Lost Creek** (970-729-5678 or 1-888-601-5678; innatlostcreek.com), 119 Lost Creek Ln., Mountain Village. The luxurious accommodations at Lost Creek are located in the heart of Mountain Village, an easy walk from the gondola. The lobby is warm and inviting, and the rooms are high-end. Rooms have flat-screen HDTVs, a fireplace, and a large jetted tub. It's a perfect place to rest after a day on the slopes. The inn offers complimentary ski waxing and deburring. Rooms and suites $195–1,900 (depending on time of year).

  ♿ **Beaumont Hotel** (970-325-7000 or 1-888-447-3255; beaumonthotel.com), 505 Main St., Ouray. The Beaumont is a quaint hotel with 12 rooms. Each room is uniquely decorated in a style reminiscent of the hotel's Victorian past, but entirely contemporary and tasteful. Rooms, junior suites, and suites are available, all with great views of the surrounding peaks. The hotel cannot "accommodate" children under 16. Rooms and suites $140–600.

BED & BREAKFASTS 🛜 ♿ **China Clipper Inn** (970-325-0565 or 1-800-315-0565; chinaclipperinn.com), 525 Second St., Ouray. Built in 1995, the China Clipper Inn was intended from the start as a B&B. The inn's exterior is not at all out of place with the historic qualities of Ouray. Inside, the inn's 12 rooms are decorated in a British colonial style. Many rooms have jetted tubs, fireplaces, decks, and private entrances. The honeymoon suites have fireplaces and Jacuzzi tubs for two. A full breakfast is served daily in the dining room. Rooms $129–259.

CAMPGROUNDS 🛜 **Ouray KOA** (970-325-4736 or 1-800-562-8026; koa.com/campgrounds/ouray),US 550 CR 23, Ouray. Open May–Sept. The campground has tent sites and RV sites with electric and full hookups. The grounds sit along the Uncompahgre River, and a stream passes through the property. The camp has a hot tub, and every weekend there is a Texas barbecue with live bluegrass music. Tent sites $46, RV sites $50–68, and Kabins $63.

✱ Where to Eat

DINING OUT Reservations are recommended.

  ♿ 🍷 **221 South Oak** (970-728-9507; 221southoak.com), 221 S. Oak St., Telluride. Open for dinner Mon.–Sat. 6–10. A short walk from the gondola, the restaurant is set in one of the town's historic homes, adding to its intimate charm. The menu is New American cuisine, with dishes such as grilled swordfish with glass noodles, mushrooms, and tea broth. Chef Eliza Gavin is also the author of *Foreplay: A Book of Appeteasers* and *Recipes from 221 South Oak Bistro*, and she was a competitor on Bravo's show, *Top Chef.* Entrées $29–50.

  ♿ 🍷 **Allred's** (970-728-7474; telluride skiresort.com/events-activities/dining /allreds-restaurant), top of the gondola. Open daily for dinner 5:30–9:30. Sitting 1,800 feet above Telluride affords fantastic views of the town—its lights a sparkling mass below. Known as much for its contemporary American cuisine and excellent wine list as for the view, Allred's offers fine dining from the top of the free gondola in San Sophia station. Local ingredients of the highest quality go into preparing the menu, which features steak and seafood, as well as elk, lamb, and duck. Dishes $27–41.

  La Marmotte (970-728-6232; lamarmotte.com), 150 W. San Juan Ave. Serving dinner daily with seating beginning at 6. The menu at La Marmotte changes daily, reflecting the availability of fresh local produce. Located in the town's 100-year-old ice house, this rustic French bistro promises an intimate dining experience. Appetizers such as yellowfin tuna tartare and hot and cold foie gras with cherry chutney, prepare the way for entrées such as sauté of Muscovy duck and seared Alaskan salmon. Dishes start at $45 for a three-course meal.

   & **New Sheridan Chop House** (970-728-9100; newsheridan.com /chop-house-restaurant-telluride), 231 W. Colorado Ave. Open daily for brunch 8–2, dinner 5:30–9. Serving diners in New Sheridan Hotel since 1895, the Chop House has a reputation for great meals. Steak and seafood top the menu, and the restaurant prides itself on stocking more than 125 bottles of excellent wine to complement every entrée. The Chop House also serves a cheese course— three cheeses nightly (selection changes often). Entrées $24–49.

EATING OUT & Ÿ **High Pie Pizzeria & Taproom** (970-728-2978; highpiepizzeria .com), 100 W. Colorado Ave. Crafted from the finest ingredients, local when available, organic and hormone free, the pizzas at High Pie are works of art. The restaurant also serves calzones and subs, and there is a wide array of beers on tap. Most pizzas $11–16.

   & Ÿ **Oak** (970-728-3985; oakstelluride .com), 250 San Juan Ave. Open daily 11–10. Carrying on the tradition of the former Fat Alley's BBQ, Oak serves excellent southern-style eats. For barbecue, there's no other restaurant in town. Oak makes it all—brisket, ribs, pulled-pork sandwiches, and roasted chicken. Sides include coleslaw, potato salad, sweet potato fries, and fried okra. The menu also includes cheeseburgers and cheesesteak, but how can anyone order a cheeseburger with all that sweet barbecue aroma in the air? Sandwiches $8.50–10 and other dishes $10–20.

   & Ÿ **The Outlaw Restaurant** (970-325-4366; outlawrestaurant.com), 610 Main St., Ouray. The Outlaw Restaurant is nothing if not a classic steakhouse. Always busy, the Outlaw serves steak, seafood, and several highly praised pasta dishes. The wine list has something for most palates. Dishes $16–27. If dining

indoors isn't your style, The Outlaw Restaurant and Colorado West Jeep Tours (970-325-4014) will drive you up into the mountains for an Outlaw Mountain Cookout. Call Colorado West for reservations and more information.

BAKERIES & COFFEE SHOPS **Baked in Telluride** (970-728-4775; bakedintel .com), 27 S. Fir St. Open daily 5:30–10. This fine dough-wrangling facility could just as likely be listed under places for lunch or dinner. The same skill that goes into the shop's delicious baked goods informs the sourdough-crust pizza making. But it's not just about the bread. Stop by for breakfast burritos or croissants, soups, sandwiches, and a menu of Mexican dishes for dinner.

   The Coffee Cowboy (970-708-0294; thecoffeecowboy.com), 131 E. Colorado Ave. Tucked between a couple of buildings on Colorado Ave., The Coffee Cowboy is a concession trailer with outdoor patio seating. It's a very nice trailer, and with the views of Telluride's great outdoors, this is an excellent choice for your morning libations.

BARS, TAVERNS, & BREW PUBS & Ÿ **New Sheridan Bar** (970-728-3911; new sheridan.com), 231 W. Colorado Ave. Open daily 3 PM–2 AM. New Sheridan Hotel boasts the oldest bar in town, looking much as it did more than 100 years ago. This is one of the town's best hangouts, and the après-ski crowd keeps the place busy.

✳ Entertainment

Telluride Repertory Theatre Company (970-728-4539; telluridetheater.com), P.O. Box 2469, Telluride. In the summer, the company puts on a three-week run of outdoor productions. In the winter, it retires to **Sheridan Opera House** (970-728-6363; sheridanoperahouse.com), 110 North Oak St., where it performs Broadway shows. All year-round, Show & Tell play readings are performed throughout town—at bookstores and galleries.

✳ Selective Shopping

Between the Covers (970-728-4504; between-the-covers.com), 224 W. Colorado Ave. This little bookstore in downtown Telluride has a great selection of books that cover regional recreation, as well as maps and other resources for travelers.

    Wilderness Wonders (970-845-7230; tonynewlin.com), 116 Beaver Creek Plaza, Beaver Creek. Tony Newlin, whose photographs make up the Wilderness Wonders gallery, strives to let nothing get between his camera and nature in the photos he displays. He uses no filters, artificial light, and no digital manipulation to create his prints. The result is a surprisingly warm and real experience of the wildness and beauty of nature in his work.

✳ Special Events

June: **Telluride Bluegrass Festival** (1-800-624-2422; bluegrass.com). Every year thousands gather in Telluride to hear great bluegrass music. The festival has featured the likes of Emmylou Harris and Béla Fleck.

    July: **Hard Rock 100** (hardrock100 .com). This 100-mile endurance race takes runners on a spectacular loop through the San Juan Mountains.

    September: **Blues and Brews** (telluride blues.com). For three days, folks come to Telluride to drink microbrews and listen to soulful music.

CRESTED BUTTE
& GUNNISON

Somewhat off the beaten path, Crested Butte is the last of the old-school Colorado ski towns. To some extent, the culture here is still governed by ski bums and laid-back hippie types (a.k.a. the granola crowd). Whereas Telluride will nix a plan to install a sculpture of an ice climber because it smacks of advertising, the folks in Crested Butte are painting their Victorian cottages every color of the rainbow, and have no qualms about a coffeehouse covered in license plates. Crested Butte may be more relaxed because the actual ski resort, Mount Crested Butte, is 3 miles away. So far, most of the resort development has remained on the mountain.

Once a mining town, Crested Butte did not suffer the fate of other mining towns. Although many got rich from the gold and silver found in the mid-19th century, it was coal (first discovered in 1879) that sustained the community into the 1950s. In the early 1960s, the ski area was developed, and Crested Butte took on a new personality. By the 1970s, hippies had taken over the slopes, and in the summers mountain biking pioneers were riding their fat-tired bikes down the mountainside.

Crested Butte is one of the most scenic spots in the state. It rests at the head of East Valley, a wide gently sloping patch of land that stretches 17 miles south of Gunnison. Mount Crested Butte, at 12,162 feet, stands out noticeably against the sky. The ski mountain in Crested Butte is technically challenging in parts and is closing in on 400,000 annual visitors. The town is surrounded by beautiful scenery. To the north and east is the Maroon Bells Snowmass Wilderness; to the west, the Raggeds.

To the south lies Gunnison. This community was here before the mining boom. In 1874, the town was established by farmers and ranchers who had moved to the valley. Gunnison still has an agricultural feel. Many visitors come for the region's recreational activities. In the winter, snowmobiling is a popular activity. In the summer, there is plenty of great fishing on local rivers and reservoirs. During hunting season, outfitters take hunters out for deer and elk.

Many folks also use Gunnison a kicking-off point for visits to Black Canyon of the Gunnison National Park or to enjoy Curecanti National Recreation Area. South of Gunnison, a day trip will take you into Lake City, and to the east is some excellent whitewater rafting in Salida.

Most of the attractions, lodgings, and restaurants listed here are open year-round. Many, however, reduce hours significantly for about six weeks in the spring and fall. Be sure to call ahead during these two off-seasons. Unless otherwise indicated, all addresses are in Crested Butte.

GUIDANCE **Crested Butte & Mt. Crested Butte Chamber of Commerce** (970-349-6438 or 1-800-545-4505; cbchamber.com), 601 Elk Ave. Open daily 9–5 in summer and winter (Mon.–Fri. 9–5 in the off-season). When you come into town from the south, CO 135 turns into Sixth Street and the visitor center is on your right at the corner of Sixth and Elk. It has all the information you could need, including town maps and trail maps.

Gunnison Chamber of Commerce (970-641-1501; gunnisonchamber.com), 500 E. Tomichi Ave. The Gunnison Chamber offices and visitor center are right on US 50—a

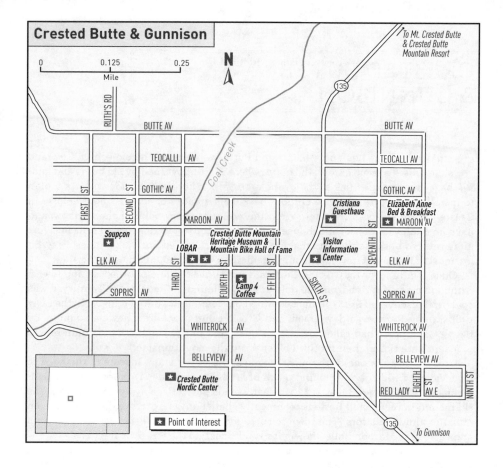

Crested Butte & Gunnison

couple of blocks east of downtown. They have information on Gunnison as well as Crested Butte.

More websites:

gunnisoncrestedbutte.com

visitcrestedbutte.com

GETTING THERE *By car:* Gunnison is located right on US 50, which begins in Pueblo and meets up with US 70 in the west by Grand Junction. The town is about 200 miles southwest of Denver (about a four-hour drive). The main road to Crested Butte, CO 135, begins in Gunnison and runs 27 miles north to the ski town.

By air: **Gunnison–Crested Butte Regional Airport** (970-641-2304; gunnison county.org/Airport), 711 Rio Grande Ave., Gunnison, sees regular flights from American and United Airlines. Shuttle service to Gunnison and Crested Butte is available through **Alpine Express** (1-800-822-4844; alpineexpressshuttle.com), P.O. Box 1250, Gunnison.

GETTING AROUND *By bus:* **Gunnison–Crested Butte RTA** (970-641-5074; gunnison valleyrta.org) offers free bus service between Gunnison and Mt. Crested Butte. **Mountain Express** (970-349-7318, mtnexp.org) is a free bus service that shuttles passengers between Crested Butte and Mt. Crested Butte.

THE VIEW ON THE WAY TO CRESTED BUTTE

✳ To See & Do

⇞ **Crested Butte Mountain Heritage Museum** (970-349-1880; crestedbuttemuseum
.com), 331 Elk Ave., Crested Butte. Open daily in the summer 10–8 and in winter 10–6.
Closed in the spring and fall. Mining, ranching, and skiing have all played a key role in
the ongoing story of Crested Butte, which is told here with artifacts, exhibitions, and
historical displays. General admission $5; children under 12 free.

West Elk Loop Scenic Byway (codot.gov/travel/scenic-byways/southwest/west-
elk-loop). This scenic byway travels through a variety of landscapes, from the high
mountain passes outside Crested Butte to Curecanti National Recreation Area along
Blue Mesa Lake. Starting in Gunnison, it heads north along CO 135 to Crested Butte,
continuing on over Keebler Pass (9,980 feet) to CO 133. The highway here offers a spur
to the north ending in Carbondale. To the southwest, CO 133 catches up with CO 92,
which turns south and connects with US 50, which you take back east to Gunnison. The
road outside Crested Butte is unpaved.

✳ Outdoor Activities

ALPINE SKIING & SNOWBOARDING **Crested Butte Mountain Resort** (970-349-
2222 or 1-800-810-7669; skicb.com), 12 Snowmass Rd., Crested Butte. Lifts operate
daily 9–4. Crested Butte offers skiers a 2,775-foot vertical drop (3,062 for those willing
to hike a little). The ski area's 1,167 acres are served by 16 lifts that could conceiv-
ably move 20,000 people up the mountain every hour. There are 121 trails, the longest

BLACK CANYON

Black Canyon of the Gunnison National Park (970-641-2337; nps.gov/blca), 102 Elk Creek, Gunnison. Black Canyon of the Gunnison is one of Colorado's most stunning natural wonders. Throughout the state, the eye is pulled up toward snowy peaks and out to breathtaking vistas. At Black Canyon, however, the eye looks out and down. From the Gunnison River below, the canyon rises 2,722 feet to Warner Point, and at its narrowest span, the canyon is only 1,100 feet wide (40 at the bottom).

South Rim Road offers the best views of the canyon. To get there from US 50, turn north on CO 347 about 15 miles east of Montrose. Begin at the visitor center at Gunnison Point. A short trail brings you down to a spectacular canyon overlook. Inside the visitor center, an impressive log structure in its own right, there is a short video on the canyon and some displays on the history and geology of the park. Along the canyon edge, numerous trails afford a more intimate experience of this impressive landscape. The trails along the top are easy to difficult. Hiking into the canyon, however, is for those in excellent physical condition. There are no trails down to the river, and "hikers are expected to find their own way down and to be prepared for self-rescue."

For more information on the canyon, the website has a large collection of videos you can watch covering geology, history, life science, and recreation as it relates to each of the overlooks along the South Rim. Single visit vehicle fee $15. Walk-ins and cyclists (motoring and pedaling) $7.

Curecanti National Recreation Area (970-641-2337 ext. 205; nps.gov/cure/planyourvisit/boattour.htm) offers another vantage point for exploring the canyon region, the Morrow Point Boat Tour. Farther downriver—outside of the towering cliffs—this 90-minute trip takes you through the upper Black Canyon on a 42-passenger pontoon. National Park rangers (or qualified volunteers) lead these guided tours. From Memorial Day to Labor Day, there are two tours daily (except Tue.) at 10 and 12:30. Reservations are required and can be made by calling the number above or by visiting the Elk Creek Visitor Center, 15 miles west of Gunnison. Adult fee $16 and seniors and children (under 13) $8.

being 2.6 miles, most of which are intermediate level. The DC Canaan Terrain Park has plenty of jumps and about a dozen rail features. There's a tubing hill for the kids, and the resort also offers ski and snowboard lessons through its Mountain School. For children's lessons, call 970-349-2211 or 1-800-544-8448; for adult lessons, 1-800-600-7349 or 970-349-2259.

CROSS-COUNTRY SKIING & SNOWSHOEING **Crested Butte Nordic Center** (970-349-1707; cbnordic.org), 620 Second St., Crested Butte. The Nordic center is a nonprofit organization that maintain 31 miles of groomed cross-country trails around Crested Butte. It also rents gear and leads tours into the Gunnison National Forest. For the complete backcountry ski experience, the center books reservations for the Forest Queen Backcountry Hut.

Crested Butte Mountain Resort Snowshoe Tours (970-349-2252; skicb.com/content/snowshoe-tours), 12 Snowmass Rd., Crested Butte. The resort offers guided snowshoe tours. Guests will snowshoe about 2.5 miles, learning about the region's history and the local ecology. This is a unique way to experience the mountains.

Elkton Cabins (970-349-1815), P.O. Box 3128 Crested Butte, maintains three cabins for backcountry stays. The cabins have gas cookstoves and wood-burning stoves for

BLACK CANYON OF THE GUNNISON

heat. A backcountry tour to consider would be from Washington Gulch to the cabins. Nightly per-person rate $18–50.

FISHING In addition to the **Gunnison River** and its three large reservoirs west of Gunnison, this region has several deep mountain lakes and rocky mountain creeks for fly fishing.

The East River, for example, starts at Emerald Lake north of Crested Butte and slowly winds its way to Almont. There are great fly-fishing stretches all along its route. Twenty-two miles northeast of Almont, Taylor Reservoir is popular with anglers as well. Although the location is somewhat remote, **Taylor Park Marina** (970-641-2922; taylorparkmarina.com), at 21700 CR 742, Almont, rents out boats and fishing equipment. It sells bait and even has a deli and grill. Check out the website—people pull huge fish out of this lake.

Dragonfly Anglers (970-349-1228 or 1-800-491-3079; dragonflyanglers.com), 307 Elk Ave., Crested Butte. The guides at Dragonfly offer walk-and-wade as well as float trips. They take anglers on all the local rivers, including Black Canyon of the Gunnison (part of a multiday trip). Two-person, half-day trips $310–350.

Willowfly Anglers (1-888-761-3474 or 970-641-1303; 3riversresort.com/fishing), 130 CR 742, Almont. This Orvis-endorsed outfitter provides guided fishing trips from spring into fall; also walk-and-wade, fly-fishing, or spin-fishing float trips. It even offers a full-day mountain lake option. Two-person, half-day trips $280–330.

GOLF **The Club at Crested Butte** (970-349- 8601; theclubatcrestedbutte.com), 385 Country Club Dr., Crested Butte. Golf is just one of the many activities, which also include tennis, skiing, etc. Guests can also find slope-side lodging at the club.

Dos Rios Country Club (970-641-1482; dosriosgolf.net), 501 Camino Del Rio, Gunnison. Two rivers wind through the 18-hole regulation course at Dos Rios. This is a semiprivate course. Greens fees $50–79.

HIKING For the ultimate hiking trip, consider walking to Aspen. This day-long hike, up through West Maroon Pass, is facilitated by a network of old roads and trails. The route is about 10.5 miles, not including the distance from the towns to their respective trailheads. You can arrange to have **Dolly's Mountain Shuttle** (office 970-349-2620, mobile 970-209-9757; crestedbutteshuttle.com) drive you from Crested Butte to local trailheads for only $20 per person with five people (or $100 minimum). For those walking from Aspen, the shuttle can return you to Aspen for $60 per person.

Alpineer (970-349-5210 or 1-800-223-4655; alpineer.com), 419 Sixth St., Crested Butte. Open daily 9–6. This shop sells and rents backcountry gear. It is also an excellent resource for learning about regional trails and hikes.

Colorado Backcountry (970-349-0800; coloradobc.com/colorado-backcountry), P.O. Box 2172, Crested Butte. This guide service offers a complete menu of hiking options, from full- and half-day trips to sunrise runs and evening strolls to all-out backcountry wilderness adventures. For longer hikes, it provides gourmet lunches and daypack rental. See website for a complete list of guided mountain tours.

HORSEBACK RIDING **Fantasy Ranch Horseback Adventures** (970-349-5425 or 1-888-688-3488; www.fantasyranchoutfitters.com), 29 Whiterock, Crested Butte. This outfitter offers true horseback adventures. The Ride and Flight of Your Life trip takes guests on a beautiful ride over East Maroon Pass on the way to Aspen. Guests then return to Crested Butte via airplane. Of course, there are also day rides and short rides in summer and winter.

MOUNTAIN BIKING One day back in 1976, the good folks of Crested Butte were visited by a bunch of ne'er-do-wells out of Aspen. These gentlemen had ridden their motorcycles up over Pearl Pass and down to Crested Butte, and spent the evening drinking at the local bar boasting of their unsurpassable feat of derring-do. Back then, CB had even more of a laid-back hippie vibe than now, but the sight of Aspenites bragging it up in their watering hole was too much to take. The next day, a group set off from Crested Butte, up the Pearl Pass Trail—on their bicycles. They had to spend the night on the mountain, but the next day they arrived in Aspen to thumb a well-deserved nose at their motorized counterparts. Every September, the feat is repeated with the Pearl Pass Tour to Aspen. It is the oldest continuous mountain biking event in the world.

Mountain biking has deep roots in Crested Butte. The trails in the surrounding country are not just plentiful and challenging; they are legendary. For a solid introduction to local trails and rides, be sure to stop by one of the local shops or sign up for a guided tour with a bike outfitter.

To get a feel for the place, ask about the **Lower Loop**, a pleasant trail that begins at Peanut Mine, northwest of town. You can begin in town and there are some alternate trails up to the mine. For a more challenging ride, one with spectacular views, try **Trail #403**—a trail for experienced riders in good physical condition. Beginning in

MOUNTAIN TOWN BIKE CULTURE

Washington Gulch, you climb and cross over to Gothic Road, which takes you back to town.

Alpineer (970-349-5210 or 1-800-223-4655; alpineer.com), 419 Sixth St., Crested Butte. Open daily 9–6. Mountain bikers will find a great selection of MTB gear and bikes for sale and rent. If you need to find a trail, ask here: They know what they are talking about.

Crested Butte Mountain Guides (970-349-5430 or 1-800-455-2307; crestedbutte guides.com), 218 Maroon Ave., Crested Butte. This outfitter leads guided tours of all the area's classic rides—Trail #401, Lower Loop, and so on. Full-day tour for one rider $275 and for two riders $175.

Crested Butte Ski and Bike Shop (1-800-970-9704; crestedbuttesports.com), 35 Emmons Loop, Crested Butte. The shop sells, rents, and repairs skis and bikes. For mountain biking, try the full-suspension Cannondale Prophet—a fine bike by any standard. Full 24-hour rental $60.

✳ Green Space

Curecanti National Recreation Area (970-641-2337, ext. 205; nps.gov/cure), 102 Elk Creek, Gunnison. Three reservoirs along the Gunnison River form the heart of this recreation area east of Black Canyon of the Gunnison. The main entry point, the Elk Creek Visitor Center, is 15 miles west of Gunnison off US 50. The park offers all sorts of recreational activities, from boating and fishing to hiking and camping. Combined with the bordering national park, the area offers 75,000 acres for you to explore. Single-visit vehicle fee $15, walk-ins and cyclists (motoring and pedaling) $7.

✷ Lodging

HOTELS (📶) **Cristiana Guesthaus** (970-349-5326 or 1-800-824-7899; cristiana guesthaus.com), 621 Maroon Ave. The Guesthaus is a lot like a B&B—a residence with three rooms for guests. The rooms are simply decorated and comfortable, and the hospitality from the innkeepers memorable. There is a hot tub on the deck with views of the mountains, and in the summer, the rock garden is quite beautiful. A continental breakfast is served daily. Rooms $85–120.

(📶) **Elk Mountain Lodge** (970-349-7533 or 1-800-374-6521; elkmountainlodge .com), 129 Gothic Ave. The lodge features 19 individually decorated rooms, each with a private bath and cable TV. Five of the rooms have balcony views of the Elk Mountains. Lodge amenities include the Lodge Bar, which is open every evening until 10 or 11, a large indoor hot tub, and a continental breakfast served daily during ski season. Rooms $89–189.

(♿ ❀ (📶)) **Grand Lodge Crested Butte** (970-349-8000 or 1-800-810-7669; skicb .com/lodging/grand-lodge), 6 Emmons Loop. This high-end, full-service hotel is located right next to the ski lifts. Amenities include a year-round heated indoor/outdoor pool, hot tub, and steam room. There's on-site dining at Woodstone Grille, Woodstone Deli, and Woodstone Lounge. The hotel offers a variety of accommodations, from simple guest rooms to suites and condos. The rooms are spacious and tastefully decorated. Rooms and suites $99–209.

(📶) **Nordic Inn** (970-349-5542 or 1-800-542-7669; nordicinncb.com), 14 Treasury Rd. Located in Mt. Crested Butte, within walking distance of the ski area, Nordic Inn has a variety of affordable rooms, many with kitchenettes. Amenities include cable TV and a continental breakfast. Rooms $85–155.

(♿ ❀ (📶)) **Water Wheel Inn** (970-641-1650 or 1-800-624-1650; waterwheel innatgunnison.com), 37478 W US 50, Gunnison. Located 2 miles west of Gunnison on US 50. The innkeeper, Dr. Jim Valenzuela, sees the Water Wheel as a home base for visitors looking to take on all the activities the Gunnison area has to offer. To that end, the inn has fostered relationships with local outfitters and can help you plan any number of trips, from hunting to snowmobiling, horseback riding, and fishing. To help guests make a good start to the day, the continental breakfast, which includes cereals, bagels, and waffles, is supplemented with fresh biscuits and hot gravy. The property is an old-school hotel, but as a new owner, Dr. Valenzuela has been making a ton of changes. Rooms along the back have beautiful views of the neighboring Dos Rios Golf Course. Rooms $69–160.

BED & BREAKFASTS **Purple Mountain Bed & Breakfast** (970-349-5888; purple mountainlodge.com), 714 Gothic Ave. Within walking distance of Elk Avenue and downtown, each of the inn's six rooms is unique—although all have private baths, WiFi, and large flat-screen TVs. Rooms $179–259.

CABINS & COTTAGES **Pioneer Guest Cabins** (970-349-5517; pioneerguest cabins.com), 2094 Cement Creek Rd. Established in 1939, Pioneer Guest Cabins offer eight log cabins nestled in the heart of the Gunnison National Forest along Cement Creek. The first four cabins were built in the 1920s to house skiers who came to tackle the Pioneer ski area. They really resonate with a sense of history. The other four cabins were built in the 1960s and are just as charming. In the winter, gas heat keeps the cabins warm, and the beds are stocked with flannel sheets and down comforters. All have kitchens, a bathroom, and can sleep larger parties. Cabins $151–179.

✷ Where to Eat

DINING OUT **Soupçon** (970-349-5448; soupcon-cb.com), 127A Elk Ave., Crested

Butte. Open Mon.–Sat. for dinner. There are two nightly seatings at 6 and 8:15. This French bistro, housed in a very American log cabin, serves an ever-changing menu of French/American cuisine. Reservations highly recommended. Dishes $35–50.

& **Garlic Mike's** (970-641-2493; garlicmikes.com), 2674 CO 135 N., Gunnison. This Italian restaurant north of Gunnison is the finest place in town for dining. The traditional Italian menu includes some gems like the New York strip steak carbonara. Entrées $13–26.

EATING OUT **Donita's Cantina** (970-349-6674; donitascantina.com), 330 Elk Ave., Crested Butte. Dinner served daily at 5:30. For classic Mexican dining, Donita's has good food, hearty portions, and affordable prices. Closed for the shoulder seasons. Dishes $12–22.95.

Izzy's (970-349-5630), 218 Maroon Ave., Crested Butte. Breakfast and lunch daily 7–2. Izzy's is tucked into an alley off Elk Avenue. It serves a great breakfast—bagels, French toast, and latkes are all favorites. For lunch, there are freshly made soups and sandwiches.

& **Paradise Café** (970-349-5622), 435 6th Ave., Crested Butte. Open daily for breakfast 7–11 and lunch 12–3. The breakfast burritos, skillets, and huevos rancheros make this one of the best places in town for a hearty breakfast. For lunch there's a decent selection of sandwiches, salads, and soups. The service is quick, friendly, and accommodating. Dishes $6–10.

Secret Stash (970-349-6245; thesecretstash.com), 303 Elk Ave., Crested Butte. Open daily 11 AM–"late." For pizza, there's no better place in town. The Secret Stash also has amazing Buffalo wings. After your meal, you might just want to sit back and take in the restaurant's funky atmosphere. Pizzas $19–36.

BAKERIES & COFFEE SHOPS & **Camp 4 Coffee** (970-349-2500; camp4coffee.com), 402½ Elk Ave., Crested Butte. Open 6:30–5:30. Outside, Camp 4 is covered with old license plates. Inside, it serves one of the best cups of coffee in town. Roasted locally, the coffee is

THE LEGENDARY COFFEEHOUSE CAMP 4 COFFEE

served at restaurants all over Crested Butte. Sledgehammer is one of the most popular blends. You might even want to buy a pound of beans for your own Crested Butte experience at home. There's also an additional Camp 4 Coffee at 161 Gillaspey Ave., open daily 5–11 AM.

BARS, TAVERNS, & BREW PUBS Ⴑ **The Eldo** (970-349-6125), 215 Elk Ave., Crested Butte. Open daily 3–2. The Eldo (short for "El Dorado") has a motto: A sunny place for shady people. The Eldo has nine beers on tap and a great selection of bottled brews. Pool table, TVs, and live music make this a great bar for just hanging out.

✳ Entertainment

Crested Butte Music Festival (970-349-0619; crestedbuttemusicfestival.com), 308 Third St. Every year in the month of July, Crested Butte is alive with the sound of music. The music festival puts on a concert every night—chamber musicians, big bands, and bluegrass pickers all take the stage throughout the month.

✳ Selective Shopping

Oh-Be-Joyful Gallery (970-349-5936; ohbejoyfulgallery.com), 409 Third St., Crested Butte. Location in Telluride as well.

Paragon Gallery (970-349-6484; paragonartgallery.com), 132 Elk Ave., Crested Butte. The gallery is a co-op of over a dozen local artists. Jewelry, pottery, stained glass, paintings, and sculpture by some of the most talented artists from Crested Butte and Gunnison are on display.

✳ Special Events

June: **Crested Butte Bike Week** (1-800-545-4505; cbbikeweek.com), Crested Butte. In the summer, the town is all about mountain biking. Events include a chainless descent down Keebler Pass, the Clunker Crit, and a whole mess of freaks on bikes.

July: **Crested Butte Wildflower Festival** (970-349-2571; crestedbuttewildflowerfestival.com), 409 Second St. Every year at the height of summer, the meadows and mountains around Crested Butte erupt into full bloom—wildflowers everywhere. Events include nature hikes, horseback rides, and four-wheel-drive rides into the mountains. There is live music, plenty of food, and art on display.

September: **Pearl Pass Tour to Aspen** (cbklunkers.com), Crested Butte. This ride commemorates the legendary Pearly Pass conquest of 1976.

Vinotok (970-349-6509 or 970-596-6681), Crested Butte. Before the snow starts falling, the town of Crested Butte comes out and makes merry. Everyone's complaints are written down and stuffed in the "grump," which is burned at festival's end.

EASTERN COLORADO

PUEBLO

TRINIDAD

EASTERN PLAINS

PUEBLO

O ften overshadowed by its northern neighbor—Colorado Springs has more than four times the population—Pueblo is the largest city in the southeast region of the state. With more than 100,000 residents, Pueblo is a thriving community. Annual events such as the Colorado State Fair and the Chile & Frijoles Festival are big draws, as is Lake Pueblo State Park. The fair alone is Colorado's biggest event—drawing nearly half a million people to Pueblo over 11 days every summer. Part mini-metropolis and part college town, Pueblo offers all the conveniences of a big city with distinctly small-town charm. This is no truer than when you visit the Union Avenue Historic District, the City Zoo, or any one of Pueblo's great restaurants.

As the southernmost city along Colorado's Front Range, Pueblo offers easy access to the mountains in the west and the state's southeastern plains. In a matter of hours, you can be driving up to view Royal Gorge outside Cañon City or buying fresh canta-loupe from a roadside stand in Rocky Ford. Closer to town, you are within minutes of museums, the zoo, and Lake Pueblo State Park.

Two waterways meet in the heart of Pueblo. For centuries, the confluence of the Arkansas River and Fountain Creek, just east of the Rockies, has been a natural place for people to meet, make camp, or trade goods. In 1706, Juan de Ulibarri, a Spanish captain leading a small expedition out of Santa Fe, crossed the Arkansas River and set up camp, becoming the first recorded European to visit the site of present-day Pueblo.

When Zebulon Pike and his men made their way up the Arkansas River in 1806, they built a small log stockade on the site. Pike then set off on a side trip north to see if he could summit a surprisingly high mountain peak he had seen on the horizon. Although he gave up the attempt and declared the mountain inaccessible, Pikes Peak still bears his name.

In 1842, legendary mountain man Jim Beckwourth, built a trading post here. Beck-wourth, who was of African descent and born into slavery in Virginia in 1798, is a fine example of the unsung role African Americans have played in settling the West. He was joined by a number of settlers, and they called the settlement Fort Pueblo. Beck-wourth would continue trading throughout the West; he fought in the Mexican-American War, lived with the Crow people, and even spent time in California during the Gold Rush. He died in 1866. Fort Pueblo did not last so long. On Christmas Day, 1854, a drunken settler opened the fort to a group of Ute and Apache. Led by Tierra Blanca, the natives killed nearly everyone inside.

Gold and silver were found in the nearby mountains in the late 1850s. The subse-quent rush of settlers established Fountain City, which was later absorbed into Pueblo.

Since its formal inception in 1860, Pueblo has had many ups and downs. In 1872, the Denver & Rio Grande Railroad came to town bringing more prosperity to the region. Colorado Coal & Iron Company built the town's first blast furnace in 1881, and coal mining and steel production remained the driving force behind Pueblo's economy into the 20th century. All this industry brought an influx of immigrants—a legacy that lives today in Pueblo's surprising cultural diversity.

On the evening of June 3, 1921, a sudden downpour, 10 miles west of Pueblo, caused the Arkansas River to rise. Rainfall 30 miles to the north had the same effect on Foun-tain Creek. When the two swollen streams met in downtown Pueblo, the result was

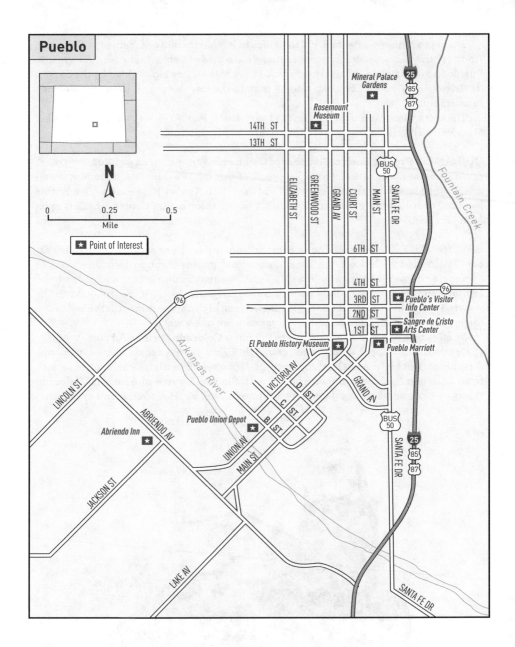

Pueblo

N

0   0.25   0.5
Mile

★ Point of Interest

14TH ST
13TH ST
ELIZABETH ST
GREENWOOD ST
GRAND AV
COURT ST
MAIN ST
SANTA FE DR
6TH ST
4TH ST
3RD ST
2ND ST
1ST ST

Mineral Palace Gardens ★

Rosemount Museum ★

BUS 50

Fountain Creek

25
85
87

96

Pueblo's Visitor Info Center ★

Sangre de Cristo Arts Center ★

El Pueblo History Museum ★

Pueblo Marriott ★

Arkansas River

VICTORIA AV
D ST
C ST
B ST
GRAND AV

Pueblo Union Depot ★

LINCOLN ST
ABRIENDO AV
UNION AV
MAIN ST

Abriendo Inn ★

JACKSON ST

BUS 50

25
85
87

SANTA FE DR

LAKE AV

SANTA FE DR

disaster. The Great Flood of 1921 wiped out a third of the businesses in Pueblo and killed hundreds of people.

It took decades for downtown Pueblo to recover from the flood. In the 1980s, the idea for a Union Avenue Historic District was born. As shops and restaurants began to move back to Union Avenue, the city began an ambitious riverwalk project: the Historic Arkansas Riverwalk of Pueblo. Millions of dollars have been pumped into building a park around the old Arkansas River channel (the river was rerouted south of town after the flood). The riverwalk serves as the perfect backdrop for many of Pueblo's festivals.

There is a higher percentage of Hispanics in Pueblo than in other cities in Colorado. And over the years, other immigrant groups have made Pueblo their home. As a result, Pueblo has unmatched cultural resources. Many of these are highlighted by the Sangre de Cristo Arts Center. They can also be seen in the town's many Italian and Mexican restaurants.

The town's largest tourist attraction today is the Pueblo Reservoir at Lake Pueblo State Park. The lake attracts more than a million visitors each year.

GUIDANCE **Greater Pueblo Chamber of Commerce** (719-542-1704 or 1-800-233-3446; pueblochamber.org), 302 N. Santa Fe Ave., P.O. Box 697, Pueblo. The chamber of commerce office is several short blocks north of the Union Avenue Historic District. At this location, the chamber maintains Pueblo's Visitors Information Center, which is open Mon.–Fri. 8–5.

GETTING THERE *By car:* If you're coming from the north or south, I-25 is your best bet. The interstate follows the Front Range and passes through Denver, Colorado Springs, and Pueblo on its way to Santa Fe, Albuquerque, and points south. From the east and the west, US 50 winds its way across the state, from Grand Junction in the west to Kansas in the east. If you take this two-lane highway, be aware that speed limits are lower in populated areas, and stoplights are not uncommon.

By air: The most accessible airport to Pueblo is **Colorado Springs Airport** (719-550-1972; flycos.com), about 45 miles to the north. Every year, it seems, more cities have direct flights in and out of Colorado Springs. If you're not renting a car, shuttle service from Colorado Springs can be arranged with **Shuttle Service of Southern Colorado** (719-545-9444 or 1-877-545-9435), 215 S. Victoria Ave. #B. However, if you are renting

PUEBLO UNION DEPOT

a car and are willing to drive a little farther, be sure to check prices for flights to Denver. **Denver International Airport** (303-342-2000 or 1-800-247-2336; flydenver.com) is about 120 miles north of Pueblo (a good two-hour drive), but it's often cheaper to land in Denver and drive the rest of the way.

By train: There is no rail service to Pueblo, although **Amtrak** (1-800-872-7245; amtrak.com) has train terminals in Denver to the north and Trinidad to the south. From both locations, you can take the Thruway bus service directly to Pueblo (see below for bus depot information).

By bus: **Greyhound** operates regular service to and from Pueblo from the **Pueblo Bus Depot** (719-543-2775; greyhound.com), which is located near I-25, north of US 50 at 123 Court St.

GETTING AROUND *By car:* The best way to get around town is by car. Aside from the usual rush-hour traffic on the interstate and major cross streets, Pueblo is a great town for driving. Interstate 25 runs north and south through town, and it's the quickest way to travel from one side of town to another. Retail businesses are plentiful around I-25, which is especially helpful if you have a sudden need to visit a Barnes & Noble or a Walmart Supercenter or a mall (located near the intersection of I-25 and US 50 along with every other retail convenience you would expect). Exit 98B for 1st St. is the quickest route for getting to the old Union Avenue Historic District. Three blocks north of 1st Street, you can pick up CO 96 (here it is also called Fourth Street). Following CO 96 to the west will take you just north of the Colorado State Fairgrounds, right by the Pueblo Zoo on your way out to Lake Pueblo State Park. Unless you are in town to go to the state fair, parking is rarely a problem (and even then it's not bad).

By bus: The city operates a transit system that can get you almost anywhere in Pueblo. The **Pueblo Transit** (719-553-2725; pueblo.us/104/Pueblo-Transit) website has a map of bus fares, routes, and schedules.

✲ To See & Do

MUSEUMS **Buell Children's Museum** (719-295-7200; sdc-arts.org/museum/about), 210 N. Santa Fe Ave. Open Tue.–Sun. 11–5 (opens at 9 on Wed.). Once you visit Buell Children's Museum, you will understand why *Child* magazine rated it as the second-best children's art museum in the country in 2002. Your kids will have a blast exploring hands-on, interactive exhibitions, making their own art in the Artrageous Studio, or visiting the Magic Carpet Theater, where they can watch a play or perform themselves. For the even younger set, the Buell Baby Barn is full of activities for children under 4. The museum isn't just about art, either; plenty of exhibitions focus on science and history. There's always something new going on, so be sure to check the website for current exhibitions and activities. Buell Children's Museum is part of the Sangre de Cristo Arts and Conference Center (see *Entertainment*). Adult admission $8 and children $6.

El Pueblo History Museum (719-583-0453; historycolorado.org/museums/el-pueblo-history-museum), 301 N. Union Ave. Open Mon.–Sat. 10–4, Thu. 10–4, Sun. noon–4. If you are interested in the history of southeastern Colorado, a great place to start is at El Pueblo History Museum, located in the heart of Pueblo, just north of the Union Avenue Historic District. The museum features an adobe trading post and plaza from the 1840s, as well as the archaeological excavation for El Pueblo's original trading post. Permanent exhibitions walk visitors through Pueblo's history, from the region's earliest inhabitants up to the present. There's a wealth of history to explore, including artifacts from early American Indian inhabitants and the armor and weapons of French and Spanish explorers. The museum building also houses the Frontier Pathways Scenic and Historic Byways Information Center (see "Scenic Drives"). Adult admission $5; seniors, children, and students $4; and children 5 and under free. On Saturday, all children 12 and under are free.

& **Pueblo Railway Museum** (for tours, call 719-251-5024; for the office, call 719-544-1773; pueblorailway.org), located adjacent to the Pueblo Union Depot on B St., at the south end of the Union Avenue Historic District. The museum has several tracks in the coach yard behind the Union Depot, and more tracks running along the Riverwalk, where you can see vintage railroad equipment such as a 100-year-old red wooden caboose. The museum also offers smaller indoor exhibitions across the street from Union Depot in the Southeastern Colorado Heritage Center. Admission is free; donations appreciated.

& ℸ **Rosemount Museum** (719-545-5290; rosemount.org), 419 W. 14th St. (at Grand Ave.). Open Tue.–Sat., from 10 until the last tour at 3:30. The most impressive feature of Rosemount, the Victorian mansion built by the Thatcher family in 1893, is that nearly everything you find inside is original to the home. Stepping into the 37-room mansion is like walking back in time. The entrance hall features a grand Tiffany chandelier, and turning toward the staircase, visitors will see the large stained-glass window that memorializes the Thatchers' two young children, who did not live to see Rosemount completed. Also on the main floor in the drawing room, you can see and listen to a unique Steinway player piano. Upstairs, as you go from room to room, you will find that different wood was used for the woodwork—mahogany, oak, cherry, maple. There's quite a lot of history in each room, and tours of the 24,000-square-foot home take about an hour. Adult admission $6, seniors (60+) $5, children (6–18) $4, and children 5 and under free. Also located on the property is **Carriage House Restaurant at Rosemount** (see "Eating Out").

ROSEMOUNT MUSEUM

♂ ♿ ⬆ **The Steelworks Museum** (719-564-9086; steelworkscenter.com), 215 Canal St. Open Mon.–Sat. 10–4 (closed on holidays). Located on the south side of town, the museum is housed in the old Colorado Fuel and Iron Corporation headquarters. The museum commemorates Pueblo's past as a major steel producer. Exhibitions illustrate the history of mining, labor issues, steel production, and the specific role played by the Colorado Fuel and Iron Company in Pueblo and the region. Adult admission $6, children (4–12) $4, and children under 4 free.

ZOOS ♿ **Pueblo Zoo** (719-561-1452; pueblozoo.org), City Park, 3455 Nuckolls Ave. Summer (Memorial Day–Labor Day) open daily 9–5; winter Mon.–Sat. 9–4 and Sun. noon–4. This 25-acre zoo, located in Pueblo's City Park, is home to 325 animals, representing 121 species. Right off the bat, you will notice that this is a small city zoo, but considering its size, there is a lot to see and do. As you walk through the various exhibitions, you will see animals from nearly every region of the world. There are lions from Africa, bears from Asia, and kangaroos from Australia. There are also river otters from Colorado, as well as a slew of small mammals, birds, and snakes. Be sure the kids don't miss Pioneer Farm, where they can feed and pet some of the animals. Adult admission $12, seniors (65+) $11, children (3–12) $10, and children 2 and under free.

HISTORIC SITES Historic Arkansas River Riverwalk of Pueblo (see "Parks" under *Green Space*).

Union Avenue Historic District (719-543-5804; historicpueblo.org/historic-districts /union-ave), centered around Union Avenue; the Historic District begins at First Street in the north and ends at B Street in the south. In 1886, the three burgs that made up Pueblo consolidated. The resulting boom made Union Avenue into a thriving center of business. In 1921, disaster struck when the nearby rivers flooded—more than 11 feet of water flowed through the city. The district took years to recover from the destruction. In the 1980s, there was a push to renew the old downtown with such projects as the city's fabulous Riverwalk. As a result, the Union Avenue Historic District has been turned upside down as numerous shops and restaurants have sprung up, making this a great place to spend an afternoon. Throughout the district, there are nearly 40 plaques that tell the history of various buildings. Local merchants can provide you with a self-guided walking tour. Numerous events are held all year long, from car shows to art walks—see website for a complete listing. Parking is free, although limited to two hours during shopping hours. (See *Entertainment*, *Selective Shopping*, and *Where to Eat* for places to see and things to do.)

SCENIC DRIVES **The Frontier Pathways Scenic and Historic Byways** (719-583-8631; frontierpathways.org), 301 N. Union Ave. (based in El Pueblo History Museum). This drive will take you up and through the Wet Mountains southwest of Pueblo. It's a beautiful drive. Head west from Pueblo on CO 96, about 55 miles to the town of Westcliffe. Return by a southern route, backtracking 15 miles on CO 96 to CO 165, through Fairview and Colorado City, and then north on I-25.

✻ Outdoor Activities

BICYCLING **Pueblo River Trails System** (see "Parks" under *Green Space*). This 35-mile network of paved trails is open to cyclists and walkers. The trails follow the Arkansas River and Fountain Creek, connecting trails as far west as Lake Pueblo State Park with downtown Pueblo and the University of Southern Colorado in the north. Cyclists must always yield to pedestrian traffic. Check out the official site for a printable PDF trail map (pueblo.us/314/Pueblo-River-Trail-System).

GOLF Because of the climate, Pueblo golf courses claim to offer more playable days a year than most other courses in the state.

Desert Hawk Golf Course at Pueblo West (719-547-2280; deserthawkgolfcourse .com), 201 S. McCulloch Blvd. Open year-round. Located in Pueblo West south of US 50. Greens fees are less than $30.

Elmwood (719-561-4946; pueblo.us/721/Municipal-Golf-Courses), City Park, 3900 Thatcher Ave. Open year-round. This course is located adjacent to the Pueblo City Park. Greens fees are $32 on weekdays and $34 on weekends.

Walking Stick (719-584-3400; walkingstickpueblo.com), 4301 Walking Stick Blvd. Open year-round. This course was given a four-star rating by *Golf Digest* and is considered one of Colorado's best. The course offers some beautiful landscape features unique to Pueblo. Given all the hype, greens fees for non-residents are reasonable, $34 on weekdays and $36 on weekends. The course also maintains a pro shop and restaurant. There is a dress code.

Hollydot (719-676-3341 or 1-866-307-2792; hollydotgolf.com), 55 N. Parkway, Colorado City. Just a quick 20-mile drive south of Pueblo brings you to Hollydot—a fine golf course, with views of the Wet Mountains. You can play nine holes on their West Course or a full 18 on the Gold Links Course. It is by far one of the most affordable courses in southeast Colorado. Prime weekend rates for 18 holes will cost you $26 (or $39 with a cart). Monday, Tuesday, and Wednesday are the best deal with an 18-hole round running $19–26 (or $32–39 with cart). Kids under 18 pay only $4 for nine holes.

PADDLING **Pueblo Whitewater Park** (pueblo.us/facilities/Facility/Details/57). Located on the Arkansas River between Union Avenue and 4th Street, this half-mile stretch of water has been designed with eight drops separated by large pools. The resulting hydraulic action makes this the perfect playground for kayakers. For more information, stop by and talk with the guys at **Edge, Ski, Paddle, and Pack** (719-583-2021; edgeskiandpaddle.com), 107 N. Union Ave.

SWIMMING The city maintains several pools at parks around Pueblo—**City Park** and **Mineral Palace Park** are particularly nice (see "Parks" under *Green Space*). If you like a more natural experience, you can swim the Arkansas River at **Rock Canyon Swim Beach** (see Lake Pueblo State Park in "Parks" under *Green Space*).

✳ Green Space

PARKS **City Park** (719-553-2790), 800 Goodnight Ave. Not only is City Park home to the Pueblo Zoo, it is a great place for recreation of all sorts. The park has a disc-golf course, horseshoe pits, tennis courts, softball fields, a swimming pool, and lakes stocked for fishing. There are even two bocce courts, built to international standards. The park is adjacent to the city golf course, Elmwood (see "Golf" under *Outdoor Activities*). One of the park highlights that visitors should not miss is a ride on the City Park Carousel—originally built in 1911.

Lake Pueblo State Park (719-561-9320; cpw.state.co.us/placestogo/parks/Lake Pueblo), 640 Pueblo Reservoir Rd. One of the area's biggest attractions is Lake Pueblo State Park, which hosts more than 1.5 million visitors every year. In the summer, this part of the country gets pretty hot, often in the triple digits—the 4,500-acre Pueblo Reservoir offers a welcome respite from the heat.

A highlight of the park is **Rock Canyon Swim Beach**. Because the lake is primarily surrounded by short prairie grass, the park has provided numerous shaded picnic areas for groups and individuals. Rock Canyon Swim Beach is no exception. There are also facilities for changing and showering—with lockers for storing your stuff. In addition to the large sandy beach, there's a five-story waterslide, bumper boats, and paddleboats. Be aware, it costs an extra $1 per person to get into the Rock Canyon Swim Beach (plus a little extra for the waterslide and boats). Also note that pets are not allowed. The beach is only open during summer months. When open the new hours of operation are 11–6; closed Tue. and Wed.

Two separate marinas serve boaters on Lake Pueblo. **North Shore Marina** (719-547-3880; noshoremarina.com), 1 N. Marina Rd., has more than 600 boat slips. It also maintains a Ship's Store where you can get everything you need for a day on the lake, from food and gear to fishing licenses. **South Shore Marina** (719-564-1043; thesouthshore marina.com), 600 Pueblo Reservoir Rd., has 370 boat slips. It has a store for boaters as well. Both offer services for maintaining, repairing, and winterizing your boat.

In addition to swimming and boating, the parks boast of 348 picnic spots, 401 campsites, 18 miles of trails for hikers and bikers, and 16 miles of trails for horseback riding. The longest of the hiking trails is the Dam Trail, which is more than 16 miles long and connects all the major sections of the park. The tree-lined Pueblo River Trail follows the Arkansas River and is a relatively easy walk. The Arkansas Point Trail is less than

PUEBLO'S WHITEWATER PARK

a mile and leads to the bluffs, where you can get a panoramic view of the reservoir. Stop at the park's visitor center for trail maps and other information. The visitor center is open Mon.–Fri. 9–4. In addition to information, it has a store where you can buy guidebooks and fishing licenses.

A fee is required to visit the park. You can purchase a day pass for $7. If you plan on making trips to other Colorado state parks, you might want to pick up an annual pass for $70.

If you simply want to see Lake Pueblo in all its grandeur but don't have the time or inclination to get a day pass and wander around the park, one overlook is easily accessed from US 50. Heading west on 50, turn south on S. Purcell Boulevard. The road gets narrower as you go, and it eventually turns into S. Liberty Point Boulevard, where it dead-ends at a small parking lot. You will find yourself on the bluffs that overlook the north side of the park. This is Liberty Point Outlook. Park and take the short hike to the outlook, where the view is spectacular. The trail is paved and not at all strenuous, and the view is well worth the detour.

Mineral Palace Park (pueblo.us/Facilities/Facility/Details/Mineral-Palace-Park-36), 1600 N. Santa Fe Ave. A greenhouse now stands on the original site of Pueblo's Mineral Palace, which opened in 1891 to showcase Colorado's rich mineral wealth and to celebrate the state's mining industry. Unfortunately, the building was demolished in 1942. Today, Mineral Palace Park is known for its spectacular gardens and annual flower displays. It is also a great place to cool off in the summer—its large, shady trees are perfect for picnicking, and the community pool has a waterslide for the kids.

Pueblo Mountain Park and the **Mountain Park Environmental Center** (719-485-4444; hikeandlearn.org), 9112 Mountain Park Rd., Beulah. Far outside the city limits, about 30 miles southwest on CO 78, the City of Pueblo owns and maintains a park at the base of the Wet Mountains, just outside Beulah. Pueblo Mountain Park was created by the city in 1918, making it Pueblo's first outdoor recreation facility. A visit to the park is a great day trip, especially if you want to get closer to the mountains and enjoy hiking. There are several miles of trails; a few connect to those in neighboring San Isabel National Forest. Trail maps are available at the Mountain Park Environmental Center. In addition to maps and general visitor information, the MPEC offers various activities throughout the year. Be sure to check its website for a schedule of guided nature hikes.

NATURAL EDUCATION **The Greenway and Nature Center** (719-549-2414), 5200 Nature Center Rd. Adjacent to Lake Pueblo State Park, just east along the Arkansas River, the Greenway and Nature Center is located in Rock Canyon. There are miles of trails for horseback riding or cycling. Bikes can be rented from the bike shack (719-251-9312). This is also the home of the **Raptor Center of Pueblo** (natureandraptor.org). Open 11–4 every day but Mon. Looking after injured birds of prey is the main mission of the Raptor Center. Birds too injured to be released back into the wild stick around to help educate visitors about these birds and their way of life. Free admission.

WALKS & **Historic Arkansas Riverwalk of Pueblo** (719-595-0242; puebloharp.com). The 32-acre Riverwalk complex is located in downtown Pueblo between D Street and Grand Avenue, easily accessible from Main Street. Although not big enough for a day-long hike, the riverwalk is perfect for an afternoon or evening stroll. Begin with a walk around Lake Elizabeth at the HARP's west end and then make your way past Kelly Falls. Hidden among the landscaping are little bronze statues of wildlife—animals, insects, even a bronze fish leaping in a side stream. Water from the Farley/

THE DAM AT LAKE PUEBLO

Reilly Fountain cascades down water steps to the river, and Confluence Fountain is lit up at night so spectators can see the jets shooting water more than 50 feet in the air.

The Daily Grind operates a coffee stand, should you need refreshment, and all of Union Avenue's fine dining is within easy walking distance. If you want to get out on the water, paddleboats can be rented at the boathouse on Lake Elizabeth (719-595-1589; puebloriverwalk.org/boatprices). The four-person pedal boat is $10 for half an hour. See website for hours. You could also ride the excursion boat or gondola—adult admission $6, seniors and military $5, children (4–12) $4, and kids 3 and under ride free. There are sunset and dinner cruises, and the boats can be chartered for private parties.

The HARP's amphitheater is often used for summer concerts and festivals, so be sure to check out the website to see which events are planned for when you're in town.

Pueblo River Trails System. Connecting with trails in the Lake Pueblo State Park, the Pueblo River Trail follows the Arkansas River to where it meets Fountain Creek and heads upstream, eventually jogging over to CSU-Pueblo. There are some side trails that take you around Runyon Lake and connect the system with the Historic Arkansas Riverwalk of Pueblo downtown. Maps are available on the **Pueblo Parks and Recreation** website (pueblo.us/parks).

✳ Lodging

If you are looking for your favorite hotel chain, Pueblo most likely has it. A gamut of hotels runs alongside I-25, north of exit 101—the majority right on Elizabeth Street. The Pueblo Chamber of Commerce can provide you with a complete list.

HOTELS ♿ **Pueblo Marriott** (719-542-3200 or 1-800-228-9290; marriott.com), 110 W. 1st St. Right off the interstate and only blocks from Pueblo's historic downtown area, the Pueblo Marriott is very conveniently located for exploring Pueblo. The hotel offers all the amenities you would expect at a Marriott—cable TV, pay-per-view, restaurant, pool, etc. Rooms and suites $100–135.

BED & BREAKFASTS ((⋅)) **Abriendo Inn** (719-544-2703), 300 W. Abriendo Ave. This B&B, located within walking distance of the Union Avenue Historic District, is one of the best things going in Pueblo. In fact, many consider it the best B&B in Colorado. Once inside, you will see what all the fuss is about. The inn maintains 10 guest rooms, all of which are located on the second or third floors. Antique furniture graces the common rooms and guest rooms, and considering the emphasis on maintaining a "period" feel, the decorating is pleasantly contemporary. The inn's amenities include free Wi-Fi Internet access, an around-the-clock supply of snacks, and afternoon tea. Each room has a private bath, air-conditioning, and cable TV. Some rooms feature whirlpool baths—especially pleasant when the weather is a bit chilly. Every morning, Kate Zamora serves a fabulous gourmet breakfast. The menu changes regularly, but beer bread toast is always available, a favorite of guests. Rooms $75–155.

((⋅)) **The Edgar Olin House** (719-544-5727; olin-house.com), 727 W. 13th St. Three rooms are available at this B&B, and like the rest of the house, they are decorated in grand Victorian style. "Victorian" always brings to mind images of heavy curtains and lots of lace, but the innkeepers did not go overboard when it came to decorating. In fact, the atmosphere is downright comfortable. Amenities include a full gourmet breakfast, afternoon tea, and, in the summer, a chance to enjoy the inn's flower garden. Rooms all have a private bathroom, air-conditioning, refrigerator, and TV with DVD player (a large collection of DVDs available). The Judge Coulter Room is particularly attractive with its Jacuzzi for two. Rooms $69–149.

CAMPGROUNDS **Lake Pueblo State Park**, (719-561-9320; cpw.state.co.us/placestogo/parks/lakepueblo), 640 Pueblo Reservoir Rd. The state park maintains 401 campsites divided into three campgrounds. Northern Plains Campground is to the north of the park, near the North Marina. The campground offers electrical and nonelectrical sites, and group camping is available. All the sites at Juniper Breaks Campground are nonelectrical. On the south side of the park is Arkansas Point Campground, located near the South Marina. This campground is all electrical sites. All sites have a fire pit and covered picnic table (shade is a lifesaver in the summer). Electrical sites have some extra amenities such as flush toilets and showers (bring coins for the shower). They also have dump stations and laundry facilities.

All of the sites at Juniper Breaks, as well as some at Arkansas Point, are open for off-season camping (Oct. 1–April 1). Shower and laundry facilities, however, are closed during the off-season. You can reserve campsites online (follow the links on the park website) or by calling 1-800-678-2267. Sites $16–20

🐾 **Pueblo KOA** (719-542-2273 or 1-800-562-7453; koakampgrounds.com/campgrounds/pueblo), 4131 I-25 N., exit 108 off I-25. For recreation, the campground has a heated pool and a "jumping pillow." There are facilities for all sorts of campers—you can park your RV, pitch your tent, or rent a Kamping Kabin. Rates run from $25 for a basic site up to $70 for their Super Site.

  ✎ 🏕 **Pueblo South/Colorado City KOA** (719-676-3376 or 1-800-562-8646; koakampgrounds.com/campgrounds /pueblo-south), 9040 I-25 South, exit 74 off I-25. Located about 20 miles south of Pueblo, this campground has a heated pool, hot tub, and a mini-golf course. Rates run from $25 for a basic site up to $70 for its Super Site.

✳ Where to Eat

Throughout the city's history, people from around the world have made their way to and through Pueblo. Spanish-speaking folks have been here since the region was considered the territory of Spain. Later, Italians and other immigrants came to Pueblo to find work in the booming mining and steel industries. Nowhere is this rich heritage as readily evident as when you look for a place to eat in Pueblo. The city serves great Italian and Mexican cuisine, and there are plenty of classic American steakhouses and burger joints. Although a lot of the action is centered on the downtown area, be sure to get in your car and see what's cooking around the city as well.

DINING OUT **The Place: An Eatery on the Riverwalk** (719-299-4966; the placepueblo.com), 102 S. Union Ave. Lunch served daily 11–4; dinner 4–close. The cuisine on the menu at The Place would be called new American. I would call it upscale comfort food. There are creative takes on steak, lamb, and seafood. Guests rave over the fried chicken. If you only have time for dessert, there's a full gelato menu. Entrées $16–32.

EATING OUT ♿ **Bingo Burgers** (719-225-8363; bingoburger.com), 101 Central Plaza. Open Mon.–Wed. 11–8, Thu.–Sat. 11–9. After visiting Pueblo for the first edition of this guide, I was raving over the fine dining at the Steel City Diner. Unfortunately, the eatery didn't last. In 2010, the restaurant's chef, Richard Warner, opened a new venture with, perhaps, a more populist appeal. On the surface, Bingo Burgers is a burgers-fries-and-shakes joint, but scratch the façade a little and you will find towering gourmet sandwiches that feature ground lamb, fresh salmon, and locally sourced chicken. Ground beef is also on the menu (it's grass fed), and, like everything they serve, is crafted from locally produced ingredients. The fries are hand-cut and come with a variety of unique dipping sauces. In addition to the location just north of downtown Pueblo, there's a Bingo Burger in Colorado Springs as well. Burgers run $10–12.

  ♿ **Cactus Flower** (719-545-8218; cactusflowerrestaurant.com), 4610 N. Elizabeth St. Open Sun.–Wed. 11–9 and Thu.–Sat. 11–10. Often cited as the best place for Southwest cuisine in Pueblo. Great atmosphere—works by local artists are displayed throughout. Entrées $11–17.

  ✎ **Do Drop Inn** (719-542-0818; dodrop innpueblo.com), 1201 S. Santa Fe Ave. Open Mon.–Sat. 6 AM–10 PM and Sun. 6 AM–9 PM. Ask around and Puebloans will tell you some of the best pizza in town is found at Do Drop Inn. The crust is thick and sweet. There are plenty of televisions if you need to keep an eye on a game. The TVs and the game room turn out to be nice distractions while you wait—since everything is made from scratch, it can take some time to get your food. Burgers and sandwiches $9.

  ♿ **Gold Dust Saloon** (719-545-0741; golddustsaloon.net), 217 Union Ave. Kitchen is open Mon.–Thu. 11–8, Fri.–Sat. 11–9, Sun. 11–4. Bar closes when folks leave. This is a great place to grab lunch when you're downtown. For a saloon it has a surprisingly bright and airy interior. In addition to burgers and fries, the saloon serves a variety of excellent sandwiches. Burgers and sandwiches $8–12.

BAKERIES & COFFEE SHOPS ♿ **The Daily Grind** (719-561-8567; thedaily grindpueblo.com), 209 S. Union Ave. Open Mon.–Fri. 6:30–11, Sat. 7–11, and Sun. 7–9. The Daily Grind's baristas pour a complete menu of hot and cold drinks. They also have bagels, danishes, and doughnuts as well as cheesecake and fantastic brownie bars. The priciest drink is $5.10—sandwiches generally in the $8 range.

♿ **Hopscotch Bakery** (719-542-4467; hopscotchbakery.com), 333 S. Union Ave. Open Tue.–Fri. 7–4 and Sat. 8–4. Proprietors Mary Oreskovich and Richard Warner opened Hopscotch Bakery in 2005. The lunch menu at the bakery maintains the couple's commitment to using quality, locally grown products to create great food. Definitely try their salad of mixed field greens. Lunch about $9.

BARS, TAVERNS, & BREW PUBS ♿ ⍦ **Phil's Radiator Service and Beer Garden** (719-584-2671; facebook.com/ philsradiator), 109 E. C St., Pueblo (within the Union Street Historic District). Open daily 4 PM–2 AM. You simply have to love a bar located in an old garage. Inside, Phil's Radiator Service offers pool. Outside in the beer garden, it often has live music throughout the summer. Located right downtown, the bar is a favorite with the younger set.

♿ ⍦ **Shamrock Brewing Company** (719-543-9974; shamrockbrewing.com), 108 W. Third St. Open Mon.–Thu. 11–midnight, Fri. and Sat. 11–1 AM, and Sun. 10–11. This pub has been around for more than 40 years. Shamrock brews its own beer, including a chili beer that's a bit on the spicy side.

⍦ **Walter's Beer Taproom and Brewery** (719-542-0766; waltersbeer.com), 126 S. Oneida St. Open Wed.–Thu. 3–9, Fri. 3–11, Sat. noon–1 AM, Sun. 11–6. The history of Walter's beer goes back to Martin Walter who bought the old Pueblo Brewery back in the 1800s. For generations this local family-owned concern brewed beer and sent it out all over the country. Things went south in the 1970s, and the brewery closed. But in recent years, a

PHIL'S RADIATOR SERVICE AND BEER GARDEN

bunch of beer enthusiasts have brought the legendary local brand back to life and added a taproom.

Entertainment

Colorado State Fair and Rodeo (1-800-876-4567; coloradostatefair.com). A highlight of the Colorado State Fair is the annual rodeo. (For more information, see Colorado State Fair under *Special Events.*)

I-25 Speedway (719-542-2277; i25speedway.com), 400 Gobatti Pl. If you are interested in auto racing, Pueblo's I-25 Speedway is located north of town at exit 108. The quarter-mile track is a favorite for racing late-model Grand Prix cars.

Pueblo Symphony (719-545-7967; pueblosymphony.com) 2200 Bonforte Blvd. Every year on the Saturday before the Fourth of July, the Pueblo Symphony provides music for Pueblo Riverwalk—a show that is punctuated by a fireworks display. The orchestra's season runs from late fall to late spring.

Sangre de Cristo Arts and Conference Center (719-295-7200; sdc-arts.org), 210 N. Santa Fe Ave. Whether you are interested in music, theater, dance, or the visual arts, the Sangre de Cristo Arts Center has it all. The Children's Playhouse Series has performers that the whole family can enjoy. Festive Fridays brings various bands to Pueblo every week throughout the summer. The center even has a ballet theater. Tickets for most events are very reasonably priced. While you're there, take the kids to Buell Children's Museum (see *To See & Do*) or visit the art galleries.

Selective Shopping

There are a several great shops in Pueblo's Union Avenue Historic District.

Deedas Corner (719-595-0500; deedascorner.com), 186 S. Union Ave. In a town that features some great antique shops, this relative newcomer really shines. The shop has a great collection of carnival and Depression glass, pottery, vintage toys, etc.

John Deaux Art Gallery (719-545-8407; johndeauxartgallery.com), 221 S. Union Ave. Sells paintings and sculptures by Colorado artists.

Pueblo Southwest Trading Co. (719-542-4998 or 1-800-224-3047; pueblo swtradingco.com), 104 S. Victoria Ave. Just a block west of Union Avenue, this shop specializes in southwestern home décor—everything from furniture to accessories.

Somewhere in Time at 220 S. Union Ave. and **Somewhere in Time Too** at 105 S. Union Ave., have a great selection of 19th- and early 20th-century antiques. If you like ornate, plush Victorian furniture, both of these places will keep your attention.

Special Events

August: **Beulah Outdoor Arts and Crafts Show** (thepinesofbeulah.com/?page_id=50). Beulah is 25 miles southwest of Pueblo on CO 78. For more than 50 years now, the town has hosted an annual arts and crafts festival. More than 100 vendors will display their wares against the backdrop of the gorgeous Beulah Valley. The fair is usually held in early August.

♿ **Colorado State Fair** (719-561-8484 or 1-800-876-4567; coloradostatefair.com), 1001 Beulah Ave. The Colorado State Fair has been a Pueblo institution since 1872, making it older than Colorado itself. It was originally billed as the Southern Colorado Agricultural and Industrial Association. The fair takes place at the end of summer—the 11-day event always closes out on Labor Day. It is clearly the biggest annual event in Pueblo. In fact, with nearly half a million people making their way from around the state to take part in the festivities, it's the biggest annual event in Colorado.

You can take in such competitive events as the rodeo, pig racing, and the Mutton Busting competition (where kids compete to stay seated on rambunctious sheep). There are various livestock and agricultural contests every day. Or you can enjoy carnival rides, firework shows, and concerts.

The main gate is on Prairie Avenue, between Tulane and Purdue streets. There are also gates on Arroyo and Beulah avenues. Tickets can be picked up on your way into the fair for $7 during the week, or $10 Fri.–Sun. For cheaper admission, check out the Colorado State Fair website for a list of Discount Days—on certain days discounts are offered for different groups (e.g., military personnel or seniors)—and for the general public, various corporate sponsors also run deals for cheaper tickets.

September: **Chile & Frijoles Festival** (1-800-233-3446; pueblochilefestivalinfo .com), downtown Pueblo. Held every year in mid-September, the Chile & Frijoles Festival celebrates the region's agricultural produce—in particular, chiles and pinto beans. Additionally, various artists and craftspeople use this opportunity to display their work. Competitions during the festival include the best bean dip in pueblo, the holy frijoles cooking contest, and a jalapeño eating contest. There's also a farmers' market, plenty of food vendors, and live entertainment.

TRINIDAD

The historic section of downtown Trinidad, with its brick-paved streets, old buildings, restaurants, and art galleries, seems tailor-made for tourists. The old Santa Fe Trail once ran down Main Street, and today this section of the trail has been made a National Historic District, called the Corazon de Trinidad (the "heart of Trinidad").

Trinidad sits at the most natural place for a town. Nearby is the confluence of the Purgatoire River and Raton Creek. To the southeast looms Fishers Peak; at an altitude of 9,627 feet, it is the highest point in the United States east of I-25. To the west lies the fertile Purgatoire River Valley, and to the east the plains of southeast Colorado.

For centuries, various people have called this region home. The first settlers of European decent were Gabriel Gutierrez and his nephew, who in 1859 built a cabin here. Strategically located on the Santa Fe Trail, by 1861 the town of Trinidad had become an important stop for travelers.

Over the years, Trinidad has had its share of colorful characters. Old West legends such as Doc Holliday and Billy the Kid walked the streets. In the 1880s, Bat Masterson served as marshal in Trinidad. Even Wyatt Earp made his way to Trinidad for a time. Later during the heydays of coal mining, Mother Jones came to town to help organize the union.

Today the town is more settled, but no less colorful. In 1969, Dr. Stanley Biber performed his first sex-change operation in Trinidad. Soon people had dubbed the town, the "Sex Change Capital of the World."

With a thriving arts community and a growing number of galleries, Trinidad is becoming a travel destination in its own right. You might hear Trinidad called "the little Santa Fe." To some extent that is the feel here, but it ignores the unique character of this distinctly Colorado town, a character well worth experiencing.

GUIDANCE **Colorado Welcome Center at Trinidad** (719-846-9512; colorado.com /colorado-official-state-welcome-center/colorado-welcome-center-trinidad), 309 Nevada Ave., also houses the **Trinidad and Las Animas County Chamber of Commerce** (719-846-9285; tlacchamber.com). The folks behind the counter are locals who are eager to tell you about their town. They are a great source of information—they know if it has been snowing near Cuchara Pass, and they can recommend a great place for lunch. As one of the state welcome centers, this has brochures for every major attraction in Colorado.

More websites:
exploresoutheastcolorado.com
historictrinidad.com
trinidadco.com

GETTING THERE *By car:* If you're coming from the north or south, I-25 is your best bet. The interstate follows the Front Range and passes through Trinidad on its way to Santa Fe, Albuquerque, and points south. From the east, US 350 cuts down from US 50 in La Junta.

By air: The most accessible airport to Trinidad is **Colorado Springs Airport** (719-550-1972; flycos.com), about 130 miles to the north.

A HISTORIC LOCOMOTIVE

By train: **Amtrak** (1-800-872-7245; amtrak.com) has a terminal in Trinidad, and the Southeast Chief makes a stop here on its way to Los Angeles.

By bus: **Greyhound** (719-846-7271 or 1-800-231-2222; greyhound.com) has a stop in Trinidad. Check the website for route information and tickets.

GETTING AROUND *By foot:* With the number of historic buildings and the brick-paved streets, Trinidad is great for walking. See "Guided Tours" below for information on the town's trolley.

✳ To See & Do

MUSEUMS ♿ ✝ **A. R. Mitchell Memorial Museum and Gallery** (719-846-4224; armitchellmuseum.com), 150 E. Main St. Open May–Oct. A. R. Mitchell was a prolific artist who was adept at capturing cowboy life. He grew up on a homestead west of Trinidad and rose to fame painting covers for western pulp magazines. Today, an impressive collection of his work is found in this museum, which also displays the work of other western artists, including painters and photographers—there's even a collection of Spanish colonial folk art. Admission $5 donation.

♿ ✝ **Louden-Henritze Archaeology Museum** (719-846-5508; santafetrailscenicand historicbyway.org/lharcmus.html), 600 Prospect at Trinidad Junior State College. Open summer Mon.–Fri. 10–4. This museum takes a deeper look at the region's history. Exhibitions include geological formations, fossils, and a dinosaur track exhibition. Kids will get a kick out of seeing the mammoth tusks and other Ice Age animal bones. Free admission.

♿ ✝ **Trinidad History Museum** (719-846-7217; historycolorado.org/museums /trinidad-history-museum-0), 312 E. Main St. Open May–Sept.: Tue.–Sat. 10–4. In the off-season, the museum is open "pending staff availability." They suggest you call for hours. The museum complex includes Baca House, Bloom Mansion, and Santa Fe Trail

Museum (312 E. Main St.). In addition to the beautifully preserved buildings, Baca House and Bloom Mansion also have impressive gardens for visitors to tour. Tickets can be bought at the museum bookstore or Santa Fe Trail Museum.

HISTORIC SITES **El Corazon de Trinidad** (corazondetrinidad.org). This 6.5-mile section of Trinidad's downtown historic district is described as "a little bit funky, a little bit weird, and a whole lotta heart." It's also a National Historic Landmark District. There are historical markers around town telling the story of individual people and places important to Trinidad. Guidebooks are also available for sale at the Carnegie Public Library, 202 N. Animas, or at any of the museums in town, which will guide you on a walking tour of the district.

Ludlow Monument. In 1914, fighting broke out between the Colorado National Guard and striking coal miners. The tent colony in which the miners and their families were living was burned to the ground. Later, 2 women and 11 children were found in a cellar beneath one of the tents, dead from asphyxiation. In addition, two union leaders were killed. The event was called the Ludlow Massacre, and union organizers put out a call to arms. For 10 days, skirmishes were fought between miners, mine companies, and the National Guard. Fighting stopped when President Wilson sent in federal troops. The massacre is commemorated at the Ludlow Monument. Next to the monument is a cellar door that leads down to the place where the women and children died.

GUIDED TOURS **Trinidad Trolley Tour** (719-846-9843 ext. 133), 309 Nevada Ave. Running free tours daily from 10 until 2. The Trinidad Trolley leaves the parking lot of the Colorado Visitor Center at the top of every hour (last tour at 2 PM). As you tour the town, you can get on and off along the way to explore various attractions.

DOWNTOWN CUCHARA

Haunted Corazón Tour (719-680-4721 for reservations), meet at Golden Eagle Gallery, 147 E. Main St. Tours run April through Oct.: Tue.–Thu. at 6 PM; Fri. and Sat. at 8 PM. The best ghost tours combine good storytelling with fascinating history. The Haunted Corazón (heart) brings the Old West back to life with stories of cowboys and outlaws, and the shades that still linger from those times. Some tours might be too spooky for little kids, so ask when you reserve tickets. Tickets $10, children $5, kids under 5 free. Purchase at Golden Eagle Gallery of Fabilis Wings, 103 E. Main St.

Yellow Pine Ranch (719-742-3528; yellowpine.us), 15880 US 12, Cuchara. Located in the Cuchara Valley, Yellow Pine Ranch has been hosting guests for closing in on 100 years. The ranch has all you might expect from the Colorado ranch experience. Day-trippers can swing by for a two-hour horseback ride through mountain pastures and forest. (There are one-hour rides in the afternoon.) To explore more, spend a couple of days in one of the ranch's cabins, then enjoy your time hiking, fishing, nightly barbeques, and marshmallow roasts.

SCENIC DRIVES **The Santa Fe Trail Scenic and Historic Byway** (santafetrailco.com). The Santa Fe Trail runs across the entirety of southeast Colorado, from Kansas to New Mexico, but there is an 80-mile stretch along US 350 that is a particularly nice drive. Starting in La Junta, US 350 winds through Comanche National Grassland on its way to Trinidad. The prairie is marked with small canyons and low buttes—much more scenic than endless fields of corn. There are several places where you can stop and make a short hike to see the old ruts left by countless wagons traveling the Santa Fe Trail.

Scenic Highway of Legends (coloradodirectory.com/maps/legends.html). This scenic drive begins in Trinidad and follows CO 12 west up the Purgatoire River Valley, through the Cuchara Pass into the Cuchara Valley. Just outside La Veta it connects with CO 160 and ends at I-25. Along the way you pass by the historic Coke Ovens in Cokedale. Before you enter Stonewall, there's a bridge on the right over the Purgatoire River with a house on it—an interesting sight. The geological feature from which Stonewall gets its name stretches out on both sides of the road and is worth a stop. From here, the terrain becomes rockier and more pronounced as you climb to Cuchara Pass. Be sure to stop in Cuchara—it's a good place to stop for a bite to eat.

✳ Outdoor Activities

GOLF **Trinidad Las Animas County Municipal Golf Course** (719-846-4015; trinidad golfcourse.com), 1417 Nolan Dr. This nicely kept municipal course has great views of the Sangre de Cristo Mountains. The course was built in 1915 and is the fourth-oldest course in Colorado. Eighteen holes $21–23.

Grandote Peaks Golf Club (719-742-3391 or 1-800-457-9986; grandotepeaks.com), 5540 CO 12, La Veta. Graced by great mountain views with the Cuchara River running through, there is no better course in the area. Grandote Peaks was named one of the top three courses in Colorado by *Golf Digest*. Eighteen holes $55–75.

SKATEBOARDING **Trinidad Skate Park**, 1415 Beshore Ave. Open daily 8–10. Rated the ninth best skate park in the world by Tony Hawk; if you are looking for a unique diversion and enjoy skateboarding, Trinidad Skate Park is just the place. The park is 15,000 square feet, and the variety built into the park's design will keep even the most avid boarder from getting bored. Access is free.

THE SPANISH PEAKS FROM TRINIDAD

✳ Green Space

Trinidad Lake State Park (719-846-6951; cpw.state.co.us/placestogo/parks/trinidad lake), 32610 CO 12, Trinidad. Open 24 hours a day, the park is just a short drive from Trinidad. Anglers come to Trinidad Lake for the great fishing for rainbow and brown trout, walleye, and bluegill. Hikers will find numerous excellent paved and unpaved trails—the more adventurous taking the Reilly Canyon Trail to the old town of Cokedale and Reilly Canyon. There are 9 miles of trails for mountain biking and several paved trails for the roadies. Daily park pass $7.

    Lathrop State Park (719-738-2376; cpw.state.co.us/placestogo/Parks/lathrop), 70 CR 502, Walsenburg. Open daily 5–10. Fishing open 24 hours. This is Colorado's oldest state park. Two lakes, Horseshoe and Martin, and several ponds make Lathrop a great spot for fishing. The lakes are stocked with everything from rainbow trout to northern pike. There's even a children's fishing pond for the young'uns. Biking is popular on the 3-mile Cuerno Verde Trail, and there's a nine-hole course for golfers. Daily park pass $7.

✳ Lodging

There are numerous places to hole up for a night or two in Trinidad as well as in the little towns along the Highway of Legends. Stonewall, Cuchara, and La Veta have their share of inns, B&Bs, and remote properties with rental cabins. The addresses listed here, however, are all in Trinidad unless otherwise noted.

HOTELS Trinidad has a view of the usual chain hotels—Quality Inn, Holiday Inn, Best Western, Super 8—all located near I-25.

BED & BREAKFASTS **Tarabino Inn** (719-846-2115 or 1-866-846-8808; tarabinoinn

.com), 310 E. Second St. This tastefully decorated B&B is located two blocks off Main Street in Trinidad. The inn has four rooms. The Walnut Suite has its own private bath. The Chestnut Suite has a detached private bath. Both the West and East Gable Rooms share a bath. A full breakfast is served daily 8–9. A continental breakfast is available before and after this time. Rooms have cable TV and a VCR. Rooms $119–129.

Heart of Trinidad (719-422-9494; heartoftrinidad.com), 402 W. Main St. Directly across the street from the singing waitstaff of Rino's Italian Restaurant and Steakhouse and catty-corner to Trinidad History Museum, this inn sits in the heart of Trinidad's historic district. The building itself is a brick Victorian, and the property also serves as an outdoor music venue, called Gilley's Place, where visitors can often catch a movie on their outdoor screen. There are only two rooms, each with a private bath and clawfoot bathtub, furnished in period antiques for that vintage Old West atmosphere. The inn was started in 2016 by two folks from Texas. Rooms $200–225.

♿ ((ı)) **Inn at the Spanish Peaks Bed & Breakfast** (719-742-5313 or 719-680-0426; www.innatthespanishpeaks.com), 310 E. Francisco St., La Veta. There are three rooms, all with unique themes—the Costa Rica Suite with wicker furniture, the St. Andrews Suite with a golfing theme, and the Colorado Suite with heavy log accents. All the rooms have private baths and decks. There is wireless Internet, but the inn does not have phones or televisions, so as to promote a peaceful stay, removed from distractions. Rooms $95–140.

CAMPGROUNDS **Trinidad Lake State Park** (719-846-6951; cpw.state.co.us/placestogo/parks/trinidadlake), 32610 CO 12. The 62 campsites at Trinidad Lake sit on a ridge 150 feet above the reservoir. The park is somewhat wooded and many sites offer shade. A number of the sites are available for winter camping. Amenities include flush toilets, showers, and laundry facilities (all available May 1–Oct. 15). Many sites have electrical hookups. Sites $16–24.

Lathrop State Park (719-738-2376; cpw.state.co.us/placestogo/parks/lathrop) 70 CR 502, Walsenberg. Located north of Trinidad, west of Walsenberg, Lathrop has 103 campsites. Amenities include vault and flush toilets, pay showers, and laundry facilities. Many sites have electrical hookups. Many sites are open throughout the winter, as are the flush toilet and shower facilities. Sites $16-20.

CABINS & COTTAGES ♿ 🐾 **Yellow Pine Ranch** (719-742-3528; yellowpine.us), 15880 CO 12, Cuchara. Open May–Oct. Yellow Pine Ranch has nine cabins and a lodge for rent. The cabins sleep 2–8, depending on the unit. The lodge sleeps 12–15. All have a full kitchen, and none has a TV or telephone. The ranch offers horseback riding for adults and children 7 and older throughout the summer. Cabins $95–160. The main lodge is $500.

✲ Where to Eat

DINING OUT ♿ **Rino's Italian Restaurant and Steakhouse** (719-845-0949; rinostrinidad.com), 400 E. Main St. Open Wed.–Sun. 5–9. If you research the family trees of Trinidad, you'll find many have Italian roots. In the late 1800s, a wave of Italian immigrants made their way west to Colorado. That heritage is seen all over Trinidad, but the most visible sign to visitors is the city's excellent Italian dining scene. Rino's Italian Restaurant and Steakhouse was launched in 2002 by two Italian brothers from Trinidad who had gone out to Las Vegas to make a name for themselves as singing waiters, combining great food and great music. After 25 years, they decided to bring their success back home. The restaurant is located in an historic church. Entrées $19–30. Reservations for dinner are recommended.

  ♿ ⛾ **Timbers Restaurant** (719-742-3838; timberscuchara.com), 23 Cuchara Rd., Cuchara. Open all summer Mon.–Fri. 4–9, Sat. 7–9, and Sun. 9–9. Nestled on the main strip of Cuchara, just off the Highway of Legends, Timbers is the best spot in Cuchara for fine dining. It has a fantastic menu of steak, chicken, and fish. Musicians are regularly engaged to provide live entertainment. The bar serves a bar menu all day. Reservations are recommended for the restaurant. Entrées $19–30.

EATING OUT **Mission at the Bell** (719-845-1513; facebook.com/missionatthe bell), 134 W. Main St. Open Mon.–Thu. 11–8 and Fri. and Sat. 11–9. Located in the basement of the Bell Block, you will be surprised how open and bright this place is—especially during the day when skylights let in some sun. The staff serve authentic Mexican food—they make their own red and green chili—and meals run $6–9.

  Nana and Nano Monteleone's Deli and Pasta House (719-846-2696), 418 E. Main St. Open Wed.–Sat. 10:30–7:30. This is the best place for Italian in Trinidad. Everything is made from scratch, and just as at the Italian restaurants in Pueblo, you can expect to wait a bit for your food. Ahhh, but it's worth it. Great sauces, lots of different pasta dishes, and the classic meatballs and Italian sausage. Sandwiches $4–6 and entrées $6–11.

  ♿ ⛾ **The Dog Bar & Grill** (719-742-6366; dogbarcuchara.com), 34 Cuchara Ave., Cuchara. Open for dinner at 5 on Fri., at noon on Sat. and Sun. Any evening in Cuchara, you will find The Dog Bar your best bet for refreshment and some live entertainment. On a summer night, the place can get so full that crowds pour out onto the front porch. If the bustling scene inside gets to be too much, there's an outside seating area away from the music and dance floor. Pizzas $16–20, sandwiches $9.

❋ Entertainment

Southern Colorado Repertory Theatre (719-846-4765; scrtheatre.com) performances at the Massari Theater, corner of State and Broom, on the college campus. See website for a complete schedule of summer shows.

❋ Selective Shopping

Corazon Gallery (719-846-0207; corazongallery.wordpress.com), 149 E. Main St. Open Mon.–Sat. 10–5 and Sun. 11–4 (in winter, Mon.–Sat. 10–4). This is Trinidad's local artist co-op, showcasing work from a number of artists from the southeast Colorado region.

❋ Special Events

June: **Trinidad Santa Fe Trail Days Festival** (719-846-9285;), downtown Trinidad. Every year Trinidad hosts this festival, which has something for everyone—live music, great food, a car show, a petting zoo, even a chili cook-off. And to celebrate the Santa Fe Trail, there are reenactments and "living history" activities.

  August: **Trinidaddio Blues Festival** (trinidaddiobluesfest.com), Central Park. The Trinidaddio Blues Festival made its appearance in 1998, and it continues to be a popular event every year. General admission $20, children 12 and under free.

  Trinidad Round-Up and Las Animas County Fair (trinidadroundup .homestead.com), 2100 N. Linden Ave. Starting a few days before and going through the Labor Day weekend, this fair is a highly anticipated regional event. There are the usual livestock shows, a carnival, and, of course, the rodeo. Admission $10 for adults, $5 for kids.

EASTERN PLAINS

The region east of the mountains, from I-25 to the Kansas border, is essentially a long, flat stretch of land—much to the chagrin of first-time visitors driving into Colorado from the east, hoping to leave behind the endless prairies when they hit the state line. For many travelers, the eastern plains don't readily come to mind when making a list of desirable Colorado travel destinations. There are no tourist towns, no revived historic districts with art gallery–lined streets. There are no ski hills, and celebrity sightings are rare. The plains, however, have a strong appeal to different travelers for various reasons.

For the purposes of this book, the region is divided into the northeast and southeast plains. The northeast is that area around I-70 and north. The other major throughway here is I-76, which connects Denver to Nebraska. The southeast section is cut by US 50, which for a time follows the old Santa Fe Trail and runs from Pueblo to Kansas.

The northeast plains are primarily farming country, with more ranching to the north. Ranchers first brought their livestock out this way in the late 19th century. Later, sheep were brought in to graze the plains. Eventually settlers came here to homestead and farm the land. For years, people farmed or ranched, and they prospered. When larger companies began buying up farmland, however, the days of the family farm were numbered. Where many small farming communities thrived now sit virtual ghost towns. Today, the biggest towns in the northeast are found along I-76—Fort Morgan and Sterling being the biggest.

Fort Morgan is best known for being Glenn Miller's hometown. Although Miller was born in Iowa, he went to high school here, and every year they celebrate with the Glenn Miller Festival. Science fiction fans may be interested to know that Fort Morgan is also the burial place of Philip K. Dick, author of *Do Androids Dream of Electric Sheep?* and *The Man in the High Castle*.

Sterling is the first big town you hit coming in from Nebraska on I-76. The story of Sterling is tied closely with the railroad. In 1881, the few settlers in the area heard the Union Pacific Railroad was planning on pushing down their way. They offered the railroad some land with the understanding that a town would be established around a train stop there. And so Sterling was born. Today, the railroad yard is an unavoidable symbol of downtown. Right off the highway you will find the Sterling Tourist Information Center, which has information on all of Colorado, and farther from the highway are a bunch of fast-food joints on Main Street.

The southeast plains are a paradise for nature lovers—especially the birdwatchers who come a long way to see the lesser prairie chicken and the annual migration of the snow geese. Some people come to hike into Picketwire Canyonlands to view 150-million-year-old dinosaur footprints—the longest set of fossilized dinosaur tracks in the world. Others simply come for the quiet—for the plains have a certain majesty that can't be compared to the mountains in the west.

The old Santa Fe Trail once passed right through the heart of southeast Colorado—roughly following US 50 from the east and then heading southwest with US 350. Although the trail has lain unused for more than a century, you can find clues to its past all over the place. There are still sections where you can find ruts left by countless wagons, driven by pioneers and traders as they made their way back and forth across

COLORADO WELCOME CENTER IN JULESBURG

the plains. Forts along the way served as way stations, where travelers could stock up on supplies and hear news from the frontier or back home. Bent's Old Fort, a National Historic Site, lies just outside La Junta.

The Arkansas and Purgatoire rivers, which meet just outside Las Animas, define the region. Tapping into that resource with irrigation ditches in the 1870s transformed the region's agricultural potential, giving Colorado some of its most productive farming land. Today, the local towns boast of prized produce, such as Rocky Ford's famous cantaloupes.

The main towns lie along US 50. La Junta, Las Animas, and Lamar are the largest and hold the greatest potential for finding a good place to eat and put up for the night. Each of these towns also has historic sites that make for great touring.

La Junta began as a small settlement next to the railroad track that ran east and west along the Arkansas River. The town was made official in 1881. For years it served as a place for farmers and ranchers to get their produce to market via the railroad. Agriculture is still a big deal. Just east of town, you can get a feel for life on the plains in the 1840s at Bent's Old Fort National Historic Site. Or you can visit Koshare Indian Museum and Kiva in town, which celebrates the Native American culture and is the home of the Koshare Indian Dancers.

Las Animas was founded in 1869 at the confluence of the Arkansas and Purgatoire rivers. In the town's early days, it was a center of commerce. Famous pioneer and mountain man Kit Carson lived in Boggsville before moving to nearby Fort Lyons, where he died. You can get a sense for the old town at the Boggsville National Historic District 2 miles south of Las Animas. The man is commemorated at Kit Carson Museum.

Lamar, founded in 1886, was named after the secretary of the interior under Grover Cleveland, Lucius Quintius Lamar. With this name, the townsfolk hoped to secure their town as the location for a new land office—and the strategy worked. For many years the town was booming as people streamed in from the east looking to claim free land. Big Timbers Museum in Lamar can teach you a lot about those days and frontier life in general. You can also learn about the Japanese-American internment camp that used to operate nearby.

GUIDANCE

NORTHEAST PLAINS

Fort Morgan Area Chamber of Commerce (970-867-6702 or 1-800-354-8660; fort morganchamber.org), 300 Main St., Fort Morgan. Open Mon.–Fri. 8–5.

    Sterling and Logan County Chamber of Commerce (970-522-5070 or 1-866-522-5070; logancountychamber.com), 109 N. Front St., Sterling. Located in the town's historic Union Pacific Depot. Sterling also has a great Colorado Tourist Information Center right off I-76.

    Colorado Welcome Center at Burlington (719-346-5554; colorado.com/colorado-official-state-welcome-center/colorado-welcome-center-burlington). The welcome center has its own on and off ramp, just west of exit 438. Open daily in the summer 8–6. The state welcome center has all the information you need for researching lodging and activities for a trip to Colorado. The staff are also well versed on local happenings and attractions.

    Colorado Welcome Center at Julesburg (970-474-2054; colorado.com/Julesburg WelcomeCenter.aspx), exit 180 off I-25. Open Memorial Day to Labor Day daily 8–6; Labor Day to Memorial Day daily 8–5. Coming into Julesburg out of Nebraska, you may feel like you haven't quite gotten to Colorado yet, but this is it. A statue out front commemorates the riders who made the Pony Express possible.

    Also visit northeastcoloradotourism.com.

SOUTHEAST PLAINS

La Junta Chamber of Commerce (719-384-7411; lajuntachamber.com), 110 Santa Fe Ave., La Junta. The LJCC website has a rather complete list of regional museums and attractions as well as links of interest for tourists.

    Las Animas/Bent County Chamber of Commerce (719-456-0453), 332 Ambassador Thompson Blvd., Las Animas. Although there's no official visitor center, the chamber office has brochures on local attractions.

    Colorado Welcome Center (719-336-3483; colorado.com/colorado-official-state-welcome-center/colorado-welcome-center-lamar) and the **Lamar Chamber of Commerce** (719-336-4379; lamarchamber.com) both reside at 109A E. Beech St., Lamar. The welcome center is staffed by locals who can answer your questions and give you a free state map. Outside, you can't miss the 18-foot-tall statue commemorating the women who traveled west along the Santa Fe Trail—the Madonna of the Trail Monument.

    More websites:

    exploresoutheastcolorado.com

    santafetrailco.com

GETTING THERE *By car:* If you are driving to Colorado from the east side of the country, people will often ask if you are taking the northern route or the southern route. By this they mean I-80 or I-70, respectively. Of course, as you come across I-80, you will veer southwest in Nebraska on I-76. These two interstates, 70 and 76, are your main routes through the region.

To get to the southeast plains, take I-25 to US 50, which runs east, eventually into Kansas. From the south, you can break off from I-25 in Trinidad and take US 350, which runs northeast to La Junta and US 50.

By air: The closest airport in the northeast is **Denver International Airport** (1-800-247-2336; flydenver.com), close to both I-70 and I-76. **Colorado Springs Airport** (719-550-1972; flycos.com) is your best bet for flying into the southeast.

By train: **Amtrak's** (1-800-872-7245; amtrak.com) California Zephyr (Chicago to San Francisco) makes stops in Fort Morgan and Denver. The Southwest Chief runs from Chicago to Los Angeles, making stops at stations in La Junta and Lamar.

By bus: **Greyhound** (greyhound.com) operates regular service along I-70 (there is a stop in Limon) and I-76 (stops at Fort Morgan, Sterling, and Brush). There is also regular service to and from Pueblo from the **Pueblo Bus Depot** (719-543-2775 or 1-800-231-2222; greyhound.com), which is located near I-25, north of US 50 at 123 Court St. From there you can travel east along US 50 and southeast to Springfield.

GETTING AROUND *By car:* Since towns are few and far between, you will need a car to get around the southeast plains.

By foot: To really experience the immensity of the plains, you have to get out of the car and do a little hiking. Remember that it gets awfully hot here in the summer, so drink lots of water.

✺ To See & Do

HISTORIC SITES

SOUTHEAST PLAINS

⚓ ♿ **Bent's Old Fort National Historic Site** (719-383-5010; nps.gov/beol), 35110 CO 194 E., La Junta. Open daily in summer (June–Aug.) 8–5:30, and daily the rest of the year

BENT'S OLD FORT

9–4. Guided tours at 10:30 and 1. The quarter-mile walk from the parking area to the fort is an easy stroll. If you are unable to walk the path, a shuttle is available. Adults (13+) $3, children $2, and children 5 and under free.

✎ **Boggsville National Historic District** (719-456-1358; bentcountyheritage .org/?s=boggsville), 2 miles south of Las Animas on CO 101. Admission and tours are free. There are three RV sites, tent camping sites, tipis to rent, full bathrooms, and showers for campers.

Sand Creek Massacre National Historic Site (719-729-3003; nps.gov/sand), 910 Wansted St., Eads (park office). The park office is in town, but the park itself is located east of Eads on CR W. (Take CO 96 east to CR 54; head north to CR W where the road Ts. Turn east and go 1.3 miles to the park entrance.) Open daily 9–4, April through Nov. The rest of the year the park is closed on the weekends. More than 150 years ago, on November 29, 1864, Col. John Chivington led 800 soldiers in an attack upon an encampment of unarmed Native Americans at nearby Sand Creek. The colonel ordered his men to, "Kill and scalp all, big and little." When the "battle" was over, nearly 200 Indians had been slain—mostly elderly men, women, and children. The park commemorates this atrocity and tries to put the event in historical context. Sand Creek Historic Site opened to the public in the summer of 2007, with rangers giving "history talks" three times a day. These days, interpretive programs are offered every day between 10 and 2. There is a visitor center and no fee to visit the site.

MUSEUMS

NORTHEAST PLAINS

& ↑ **Fort Morgan Museum** (970-542-4010; cityoffortmorgan.com/index.aspx?nid=238), 414 Main St., Fort Morgan. Open Mon. 10–5, Tue.–Thu. 10–8, Fri. 10–5, and Sat. 11–5. Fort Morgan Museum preserves and commemorates pieces of Fort Morgan history, from archaeological artifacts found on local digs to Hillrose Soda Fountain that closed in the 1970s. Admission is "by donation."

✎ & ↑ **Kit Carson County Carousel & Museum** (719-346-7666; kitcarsoncounty carousel.com), 815 15th St., Burlington. Open Memorial Day–Labor Day 11–6. Recently completed, the Kit Carson County Carousel now has a fantastic museum. Although the museum is small, a lot is presented, and presented well. Visitors can see how carousel horses are made or learn how the organ works. Rides on the carousel cost just a quarter. Museum admission $1 (under 9 free).

KIT CARSON COUNTY CAROUSEL & MUSEUM

& ↑ **Old Town Museum** (719-346-7382 or 1-800-288-1334), 420 S. 14th St., Burlington. Open year-round Mon.–Sat. 9–5 and Sun. noon–5. This 6½-acre complex offers visitors a chance to tour several historic buildings. There's a sod house and an old jailhouse. There's even a saloon complete with a piano player and dancing girls. Throughout you will find artifacts from the turn of the century— there are plenty of cars and old tractors. In the summer, you can enjoy entertainment and ice cream and wagon rides.

WHEN THE GENOA TOWER AND MUSEUM CLOSED, IT MARKED THE END OF AN ERA

Adult admission $6, seniors $5, children 12–17 $4, children 3–11 $2, and kids under 3 free.

🕇 **Overland Trail Museum** (970-522-3895; sterlingcolo.com/?page_id=145) 21053 CR 26.5, Sterling. Open April–Oct., Tue.–Sat. 9–5; Nov.–Mar. Tue.–Sat. 10–4. This is a museum and an entire village of pre-1915 structures. The museum is housed in a fieldstone building from 1936 and commemorates the many people who traveled the Overland Trail, which was a spur off the Oregon Trail that ran east and west across Nebraska. Would-be gold miners and pioneers made the Overland Trail the most traveled road in the world from 1862 to 1868. Call for cost of admission.

MUSEUMS

SOUTHEAST PLAINS

& 🕇 **Big Timbers Museum** (719-336-2472; bigtimbersmuseum.org), 7515 W. US 50, Lamar. Open Tue.–Sat. 10–5 during summer, 1–4 in winter. The museum is named after the giant cottonwood trees that once lined the Arkansas River near Lamar. The area was once a spot where Native Americans camped for the winter. The everyday lives of past residents of southeast Colorado are chronicled by the artifacts such as agricultural tools used by early pioneers. The museum also tells the story of nearby Camp Amache, a World War II internment camp.

Kit Carson Museum is closed. The artifacts once housed there are now on display at the **John W. Rawlings Heritage Center** (719-456-6066; bentcountyheritage.org /Heritage.html) at 560 Bent Ave. in Las Animas.

& 🕇 **Koshare Indian Museum and Kiva** (719-384-4411; kosharehistory.org), 115 W. 18th St., La Junta. Open daily in summer 10–5 (open until 9 when there is a show); in winter, open daily noon–5, except Mon. and Wed. open 5–9. Back in 1933, a group of Boy Scouts gathered together to form an Indian club. They began performing Native American dances. Soon the Koshare Indian Dancers, as they were named, gathered quite a following—inspiring boys from various troops to work hard and meet the requirements of becoming Koshare Indian Dancers themselves. Their celebration of Native American culture culminated in the creation of Koshare Indian Museum and Kiva, which reportedly houses one of the world's finest collections of Native American art and artifacts. The Koshare Indian Dancers are still around today and regularly perform in the Kiva. Adult admission $5, seniors and students $3, and children under 6 free.

⊤ **Otero Museum** (719-384-7500; oteromuseum.org), 706 W. Third St., La Junta. Open in summer (June–Sept.) Mon.–Sat. 1–5. Open by appointment in the off-season. Several historic buildings make up the Otero Museum complex, which strives to preserve the history of La Junta and Otero County. There's the blacksmith shop and the old-time grocery. There is also the requisite schoolhouse—in this case, a log cabin replica of the first schoolhouse in Otero County. Among the many artifacts, of particular interest is the 1865 stagecoach, built in Concord, New Hampshire. Admission is free.

SCENIC DRIVES **Pawnee Pioneer Trails**. This scenic and historic byway takes you across Pawnee National Grassland with views of the Pawnee Buttes. The trip is a great introduction to the beauty of shortgrass prairie. The trail starts in Sterling (and Fort Collins, the two legs meeting in Raymer), and then makes its way west to Ault. The route follows some back roads, so stop by the Sterling Tourist Information Center for a map and directions.

The Santa Fe Trail Scenic and Historic Byway (santafetrailco.com). The drive begins in Trinidad and follows US 350 up to La Junta and then US 50 east to Lamar. Along the way you will pass close to various historical sites and markers that track the history of the Santa Fe Trail.

✳ Outdoor Activities

BIRDWATCHING **Bent's Bird Sanctuary** (719-456-0011), 10950 E. US 50, Las Animas. There are feeding stations, and many trails wind through the sanctuary, which is located right behind Bent's Fort Inn. You can purchase bird feed in the hotel lobby.

Comanche National Grassland (719-523-6591; www.fs.usda.gov/goto/psicc/com), 27162 US 287, Springfield. The lesser prairie chicken is pretty unique to southeast Colorado. At one time, the bird thrived in this region's prairies. As the prairies were tilled under for farmland, the lesser prairie chicken population dropped. But the restoration of prairie in Comanche National Grassland has helped stabilize bird numbers. Every year, from March to June, male prairie chickens perform an elaborate courtship ritual for the females. Year after year they return to the same display grounds, called leks. You need to reserve a spot to view this annual event—the number of cars and people allowed out to view the display grounds is limited, and you must follow certain rules to participate. Call the Grassland office for more information.

John Martin State Park (719-227-5250; cpw.state.co.us/placestogo/parks/johnmartinreservoir), 30703 CR 24, Hasty. Nearly 400 species of birds can be found around the John Martin Reservoir and nearby Lake Hasty. In the winter, the area is a regular roosting place for bald eagles.

FISHING **John Martin Reservoir and Lake Hasty** (719-227-5250; cpw.state.co.us /placestogo/parks/johnmartinreservoir), 30703 CR 24, Hasty. People fishing the reservoir have caught everything from walleye and bass (largemouth and smallmouth) to bluegill and catfish. Lake Hasty has many of the same species but is also stocked with rainbow trout.

Queens State Wildlife Area, 15 miles south of Eads on US 287. There are a number of lakes in the wildlife area for fishing. The Nee Noshe, Nee So Pah, and Nee Grande lakes, as well as Upper and Lower Queens reservoirs, offer anglers a chance at landing a variety of species such as catfish, walleye, and largemouth and smallmouth bass.

HIKING **Pawnee Grasslands**. See "Parks" under *Green Space*.
Picketwire Canyonlands. See "Parks" under *Green Space*.
Vogel Canyon. See "Parks" under *Green Space*.

✳ Green Space

NORTHEAST PLAINS

Jackson Lake State Park (970-645-2551; cpw.state.co.us/placestogo/parks/jackson lake), 26363 MCR 3, Orchard. Open 24 hours a day. The park is located 20 miles northwest of Fort Morgan. Some of the biggest attractions at Jackson Lake are the excellent swimming beaches. The lake is relatively shallow, so it warms up nicely. Visitors also take advantage of the other water sports—fishing, boating, and jet skiing. It is a popular park with hunters as well. There are some trails for hiking and biking. Daily park pass $7.

North Sterling State Park (970-522-3657; cpw.state.co.us/placestogo/parks/north sterling), 24005 CR 330, Sterling. Visitor center open daily 8–4:30. Park open 24 hours, no day use after 10 PM. More than 3,000 acres of water make this a great getaway in the summer. Trails for mountain biking and hiking and opportunities to swim, boat, and fish attract thousands of guests to North Sterling annually. Daily park pass $7.

Pawnee National Grassland and Pawnee Buttes (970-295-6600; fs.usda.gov/goto /arp/pngrecreation), 2150 Centre Ave., Bldg. E, Fort Collins. The offices for Pawnee Grassland are in Fort Collins, but the grassland itself is farther north. The Pawnee Buttes are well worth the drive into the country. They sit alone on the plains, rising 250 feet above the prairie floor. To get there, take CO 14 to CR 103, head north to Keota, and follow the signs to the parking area. Once you are there, it's a level 1.5-mile walk to the buttes. There are other trails in the Pawnee Grassland, so stop by the offices in Fort Collins for maps and more information.

SOUTHEAST PLAINS

Comanche National Grassland. The nearly 420,000 acres of shortgrass prairie that make up Comanche National Grassland are fairly inhospitable. It is a dry region and the days are either very hot or very cold. The delicate balance that allowed the prairie to thrive in these conditions was tipped by years of ranching and farming. By the time of the Dust Bowl years, the prairies were no longer viable for agriculture. So in 1938, the government started buying back the land. The grasslands are found primarily in two areas, just south of La Junta and just south of Springfield.

John Martin State Park and Lake Hasty (719-227-5250; cpw.state.co.us/placestogo /parks/johnmartinreservoir), 30703 CR 24, Hasty. East of Las Animas, the Arkansas River was dammed to create John Martin Reservoir. Below the dam is the well-stocked

Lake Hasty. This is a popular park for boaters, anglers, and birdwatchers. Lake Hasty has a swim beach, the only one in the park. Hikers can get some exercise walking Red Shin Trail, a 4.5-mile hike that ends at a marker for the Santa Fe Trail. Daily park pass $6.

Picketwire Canyonlands and Dinosaur Tracks. Take CO 109 south of La Junta 13 miles to CR 802. Head west 8 miles and turn south on CR 25. After 6 miles, you will find the Corral Parking Area. The paleontological jewel of southeast Colorado is found here at Picketwire Canyonlands: more than 1,300 dinosaur footprints, Native American rock art, early Hispanic settlements, and an historic ranch. The tracksite is considered the largest in North America.

Vogel Canyon. The directions to the Vogel Canyon parking lot are pretty simple. Head north of La Junta 13 miles on CO 109. There's a sign there directing you to turn west on CR 802 (also known as Vogel Canyon Road). After 1.5 miles, turn south on 505A and go another 1.5 miles to the parking lot. Four different trails provide the best way to explore the sandstone canyon. The Canyon Trail is particularly exciting—several spurs get you close to the canyon walls, where you can see Native American rock art, some nearly 800 years old. The Overlook Trail is handicapped accessible. The gravel path leads along the top of the canyon and lets you see a good bit of the scenery. Just as at Picketwire Canyonlands, you may stumble upon the ruins of some old building, which makes a hike here that much more interesting. The trails are not just used for hiking, but horseback riding and mountain bike riding as well.

✳ Lodging

SOUTHEAST PLAINS

HOTELS The pickings are mighty slim when it comes to hotels in southeast Colorado. Your best places to stay are closer to I-25 in Pueblo or Trinidad. There are Best Westerns in Las Animas (719-456-0011; 10950 E. US 50) and Lamar (719-336-7753; 1301 N. Main St.), but reviews are mixed. There is also a Holiday Inn Express in La Junta (719-384-2900; 27994 Frontage Rd.).

🐾 (ȵ) **Mid-Town Motel** (719-384-7741), 215 E. Third St., La Junta. Located near the main drag, the Mid-Town Motel offers clean (although somewhat dated) rooms at extremely affordable rates. If you are looking for a place to crash for the night, you won't be disappointed. Rates $40–50.

BED & BREAKFASTS (ȵ) **Finney House** (719-384-8758), 608 Belleview Ave., La Junta. This beautifully restored 1899 Victorian home is a jewel, located in a quiet neighborhood close to downtown.

Four rooms are available, and if you are looking for a longer stay, one room even has its own kitchen. The owner/innkeeper Shirley Flock serves a fine gourmet breakfast, and dinner is available (just be sure to set it up with Shirley in advance). Rates $70–85.

🐾 (ȵ) **3rd Street Nest Bed & Breakfast** (719-336-5217; 3rdstnestbb.com), 304 S. Third St., Lamar. Just a couple of blocks from downtown Lamar, 3rd Street Nest has two rooms. During the week, innkeeper Jane Felter maintains a "Super Continental" breakfast and prepares a gourmet breakfast on weekends. Cable TV in each room. Both rooms have a private bath, although the Garden Room's bath is in the hall. There's a garden hot tub out back. Lavender 'n' Lace Suite (with whirlpool tub) $65–75. The Garden Room $60–70.

CAMPGROUNDS **Boggsville National Historic District** (719-456-1358), 2 miles south of Las Animas on CO 101. You can camp at Boggsville. There are three RV sites, tent camping sites, tipis to rent, full bathrooms, and showers for campers. (See "Historic Sites" under *To See & Do* for more information on the historic side of things at Boggsville.)

John Martin State Park (719-227-5250; cpw.state.co.us/placestogo/Parks/JohnMartinReservoir), 30703 CR 24, Hasty. The state park maintains 213 campsites divided into two campgrounds. Lake Hasty Campground is east of the John Martin Dam next to Lake Hasty. The site is rather wooded, offering nice shade in the summer. Fifty-four of the campground's 109 sites are open year-round. All are wired for electricity. The campground has flush toilets and showers (bring coins for the shower). There are also dump stations and laundry facilities. Point Campground is more open than Lake Hasty, as it is surrounded by the reservoir on three sides with desert prairie to the north. Camping facilities here are a little more rustic. Three sets of vault toilets serve the 104 sites, which run $20.

NORTHEAST PLAINS

BED & BREAKFASTS ♿ (ᵰ) **Claremont Inn** (1-888-291-8910; claremontinn.com), 800 Clairmont, Stratton. This B&B calls itself "an oasis on the Colorado Plains." In many respects it is true—lodging of this caliber is not found for miles. And just as you can charge a mint for water in the desert, the rates here are pretty highfalutin. You will not, however, be disappointed by your stay. You might even want to plan on staying over on one of the inn's special weekends, where you can take cooking classes, enjoy a murder mystery, or simply sweep your beloved away for a romantic getaway. Rates $150–280.

CAMPGROUNDS **Jackson Lake State Park** (970-645-2551; cpw.state.co.us/placestogo/parks/jacksonlake), 26363 MCR 3, Orchard. Many of the park's 260 campsites are open year-round. Restrooms, showers, and laundry facilities are located throughout the campground. Sites $18–24.

Limon KOA (719-775-2151 or 1-800-562-2129; koa.com/campgrounds/limon), 575 Colorado Ave., Limon. Hookups include electrical, telephone, and cable television. There is a camp swimming pool, and the campground rents bikes for those who want to take a ride. In addition to RV and tent sites, Limon also has one- and two-room Kabins for rent.

North Sterling State Park (970-522-3657; cpw.state.co.us/placestogo/parks/northsterling), 24005 CR 330. Sterling. The three campgrounds at North Sterling have a total of 191 sites. Electric hookups are available. Restrooms, showers, and laundry facilities are located conveniently in each campground. Sites $18–24.

✳ Where to Eat

EATING OUT **Hog's Breath Saloon** (719-384-7879), 808 E. Third St., La Junta. The name may sound intimidating, ill-conceived, or just plain humorous, but the Hog's Breath is one of the best places in town for family dining. In addition to the usual American dishes, there are some unusual items. For an appetizer try the snake eggs, which are bacon-wrapped jalapenos stuffed with cream cheese. Burgers start around $6 and dinner entrees $10–15 (more for the lobster tail).

ENTERTAINMENT **Koshare Indian Dancers**. See Koshare Indian Museum and Kiva in "Museums" under *To See & Do*, page 289–290.

✳ Special Events

February: **High Plains Snow Goose Festival and Nature Arts and Crafts Fair** (highplainssnowgoose.com), Lamar. Celebrating the annual migration of the snow geese, the city of Lamar has also planned an annual arts-and-crafts fair that allows artists who try to capture the beauty of nature a chance to show their stuff.

Late July/early August: **Kit Carson County Fair** (719-346-7382 or 1-800-288-1334; kitcarsoncounty.org/County_Fair.html), 815 15th St., Burlington. First week in August.

Arkansas Valley Fair (719-254-7723; arkvalleyfair.com), 800 N. Ninth St., Rocky Ford. The first Arkansas Valley Fair was back in 1878, and it's the oldest continuous annual fair in Colorado. The fair has the usual events—truck and tractor pulls, rodeo events, and even a demolition derby.

INDEX

Photographs indicated in bold.